Inventory Optimization

Inventory management is a very tedious task faced by all the organizations in any sector of the economy. It makes decisions for policies, activities and procedures in order to make sure that the right amount of each item is held in stock at any time. Many industries suffer from indiscipline in ordering and production mismatch. Providing best policy to control such mismatch would be invaluable to them.

The primary objective of this book series is to explore various effective methods for inventory control and management using optimization techniques. The series will facilitate many potential authors to become the editors or author in this book series. The series focuses on an aspect of Operations Research which does not get the importance it deserves. Most researchers working on inventory management are publishing under different topics like decision making, computational techniques and optimization techniques, production engineering etc. The series will provide the much needed platform for them to publish and reach the correct audience.

Some of the areas that the series aims to cover are:

- Inventory optimization
- Inventory management models
- Retail inventory management
- Supply chain optimization
- Logistics management
- Reverse logistics and closed-loop supply chains
- Green supply chain
- Supply chain management
- Management and control of production and logistics systems
- Datamining techniques
- Bigdata analysis in inventory management
- Artificial intelligence
- Internet of things
- Operations and logistics management
- Production and inventory management
- Artificial intelligence and expert system
- Marketing, modelling and simulation
- Information technology

This book series will publish volumes of books which will be edited and reviewed by the reputed researcher of inventory optimization area. The beginner and experienced researchers both can publish their innovative research work in the form of edited chapters in the books of this series by getting in touch with the contact person. Practitioners and industrialist can share their real time experience bolstered with case studies. The objective is to provide a platform to the practitioners, educators, researchers and industrialist to publish their valuable work in the area of inventory optimization.

This series will be beneficial for practitioners, educators and researchers. It will also be helpful for retailers/managers for improving business functions and making more accurate and realistic decisions.

Nita H. Shah · Mandeep Mittal
Editors

Sustainable Inventory Management

Perspectives from India

Springer

Editors
Nita H. Shah
Department of Mathematics
School of Emerging Science
and Technology
Gujarat University
Ahmedabad, Gujarat, India

Mandeep Mittal
Department of Mathematics
School of Computer Science Engineering
and Technology (SCSET)
Bennett University
Greater Noida, India

ISSN 2730-9347 ISSN 2730-9355 (electronic)
Inventory Optimization
ISBN 978-981-97-6764-9 ISBN 978-981-97-6765-6 (eBook)
https://doi.org/10.1007/978-981-97-6765-6

This Springer imprint is published by the registered company Springer Nature Singapore Pte Ltd.
The registered company address is: 152 Beach Road, #21-01/04 Gateway East, Singapore 189721, Singapore

Preface

Global warming, environmental disasters, and heightened public awareness about environmental issues are driving countries to reduce greenhouse gas (GHG) emissions. The Kyoto Protocol, signed in 1997 by 37 industrialized countries and the European Union (EU), enabled nations to collectively address GHG emissions. Sustainable inventory management is a crucial and challenging task to reduce the environmental and social impacts of industries without compromising profitability. This complex challenge affects organizations across all economic sectors, necessitating decisions on policies, activities, and procedures to reduce carbon emissions and maintain a clean environment. Many industries in India struggle with managing carbon emissions effectively, emphasizing the need to follow government guidelines and regulations.

Chapter 1 explores the necessity of economical sourcing and procurement procedures. Organizations face increasing pressure to integrate sustainable practices into their supply chains due to global awareness and concerns about ecological and social issues.

Chapter 2 examines carbon emissions as a primary driver of global warming, posing a significant risk to the planet. As consumer concerns about quality and environmental impact grow, businesses are compelled to adopt sustainable practices. Developing inventory models that incorporate sustainability is essential for businesses to remain competitive while addressing issues like shortages and pricing.

Chapter 3 formulates a low-carbon inventory model for imperfect items with screening, preservation, and green investment under inflationary conditions in a fuzzy environment. It highlights the significant impact of carbon emissions from various sources and the need to reduce environmental consequences through green technologies and lower emissions.

Chapter 4 addresses the role of warehouses in inventory management, providing a controlled environment for storing, sorting, and managing products. Strategic warehouse placement helps businesses manage inventory during low demand and position goods closer to end customers.

Chapter 5 proposes a methodology for optimizing green logistics in the textile supply chain, focusing on reducing carbon emissions and water footprints. The study incorporates life cycle assessment (LCA) methods to evaluate the environmental impact of each supply chain stage and identifies efficiency gains and emission reductions.

Chapter 6 considers market price fluctuations, enabling cost-effective procurement decisions. It examines stock-dependent demand, dynamic pricing strategies, and volume flexibility within flexible manufacturing systems. The chapter also emphasizes optimizing transportation logistics to reduce carbon footprints and operational costs.

Chapter 7 develops an environmentally conscious inventory model for producers using a markdown strategy for fresh products. The model accounts for product deterioration, factors influencing demand, and the implementation of markdown strategies to maximize profit while managing carbon emissions.

Chapter 8 introduces a deteriorating inventory model addressing stock and advertisement-sensitive demand dynamics within a prepayment framework. The model integrates product deterioration, fluctuating demand, and prepayment arrangements to optimize inventory levels, pricing strategies, and advertising investments.

Chapter 9 focuses on inventory management for online B2C businesses with JIT (Just in Time) deliveries. It includes the Kanban system to manage workflow effectively and addresses the challenges of unpredictable online demands.

Chapter 10 presents an inventory model incorporating trade-credit policy and price-dependent demand, along with preservation technology. The model aims to maximize profit by extending the producer's credit period beyond the cycle time.

Chapter 11 develops a leakage inventory model in a fuzzy environment, avoiding shortages and incorporating carbon emission costs. The model uses fuzzy numbers for uncertain parameters and defuzzifies results using the signed distance method.

Chapter 12 highlights the importance of integrating sustainability into traditional inventory systems to align financial and environmental goals. It examines the interplay between inventory management, carbon emissions, partial backlogging, price-stock-dependent demand, and deterioration.

Chapter 13 derives an EOQ model for medication inventory during medical emergencies or epidemics, using time-dependent exponential demand and considering drug shortages and lead time.

This book compiles research methods and ordering policies for sustainable inventory management in India. It addresses a critical gap in sustainable inventory management research in India and provides valuable insights for practitioners, educators, researchers, and retailers/managers to reduce carbon emissions while effectively managing inventory.

Ahmedabad, India — Nita H. Shah
Greater Noida, India — Mandeep Mittal

Contents

About the Editors

Prof. Nita H. Shah heads the School of Emerging Science and Technology at Gujarat University, India. She is a post-doctoral visiting research fellow at the University of New Brunswick, Canada. Professor Nita's research interests include inventory modeling in the supply chain, robotic modeling, mathematical modeling of infectious diseases, image processing, dynamical systems and their applications, etc. She has completed 3-UGC sponsored projects. She has published 13 monographs, five textbooks, and 525+ peer-reviewed research papers and book Chapters. Her five edited books have been published by international publishers such as Springer. She has guided 34 Ph.D. students and 15 M.Phil. students till now. She has travelled in the USA, Singapore, Canada, South Africa, Malaysia, and Indonesia for lectures and visiting faculty posts. She was the Vice-President of the Operational Research Society of India and council member of Indian Mathematical Society. She is the secretary of Gujarat Science Academy.

Prof. Mandeep Mittal has 24 years of experience in higher education institutions. Currently, he serves as a Professor and Head of the Department of Mathematics in the School of Computer Science, Engineering, and Technology at Bennett University, part of The Times Group in Greater Noida, India. He earned his post-doctorate from Hanyang University, South Korea, his Ph.D. from the University of Delhi, India, and his postgraduation from IIT Roorkee, India. Professor Mittal has published over 100 research articles in international journals, book chapters, and conferences. He has authored and edited 10 books with IGI Global, USA, and Springer, Singapore. Additionally, he is a series editor of Inventory Optimization for Springer Singapore Pvt. Ltd. He has guided seven Ph.D. scholars and is currently supervising six students in Inventory Control and Management. Previously, he was the Head of the Department of Mathematics and Dean of Student Activities at Amity School of Engineering and Technology. Professor Mittal has also actively participated as a core member of organizing committees for international conferences in India and abroad.

Chapter 1
Sustainable Inventory Control and Management

Gurjapna Anand, Priyanka Vashisht, Simar Preet Singh, and Mandeep Mittal

Abstract This book chapter investigates the imperative requirement of economical sourcing and acquirement procedures. Associations are under developing weight to coordinate feasible hones into their supply chains due to the worldwide mindfulness and concerns concerning biological and social issues. The chapter commences by underscoring the basic principles of feasible sourcing, with a particular accentuation on the centrality of social obligation, assessments of environmental consequences, and moral consultations within the provider choice preparation. This paper looks at the focal points of feasible shopping that go past insignificant adherence to rules and controls. It can result in taking a toll on reserve funds, expanding brand mindfulness, and making strides in the capacity to handle supply chain interferences. The article investigates numerous methodologies and strategies for consolidating supportability into acquirement forms, such as executing green acquirement enactment, conducting provider supportability reviews, and locking in collaborative activities with providers to empower eco-efficiency and advancement. Moreover, it investigates the obstructions that companies confront when receiving economical sourcing and acquirement strategies, counting constrained assets, resistance from providers, and the need for progressing appraisal and upgrade. The introduction highlights case ponders and real-world illustrations that illustrate fruitful procedures and profitable experiences for accomplishing maintainable obtainment fabulousness.

Keywords Supply chain management · Inventory · Green inventory · Inventory optimization · Sustainability

G. Anand · P. Vashisht (✉)
Department of Computer Science and Engineering, Amity University Haryana, Gurugram, Haryana, India
e-mail: priyanka.vashisht@gmail.com

S. P. Singh
School of Computer Science Engineering and Technology, Bennett University, Greater Noida, UP, India

M. Mittal
Department of Mathematics, School of Computer Science Engineering and Technology, Bennett University, Greater Noida, UP, India

N. H. Shah and M. Mittal (eds.), *Sustainable Inventory Management*, Inventory Optimization, https://doi.org/10.1007/978-981-97-6765-6_1

1.1 Introduction

The concept of maintainability has picked up noteworthy significance within the modern, energetic, and interconnected worldwide economy, affecting different financial segments. Businesses are progressively perceiving the requirement of maintainable stock administration in accomplishing a concordant combination of social obligation, natural care, and financial proficiency. This chapter offers a comprehensive examination of maintainable stock control and administration Srivastava and Srivastava (2023), highlighting its importance, crucial standards, and essential components. The chapter commences by explaining the elemental concepts of supportability in stock administration, with a specific accentuation on the triple foot line approach, which coordinates social, natural, and financial measurements. This highlights the interconnecting of these viewpoints and their effect on an organization's execution, capacity to persevere difficulties, and position in a showcase where clients put significance on supportability. The chapter looks at the center standards that direct economical stock administration, counting:

(I) Natural Duties: This involves diminishing asset consumption, limiting squander era, and moderating natural results all through the complete stock handle. Social equity incorporates the advancement of ethically upright work practices, ensuring the security of workers in their work environments, and cultivating comprehensive collaborations over the complete supply chain (Dubey et al. 2015). (ii) Financial practicality: Accomplishing taken a toll decrease by utilizing feasible hones, diminishing stock levels, and improving operational effectiveness.

This book chapter traces an exhaustive methodology for accomplishing maintainable stock administration. The approach incorporates the enhancement of forms, integration of innovation, engagement of partners, vital arranging, and continuous enhancement. This explanation underlines the significance of cross-functional collaboration in successfully building and keeping up feasible stock frameworks, which includes a few offices counting fabricating, obtainment, coordination's, and client benefit. In addition, it investigates the effect of industry standards, streamlined forms, and advancing enactment on around the world feasible stock administration endeavors. In addition, it recognizes the importance of progression, data analytics, and digitization in making a distinction businesses overview execution pointer, make taught choices, and development diligent improvement in attainable stock organization (Raut and Singh 2022).

1.2 Literature Review

Mandeep Mittal's paper on credit financing explores how monetary instruments influence supply chain operations for things that are both falling apart and blemished, whereas too considering carbon emanations. Past investigations have inspected the impact of credit terms on stock arrangements, recognizing the significance of money related contemplations in optimizing supply chains (Goyal 1985; Chung and Huang 2003). Mittal expands these foundational ponders by coordinating the complexities related with item weakening and defects. Besides, the incorporation of carbon emanations reflects the developing significance of natural supportability in supply chain administration (Giri and Sharma 2015). By consolidating natural costs into the supply chain show, Mittal gives a comprehensive approach that adjusts budgetary, operational, and natural goals, contributing essentially to the field of maintainable supply chain administration in Optimizing Stock Administration.

"A Comprehensive Investigation of Models Joining Assorted Fluffy Request Capacities," Mittal looks at how stock administration can be optimized utilizing fluffy rationale to handle dubious requests. Fluffy rationale, presented by Zadeh (1965), has been broadly recognized for its capacity to oversee instability and imprecision, making it especially reasonable for stock administration where request is frequently eccentric (Dubois and Prade 1980). Mittal audits different models that apply fluffy rationale to stock control, highlighting their adaptability and vigor in managing with real-world complexities (Tanaka et al. 1983; Petrovic et al. 1999). This comprehensive examination underscores the significance of progressed numerical methods in making strides stock administration hones, emphasizing how fluffy request capacities can lead to more precise decision-making and diminished occurrences of stock-outs or overstock circumstances. Mittal's investigation on stock models for flawed, breaking down things inside a fluffy environment addresses the challenges posed by item quality and request instability. Conventional stock models frequently accept idealize things and deterministic requests, which don't reflect real-world conditions (Nahmias 1982; Raafat 1991). Mittal's show consolidates fluffy rationale to oversee the instability inborn in supply and request, building on prior work by Crutzen (1991) and Wang and Tooth (2001). By bookkeeping for the continuous misfortune of item esteem over time, Mittal gives a more versatile and reasonable approach to stock control, especially in businesses where item quality and shelf-life are basic components. This investigation highlights the significance of considering both disintegration rates and request inconstancy to create successful stock methodologies. Mittal's paper on optimizing supply chain procedures for falling apart things and defective fabricating beneath carbon outflow controls investigates the basic crossing point of fabricating flaws, item disintegration, and natural directions. Past thoughts have inspected the complexities of overseeing falling apart things and flawed generation forms (Goyal and Giri 2001; Papachristos and Konstantaras 2006). Mittal builds on this work by joining the extra measurement of carbon emanation controls, reflecting the expanding significance of maintainability in supply chain administration (Pachauri et al. 2014). His show gives a comprehensive system for optimizing supply chain operations, adjusting the trade-offs between generation proficiency, item quality, and natural affect. These inquiries about emphasizes the require for all encompassing approaches that consider numerous facets of supply chain administration, counting administrative compliance and supportability objectives, subsequently contributing to more economical and productive supply chain procedures. In brief, Mandeep Mittal's investigation progresses the field of supply chain and stock administration by tending to complex issues such as budgetary techniques, request vulnerability, item weakening, and natural supportability. His integration of fluffy rationale, monetary contemplations, and natural impacts into conventional stock and supply chain models gives a more all-encompassing and practical approach to overseeing cutting edge supply chains. These commitments are significant for creating maintainable and effective supply chain methodologies that can meet the advancing requests of businesses and administrative situations.

1.3 Environmental Impacts of Inventory Management

Managing inventory is an influential factor of supply chain-based operations, since it has a substantial influence on both the profitability and environmental sustainability of a company. This chapter examinations the eminent natural impacts connected to stock administration methodologies inside the setting of feasible stock control and administration. This explains the relationship between stock strategies and natural results. Figure 1.1 analyzes the most natural issues that emerge from conventional stock administration approaches.

Lifted stock levels result in expanded usage of assets such as water, control, and crude materials, driving to the consumption of assets and natural strain. However, inefficient inventory management methods sometimes result in surplus or outdated inventory, leading to the development of waste, disposal in landfills, and subsequent environmental pollution. The administration, capacity, and development of stock contribute to the discharge of nursery gases, which decline natural corruption and climate alteration. In expansion, it surveys the natural impacts at a few stages of the stock lifetime, counting fabricating, acquirement, conveyance, and transfer. This paper analyzes the concept of life cycle evaluation (LCA) as an intensive strategy for surveying the natural impacts of stock administration techniques. The chapter emphasizes the significance of using sustainable inventory techniques to reduce the environmental impact, as seen in Fig. 1.2.

Inventory optimization entails the application of lean inventory principles, just-in-time (JIT) inventory methods, and demand forecasting to reduce surplus inventory and optimize resource utilization. Green procurement minimizes environmental

Fig. 1.1 Environmental impacts [*Source* Own]

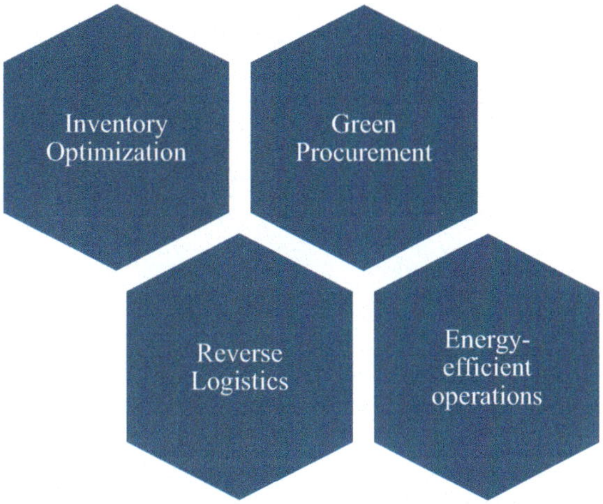

Fig. 1.2 Sustainable inventory methods [*Source* Own]

harm along the whole supply chain (Kannan et al. 2021) by adopting environmentally conscious suppliers, eco-friendly materials, and sustainable sourcing. Reverse Logistics aims to minimize waste and promote the principles of the circular economy by implementing efficient systems for product returns, recycling, and reuse. Energy-efficient operations (Vashisht et al. 2024) decrease energy usage and greenhouse gas emissions by employing energy-efficient (Vashisht et al. 2017) equipment, warehouse configurations, and transportation methods. This book chapter aims to promote the adoption of holistic approaches that connect business goals with environmental stewardship to achieve sustainable inventory control and management. It does so by assessing the environmental impacts of inventory management and advocating for the implementation of sustainable practices. Green inventory control aims to reduce the environmental impact of inventory management while maintaining efficiency and meeting customer needs. Certainly, there are some principle concepts of green inventory control such as demand forecasting and lean principles, ssustainable sourcing and procurement, inventory optimization strategies, effective storage and handling, integration of reverse logistics procedures etc. that will be explored in the following section.

1.4 Principles of Green Inventory Control

This section focuses on the set of ideas and procedures that emphasis on environmental sustainability and maximizes inventory management. Within the larger context of sustainable inventory management, it also explains the core ideas as shown in Fig. 1.3 that underpin green inventory control.

In Demand Forecasting and Lean Principles, predicting customer needs through data analytics and historical trends is the first step in green inventory control. By

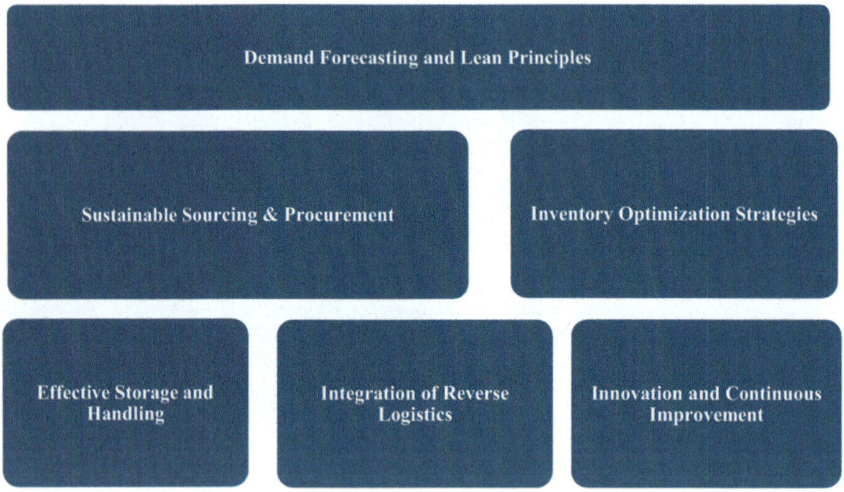

Fig. 1.3 Principles of green inventory control [*Source* Own]

synchronizing inventory levels with actual demand, implementing lean concepts that involve reducing waste, minimizing excess inventory, and optimizing manufacturing processes results in improved resource efficiency and reduced environmental footprint. Executing maintainable obtainment techniques incorporate choosing items with least natural affect, inclining toward providers that follow to moral work benchmarks, and selecting providers with eco-friendly certifications. Green acquirement approaches ensure the moral procurement of stock items and progress natural stewardship over the whole supply chain (Kannan et al. 2021). By consolidating procedures like financial arrange amount (EOQ), security stock enhancement, and ABC examination, stock administration can be made strides through the diminishment of squander and carrying costs. Just-in-time (JIT) stock frameworks advance asset preservation by decreasing abundance stock and the coming about natural costs. Green stock control centers on actualizing proficient capacity and taking care of procedures to enhance space usage, diminish vitality utilization, and limit squander. Robotized distribution center innovations, eco-friendly capacity arrangements, and upgraded stock format all contribute to maintainable operations. The execution of turn around coordination's components for item returns, reusing, and remanufacturing encourages the selection of a circular economy worldview Carter and Rogers (2008). Green stock control includes the execution of methodologies to reuse, repair, and reuse items. These methods have the objective of lessening squander generation, drawing out the life expectancy of things, and advancing natural maintainability. A basic component for establishing environmentally friendly stock control may be a solid commitment to development and persistent advancement. Associations can improve proficiency and empower supportability by actualizing cutting-edge innovation like as fake insights (AI) (Narang et al. 2024) and the Web of Things (IoT), encouraging participation over distinctive capacities, and expanding representative association. Besides, accomplishing stock enhancement for maintainability involves executing strategies that limit the natural impression while concurrently keeping up or making strides operational viability. Another area investigates diverse stock enhancement strategies that are particularly equipped to improve supportability.

1.5 Inventory Optimization Techniques for Sustainability

The chapter on stock advancement procedures for maintainability in this book analyzes the critical part that stock enhancement approaches play in progressing maintainability within the space of stock control and administration (Sarkis et al. 2011). To follow feasible commerce hones, the archive presents an assortment of methodologies and strategies pointed at enhancing stock levels, limiting squander, and improving asset productivity, as portrayed in Fig. 1.4.

Organizations can enhance their ability to forecast client demand more accurately by leveraging data analytics and advanced demand forecasting algorithms. By effectively controlling inventory levels and minimizing excess inventory, the potential for waste and adverse environmental impacts can be mitigated. This approach also reduces the likelihood of having either excessive stock or stockouts. ABC Analysis is put into practice organizations can allocate resources and focus more heavily on high-value items by using ABC analysis (Govindan and Soleimani 2021), which classifies inventory items according to their relative importance. For lower-value products, leaner inventory procedures can be implemented. To support sustainability goals, this

Fig. 1.4 Inventory optimization techniques [*Source* Own]

segmentation makes inventory management (Sarkis et al. 2011) and resource allocation more efficient (Vashisht et al. 2014). However, the Economic Order Quantity (EOQ)is the best practice (Bal and Singh 2023) for order quantity to reduce overall inventory costs, including ordering and holding expenses, can be found by computing the EOQ. Organizations can lessen their need for storage space, the environmental impact of surplus inventory, and excessive inventory by placing the proper orders at the right time. Another concept, namely, Just-in-Time (JIT) inventory systems focus on delivering goods and supplies exactly when needed, doing away with the need to retain excess inventory and cutting down on waste. JIT principles reduce waste production, energy use, and resource consumption associated with inventories, which is in line with sustainability goals. Subsequently, Safety Stock Optimization guarantees sufficient inventory availability while avoiding excessive safety stock that could result in waste. It fulfills this by enhancing the amount of security stock, considering the inconstancy of request, lead times, and the necessities for benefit measures. Energetic security stock models upgrade maintainability by viably overseeing stock levels based on fluctuating request designs. Vendor-Managed Stock (VMI) understandings include providers expecting obligation for controlling stock levels at client locales concurring to indicated stock objectives. Merchant Overseen Stock (VMI) cultivates collaboration, limits the natural impression of stock, limits costs related to stock administration, and makes strides renewal cycle effectiveness. Advancing the sizes of bunches in acquirement and fabricating operations leads to take a toll reserve funds in setup, evasion of squander, and more noteworthy effectiveness in generation. Advancing group measures contribute to the accomplishment of supportability goals by limiting fabric squander, vitality utilization, and asset usage over the supply chain. Checking the rate at which stock is turned over permits the assessment of stock effectiveness and the distinguishing proof of zones that require enhancement. Embracing compelling stock administration procedures can progress stock turnover rates, driving to less natural effect, lower dangers of out-of-date quality, and diminished holding costs related with abundance stock.

1.6 Mathematical Model

The objective of the model is to minimize the total cost associated with inventory control and management. This total cost comprises four main components:

Holding Fetched: This component speaks to the taken a toll of holding stock over time. It is calculated as the item of the holding taken a toll per unit of stock per period (C_{h}) and the normal stock level over the period.

Deficiency Fetched: This component speaks to the fetched caused when request surpasses stock levels, driving to deficiencies. It is calculated as the item of the deficiency taken a toll per unit of stock per period (C_{s}) and the overall number of units that are brief of request.

Requesting Fetched: This component speaks to the taken a toll of putting orders for stock. It is calculated as the item of the ordering taken a toll per arrange (C_o) and the whole number of orders put over the period.

Natural Taken a toll: This component speaks to the natural effect related to stock administration. It is calculated as the item of the natural taken a toll per unit of stock per period (C_e) and the normal stock level over the period.

The objective function looks to play down the entirety of these four taken a toll component over the whole-time skyline.

Let:

It is the inventory level at time t.

D_t be the demand for inventory at time *t*.
O_t be the order quantity at time *t*.
C_h be the holding cost per unit of inventory per time period.
C_s be the shortage cost per unit of inventory per time period.
C_o be the ordering cost per order.
C_e is the environmental cost associated with inventory management.

Assumptions

Constant demand rate $D_t = D$ for simplicity.

Ordering costs and environmental costs are proportional to the order quantity and inventory level, respectively.

Holding costs are incurred based on the average inventory level over the time period.

Shortages are allowed.

The objective function to be minimized is the total cost, considering both economic and environmental aspects:

$$\text{Total Cost} = C_h \times \frac{\sum_{t=1}^{T}\left(I_t + \frac{O_t}{2}\right)}{T} + C_s + \frac{\sum_{t=1}^{T}\max(0, +D - I_t)}{T} + C_o * \frac{\sum_{t=1}^{T} o_t}{T} + C_e * \frac{\sum_{t=1}^{T} I_t}{T} \tag{1.1}$$

Equation (1.1) is applicable with subject to below criteria's:

Inventory balance equation: $I_t + 1 = I_t + O_t - \mathrm{D}$
Non-negativity constraints: $I_t \geq 0, \forall t$
Order quantity constraints: $O_t \geq 0, \forall t$.

This model aims to find the optimal order quantity O_t at each period that minimizes the total cost, considering holding costs, shortage costs, ordering costs, and environmental costs associated with inventory management while ensuring the inventory balance over time. Solving this model provides insights into how businesses can effectively manage their inventory in a sustainable manner by considering both economic and environmental factors.

1.7 Green Packaging and Materials Handling

This region looks at the noteworthiness of utilizing ecologically inviting bundling and grasping capable methodologies for managing with materials in organize to advance practicality inside the field of stock control and organization. This substance analyzes strategies, concepts, and perfect techniques pointed at reducing the common impact, progressing resource utilize, and pushing for eco-friendly operations all through the full supply chain.

A few characteristics are pivotal for supportability, counting eco-friendly bundling materials, plan enhancement, reusability, squander decrease, and others, as portrayed in Fig. 1.5. Utilizing ecologically inviting pressing materials diminishes squander, reduces its effect on the environment, and advances the thoughts of the circular economy. It is essential for maintainability to optimize bundling plan to play down fabric utilize, maximize space utilize, and progress item security. Compelling bundling plan cuts down on bundling squander, transportation costs, and packaging-related nursery gas outflows. Utilizing bundling that's reused and returnable, counting beds, cartons, and holders, makes a difference decrease squander and moderate assets. It moreover makes a difference with switch coordination, diminish bundling squander, and make the supply chain more naturally inviting. Utilizing lightweight and moderate bundling plans brings down the number of materials utilized, the weight of the shipment, and the carbon emanations (Zhang et al. 2021) caused by bundling. It also maximizes space usage, saves transportation expenses, and lessens environmental effect when being distributed. Resolving issues with over-packaging and unnecessary void fill materials in e-commerce packaging is critical to sustainability. Online retail businesses can increase efficiency and lessen their environmental impact by implementing eco-friendly packing procedures, sustainable cushioning materials, and appropriately sized packaging. Energy consumption and carbon emissions (Zhang et al. 2021) in warehouse operations are decreased by using environmentally friendly and energy-efficient materials handling equipment (Vashisht et al. 2014), such as automated storage solutions, conveyor systems, and electric forklifts. Sustainable logistics methods benefit from having equipment for handling commodities that is efficient. Reducing packaging waste and advancing a circular economy approach are two benefits of implementing waste reduction techniques, such as source reduction, recycling programs, and waste-to-energy efforts. Recycling pallets and packing materials saves natural resources and lessens waste going to landfills. Innovation and sustainability are promoted throughout the packaging and materials handling value chain through cooperation with logistics partners, packaging suppliers, and stakeholders. A more sustainable inventory environment is facilitated by collaborations on waste management (Seuring and Muller 2008), eco-friendly material procurement, and sustainable packaging projects.

Apart from smart packaging, its handling, reusability etc. waste management strategies are very crucial parameters for sustainable inventory management and are discussed in the following section.

Fig. 1.5 Importance of green packaging [*Source* Own]

1.8 Waste Reduction Strategies in Sustainable Inventory Management

This section explores the waste reduction strategies into sustainable inventory management practices (Seuring and Muller 2008) and how it can significantly contribute to environmental conservation and operational efficiency. Various waste management points are shown in Fig. 1.6.

While implementing the lean manufacturing concepts the application embraces effective waste reduction at every stage of the production process. This involves reducing excess inventory, streamlining processes, and optimizing resource utilization. A just-in-time (JIT) inventory management system (Pagell and Wu 2009) seeks to decrease surplus inventory levels and minimize waste related to excessive production, unnecessary storage, and obsolescence. This methodology guarantees that stock is procured and moved as it were when it is fundamental for fabrication or dissemination. Setting up a solid association with providers is exceedingly critical in arranging materials and components that have the properties of being strong, recyclable, and naturally inviting. Select providers that organize supportability in their operations and offer items with less bundling and squander. Moreover, by actualizing stock enhancement procedures like request determining, stock segmentation, and security stock enhancement, we will guarantee that stock levels are adjusted with genuine request and generation necessities. This methodology decreases the likelihood of storing up an intemperate sum of stock and reduces the amount of squander coming about from overloading products. Maintainable Item Plan is critical as maker make things with a center on supportability, by utilizing materials that can be reused,

Fig. 1.6 Waste reduction strategies [*Source* Own]

decayed normally, or utilized once more. Enhance the efficacy of item bundling to limit squander generation and relieve the natural effect over the total item lifecycle. Actually, squander reduction and reusing programs interior of the association is done to limit squander generation and advance the recovery and reutilization of materials. This includes the method of classifying and reusing undesirable materials, such as paper, cardboard, plastics, and metals. Be that as it may, the objective is to upgrade vitality and asset proficiency in generation and dissemination operations to limit squander related to vitality utilization, water utilization, and extraction of crude materials. To moderate the adverse impact on the environment, it is prudent to spend budgetary assets towards obtaining energy-efficient hardware, embrace water preservation strategies, and explore the use of renewable vitality sources. Eventually, the objective is to make a structure that advances progressing upgrade and following of performance, fostering a mentality that effectively looks for ways to decrease wasteful aspects and improve maintainability. Reliably assess basic execution measurements (KPIs) related with squander generation, stock control, and natural impact, and execute appropriate remedial measures.

1.9 Energy-Efficient Warehouse Operations

This section investigates the basics that must be integrated with energy-efficient innovations in distribution center operations in order to attain economical stock control and administration. This segment offers a comprehensive investigation of the procedures, advances, and strategies that are very effective in diminishing vitality utilization, decreasing carbon emanations, and upgrading environmental maintainability within the space of distribution center administration (Pagell and Wu 2009). A vitality review and appraisal involve a careful examination of distribution center offices to pinpoint regions of vitality wastefulness and potential openings for improvement, as illustrated in Fig. 1.7. Through the examination of vitality utilization designs, hardware viability, and building framework execution, associations can create focused plans to progress vitality effectiveness.

Executing energy-efficient lighting arrangements, such as Driven lighting and movement sensor controls, in distribution centers leads to diminished power utilization and decreased lighting-related vitality costs.

Lighting optimization arrangements upgrade perceivability, security, and supportability whereas minimizing the antagonistic effect on the environment.

HVAC Framework Optimization alludes to the method of making strides the viability of warming, ventilation, and discuss conditioning (HVAC) frameworks by utilizing energy-efficient hardware, programmable indoor regulators, and upgrading cover. As a result, there is a reduction in energy consumption and a drop in the costs related to HVAC systems. Enhancing the HVAC system enhances the indoor air quality, enhances comfort, and supports energy sustainability in warehouses.

When designing warehouses, using energy-efficient elements like insulated walls, energy-efficient windows, and natural ventilation helps to decrease the transfer of heat, Minimize the requirement for heating or cooling systems and promote energy sustainability. Improvements made to the building envelope led to energy preservation and enhanced environmental resilience.

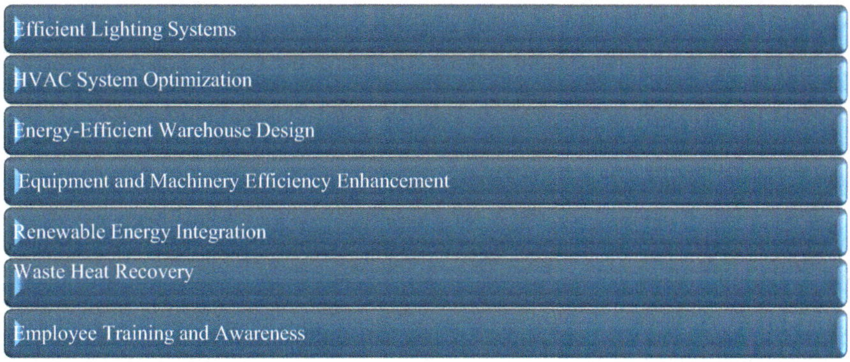

Fig. 1.7 Energy efficiency areas [*Source* Own]

Improving the proficiency of hardware and apparatus:

By transitioning to energy-efficient gear and apparatus, such as electric forklifts, transport frameworks, and robotized taking care of innovations, distribution center operations can essentially diminish vitality utilization and carbon emanations. Upgrading hardware effectiveness leads to expanded efficiency and supportability.

Renewable Vitality Integration includes joining renewable vitality sources such as sun powered boards, wind turbines, or geothermal frameworks into distribution center buildings. This decreases dependence on conventional vitality sources, brings down vitality costs, and advances the utilization of renewable vitality. Joining renewable vitality advances the accomplishment of maintainability destinations and the mindful administration of the environment.

Squander Warm Recuperation:

The execution of squander warm recuperation frameworks includes capturing and utilizing excess warm delivered by distribution center operations, such as gear operation or HVAC frameworks, for the reason of warming or other energy-intensive forms. Endeavors to recoup squander warm improve vitality proficiency and lessen natural results.

Employee Training and Awareness: Imparting knowledge and increasing consciousness among warehouse personnel regarding energy-saving methods, ways for conserving energy, and sustainability efforts cultivates a culture of energy efficiency. Encouraging staff to participate in energy-conserving actions and adopting optimal methods improves the sustainability initiatives in warehouse operations.

Warehouses can achieve substantial energy savings, operational efficiency, cost reductions, and environmental advantages in sustainable inventory control and management by implementing energy-efficient processes, utilizing sustainable technologies, and fostering a culture of energy conservation.

1.10 Sustainable Transportation and Logistics

This section examines the crucial significance of sustainable transportation and logistics methods in the context of attaining sustainable inventory control and management. The content explores tactics, advancements, and exemplary methods as shown in Fig. 1.8 and more focused on diminishing carbon emissions, maximizing supply chain effectiveness, and advocating for environmental sustainability in Transportation and logistics activities.

Green Fleet Management (Hall and Williams 2013) entails the implementation of fuel-efficient cars, alternative fuel choices (such as electric or hybrid vehicles), and the optimization (Yu et al. 2023) of route planning to minimize fuel usage and carbon emissions in transportation operations. Green fleet initiatives have a role in promoting environmental sustainability and achieving cost savings.

Transportation Mode Optimization involves optimizing various modes of transportation, such as rail, canals, or multimodal transport, by considering factors such as distance, cargo volume, and environmental impact. The point of this advancement

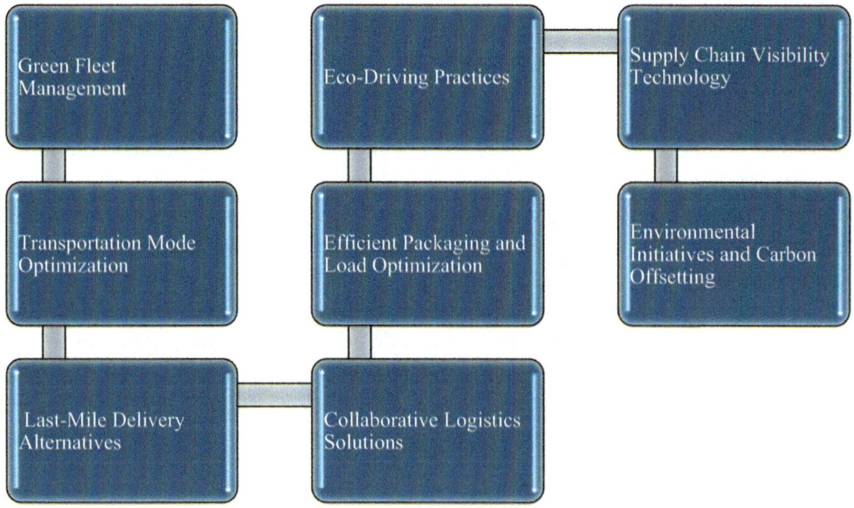

Fig. 1.8 Importance of sustainable transportation and logistics [*Source* Own]

strategy (Yu et al. 2023) is to limit both the emanation of nursery gasses and the costs related to transportation. Advancing the utilize of economical choices cultivates the integration of naturally mindful calculated forms.

Implementing diverse last-mile delivery methods, such as using bicycle couriers, electric vans, or micro-hubs, can effectively reduce emissions and alleviate traffic congestion in metropolitan areas. Last-mile optimization solutions aim to minimize delivery times, improve customer happiness, and promote sustainability in logistics operations.

Companies can enhance the efficiency of their resource utilization, reduce the distance travelled with empty loads, and mitigate the environmental impact of their supply chain transportation by adopting collaborative logistics solutions like freight pooling, shared warehouses, or collaborative shipping. This can be achieved by reducing carbon emissions. Collaboration improves the efficiency and long-term sustainability of logistics networks.

Optimized Packaging and Load Efficiency: Through the utilization of eco-friendly packaging materials, precise sizing of packaging to match contents, and maximizing load capacities, we can minimize waste, decrease the usage of packaging materials, and reduce fuel consumption during transportation. Implementing efficient packing and load optimization solutions improves the sustainability and cost-effectiveness of transportation.

Encouraging eco-driving practices and giving driver training on fuel-efficient approaches, while also rewarding sustainable behaviors, can effectively optimize fuel economy, decrease emissions, and improve driver safety in transportation operations. Eco-driving activities contribute to the achievement of sustainability objectives and enhance environmental performance.

By utilizing supply chain (Chabowski and Mena 2015) visibility technology, such as real-time tracking, data analytics, and predictive modeling, logistics efficiency may be improved, transportation delays can be reduced, and carbon emissions can be minimized. Supply chain optimization (Chabowski and Mena 2015) promotes the use of sustainable transportation methods and aims to achieve operational excellence.

Participating in carbon offsetting programs, investing in renewable energy projects, and engaging in environmental initiatives like tree planting or waste reduction campaigns show dedication to environmental responsibility and sustainability in transportation and logistics.

The organizations can attain substantial environmental advantages, cost reductions, supply chain durability, and stakeholder contentment in sustainable inventory control and management by incorporating sustainable transportation and logistics practices, utilizing technology, encouraging collaboration, and advocating for eco-friendly initiatives.

1.11 Technology Applications for Sustainable Inventory Management

This section examines how technological applications can facilitate the development of sustainable inventory management techniques as depicted in Fig. 1.9. It also explores cutting-edge technology, digital solutions, and data-driven strategies that focus on improving inventory management (Karkkainen and Holmstrom 2021), reducing environmental harm, and advancing sustainability across the supply chain.

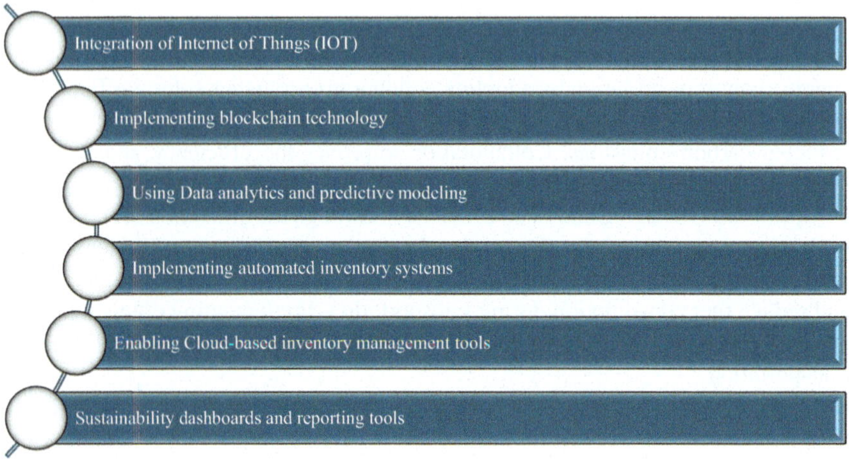

Fig. 1.9 Applications for sustainable inventory management [*Source* Own]

The integration of Internet of Things (IoT) devices, such as RFID tags, sensors, and linked devices, improves the process of inventory tracking, monitoring, and management. IoT-enabled systems offer immediate data on inventory levels (Karkkainen and Holmstrom 2021), conditions, and movements, allowing for proactive decision-making and minimizing waste.

Implementing blockchain technology improves supply chain transparency, traceability, and trust by securely documenting transactions and data along the supply chain. Blockchain technology guarantees the integrity of sourcing, minimizes the chances of counterfeit products, and fosters sustainability by implementing transparent and verifiable procedures.

Data analytics and predictive modeling are utilized to enhance inventory planning, demand forecasting, and supply chain optimization by employing techniques such as machine learning. Using data-driven bits of knowledge permits for proactive hazard administration, fetched reserve funds, and supportability points of interest in stock administration operations.

Executing robotized stock frameworks, such as mechanical technology, robotized capacity and recovery frameworks (AS/RS), and independent vehicles, upgrades distribution center operations, decreases human blunders, and improves effectiveness. Mechanization innovations improve stock precision, work efficiency, and maintainability in stock administration.

Cloud-based stock administration devices empower real-time communication, consistent information trade, and adaptable versatility among accomplices within the supply chain. Cloud arrangements make strides the capacity to see, work together, and get to inventories, whereas moreover diminishing costs and the environmental effect of IT foundation.

Devices for observing and detailing maintainability incorporate supportability dashboards, announcing devices, and Key Execution Markers (KPIs). These devices help track and upgrade natural information and maintainability execution. Information use moves forward supportability administration by empowering well-informed decision-making and guaranteeing duty for maintainable stock control.

Associations can achieve economical stock administration hones, improve asset usage, diminish natural affect, and give enduring esteem by receiving mechanical applications, advanced advancements, and data-driven arrangements.

1.12 Metrics and Key Performance Indicators for Sustainability

This section investigates the fundamental work of measurements and key execution pointers (KPIs) in measuring and managing maintainability inside the domain of stock control and administration, as portrayed in Fig. 1.10. This article analyzes the method of making, executing, and understanding measurements and key execution pointers (KPIs) that are in line with economical hones and objectives for natural

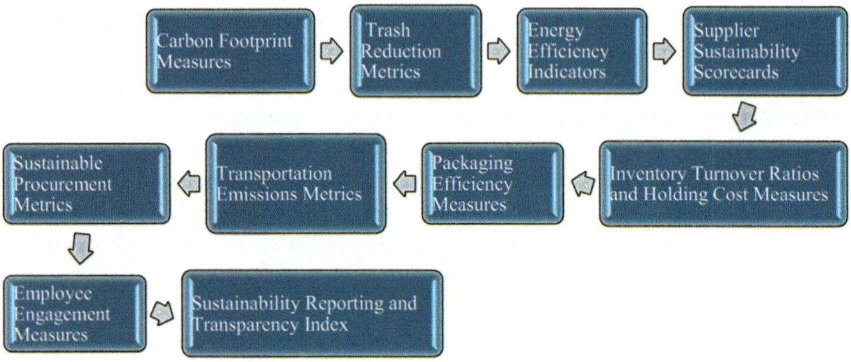

Fig. 1.10 Key performance indicators [*Source* Own]

stewardship. This article looks at the method of making, executing, and understanding measurements and key execution pointers (KPIs) that are in line with maintainable hones and objectives for natural stewardship.

Carbon impression calculations evaluate the amount of nursery gas outflows created by stock administration exercises, transportation, and warehousing operations. Measuring the sum of carbon emanations created for each unit of stock or shipment gives imperative data around the natural effect and conceivable ways to decrease it.

Squander diminishment measurements track the sum of squander produced, reused, or arranged of amid stock forms. The user's content is designed as a bullet point. Measurements such as waste preoccupation rates, reusing rates, and waste-to-energy proportions are utilized to survey the viability of squander administration and advance the standards of a circular economy.

Vitality proficiency markers give an exact implied of measuring the amount of vitality expended, the vitality utilization designs, and the energy-saving measures actualized in stockrooms, transportation armadas, and coordination exercises. Measurements like as vitality escalated per unit of stock or per transportation mile are used to evaluate vitality execution (Boon-itt and Wong 2022) and offer a course for upgrading productivity.

Provider maintainability scorecards survey provider execution utilizing maintainability criteria, counting natural measures, moral sourcing, and social obligation (Preuss et al. 2009). Scorecards assess the degree to which providers comply with, uncover, and impact maintainability objectives inside the supply chain.

Stock turnover proportions and holding fetched measurements assess the adequacy of stock administration by measuring the speed at which stock is sold and the costs caused in keeping up stock. Maximizing inventory turnover reduces excess inventory, lowers holding costs, and encourages efficient use of resources.

Bundle proficiency evaluations evaluate the viability of utilizing bundle materials, utilizing legitimate measuring strategies, and embracing ecologically neighborly bundling. Metrics such as packaging waste per unit of inventory or weight of packing materials per shipment are utilized to assess packaging sustainability and efforts to minimize waste.

Transportation emissions metrics measure the amount of greenhouse gas emissions produced by transportation activities, as well as the amount of fuel consumed and the efficiency of fuel usage in logistical operations. Tracking emissions per mile, enhancing fuel economy, and increasing the utilization of alternative fuels support the adoption of sustainable (Pagell et al. 2010) transportation practices.

Sustainable procurement metrics (Pagell et al. 2010) measure supplier variety, ethical sourcing standards, and environmental impact assessments in procurement procedures. Procurement sustainability is measured by metrics such as supplier sustainability ratings, percentages of eco-friendly product sourcing, and fair-trade certifications.

Employee engagement measures evaluate the extent to which employees are informed, actively involved in training, and embracing sustainability methods in inventory management (Pagell and Shevchenko 2014). Metrics such as the number of hours spent on staff training, the results of sustainability surveys, and the level of participation in sustainability initiatives are used to measure employee engagement and the extent of their impact.

The Sustainability Reporting and Transparency Index is a compilation of essential sustainability measures, KPIs, and performance indicators that are consolidated into a comprehensive sustainability report. The index improves clarity, responsibility, and communication with stakeholders regarding sustainability accomplishments and advancements.

Case Studies in Sustainable Inventory Control and Management

This section presents a case study detailing the approaches adopted by Toyota company to achieve its successful outcomes. The case study, Toyota: Enforcing Lean Principles to Minimize Waste highlights the summary, approach, and results of sustainable sourcing and green procurement in real-world scenarios of the Toyota organization as described in Fig. 1.11.

Sustainable inventory control and management are crucial in modern manufacturing and supply chain operations. They ensured that resources are used efficiently, waste is minimized, and environmental impacts are appropriately reduced. One company that exemplifies these principles is Toyota. Renowned for its innovative approaches, Toyota has implemented lean principles to minimize waste, creating a model for sustainable inventory management. This case study explores Toyota's methodologies, strategies, and the impact of its lean principles on inventory control.

The Incline Standards of Toyota include the application of incline fabricating, commonly known as the Toyota Generation Framework (TPS). This method utilizes systematic preparation with the objective of lessening squander whereas too maintaining ideal levels of effectiveness. Toyota applies incline standards by joining key concepts such Just-in-Time (JIT), Kaizen, Jidoka, Heijunka, and the Poke-Yoke approach.

The Just-in-time (JIT) fabricating approach centers on boosting company return on speculation by diminishing in-process stock and the related costs of stock keeping.

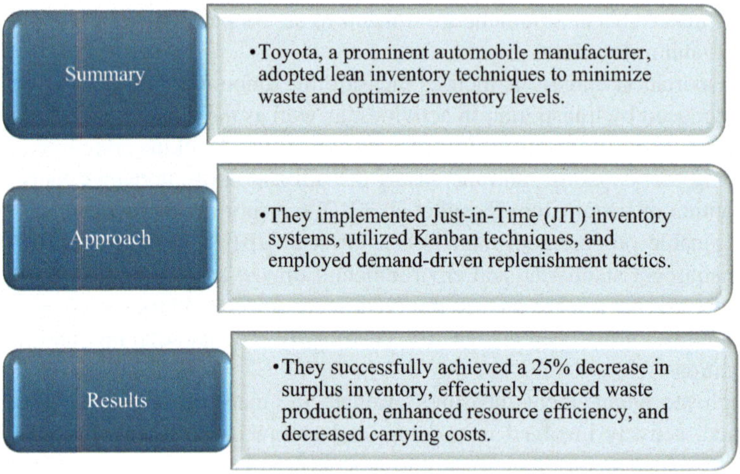

Fig. 1.11 Case study: Toyota [*Source* Own]

Toyota actualizes the just-in-time generation strategy, which includes creating things within the correct amount required at the exceptionally time they are required. This approach limits the sum of excess stock and viably diminishes the sum of squander produced. The Kaizen guideline, frequently known as Ceaseless Advancement, centers on making continuous and slow improvements to forms. The Jidoka guideline, moreover, known as Mechanization with a Human Touch, ensures that any fabricating handle ends right away upon the location of an issue. This measure prevents the passage of faulty products throughout the production line, therefore diminishing the amount of waste generated. The Heijunka, also known as Levelling Production, seeks to optimize production schedules by minimizing variations in production rates.

By leveling the type and quantity of production, Toyota reduces bottlenecks and maintains a consistent workflow, minimizing idle time and overproduction. The Poka-Yoke (Mistake-Proofing) technique involves designing processes to prevent errors or make them immediately apparent. By incorporating simple, fail-safe mechanisms, Toyota ensures quality control at every step of production.

The implementation of Toyota's lean principles is very much comprehensive and integrated into every aspect of its real time operations by maintaining Supplier Relationships, production processes and healthy employee involvement. Toyota maintains close relationships with its suppliers, ensuring they also adhere to lean principles. This collaboration also extends the benefits of lean practices throughout the supply chain, from raw materials to finished products. At Toyota's manufacturing plants, JIT and Jidoka principles are paramount. Production lines are highly flexible, capable of adjusting quickly to changes in demand without accumulating excess inventory. Automation and robotics are employed, yet human oversight ensures quality and timely response to any issues. The principle of Kaizen is deeply ingrained in the culture of Toyota. Staff members are highly encouraged to actively discover any inefficiencies and suggest potential enhancements. Regular training and workshops enable personnel to proficiently implement lean ideas.

The usage of Incline Standards offers a huge number of points of interest, counting squander lessening, quality upgrade, productivity enhancement, and supportability advancement. Toyota successfully kills fabric squander by diminishing overabundance stock and generation wasteful aspects. This not as it were decreases costs but mitigates the biological impression. By applying Jidoka and Poka-Yoke methods, the recognizable proof and determination of deficiencies can be assisted, coming about in made strides item quality and less squander created by inadequate things. Besides, incline standards progress mechanical forms by limiting downtime and amplifying the effective utilize of assets. As a result, there's a diminishment in operational costs and an increment in efficiency. Toyota's commitment to supportability is clear in its execution of incline hones. The company accomplishes natural maintainability by limiting squander and expanding asset use, consequently cultivating an agreeable environmental adjust.

In outline, Toyota's joining of incline standards in its stock control and administration frameworks sets a standard for the appropriation of feasible fabricating strategies. Toyota accomplishes operational brilliance and underpins natural supportability by organizing squander lessening, ceaseless enhancement, and successful asset use.

1.13 Results

After solving the mathematical model presented for sustainable inventory control and management, several key insights had emerged, shedding light on the optimal strategies to balance economic efficiency with environmental sustainability in inventory management practices.

- Ideal Arrange Amounts: The optimization show gives the ideal arrange amounts (O_t) at each period, guaranteeing that stock levels are overseen viably to meet the request whereas minimizing holding, deficiency, and requesting costs. These ideal arranged amounts reflect a cautious adjust between keeping up satisfactory stock levels and minimizing costs.
- Add up to Taken a toll Reserve funds: By joining natural costs into the stock administration system, businesses can accomplish critical add up to take a toll investment funds compared to conventional approaches that as it were considered financial components. The demonstration illustrates that by embracing economical stock methodologies, companies can at the same time decrease their natural effect and upgrade their budgetary execution.
- Natural Affect Diminishment: The consideration of natural costs within the optimization show highlights the significance of considering maintainability components in stock administration choices. The show distinguishes openings

to diminish natural effect through measures such as optimizing transportation courses, minimizing overabundance stock, and receiving green sourcing hones.
- Long-Term Supportability: about the outcomes emphasize the significance of receiving a long-term viewpoint in stock administration hones. By contributing to feasible stock control methodologies, businesses cannot as it were accomplish prompt taken a toll reserve funds but too position themselves for long-term victory in a progressively ecologically cognizant commercial center.
- Vital Experiences: The bits of knowledge picked up from the optimization demonstrate give profitable direction for businesses looking for to make strides their stock administration hones. By recognizing the ideal adjustment between financial effectiveness and natural supportability, companies can create key activities to improve their competitiveness while contributing to a more economical future.

1.14 Conclusion and Future Scope

This chapter highlights the vital significance of coordination maintainability standards into stock operations in arranging to attain economical stock control and administration. It is vital to coordinate natural and social components near the conventional center on taken a toll viability and benefit measures. This worldview alter involves joining strategies like squander lessening, ideal asset usage, and the appropriation of ecologically feasible hones over the complete supply chain. Receiving maintainable stock administration arrangements not as it were shielding the environment but too boosts a company's long-term benefit by making strides its brand notoriety, guaranteeing adherence to laws, and cultivating advancement.

A compelling and long-lasting stock administration requires a comprehensive arrangement that incorporates numerous basic components. Data-driven decision making includes the utilize of progressed advances just like the Web of Things (IoT), Counterfeit Insights (AI), and Huge Information analytics to assemble real-time information and create taught assessments. Besides, the execution of inclined stock arrangements is fundamental for limiting squander, diminishing excess stock, and upgrading operational productivity. Moreover, the usage of circular economy models streamlines the forms of reusing, remanufacturing, and reutilizing assets. Moreover, it is basic to encourage collaborative tries by effectively including providers, shoppers, and other partners to progress supportability along the whole supply chain. Administrative compliance ensures strict adherence to natural laws and directions, subsequently maintaining a strategic distance from punishments and making strides market entry. End of the presents broad and promising prospects for feasible stock control and administration. With the developing conspicuousness of natural concerns, both companies and customers will progressively look for maintainable methods.

Crucial areas for future exploration and progress involve the incorporation of sophisticated predictive analytics. This involves the need for increased precision and incorporation to boost the accuracy of predicting demand and optimize the management of inventory, leading to a decrease in waste and improved use of resources.

Utilizing blockchain technology can improve transparency and traceability in the supply chain, ensuring sustainable sourcing and ethical conduct. Artificial intelligence (AI) (Tiwari and Choudhary 2022) and machine learning are essential for automating and enhancing inventory management processes, leading to smarter and eco-friendly operations. Enabling the extensive use of IoT devices will enable real-time monitoring and management of inventory levels, storage conditions, and movements throughout the supply chain. It is essential to adopt sustainable packaging options to reduce the environmental impact of storing and transporting goods. The advancement of circular economy principles will give priority to the management of product life cycles and encourage the production of long-lasting and recyclable things. Developing future standards and regulations will promote and incentivize the use of sustainable inventory methods, ensuring broad acceptance throughout the sector. Enhancing customer knowledge and education regarding sustainable products and processes would boost the demand for inventory that is sustainably managed. Promoting global collaboration to build standardized and sustainable inventory management practices will be beneficial as it allows for the sharing of knowledge and resources. In summary, the transition towards sustainable inventory control and management is not a fleeting fad, but a necessary imperative for the future. By adopting cutting-edge technology and implementing efficient procedures, businesses may successfully attain their sustainability objectives, strengthen their competitive advantage, and actively contribute to the betterment of the environment and society.

References

Bal A, Singh S (2023) Sustainable inventory management: practices, challenges, and opportunities. Resour Conserv Recycl 180:106023

Boon-itt S, Wong CY (2022) Sustainable inventory management practices and performance: the role of environmental uncertainty and green supply chain integration. Int J Prod Econ 242:108406

Carter CR, Rogers DS (2008) A framework of sustainable supply chain management: moving toward new theory. Int J Phys Distrib Logist Manage 38(5):360–387

Chabowski BR, Mena JA (2015) The role of information in sustainable supply chain management. Int J Phys Distrib Logist Manage 45(1/2):56–87

Chung KJ, Huang YF (2003) The optimal cycle time for EPQ inventory model under permissible delay in payments. Int J Prod Econ 84(3):307–318

Crutzen PJ, Zimmermann PH (1991) The changing photochemistry of the troposphere. Tellus A: Dyn Meteorol Oceanogr 43(4):136–151

Dubois D, Prade H (1980) Systems of linear fuzzy constraints. Fuzzy sets sys 3(1):37–48

Dubey R, Gunasekaran A, Childe SJ (2015) Big data analytics capability in supply chain agility: the moderating effect of organizational flexibility. Int J Prod Econ 176:30–43

Giri BC, Sharma S (2015) Optimizing a closed-loop supply chain with manufacturing defects and quality dependent return rate. J Manuf Sys 35:92–111

Govindan K, Soleimani H (2021) Sustainable inventory management: a bibliometric analysis and future research directions. J Clean Prod 280:124369

Goyal SK, Giri BC (2001) Recent trends in modeling of deteriorating inventory. Eur J Oper Res 134(1):1–16

Hall JW, Williams CA (2013) Greening the supply chain: interpreting the importance of integration for sustainability outcomes. Int J Prod Econ 146(1):351–366
Kannan D, Kannan PK, Haq AN (2021) Sustainable inventory management in closed-loop supply chains: a review and research agenda. Int J Prod Econ 237:108248
Karkkainen H, Holmström J (2021) Sustainability-driven inventory management: a literature review and research agenda. Int J Prod Econ 240:108220
Nahmias S (1982) Perishable inventory theory: a review. Oper Res 30(4):680–708
Narang A, Vashisht P, Bajaj SB (2024) Artificial intelligence in banking and finance. Int J Innov Res Comput Sci Technol 12(2):130–134
Pagell M, Shevchenko A (2014) Why research in sustainable supply chain management should have no future. J Supply Chain Manage 50(1):44–55
Pagell M, Wu Z (2009) Building a more complete theory of sustainable supply chain management using case studies of 10 exemplars. J Supply Chain Manage 45(2):37–56
Pagell M, Wu Z, Wasserman ME (2010) Thinking differently about purchasing portfolios: an assessment of sustainable sourcing. J Supply Chain Manage 46(1):57–73
Papachristos S, Konstantaras I (2006) Economic ordering quantity models for items with imperfect quality. Int J Prod Econ 100(1):148–154
Pachauri S (2014) Household electricity access a trivial contributor to CO2 emissions growth in India. Nature Clim Change 4(12):1073–1076
Petrovic D, Roy R, Petrovic R (1999) Supply chain modelling using fuzzy sets. Int J prod Econ 59(1–3):443–453
Preuss L, Haunschild K, Matten D (2009) A review of the literature on corporate social responsibility in international business: the role of government, NGOs and multinational companies. Int J Manage Rev 12(1):7–28
Raafat F (1991) Survey of literature on continuously deteriorating inventory models. J Oper Res Soc 42(1):27–37
Raut RD, Singh S (2022) A systematic literature review of sustainable inventory management: trends, challenges, and future directions. J Clean Prod 330:129922
Sarkis J, Zhu Q, Lai KH (2011) An organizational theoretic review of green supply chain management literature. Int J Prod Econ 130(1):1–15
Seuring S, Müller M (2008) From a literature review to a conceptual framework for sustainable supply chain management. J Clean Prod 16(15):1699–1710
Srivastava SK, Srivastava R (2023) Sustainable inventory control and management: a review. Int J Prod Res 61(1):1–19
Tanaka M (1983) The stability of steep gravity waves. J phys Soc Japan 52(9):3047–3055
Tiwari MK, Choudhary AK (2022) Sustainable inventory management using artificial intelligence techniques: a systematic review and future research directions. Comput Industr Eng 166:107328
Vashisht P, Kumar R, Sharma A (2014) Efficient dynamic replication algorithm using agent for data grid. Sci World J 2014(1):767016
Vashisht P, Sharma A, Kumar R (2017) Strategies for replica consistency in data grid—a comprehensive survey. Concurr Comput Pract Exp 29(4):e3907
Vashisht P, Bajaj SB, Narang A (2024) Energy-efficient fog computing: a review and future directions. Int J Innov Res Comput Sci Technol 12(2):135–139
Wang W (2001) Early detection of gear tooth cracking using the resonance demodulation technique. Mech Sys Signal Process 15(5):887–903
Yu W, Zhang M, Zhang G (2023) A novel bi-objective optimization model for sustainable inventory management considering green practices and carbon emission constraints. J Clean Prod 344:130273
Zadeh LA (1965) Fuzzy sets. Information and control
Zhang Y, Lu W, Lai KH (2021) Sustainable inventory management under carbon emission constraints: an EOQ model. Transp Res Part E Logist Transp Rev 146:102232

Chapter 2
Imperfect Inventory Model with Exponential Demand Having Carbon Emission and Backlog

Rakhi Trivedi and Vinti Dhaka

Abstract It is commonly known that carbon emissions are one of the main causes of global warming, which poses a serious risk to the world. As it is often known, carbon emissions are one of the primary drivers of global warming, which is considered a major environmental problem. Because of this, consumers are now more concerned with quality and the environment than ever before, and as a result, they demand that businesses practice sustainability. In this case, business should develop and apply inventory models that consider sustainability. The company must also deal with issues like shortages and pricing in order to survive in a cutthroat industry. In addition, some products are distinct from the norm and call for feeding them until they reach a certain weight before being slaughtered and sold to customers. All the items are considered in the form of imperfect items. In this regard, the study suggests an inventory model for producing mediocre quality when there are backlogs and exponential demand with carbon emissions. The backorder is complete. As demand is an exponential function. In order to maximise the expected total profit per unit of time, the recommended inventory model takes into account the order amount, backorder quantity, and retail cost of perfect quality developing products. To demonstrate the application and pertinence of the inventory model, some numerical examples are resolved in order to illustrate the use and the applicability of the inventory model. Finally, a sensitivity analysis is conducted and some managerial insights are given.

Keywords Inventory · Exponential demand · Carbon emission · Shortages · Imperfect items

R. Trivedi · V. Dhaka (✉)
School of Basic and Applied Sciences, IILM University, Greater Noida, U.P. 201310, India
e-mail: drvintidhaka@gmail.com

N. H. Shah and M. Mittal (eds.), *Sustainable Inventory Management*, Inventory Optimization, https://doi.org/10.1007/978-981-97-6765-6_2

2.1 Introduction

In today's market, the inventory management is a valued function. It is control system of the firm. It is a buffer system between the demand and supply. The researcher Harris (1913) firstly introduced the EOQ model in the development of market. He gave the basic key for all the firms. Climate change is mostly caused by emissions of carbon from logistics and supply chain activities. After the Kyoto Protocol was passed in 2005, governments and environmental organisations made a concerted effort to embrace technical solutions and policies aimed at reducing carbon emissions. Businesses collaborated with government policies and laws to reduce carbon emissions, encouraging a balance between each party in strategic decision-making to optimise profit goals while adhering to carbon reduction requirements. The proposed model takes into account the roles of the manufacturer as the leader and the retailer with the best ordering, selling price, shipping, and investment decisions made by both parties as the equilibrium is reached. Nowadays competition is too much high as every company uses different advertisement technique to sell their product and customers have different choice in their hand so the best quality product is always sold. Hence, the company focused on the quality of the product.

This chapter is divided into eight sections, in the Sect. 2.2 there is literature review. Section 2.3 contain the assumptions and notation. Mathematical modelling is in Sect. 2.4. The solution procedure is in Sect. 2.5. Section 2.6 defines the result with its sensitivity analysis. Section 2.8 concludes the chapter.

2.2 Literature Review

"Carbon dioxide emissions and carbon footprint control have become more popular topics in supply chain management. Policies to reduce carbon emissions, such as carbon emission caps, carbon taxes, carbon quotas, emissions trading, and carbon offsets, have been addressed in several previous studies. Previous studies have mainly focused on the equal decision-making ability of retailers involved in the supply chain. Companies are increasingly aware of the need to reduce carbon footprints and the fact that the cultivation of products is a source of emissions at many points in the supply chain, including cultivation, inventory management, and shipping. Thus, Zhang et al. (2016a) presented an inventory model that integrates carbon constraint mechanisms and extends the EOQ framework. Similarly, Dhanam and Jesintha (2017) developed a fuzzy inventory model specialized for fast and slow growing commodities, such as baby carrots and corn. The model considers the limits of deterioration within a single period to determine the maximum inventory level per period. Sebatjane (2018a) identified three problems that may arise in an inventory system with growing items. To evaluate whether shortages are economically desirable and therefore more beneficial than a situation in which shortages are not allowed, Garza Cabello (2019) created an inventory model for growing raw materials, taking into account planned shortages and quality deterioration. Sebatjane and Adetunji (2020a) presented a three-tier supply chain inventory management model for growing commodities. The model consists of processing plants, farms, and retail stores that are responsible for meeting consumer demand. Later after a long time, an unused theme, that is, stock administration for developing things, has too been included in the induction of stock models. A developing thing is a kind of item which is competent of development amid time like yard creatures, and is not at all like idle items that do not obtain increment in weight amid capacity. Developing things are joined for to begin with time in an EOQ stock demonstrated by Rezaei (Zhang et al. 2016b). Here, the weight increase of things is the primary distinction between the stock models proposed by Rezaei (Zhang et al. 2016b) and Harris (1913). Rezaei (Zhang et al. 2016b) created an EOQ for developing things for diverse sorts of creatures, particularly for a kind of poultry. Zhang et al. (Sebatjane 2018b) returned to and amplified the investigate work of Rezaei (Zhang et al. 2016b) by making a stock show for developing things decreasing the carbon emanations in operations. Sebatjane (Khalilpourazari and Pasandideh 2019) displayed three stock models for developing things. A while later, Khalilpourazari and Pasandideh (Gharaei and Almehdawe 2020) worked with developing things as well. They defined a scientific demonstrate for multi-item financial arrange amount subjected to a few operational obliges. Gharaei and Almehdawe (Hidayat et al. 2020) given an financial developing amount (EGQ) stock show to decide the ideal financial development and butcher period and the financial developing amount to minimize the add up to taken a toll of the stock framework. Hidayat et al. (Mokhtari et al. 2020) presented an EOQ stock show with a capacitated product house office and constrained budgetfor developing items when the vender gives an incremental amount rebates conspire.

The selling price and expiry date of the processed inventory affect the demand rate. An integrated four-tier supply chain inventory management model for growing raw materials with various activities of cultivation, sorting, processing and retailing was first proposed by Sebatjane and Adetunji (2020b). In other words, it was found that many inventory issues related to carbon emissions cannot be adequately addressed by traditional inventory analysis techniques in inventory models, including the Bonney and Jaber technique (Bonney and Jaber 2011). Building a responsible inventory system that complies with environmental regulations and considerations is also one of these challenges. An integrated inventory model for a seller-buyer system was developed by Saga et al. investigated. Authors in Saga et al. (2019), considered the energy impact and carbon emissions from production and transportation. A study on mathematical inventory optimization problems focusing on fresh food products was carried out by Yu et al. (2020). The objective of the study was to optimize retailers' profits within a limited planning horizon, taking into account the possible introduction of a carbon tax or an emissions trading scheme. Wee and Daryanto (2020) focused on a supply chain that handles a certain percentage of out-of-spec products in delivered batches. This study specifically considered the impact of CO_2 emission pricing in the context of CO_2 tax policies. In 1963, Hadley and Within (1963) considered an inventory model that included multiple items and considered overall storage space scarcity and limitations. The objective of the model is to develop an ordering strategy for each product that minimizes the cost per unit time of ordering and long-term storage. Mashud et al. (2019) considered two different demand functions and a two-stage trade credit policy to optimize an EOQ model that considered wear and tear. According to this paradigm, shortages are fully deferred and allowed to worsen. Mashud (2020) studied an EOQ inventory shrinkage model that considered variables such as price, inventory-dependent demand, and fully deferred shortages. Khanna et al. (2021) investigated and modified the conceptual and mathematical problems of Mishra et al. (2017) and proposed an EOQ model for seasonally deteriorating goods that considers demand as a function of inventory and selling price. Price-based demand models are widely used by researchers. San Jose et al. For example, (San-José et al. 2018) considered an inventory model for a product whose demand, represented by a bivariate function, depends on both price and time. In the context of various carbon emission regulation systems, Ruidas et al. (2021) developed a production inventory model that takes into account the possibility of defective items. They assumed that demand decreases linearly with the selling price of the product. A fully integrated inventory model focused on maximizing profits was developed by Dey et al. and presented (Dey et al. 2019). This incorporates sustainable techniques such as the careful reduction of setup costs, predictable lead times, and environmental considerations. Selling price, inventory cost per unit (which varies linearly over time), and, in a scenario with any unit discounts, purchasing price per unit all affect the demand for a product.

2.3 Assumptions and Notation

2.3.1 Assumptions

The presumptions of the model:

(1) One type of product in particular is purchased with an unlimited planning horizon.
(2) Completely back-ordered shortages are allowed.
(3) A 100% successful inspection procedure is in place.
(4) Items of inferior quality are not repaired or changed.
(5) The weight that these acquire is closely correlated with the feeding expense for developing the goods.
(6) The holding costs to maintain the item in storage occur both throughout the inspection procedure and the time of consumption.
(7) The exponential demand rate function of the goods is d, where $d = \pi e^{-\rho\lambda n}$
(8) The optimal selling price of flawless things is determined by their superior quality.
(9) The system account with the carbon emissions.

2.3.2 Notation

In order to create a uniform notation for inventory models with expanding item counts.

a''	The quantity of lower-quality assessment of inventory which are unidentified in nature higher-quality finished inventory
a	Specified percentage of finished inventory
C_f	Inventory of expense per weight, per unit of time, and live inventory
d	The demand rate of the commodities per unit time
h_p	Holding cost per unit time
h_i	The facility of inspection of the processor maintains the expense per weight unit per unit of time
s_f	Setting up cost each cycle for customer's profit
s_p	The cost of setup per cycle for processing expenses
s_s	The setup costs for the quality check
s_r	The setup costs for quality of inspection
i_r	Expense weight unit of processed inventory with lower quality
i_s	Expense weight for each unit of discarding finished inventory of good quality
m_f	Weight in mortal inventory units divided by time units
q_p	The quantity of batches of finished inventory to the inspection facility after each processing cycle unit
q_s	The quantity of well-finished inventory batches that the processor sends to the retailer from the facility of inspection in a single inspection run
c_F	The cost of live goods per weight unit
c_p	The cost at which a processor sells live goods per weight unit of processed inventory
c_Q	The cost at which a processor sells live goods per weight unit of processed inventory of poorer quality after the inspection
c_R	The price at which a retailer sells live goods per weight unit of good quality
c_V	The price of a live newborn item per weight unit at purchase
R	Weight of units per unit time of processing rate
t	Total time of retailer's cycle
t_f, t_p and t_s	Time spans of the growth cycle, processor's cycle and the inspection of total lot
$d = \gamma e^{-\rho\lambda n}$	Demand function Where, γ = exponential dependent demand scale parameter ρ = sensitivity demand parameter λ = selling price of the imperfect items
p_1	Type I error probability
p_2	Type II error probability
w_0	The weight of each brand-new product

(continued)

(continued)

w_1	The target weight of each product
w_t	Product's weight at time t
x	The portion of living products that endure during the growing phase
z	Rate of inspection in weight units per unit of time
α	The product's asymptotic weight
β	Constant of integration
γ	Rate of exponential growth
μ	The interval between consecutive shipments to the merchant from the inspection facility of high-quality batches of processed inventory
T	Total cycle period
y	Order quantity of model
λ	Selling price of the perfect items
B	Backordering quantity
TPU	Total profit function of the model which is dependent on ($y*$, $B*$ and $\lambda*$)

2.4 Mathematical Modelling

The earnings made for the customers, the processor (which includes the facilities for processing and inspection), and the retailer make up the total profit made across the supply chain.

2.4.1 The Customer's Profit

With the start of new cycle of replenishment, we planned to purchase $q_p y$ items. Weight of each product is w_0. So the total weight of all new born items is $q_p Q$, it can also be written as $q_p y w_0$. During the replenishment cycle, the weight of each item increases until it reaches a target of w_1. Every infant item in the order grows at the same rate, and when their combined weight reaches the desired weight w_1, transferred to further process. However, diseases and scavengers cause certain objects to not make it to the conclusion of the rising cycle. The total mass of everything that survived in order $xq_p y w_1$ at the end of the growth, based on a survival rate of x. The processor receives this quantity for processing and quality assurance (Fig. 2.1).

The growth function of the objects is represented by

$$w_t = \frac{\alpha}{1 + \beta e^{-\gamma t}}. \tag{2.1}$$

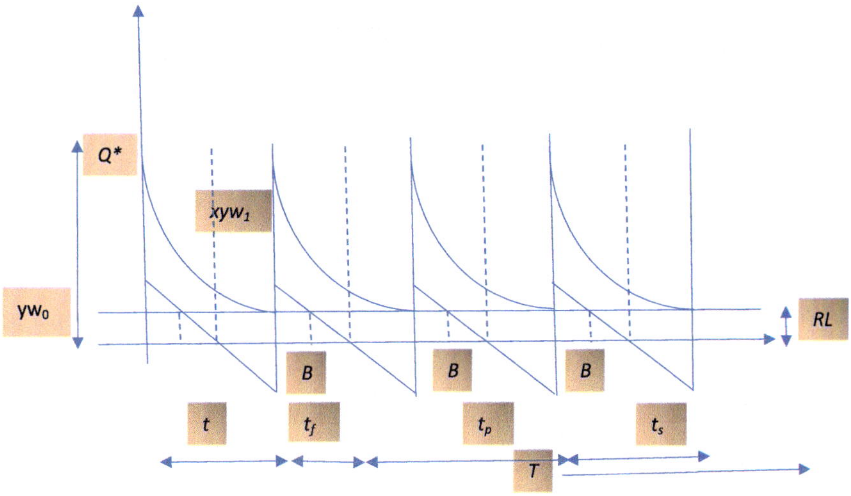

Fig. 2.1 Structure of the inventory management [*Source* Own]

Three factors are used by the logistic growth function to show the evolution of a product over time. They are γ, β and α, which stand for the asymptotic weight of the items, the exponential growth rate, and integration constant, correspondingly.

$$t = -\frac{\log_e\left[\frac{1}{\beta}\left(\frac{\alpha}{w_1} - 1\right)\right]}{\gamma} \tag{2.2}$$

$$\begin{aligned}\text{Area}(f) &= \int_0^{t_f} q_p y w_t \mathrm{d}t \\ &= q_p y\left\{\alpha t_f + \frac{\alpha}{\gamma}\left[\log_e\left(1 + \beta e^{-\gamma t_f}\right) - \log_e(1+\beta)\right]\right\}\end{aligned} \tag{2.3}$$

The expenditure per unit of time $\left(C_f\right)$ for the customer. Consequently,

$$f * C_f = C_f x q_p y\left\{\alpha t_f + \frac{\alpha}{\gamma}\left[\log_e\left(1 + \beta e^{-\gamma t_f}\right) - \log_e(1+\beta)\right]\right\} \tag{2.4}$$

During the inspection period. The backorder cost is

$$t = \frac{B}{z}. \tag{2.5}$$

And the backordering inspection quantity with the screening process is

$$t_f = \frac{y w_1 - B}{z}. \tag{2.6}$$

After the inspection, the imperfect quality items defined as

$$E[t_s] = \frac{yw_1 - B - \mathrm{d}t_f - E[x]yw_1}{d} \tag{2.7}$$

The shortages accumulation during this period is obtain as

$$t_s = \frac{B}{z}. \tag{2.8}$$

The expected cycle time for the behaviour of growing items with the imperfect items is calculated as

$$E[T] = \frac{yw_1(1 - E[x])}{d}. \tag{2.9}$$

The customer's average inventory level, the percentage of things that don't survive $(1 - x)$, and the cost of mortality per unit of weight and time (m_f) are multiplied to get the mortality cost per cycle

$$m_f * f = m_f(1 - x)q_p y\left\{\alpha t_f + \frac{\alpha}{\gamma}\left[\log_e\left(1 + \beta e^{-\gamma t_f}\right) - \log_e(1 + \beta)\right]\right\} \tag{2.10}$$

The discrepancy between total expenses and income is used to compute the profit per cycle TP_f is :

$$\begin{aligned} \mathrm{TP}_f &= C_F q_p x y w_1 - C_V q_p y w_0 - S_f \\ &\quad - q_p y\left\{\alpha t_f + \frac{\alpha}{\gamma}\left[\log_e\left(1 + \beta e^{-\gamma t_f}\right) - \log_e(1 + \beta)\right]\right\} \\ &\quad \left[c_f x + m_f(1 - x)\right] \end{aligned} \tag{2.11}$$

The equation, which is derived as the product of the price the farmer charges the processor for mature live inventory (C_F) and the quantity of live inventory $(q_p x y w_1)$ that the farmer sells to the processor each cycle in weight units, represents the revenue gained per cycle. The farmer's procurement cost each cycle is the next component. This cost is calculated by multiplying the procurement cost for the newborn inventory (C_V) by the total weight of inventory from purchases made throughout each cycle $(q_p y w_0)$. The final part is the sum of the costs associated with feeding and death, as indicated by the formulae, respectively. The third term is the fixed setup cost spent at the start of each cycle for setting up the growing facility (S). The goods chosen maturity weight determines how long it can develop during that time. The duration of the processor's cycle of replenishment $(q_p T)$, the total gain per unit time, or TPU_f, is calculated.

$$\mathrm{TPU}_f = \frac{C_F x y w_1}{T} - \frac{C_V y w_0}{T} - \frac{S_f}{q_p T}$$

$$
-\frac{y}{q_pT}\left\{\alpha t_f+\frac{\alpha}{\gamma}\left[\log_e\left(1+\beta e^{-\gamma t_f}\right)-\log_e(1+\beta)\right]\right\}
\left[c_f x+m_f(1-x)\right]\cdot \tag{2.12}
$$

2.4.2 Expenses Incurred in the Processing Centre

At the start of each cycle, the weighs $q_pQ = q_pxyw_1$, providing the processor with a live inventory. The live inventory is converted into processed inventory at a rate of R weight units per unit time. During a single production cycle (duration t_p), the processor sends q_p equally-sized batches of processed inventory to the facility of inspection. This indicates that each batch sent to the inspection facility weighs xyw_1 because the batches are of similar size. Consequently, the area beneath the inventory profit, as

$$
\begin{aligned}
\text{Area}_p &= \frac{q_pQ}{2R}+Q^2\left(\frac{1}{d}-\frac{1}{R}\right)+2Q^2\left(\frac{1}{d}-\frac{1}{R}\right)+\ldots+(q_p-1)Q^2\left(\frac{1}{d}-\frac{1}{R}\right)\\
&=\frac{(q_pQ)^2}{2R}+\frac{q_p(q_p-1)(q_pQ)^2}{2}\left(\frac{1}{d}-\frac{1}{R}\right)\\
&=\frac{(q_pxyw_1)^2}{2R}+\frac{q_p(q_p-1)(q_pxyw_1)^2}{2}\left(\frac{1}{d}-\frac{1}{R}\right)\cdot
\end{aligned} \tag{2.13}
$$

The total cost incurred by the processor is represented by the sum of the purchasing, processing setup, and holding charges for each cycle at the processing facility, as shown by.

$$
\text{TC}_p = C_F q_pxyw_1 + S_p + h_p\left[\frac{(q_pxyw_1)^2}{2R}+\frac{q_p(q_p-1)(q_pxyw_1)^2}{2}\left(\frac{1}{d}-\frac{1}{R}\right)\right] \tag{2.14}
$$

2.4.3 Profit in Supply Chain

Under the assumption that the survival probabilities (x), Type I errors (p_1), Type II errors (p_2), and the fraction of lower quality treated inventory (a) are random variables with recognized probability density function are as follows $f(x), f(u_1), f(u_2), f(a)$ relatively, the supply chain profit's Expected Value is determined by as $E[\text{TGU}_{sc}]$. This whole supply chain gain per unit time, TGU_{sc}, is as calculated

$$E[\mathrm{TGU}_{sc}] = C_R d + \frac{C_Q E[a]E[w_2]d}{E[1-a]E\left[1-p_1\right]} + \frac{C_Q E\left[p_1\right]d}{E\left[1-p_1\right]} + \frac{C_Q E[a]E\left[1-p_2\right]d}{E[1-a]E\left[1-p_1\right]}$$
$$-\frac{S_r d}{E[x]yw_1 E[1-a]E\left[1-p_1\right]} - \frac{i_r E[a]E\left[p_2\right]}{E[1-a]E\left[1-p_1\right]}$$
$$-\frac{u_r u}{E[1-a]E\left[1-p_1\right]}\left\{\frac{^2[\lambda]yw_1}{2}\right.$$
$$\left.-\frac{\{(q_s-1)E[x]yw_1 d\}\left\{E[1-a]E\left[1-p_1\right]+E[a]E\left[p_2\right]\right\}}{2q_s z E[1-a]E\left[1-p_1\right]}\right\} - \frac{i_s E\left[p_1\right]d}{E\left[1-p_1\right]}$$
$$-\frac{vd}{E[1-a]E\left[1-p_1\right]} - \frac{K_f d}{q_p E[x]yw_1 E[1-a]E\left[1-p_1\right]}$$
$$-\frac{\left\{C_f E[x]+mE[1-x]\right\}d}{g_p E[x]w_1 E[1-a]E\left[1-p_1\right]}\left\{at_f\right.$$
$$\left.+\frac{\alpha}{\gamma}\left[\log_e\left(1+\beta e^{-\gamma t_f}\right)-\log_e(1+\beta)\right]\right\} - \frac{C_V w_0 d}{E[x]w_1 E[1-a]E\left[1-p_1\right]}$$
$$\left(\text{subject to: } q_p \varepsilon Z,\ q_s \varepsilon Z,\ t_f \le q_p t\right) \tag{2.15}$$

2.4.4 *Inspection Facility for the Cost*

During a single processing run, the processor moves n_p processed goods batches to the inspection warehouse from the facility of processing. Every batch is $Q = xyw_1$ in weight.

This is presumable that a specific percentage (a) of the finished inventory that the facility of processing sends to us is of lower quality. Accordingly, for each batch that is received from the to the inspection warehouse processing facility weighing xyw_1, the weight of processed inventory of bad quality is $xyw_1(1 - a)$, while the processed inventory of higher quality weighs $xyw_1(1 - a)$. To differentiate the finished inventory of fine quality from the worse quality at the rate of z weight units each unit time, the complete lot received from the facility of processing (i.e., xyw_1) is checked for each inspection cycle. This suggests that the checking period is

$$t_s = \frac{xyw_1}{z}$$

The processor provides the retailer with an integer (q_s) of a lot of high-quality finished goods at regular intervals of time μ during a single inspection cycle. The computation of τ's duration involves dividing t_s by q_s, where t_s represents the duration of a single inspection cycle. Consequently,

$$\mu = \frac{xyw_1}{q_s z}$$

A Type II error occurs when good quality finished inventory is categorized as bad quality finished inventory after the checking process has concluded. A Type I error occurs when lower quality processed inventory is categorized as good quality processed inventory after the inspection process p_1 and p_2, respectively, indicate the likelihood of making Type I and Type II errors. Accordingly, the odds of properly identifying processed inventory that is of higher quality $(1 - p_1)$ and lower quality $(1 - p_2)$ are, respectively.

The weights of the finished inventory for each of the four situations are

Situation 1: $xyw_1(1 - a)(1 - p_1)$.
Situation 2: $xyw_1(1 - a)p_1$.
Situation 3: $xyw_1 a p_2$.
Situation 4: $xyw_1 a(1 - p_2)$.

The total of the weights for Situation 1 and 3 represents the weight of finished inventory classified as good in each inspection run. Situation 1 was classified correctly and Situation 3 was classified $s\mu$. This indicates that, after τ units of time, the weight of each batch supplied to the store is

$$w = \frac{xyw_1(1 - a)(1 - p_1) + xyw_1 a p_2}{q_s} \tag{2.16}$$

Similarly, the total of the weights for Situation 2 and 4 signifies the weight of finished inventory classified as low worth in each inspection cycle. Situation 2 was incorrectly classified and Situation 4 was appropriately classified. This shows that the processor allows all μ time units.

$$w = \frac{xyw_1(1 - a)p_1 + xyw_1 a(1 - p_2)}{q_s} \tag{2.17}$$

weight units of finished inventory that are categorized as very poor quality to build up This shows that the weight of each batch that the processor sells to secondary markets at the end of each inspection cycle is $xyw_1(1 - a)p_1\ xyw_1 + a(1 - p_2)$.

The total cost in the equation is the amount spent on each inspection run. Because the processor transports q_s batches of processed goods from the processing plant to the inspection warehouse during each processing run, the total cost incurred at the inspection facility is as high as it is. The area and profit function is

$$\text{Area} = \frac{x^2y^2w_1^2}{z} - \frac{\left[(q_s - 1)x^2y^2w_1^2\right]\left[(1 - a)(1 - p_1) + ap_2\right]}{2zq_s} \tag{2.18}$$

$$\text{TC} = q_s S_s + vxyw_1 + xyw_1 i_s(1 - a)p_1$$

$$+ h_1\left[\frac{x^2y^2w_1^2}{z} - \frac{[(q_s-1)x^2y^2w_1^2][(1-a)(1-p_1)+ap_2]}{2zq_s}\right] \quad (2.19)$$

2.4.5 Profit Generated by the Processor

The processor makes money during each processing setup by selling processed merchandise, both high quality and low quality. The money is provided by

$$\begin{aligned}\mathrm{TP} = {} & q_pC_Pxyw_1(1-a)(1-p_1) + q_pC_Pxyw_1ap_2 \\ & + q_pC_Pxyw_1(1-a)p_1 + q_pC_Pxyw_1a(1-p_2)\end{aligned} \quad (2.20)$$

The revenue from sales of processed inventory that has been rated as good quality after the inspection procedure is represented by the first two terms from the equation. For these two terms, the processed inventory weights correspond to Situation 1 and 3. The profits from each inspection run of high-quality inventory are calculated by multiplying these weights $[[yw_1(1-a)(1-p_1)$ and $xyw_1ap_2]$ by the price the processor bills the retailer for each weight of processed merchandise that has been rated as being of exceptional quality.

The total profit (TP) of the processor for each cycle is the same as the total revenue for each cycle.

$$\begin{aligned}\mathrm{TP} = {} & q_pC_Pxyw_1(1-a)(1-p_1) + q_pC_Pxyw_1ap_2 \\ & + q_pC_Pxyw_1(1-a)p_1 + q_pC_Pxyw_1a(1-p_2)C_F \\ & - C_Fxyw_1 - S_p - h_p\left[\frac{(q_pxyw_1)^2}{2R} - \frac{q_p(q_p-1)(q_pxyw_1)^2}{2}\left(\frac{1}{d}-\frac{1}{R}\right)\right] \\ & - q_pq_sS_s - q_pvxyw_1 - q_pi_sxyw_1(1-a)p_1 \\ & - q_ph_i\left\{\frac{(xyw_1)^2}{z} - \frac{[(q_s-1)(xyw_1)^2][(1-a)(1-p_1)+ap_2]}{2q_sz}\right\}\end{aligned} \quad (2.21)$$

The processor's total revenue per cycle, as provided by formulation, is divided by the length of the processor's refill cycle (i.e., q_pT) to determine the processor's final profit per unit time, or TPU_p.

$$\begin{aligned}\mathrm{TPU}_p = {} & \frac{C_Pxyw_1(1-a)(1-p_1)}{T} + \frac{C_Pxyw_1ap_2}{T} \\ & + \frac{C_Qxyw_1(1-a)p_1}{T} + \frac{C_Qxyw_1a(1-p_2)}{T} - \frac{C_Fxyw_1}{T}\end{aligned}$$

$$-\frac{S_p}{q_pT}-\frac{h_p}{q_pT}\left[\frac{(q_pxyw_1)^2}{2R}-\frac{q_p(q_p-1)(q_pxyw_1)^2}{2}\left(\frac{1}{d}-\frac{1}{R}\right)\right]$$
$$-\frac{q_sS_s}{T}-\frac{vxyw_1}{T}-\frac{i_sxyw_1(1-a)p_1}{T}$$
$$-\frac{h_i}{T}\left\{\frac{(xyw_1)^2}{z}-\frac{[(q_s-1)(xyw_1)^2][(1-a)(1-p_1)+ap_2]}{2q_sz}\right\} \tag{2.22}$$

2.4.6 *Profit Generated by the Retailer*

Every μ time units, the processor's inspection facility sends batches of processed inventory that has been deemed good quality inventory to the retailer. The weight of each batch is obtained using an equation. It computes the profile for the processed inventory of the retailer. During a single replenishment cycle, which is defined as the series of time intervals of T duration at which the retailer's processed inventory level falls to zero, *ns* batches of processed inventory are delivered to the retailer.

This indicates that multiplying the answer to the equation by q_s will yield the weight of processed inventory received during the retailer's replenishment cycle, a''. Therefore,

$a'' = xyw_1(1-a)(1-p_1) + xyw_1ap_2$ and $a'' = xyw_1ap_2$ the duration of the retailer's cycle time can be computed as

$$t=\frac{xyw_1(1-a)(1-p_1)}{d} \tag{2.23}$$

It is presumed that the retailer provides customers with a complete refund in the event that improperly classified. Consequently, the retailer's cycle revenue is

$$\mathrm{TR}=C_Rxyw_1(1-a)(1-p_1)+C_Qxyw_1ap_2 \tag{2.24}$$

The retailer's profit each cycle. Consequently

$$\mathrm{TP}_r=C_Rxyw_1(1-a)(1-p_1)+C_Qxyw_1ap_2-C_Pxyw_1(1-a)(1-p_1)$$
$$-C_Pxyw_1ap_2-S_r-i_rxyw_1au_2$$
$$-h_r\left[\frac{xyw_1(1-a)(1-p_1)T}{2}-\frac{[(q_s-1)(xyw_1)^2][(1-a)(1-p_1)+ap_2]}{2q_sz}\right] \tag{2.25}$$

By dividing the retailer's total profit per cycle, as given in equation, by the length of the retailer's replenishment cycle (i.e., TPU_r), the total profit per unit time, or TR, is calculated.

$$
\begin{aligned}
\mathrm{TPU}_r = C_R d &+ \frac{C_Q a u_2 d}{(1-a)(1-p_1)} - C_P d - \frac{C_P a p_2 d}{(1-a)(1-p_1)} - \frac{S_r \mathrm{d}}{(1-a)(1-p_1)} \\
&- \frac{S_r d}{x y w_1 (1-a)(1-p_1)} - \frac{i_r a p_2}{(1-a)(1-p_1)} \\
&- h_r \left[\frac{x y w_1 (1-a)(1-p_1)}{2} - \frac{\left[x y w_1 (q_s - 1) d \right] \left[(1-a)(1-p_1) + a p_2 \right]}{2 q_s z (1-a)(1-p_1)} \right]
\end{aligned}
\tag{2.26}
$$

The total generated profit

$$
\begin{aligned}
\mathrm{TPU} = C_R &+ \frac{C_Q a u_2}{(1-a)(1-p_1)} - C_P \frac{C_P a p_2}{(1-a)(1-p_1)} \\
&- \frac{S_r}{(1-a)(1-p_1)} - \frac{S_r}{x y w_1 (1-a)(1-p_1)} - \frac{i_r a p_2}{(1-a)(1-p_1)} \\
&- h_r \left[\frac{x y w_1 (1-a)(1-p_1)}{2} - \frac{\left[x y w_1 (q_s - 1) \pi e^{-\rho \lambda n} \right] \left[(1-a)(1-p_1) + a p_2 \right]}{2 q_s z (1-a)(1-p_1)} \right] \\
&+ \frac{C_P x y w_1 (1-a)(1-p_1)}{T} + \frac{C_P x y w_1 a p_2}{T} \\
&+ \frac{C_Q x y w_1 (1-a) p_1}{T} + \frac{C_Q x y w_1 a (1-p_2)}{T} - \frac{C_F x y w_1}{T} \\
&- \frac{S_p}{q_p T} - \frac{h_p}{q_p T} \left[\frac{\left(q_p x y w_1 \right)^2}{2R} - \frac{q_p (q_p - 1) \left(q_p x y w_1 \right)^2}{2} \left(\frac{1}{\gamma e^{-\rho \lambda n}} - \frac{1}{R} \right) \right] \\
&- \frac{q_s S_s}{T} - \frac{v x y w_1}{T} - \frac{i_s x y w_1 (1-a) p_1}{T} \\
&- \frac{h_i}{T} \left\{ \frac{(x y w_1)^2}{z} - \frac{\left[(q_s - 1)(x y w_1)^2 \right] \left[(1-a)(1-p_1) + a p_2 \right]}{2 q_s z} \right\} \\
&+ \frac{C_F x y w_1}{T} - \frac{C_V y w_0}{T} - \frac{S_f}{q_p T} \\
&- \frac{y}{q_p T} \left\{ \alpha t_f + \frac{\alpha}{\gamma} \left[\log_e \left(1 + \beta e^{-\gamma t_f} \right) - \log_e (1 + \beta) \right] \right\} \left[c_f x + m_f (1 - x) \right] \\
&+ \frac{y w_1 - B - d t_f - E[x] y w_1}{\gamma e^{-\rho \lambda n}} + \frac{y w_1 - B - d t_p - E[x] y w_1}{\gamma e^{-\rho \lambda n}} \\
&+ \frac{y w_1 (1 - E[x])}{\gamma e^{-\rho \lambda n}} + \frac{B}{z}
\end{aligned}
\tag{2.27}
$$

2.5 Solution Procedure

The unconstrained optimization problem is considered in order to obtain some theoretical results. Then consider the algorithm for finding the optimal solution of the constrained from the given problem which is given in Eq. (2.27). The aim is to find the optimal values for the order quantity (y^*), with its backordering cost or with the exponential dependent demand. This function obtained the maximization function of the total profit per unit time.

For finding the numerical analysis and sensitivity analysis for different parameters, the algorithm is used as follows

1. Firstly give the all parametric values of C_F;R; h_p; h_i ; s_f; s_p;s_s; s_r; i_r; i_s; c_f; C_V; C_p; C_Q; C_R; m_f; w_0; w_1; α; β; μ; w_t; z; x; n; γ, ρ; a; a''. Compute the order quantity with its total profit function from Eqs. (2.7–2.26).
2. If the optimal values satisfied, the optimal condition then go to step *4* to check, otherwise go to next step.
3. If the situation is optimal then go to step *5*, otherwise back to the last step for the optimal solution.
4. Calculate the expected total profit per unit of time E[TPU] from Eq. (2.27).
5. Report the solution of ($\lambda*$, $y*$, $T*$) and E[TPU]
6. Stop the program.

By this procedure, it is observed that the expected total profit of the model is taken into the account.

2.6 Numerical Analysis

This is an example that takes into account of the production value chain. The sample takes into account the subsequent input parameters: C_F = 15/kg;R = 300/kg; h_p = 0.2/kg; h_i = 0.25 ZAR/kg; s_f = 30,000; s_p = 20,000;s_s = 10,000 ZAR; s_r = 2500; i_r = 500/kg; i_s = 200/kg; c_f = 0.1 /kg; C_V = 5/kg; C_p = 55/kg; C_Q = 20/kg; C_R = 60/kg; m_f = 0.2/kg; w_0 = 8.5 kg; w_1 = 30 kg; α = 51 kg; β = 5; μ = 0.12; w_t = 30 kg; z = 1000/kg; x = 525/kg; n = 2; γ = 10,000, ρ = 0; a = 1000ZAR/cycle; a'' = 150/year are assumed to be random variables uniformly distributed over [0.8, 1], [0, 0.05], [0, 0.05] and [0, 0.05], respectively. Then the optimal solution is y^* is 1500.51 with its expected total profit to be 35,013. From the other situation, the optimal value is 142.50 with the expected total profit 449,374 and the backorder cost with its exponential rate is 51509.93 and 0.6939 (Table 2.1).

Even while supply systems with more centralization operate better, some individual supply chain participants may still benefit from decentralized supply chains. This suggests that certain participants in the supply chain might prioritize their personal financial gains over the profit of the network as a whole. Profit-sharing arrangements, which are intended to motivate individual supply chain participants

Table 2.1 Optimal values for the objective function [*Source* Own]

Situation 1	$y*$	E[TPU∗]	150.51	35,013				
Situation 2	$y*$	E[TPU∗]	155.21	35,009.38				
Situation 3	$y*$	$B*$	E[TPU∗]	171.75	56,624	35,880.02		
Situation 4	$y*$	$B*$	$\lambda*$	E[TPU∗]	142.50	51,509.93	0.6939	449,374

to work together and maximize the profit of the entire supply chain, may be useful in discouraging this (Figs. 2.2, 2.3 and 2.4).

Fig. 2.2 The concavity graph with respect to the B and λ [*Source* Own]

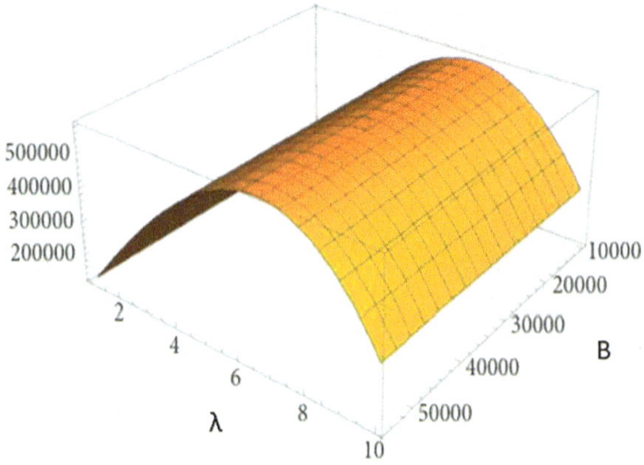

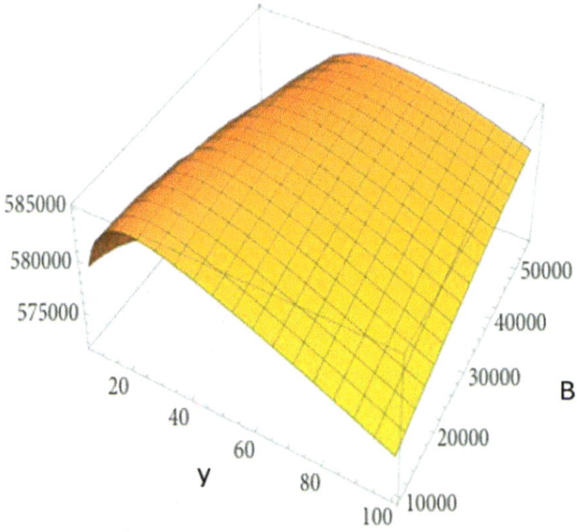

Fig. 2.3 The concavity graph with respect y and B [*Source* Own]

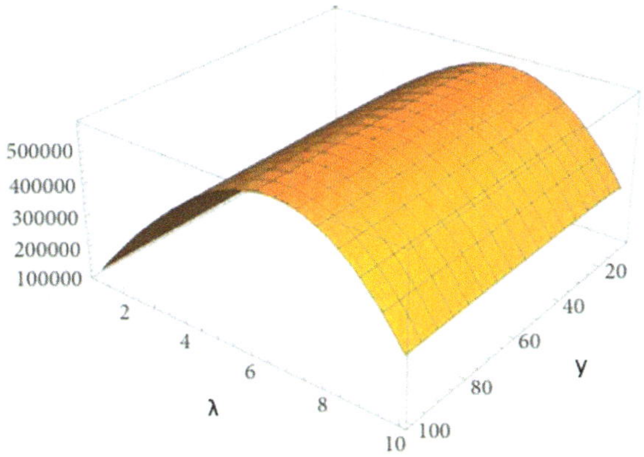

Fig. 2.4 The concavity graph with respect to the λ and *y* [*Source* Own]

2.6.1 Sensitivity Analysis

Since most of the input parameters in previous studies had already undergone sensitivity analyses, only a subset of the input parameters in the current study particularly those that are unique to the study were exposed to sensitivity analysis. Several findings from the analysis were as follows (Figs. 2.5, 2.6; Table 2.2).

- In relation to the anticipated total profit, the expected value of the rising products that are defective lowers.
- Order quantity and overall profit both rise as ordering costs rise relative to cycle time.
- Change in the increasing value of selling price gave the increment in the total cycle time, ordering size and total profit.

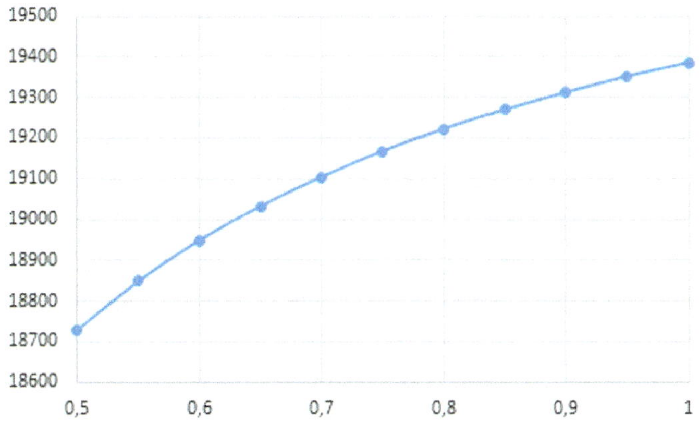

Fig. 2.5 Profit graph with respect to time [*Source* Own]

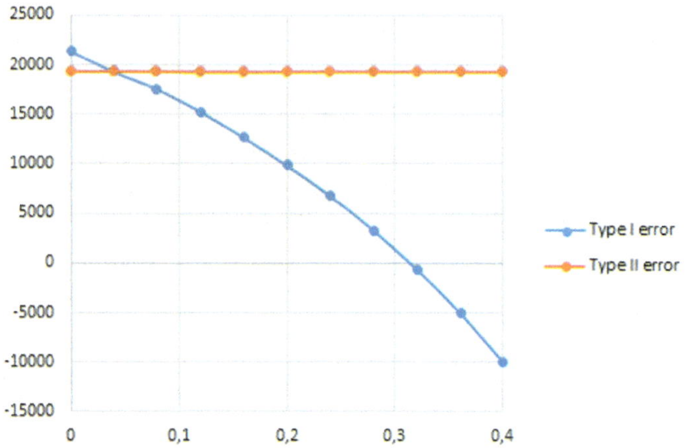

Fig. 2.6 Error graph with respect to the profit [*Source* Own]

- Change in the value of change in holding policy per weight per unit time for the processor and retailers gives the increasing order gives the increment in the corresponding value such as cycle time, ordering size and total gain.
- As the inspection policy per weight per unit time is increased in this model, it increases the total cycle time but decreases the value of total profit and ordering quantity.
- The corporation must raise the selling price parameter if the setup costs increase, and it must raise the selling price parameter when the demand parameter grows. These actions have an immediate effect on the overall profit.
- Economically speaking, the strategy that allows shortages with complete backordering is preferable to the one that prevents shortages.
- Parameters gave more attention to quality and ensure that the percentage of defective items is kept to a minimum.
- This paper developed inventory for unsatisfactory quality items with the exponential demand, which is more effective for online marketing with respect to the growing items.

2.7 Managerial Insights

Some practical applications exist for this paper. Because some of the previously published inventory models are specific instances. It was discovered that the more cost-effective approach is the one that allows shortages with complete backordering. Furthermore, it was discovered that the suggested inventory model performs better. Since the deterministic demand assumption is unreal, another possible field for investigation could be stochastic demand patterns. The suggested approach addresses carbon emissions in addition to a wide range of price-dependent demand. The

Table 2.2 Sensitivity analysis with the parameters [*Source* Own]

Parameters	Change in parameters	Cycle time ($T*$)	Total profit	Order quantity ($y*$)
s_r	50	0.1714	36,975	343
	100	0.24253	34,555	485
	150	0.2970	32,705	594
	200	0.3429	31,134	685
C_V	6	0.1714	36,974	343
	6.2	0.3429	21,163	576
	6.4	0.3429	21,194	566
	6.6	0.3429	31,233	557
C_R	7	0.1714	26,974	343
	7.5	0.3338	21,163	676
	8	0.3333	31,195	666
	8.5	0.3287	41,236	657
h_i	2.5	0.2714	59,754	444
	3	0.2626	57,232	583
	3.5	0.2424	58,423	582
	4	0.2729	58,545	581
h_p	2.5	0.1714	59,867	248
	3	0.4425	37,533	483
	3.5	0.4426	37,523	485
	4	0.4428	37,467	480
Γ	2000	0.4718	26,975	343
	2500	0.1533	21,984	383
	3000	0.1400	27,053	420
	3500	0.1296	32,186	453
$E[x]$	0.01	0.111	58,501	33.9
	0.02	0.123	58,500	34.2
	0.03	0.212	58,499	34.5
	0.04	0.132	58,498	34.9
s_p	2.5	0.1714	56,977	343
	3	0.3429	57,345	685
	3.5	0.3429	57,389	685
	4	0.3429	57,390	685

suggested that models can be used in online markets, corporate sectors, and industrial enterprises provided the decision-maker accepts the model's suppositions and uses the numerical values of the input parameters.

2.8 Conclusion

In order to account for items with unsatisfactory quality and the risk of errors during the quality inspection process, this study developed an inventory model for the supply chain in which the demand rate is an exponential function. Additionally, as items are completely backordered, the shortages are acceptable. Some theoretical results are produced to optimize the projected total profit per unit of time. Based on these findings, a successful and efficient solution technique is devised. Sensitivity analysis and numerical examples provide some crucial managerial insights. It is critical to focus on quality and make sure that the proportion of faulty products is as low as possible. Additionally, the corporation must raise the selling price in the event that setup costs rise, and it must raise the selling price in the event that the demand elasticity parameter rises. These actions have a direct impact on the overall profit. Even in situations where there is little chance of making such mistakes. As such, minor modifications to these odds could result in large variations in the supply chain's earnings. Production managers should strive to minimize these mistakes for the benefit of both consumer health protection and profit maximization. The numerical results also illustrated the advantages of a profit-sharing arrangement in a centralized supply chain, which was found to outperform a decentralized supply chain. Numerous approaches exist for further developing the suggested model. One example of this would be to include how learning affects processes related to processing and inspection. Furthermore, an investigation of the efficacy of implementing other shipment policies, such as power-of-two policies in lieu of the integer shipment policy, can be conducted. This paper can be extended with rework system in the environment, stochastic demand parameter and so on.

References

Bonney M, Jaber MY (2011) Environmentally responsible inventory models: non-classical models for a non-classical era. Int J Prod Econ 133:43–53

Dey BK, Sarkar B, Sarkar M, Pareek S (2019) An integrated inventory model involving discrete setup cost reduction, variable safety factor, selling price dependent demand, and investment. RAIRO-Oper Res 53:39–57

Dhanam K, Jesintha W (2017) Fuzzy inventory model for slow and fast growing items with deterioration constraints in a single period. Int J Manag Soc Sci 5:308–317

Garza Cabello E (2019) Modelo de Inventarios para Ítems con Crecimiento, Calidad Imperfecta y Faltantes Planeados. Master's Thesis, Tecnológico de Monterrey, Monterrey, Mexico

Gharaei A, Almehdawe E (2020) Economic growingquantity. Int J Prod Econ 223:107517

Hadley G, Whitin T (1963) Analysis of inventory systems. Prentice-Hall, Englewood Cliffs NJ USA

Harris FW (1913) How many parts to make at once. Fact Mag Manag 152:135–136

Hidayat YA, Riaventin VN, Jayadi O (2020) Economic order quantity model for growing items with incremental quantity discounts, capacitated storage facility, and limited budget. Jurnal Teknik Industri 22(1):1–10

Khalilpourazari S, Pasandideh SHR (2019) Modeling and optimization of multi-item multi-constrained EOQ model for growing items. Knowledge-Based Syst 164:150–162

Mashud AHM (2020) An EOQ deteriorating inventory model with different types of demand and fully backlogged shortages. Int J Logist Syst Manag 36:16

Mashud AHM, Uddin S, Sana SS (2019) A two-level trade-credit approach to an integrated price-sensitive inventory model with shortages. Int J Appl Comput Math 5:121

Mishra U, Cárdenas-Barrón LE, Tiwari S, Shaikh AA, Treviño-Garza G (2017) An inventory model under price and stock dependent demand for controllable deterioration rate with shortages and preservation technology investment. Ann Oper Res 254:165–190

Mokhtari H, Salmasnia A, Asadkhani J (2020) A new pro duction-inventory planning model for joint growing and deteriorating items. Int J Supply Oper Manage 7(1):1–16

Priyamvada R, Khanna A, Jaggi CK (2021) An inventory model under price and stock dependent demand for controllable deterioration rate with shortages and preservation technology investment: revisited. OPSEARCH 2021 58:181–202

Ruidas S, Seikh MR, Nayak PK (2021) A production inventory model with interval-valued carbon emission parameters under price-sensitive demand. Comput Ind Eng 154:107154

Saga RS, Jauhari WA, Laksono PW, Dwicahyani AR (2019) Investigating carbon emissions in a production-inventory model under imperfect production, inspection errors and service-level constraint. Int J Logist Syst Manag 34:29–55

San-José LA, Sicilia J, Alcaide-López-De-Pablo D (2018) An inventory system with demand dependent on both time and price assuming backlogged shortages. Eur J Oper Res 270:889–897

Sebatjane M (2018) Selected deterministic models for lot sizing of growing items inventory. Master's Thesis, University of Pretoria, Pretoria, South Africa

Sebatjane M (2018) Selected deterministic models for lot sizing of growing items inventory. M.S. thesis, University of Pretoria, South Africa

Sebatjane M, Adetunji O (2020a) A three-echelon supply chain for economic growing quantity model with price-and freshness dependent demand: pricing, ordering and shipment decisions. Oper Res Perspect 7:100153

Sebatjane M, Adetunji O (2020b) Optimal inventory replenishment and shipment policies in a four-echelon supply chain for growing items with imperfect quality. Prod Manuf Res 8:130–157

Wee H-M, Daryanto Y (2020) Imperfect quality item inventory models considering carbon emissions. In: Optimization and inventory management. Springer, Singapore, pp 137–159

Yu C, Qu Z, Archibald TW, Luan Z (2020) An inventory model of a deteriorating product considering carbon emissions. Comput Ind Eng 148:106694

Zhang Y, Li L-Y, Tian X-Q, Feng C (2016) Inventory management research for growing items with carbon-constrained. In: Proceedings of the 2016 35th Chinese control conference (CCC), Chengdu, China, 27–29 July 2016, pp 9588–9593

Zhang Y, Li LY, Tian XQ, Feng C (2016) Inventory management research for growing items with carbon-con strained. In: Proceedings of the 2016 35th Chinese control conference (CCC). IEEE, Chengdu, China, July 2016, pp 9588–9593

Chapter 3
Low Carbon Inventory Model of Imperfect Items with Screening, Preservation and Green Investment Under Inflationary and Fuzzy Environment

Vaishali Singh, S. R. Singh, and Surendra Vikram Singh Padiyar

Abstract There are so many environmental problems in the current world. A significant factor is the emission of carbon from diverse sources, encompassing multiple industries and modes of transportation. The terminology associated with the sustainable inventory model has garnered considerable attention in recent years, especially regarding its economic and environmental impacts. The emphasis has turned to reduce environmental consequences through the implementation of green technologies and a reduction in carbon emissions. Another typical element of the current inventory system is the inflation phenomenon. Considering this issue, we have proposed a sustainable inventory model with imperfect products under an inflationary environment. This study involves the adoption of green techniques to mitigate carbon emissions resulting from the operation of the inventory system. Additionally, preservation technologies are employed to decrease the deterioration rate of the products. Preservation techniques are still uncommon in the literature due to concerns about carbon emissions. An inspection method has been implemented to distinguish defective items from perfect ones. To encourage the sale of defective items; a discount strategy is introduced in this model. This research aims to obtain the optimal selling price for a retailer's total profit when demand price and carbon emission reduction sensitive. The findings of the proposed model demonstrate how an appropriate investment in green might help to reduce the environment's rising carbon emissions. The suggested model is also created within a fuzzy environment, and the overall profit is de-fuzzified using graded mean integration and the signed distance method. The impact of variable holding cost has been considered throughout the analysis. A numerical illustration has been performed in a both crisp and fuzzy sense to validate

V. Singh · S. R. Singh
Department of Mathematics, Chaudhary Charan Singh University, Meerut, Uttar Pradesh, India

S. V. S. Padiyar (✉)
Department of Mathematics, H.N.B. Government Post Graduate College Khatima, Khatima, Uttrakhand, India
e-mail: surendrapadiyar1991@gmail.com

N. H. Shah and M. Mittal (eds.), *Sustainable Inventory Management*, Inventory Optimization, https://doi.org/10.1007/978-981-97-6765-6_4

the proposed model. Also, the concavity of the total profit for each case is shown by MATHEMATICA 12 software. Finally, sensitivity analysis is carried out for various parameters to gather insightful observations.

Keywords Inflation · Imperfect products · Deterioration · Investment in preservation · Green technology · Fuzzy environment

3.1 Introduction

Sustainable business practices are gaining increasing significance in modern society due to growing environmental concerns and shifting consumer preferences. Businesses, governments, and worldwide people are actively looking for solutions that mitigate carbon emissions and the effects of climate change. A critical aspect of this transformation is developing and implementing effective low-carbon inventory models that consider both preservation and green technology, as well as accounting for the price and carbon reduction-dependent demand. As organizations strive to meet the needs of environmentally concerned customers, it becomes essential to create such inventory models that incorporate sustainability principles while taking demand based on price and carbon reduction into account. This innovative approach combines inventory level optimization with cost and emission reduction, balancing financial objectives with environmental consciousness.

Researchers worldwide are paying close attention to the rising concern for environmental problems and sustainable development. Carbon emissions, including industries and transportation, are among the most critical factors. Many countries are working hard to develop CO_2 emission reduction strategies. Carbon Tax is one of the standard policies used by governing agencies worldwide to reduce carbon emissions. Carbon pricing, sometimes known as a carbon tax, imposes a penalty on carbon emissions. A payroll tax exemption of revenues to consumers would be produced using the tax returns. Thus, the concept of controlling supply chains under various carbon regulations is developing rapidly. The operational choices have attracted considerable attention for a sustainable transition, including the carbon emission penalty or the idea of punishing the emitters by adding a penalty factor to the amount of carbon emissions. Governments and researchers have made many efforts to quantify and reduce GHG emissions.

There are many other environmental issues affecting today's world as well. The effectiveness of a product is limited by natural processes such as deterioration and emissions. Most items in greenhouses, such as vegetables and flowers, decay naturally over time. Greenhouse managers may use green technology investment to minimize carbon emissions. As a result, investment in exclusive preservation technology (PRT) and green technology (GRT) should be made to prevent inventory deterioration and environmental emissions. Preservation and green technology are vital to a sustainable low-carbon inventory model. Preservation refers to efficiently utilizing resources, minimizing waste, and adopting strategies that extend the lifespan of products and materials. Green technology, on the other hand, involves using environmentally friendly innovations and practices throughout the supply chain to reduce carbon emissions and enhance sustainability. Combining these principles with price and carbon reduction-dependent demand, businesses can optimize their inventory management processes to align with economic and environmental objectives. The idea of demand that relies on price and carbon reduction in this model considers customer preferences that consider both the price and the environmental effect of items they buy. These customers are prepared to pay more for products made, stored, and shipped with less carbon emissions while maintaining sustainability. Businesses may efficiently meet the demands of environmentally sensitive customers while advancing their sustainability initiatives by including this need in the inventory model.

3.2 Literature Review

3.2.1 Inventory Models Based on Sustainability

In today's world, sustainable business practices are gaining increasing importance due to growing environmental concerns and shifting consumer preferences. Organizations are actively looking for solutions that mitigate carbon emissions and develop a sustainable business. O'Connor (1994) makes one of the earliest allusions to sustainability, stating that the issue of "sustainability" is not simply an ecological (or even economic) debate, but rather one of politics and ideology. The integration of sustainability principles within supply chains has become a focal point of extensive research. Ahi and Searcy (2013) contributed significantly to this area, exploring how the concept of sustainability can be effectively incorporated into supply chain management practices. Their work has laid a foundation for understanding the implications and potential benefits of sustainable supply chain practices. Dissorn (2018) extended this exploration by highlighting the emerging trend of green logistics in SIM, particularly within the corporate community involved in the agricultural and food product sectors. This trend reflects a growing awareness and commitment to environmentally friendly practices in the handling and distribution of goods. In the domain of inventory management, Khan et al. (2020) proposed a two-warehouse inventory system specifically designed for deteriorating items, considering the impact of advance payments on the overall inventory strategy. Their research addressed the complexities associated with managing deteriorating inventory while incorporating financial considerations. Mashud et al. (2021a, b) took a novel approach by developing a sustainable inventory framework that focused on innovative strategies for controlling carbon emissions. Their work contributes to the ongoing efforts to align inventory management practices with environmental sustainability goals, acknowledging the role of carbon footprint reduction in supply chain operations. Taleizadeh et al. (2022) delved into environmental concerns within inventory systems, specifically investigating an Economic Order Quantity (EOQ) model. This model took into account partial trade credit policies and situations involving partial backordering, providing insights into the optimization of inventory decisions while considering environmental factors. In the pursuit of sustainable inventory practices, Kumar et al. (2023) introduced a model for managing deteriorating items that incorporated preservation techniques and green technology. This approach acknowledges the importance of adopting eco-friendly technologies and preservation methods to enhance the sustainability of inventory management practices. The study also considered the impact of learning on the overall effectiveness of the sustainable inventory model. Collectively, these studies contribute to the evolving landscape of sustainable inventory management, addressing various aspects such as environmental concerns, financial considerations, and technological innovations. They provide valuable insights and frameworks for organizations seeking to align their inventory practices with sustainable and environmentally conscious strategies.

3.2.2 Inventory Models Based on Inflation

Inflation has a variety of effects on the economy. A rise in the inflation rate signifies a decrease in the purchasing power of money. Many companies have seen a large decay in their purchasing power as a result of high inflation rate. As a consequence, the impact of inflation on the progress of any inventory system cannot be ignored. Therefore to involve inflation in a system is a realistic access. The evolution of inventory models under the influence of inflation has seen several notable contributions. Firstly, Buzacott (1975) laid the groundwork by introducing an Economic Order Quantity (EOQ) model that considered the impact of inflation on inventory management. Building upon Buzacott's foundational work, Bierman and Thomas (1977) extended the EOQ model by incorporating discount rates and further accounting for inflationary effects. Ray and Chaudhuri (1997) added complexity to the understanding of EOQ models by introducing the element of inflationary time discounting under stock-dependent demand. This nuanced perspective aimed to enhance the accuracy of inventory management strategies, Sarkar and Moon (2011) extended an Economic Production Quantity (EPQ) model. Their work aimed to provide insights into optimal production quantities, taking into account both imperfections in the production process and the impact of inflation. Shah and Shah (2014) contributed to the literature by discussing an EPQ model with imperfect production in the context of time-varying demand. Their model accounted for the effects of inflation and reliability, offering a comprehensive view of inventory management under dynamic conditions. Esmaeili and Nasrabadi (2021) delved into the intricacies of supply chain dynamics by investigating the effect of inflation on an inventory model within a single vendor-multiple retailer supply chain. This research sought to understand how inflation influences decision-making processes and inventory levels within a complex supply chain network. Hatibaruah and Saha (2022) extended the exploration of inflationary effects on inventory models by outlining an EPQ model for items experiencing both amelioration and deterioration. This comprehensive model aimed to capture the dual nature of product conditions in the presence of inflation. In a more recent contribution, Singh and Chaudhary (2023) formulated an economic order quantity model that considered the impact of inflation on imperfect products, incorporating the additional complexity of a carbon tax policy. This work aimed to address environmental considerations alongside economic factors in inventory decision-making. Further expanding on the understanding of inflationary effects, Singh and Ambedkar (2023) investigated the impact of inflation on a sustainable inventory model for deteriorating and expiring items. Their study considered the intricate dependencies of product demand on stock levels, pricing, and product lifetime, providing a holistic view of sustainable inventory management under the influence of inflation.

3.2.3 Inventory Models Based on Controllable Deterioration

In the existing inventory system, the management of deterioration stands out as another crucial task. In reality, every product undergoes a loss of freshness and utility after a certain period, with this effect continuing over time-a natural phenomenon known as deterioration. Consequently, this phenomenon significantly impacts the inventory system and cannot be overlooked. The exploration of continuous deterioration inventory methods traces back to Ghare and Schrader's pioneering work in 1963. Acknowledging the pivotal role of preservation technology in mitigating the impact of deterioration, numerous industrial enterprises and organizations have recognized the need to incorporate preservation techniques into their inventory control systems. This concept of preservation technology was formally introduced by Hsu et al. (2010), who, through their work, advocated for the adoption of preservation measures in inventory management systems. Their efforts culminated in the development of an inventory model that is considered constant demand alongside the strategic implementation of preservation technology. Expanding on the realm of production inventory systems, Dye and Hsieh (2012) delved into the examination of the effects resulting from investments in preservation technology. Their research sheds light on how preservation technology influences the dynamics of production inventory systems, providing valuable insights for organizations seeking to enhance their production processes. Addressing the intricacies of shortage considerations in preservation inventory models, Mishra et al. (2017) proposed a model that factored in the impact of price-dependent demand. This work aimed to offer a comprehensive understanding of how preservation measures align with inventory management strategies in the presence of demand fluctuations. In the context of non-instantaneous decaying items, emphasizing the broader perspective of sustainability, Gautam et al. (2023) took a holistic approach by developing a sustainable inventory model for deteriorating items. Their model considered selling price and green-level-dependent demand while incorporating investments in preservation technology. This research aimed to provide organizations with a framework that aligns with sustainability goals, offering a nuanced understanding of the interplay between preservation technology, demand dynamics, and environmental considerations in inventory management. Singh et al. (2024) discussed the benefits of preservation techniques in a sustainable inventory model in both crisp and fuzzy environment. Their research highlighted how these preservation techniques can enhance the longevity and quality of inventory items, thereby reducing waste and promoting sustainability.

3.2.4 Inventory Models Based on Fuzzy Environment

A review of the inventory literature indicates that, for the purpose of simplicity, various models have been developed in a static nature. It is discovered that defining distinct inventory cost factors exactly is challenging due to a rapid development in the complexity of the environment. Academics and researchers developed fuzzy set theory to overcome this challenge. Zadeh (1965) was the first to present the concept of fuzzy set theory. After that numerous studies were performed on fuzzy number defuzzification algorithms. In a comprehensive examination of inventory management, Chen et al. (2018) extended the exploration of inventory systems by introducing a fuzzy multi-cycle remanufacturing production model. This model specifically considered a preference for low carbon footprint and accounted for the challenges posed by an inflationary environment. The integration of fuzzy logic aimed to capture the nuances and uncertainties inherent in the remanufacturing and production processes. Further advancements in the realm of fuzzy inventory systems were made by Mahapatra et al. (2019). Their study presented a model where holding costs were explicitly modeled as a function of time, and the deterioration of items followed a Weibull distribution. The complexity of the model is increased by considering dependencies on price, stock levels, reliability, and advertising in the context of demand. This holistic approach provided a nuanced perspective on the interplay of various factors affecting inventory systems. In a more recent contribution, Poswal et al. (2022) extended the understanding of inventory dynamics within a fuzzy environment. Chaudhary et al. (2023) introduced a two echelon sustainable integrated inventory model for defective products in fuzzy environment considering the deleterious effects of environmental pollution due to production.

Research Gap

Based on the abovementioned literature, various researchers looked at preservation and green investments that reduced carbon emissions and maximized their performance. Taking all of this into account, the following research question emerges: In an inflationary and fuzzy climate, how would SEOQ with defective products be constructed, taking preservation and green investment into account?

To fill this gap, the proposed research created a sustainable low-carbon inventory model with defective products under a fuzzy environment that simultaneously invests in both preservation and green. Also, the impact of inflation and time-varying holding costs on the progress of any inventory model must be addressed. Therefore to involve inflation and variable holding cost in a system is realistic access. The main objective of this study is to develop a model for a retailer that can maximize the total average profit with less environmental damage.

Contribution of this Study

Table 3.1 provides a summary of the contributions made in the current model along with findings from previous research. Except for the introduction, the paper is organized into eight sections, ensuring a thorough and structured analysis. In Sect. 3.2, a review of relevant studies is conducted, with a focus on highlighting existing gaps and limitations. Section 3.3 outlines the notations and fundamental assumptions of the current model. The mathematical formulation describing the integrated inventory system, incorporating the previously mentioned elements, is presented in Sect. 3.4. Section 3.5 discusses the solution methodology for determining the optimal solution, whereas Sect. 3.6 offers a numerical illustration of the proposed inventory system. A sensitivity analysis is carried out in Sect. 3.7 to assess the applicability of the proposed model. Section 3.8 delivers insightful managerial implications and valuable outcomes from the current model. Finally, Sect. 3.9 provides a conclusion and suggests future extensions in this field.

3.3 Problem Definition, Notations and Assumptions

3.3.1 Problem Definition

In today's world, decision-makers encounter numerous challenges in supply chain operations. A key factor among these challenges is the waste and emission of carbon from various sources, including various industries and transportation modes. The concept of a sustainable inventory system has garnered significant attention in recent years, particularly with regard to its economic and environmental implications. The focus of the current study revolves around a sustainable supply chain model, where a retailer receives products from a global supplier. A notable issue arises when a portion of these delivered products is found to be defective due to the transportation process. Returning the defective products to the supplier poses a significant problem for the buyer due to its high cost, which contributes to transportation expenses and ultimately impacts the overall profit of the inventory system and the environment. To address this challenge, the proposed policy suggests selling the defective items at a discounted price. This approach proves beneficial for decision-makers in mitigating the additional transportation or delivery costs associated with imperfect items. Furthermore,

Table 3.1 Research gap table [*Source* Own]

References	Price and carbon reduction dependent demand	Variable holding cost	Inflation	Deterioration	Preservation technology	Carbon emission	Fuzzy parameters	Imperfect products
Chen and Ouyang (2006)				✓			✓	✓
Tsao (2015)			✓	✓	✓	✓	✓	
Chen et al. (2018)			✓				✓	
Mahapatraet al. (2019)		✓	✓	✓	✓		✓	
Lu et al. (2020)	✓			✓		✓		
Mashudet al. (2020)	✓	✓		✓	✓	✓		✓
Padiyar et al. (2021)		✓	✓	✓			✓	
Alamriet al. (2022)			✓	✓	✓	✓		✓
Kumaret al. (2023)				✓	✓	✓	✓	
Present paper	✓	✓	✓	✓	✓	✓	✓	✓

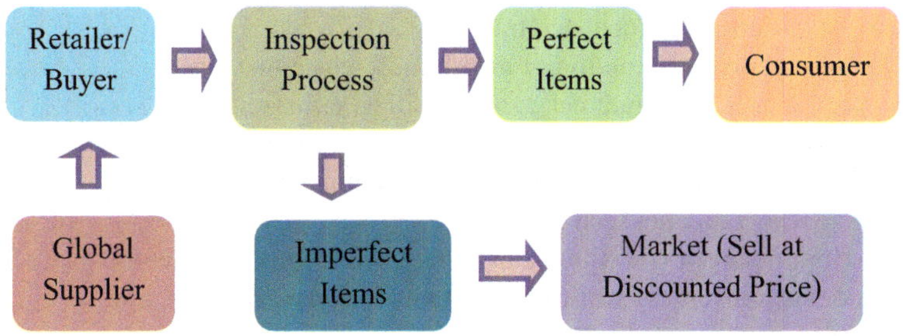

Fig. 3.1 Graphical representation for low carbon inventory model [*Source* Own]

this policy proves effective in managing and controlling the environmental impact of imperfect items (Fig. 3.1).

3.3.2 Notations

a_1	The demand function's scale parameter for perfect items.
a_2	The demand function's scale parameter for imperfect items.
b	Coefficient of price sensitivity ($b > 0$).
j	Coefficient of preference for low carbon ($j > 0$).
λ	Emission reduction percentage per unit product.
C_o	Cost of ordering/cycle.
C_p	Cost of purchasing/unit.
C_{h1}	Storage cost parameter for perfect items.
C_{h2}	Storage cost parameter for imperfect items.
C_{d1}	Deterioration cost/unit time for perfect items.
C_{d2}	Deterioration cost/unit time for imperfect items.
ω_1	Rate of deterioration for perfect items ($0 < \omega_1 \ll 1$).
ω_2	Rate of deterioration for imperfect items ($0 < \omega_2 \ll 1$).
C_s	Screening cost/unit/unit time.
r	Rate of discount on imperfect items.
δ	Percentage of Imperfect items.
k	Rate of inflation.
q	Preservation technology's sensitive parameter.
χ	Investment in Preservation technology.
u	Per trip transportation fixed cost.
v	Cost/unit transported/distance traveled.
m	Capacity of truck.
n	Number of trips.
d	Distance traveled.
w	Weight of product.
F	Per trip fixed cost for each truck.

N **No**. of gallons/truck/distance traveled.
C_e Tax of carbon emission/ton of green house gas emissions.
C_g Cost of diesel truck fuel per gallon of GHG emission.
C_f Constant part of carbon emission due to storage inventory.
C_v Per holding cost variable factor of carbon emission.
η Efficiency of greener technology.
π Maximum part of CE which can be reduced from investment in green.
t_1 Time when inventory of imperfect items becomes zero.
T Retailer's cycle time.

Decision variables

P Selling Price.
G Investment in green.

3.3.3 *Assumptions*

(1) A δ portion of total products is damaged due to the travelling process and is found to be defective, however the remaining $(1-\delta)$ part is perfect.
(2) The demand function for perfect goods is taken to be $D(p,\ \lambda) = (a_1 - bp + j\lambda)$, while for the imperfect items is taken $D_1(p,\ \lambda) = (a_2 - b(1-r)p + j\lambda)$ where $a_1, a_2, b > 0$.
(3) Because imperfect objects deteriorate more quickly than perfect ones, therefore the rate of deterioration for defective objects is higher than for perfect objects.
(4) Since there are different types of demand for both perfect and imperfect products, there is a time length, t_1, where the inventory of imperfect items becomes zero, and a time length, T, where the retailer's cycle time is considered. In the current context, green investment plays a vital role in inventory management and has a direct impact on the selling price. Therefore, an attempt has been made to present results in a new way for this model by considering green investment and selling price as decision variables. Additionally, the cycle length is assumed to be a constant parameter for all types of time.
(5) To mitigate the rate of deterioration, preservation techniques are used. After investing in preservation, the rate of decay is decreased by $\psi(\chi) = e^{-q\chi}$.
(6) Inflation is considered in the proposed inventory system with rate k.
(7) Shortages are not permitted.
(8) Holding cost is taken to be a linear function of time i.e. $C_{h1}(g + ht)$ and $C_{h2}(g + ht)$ are the unit holding cost parameters for perfect and imperfect items respectively where $g_1(= gC_{h1}) > h_1(= hC_{h1}) > 0$, $g_2(= gC_{h2}) > h_2(= hC_{h2}) > 0$.

3.4 Mathematical Formulation

3.4.1 Crisp Model

The proposed inventory model considers two types of products (perfect and imperfect). As a result, because of their distinct characteristics, both products have different levels of inventory than one another. The inventory for perfect goods is represented by:

$$q_1'(t) + \omega_1\psi(\chi)q_1(t) = -D, 0 \le t \le T \tag{3.1}$$

In the presence of boundary restrictions $q_1(0) = (1-\delta)Q$ and $q_1(T) = 0$.

The level of inventory for imperfect items is represented by (Fig. 3.2).

$$q_2'(t) + \omega_2\psi(\chi)q_2(t) = -D_1, 0 \le t \le t_1 \tag{3.2}$$

In the presence of boundary restrictions $q_2(0) = \delta S$ and $q_2(t_1) = 0$.

The solution to Eq. (3.1) is given by using the boundary condition $q_1(T) = 0$,

$$q_1(t) = \frac{D}{\omega_1\psi(\chi)}\left(e^{\omega_1\psi(\chi)(T-t)} - 1\right) \tag{3.3}$$

Again, using the boundary condition $q_2(t_1) = 0$, the solution of Eq. (3.2) is given by

$$q_2(t) = \frac{D}{\omega_2\psi(\chi)}\left(e^{\omega_2\psi(\chi)(t_1-t)} - 1\right) \tag{3.4}$$

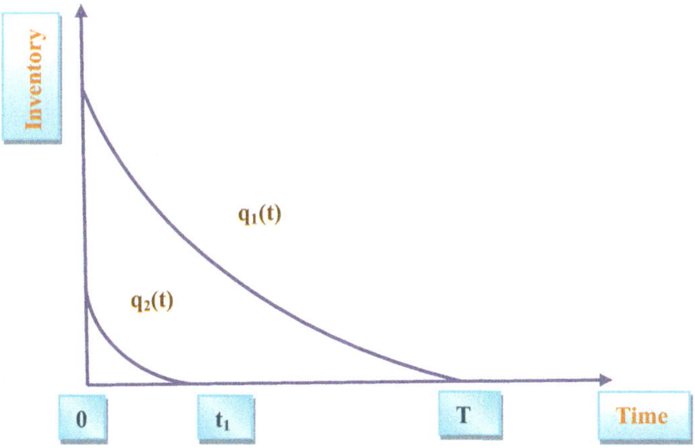

Fig. 3.2 Depiction of an inventory with perfect and imperfect quality products [*Source* Own]

Using the boundary condition $q_1(0) = (1-\delta)Q$ in Eq. (3.3), we get the initial inventory level

$$\left(Q = \frac{D}{(1-\delta)\omega_1\psi(\chi)}\left(e^{\omega_1\psi(\chi)T} - 1\right)\right) \tag{3.5}$$

Now the inventory costs are

Sales Revenue: To boost sales income, the retailer opts to decrease the price of the defective goods by r percent. This decision is based on the recognition that defective products typically experience lower demand than perfect ones, and the rate of deterioration for imperfect items is somewhat faster than that for perfect items. As a result,

$$\begin{aligned}\text{Sales Revenue SR} &= Dp\int_0^T e^{-kt}\mathrm{d}t + (1-r)D_1p\int_0^{t_1} e^{-kt}\mathrm{d}t \\ &= \frac{pD}{k}\left(1-e^{-kT}\right) + \frac{(1-r)pD_1}{k}\left(1-e^{-kt_1}\right)\end{aligned} \tag{3.6}$$

Ordering Cost: Cost of ordering the stock per cycle is:

$$\text{O.C.} = \frac{C_o}{T}\int_0^T e^{-kt}\mathrm{d}t = \frac{C_o}{Tk}\left(1-e^{-kT}\right) \tag{3.7}$$

Purchasing Cost: The OQP during the cycle and the material's per-unit cost determines the material's cost. Considering that the cost per unit of purchase is C_p. Then, the cost of purchasing per cycle is:

$$\text{P.C.} = \frac{C_pQ}{T} = \frac{C_pD}{T(1-\delta)\omega_1\psi(\chi)}\left(e^{\omega_1\psi(\chi)T} - 1\right) \tag{3.8}$$

Screening Cost: The cost of screening per cycle is:

$$\text{S.C.} = \frac{C_sQ}{T} = \frac{\text{DC}_s}{T(1-\delta)\omega_1\psi(\chi)}\left(e^{\omega_1\psi(\chi)T} - 1\right) \tag{3.9}$$

Holding Cost: To keep perishable items from decaying or deteriorating, they must be stored properly. As a result, the retailer incurs inventory holding costs in order to keep things in stock. If C_{h1} and C_{h2} are per unit per unit time holding costs for perfect and imperfect items respectively. Then the per-cycle holding cost for ideal items is:

$$\mathrm{HC}_1 = \frac{1}{T}C_{h1}\int_0^T (g+ht)e^{-kt}q_1(t)\mathrm{d}t$$
$$= \frac{\mathrm{D}C_{h1}}{T\omega_1\psi(\chi)}\left(\begin{array}{l}\left(\frac{g}{(\omega_1\psi(\chi)+k)}+\frac{h}{(\omega_1\psi(\chi)+k)^2}\right)e^{\omega_1\psi(\chi)T}+\left(\frac{g+hT}{k}+\frac{h}{k^2}\right)e^{-kT}\\ -\left(\frac{g+hT}{(\omega_1\psi(\chi)+k)}+\frac{h}{(\omega_1\psi(\chi)+k)^2}\right)e^{-kT}-\left(\frac{g}{k}+\frac{h}{k^2}\right)\end{array}\right)$$

The per-cycle holding cost for imperfect items is:

$$\mathrm{HC}_2 = \frac{1}{T}C_{h2}\int_0^{t_1} (g+ht)e^{-kt}q_2(t)\mathrm{d}t$$
$$= \frac{D_1 C_{h2}}{T\omega_2\psi(\chi)}\left(\begin{array}{l}\left(\frac{g}{(\omega_2\psi(\chi)+k)}+\frac{h}{(\omega_2\psi(\chi)+k)^2}\right)e^{\omega_2\psi(\chi)t_1}+\left(\frac{g+ht_1}{k}+\frac{h}{k^2}\right)e^{-kt_1}\\ -\left(\frac{g+ht_1}{(\omega_2\psi(\chi)+k)}+\frac{h}{(\omega_2\psi(\chi)+k)^2}\right)e^{-kt_1}-\left(\frac{g}{k}+\frac{h}{k^2}\right)\end{array}\right)$$

Thus the total holding cost per cycle

$$\mathrm{H.C.} = \mathrm{HC}_1 + \mathrm{HC}_2 \tag{3.10}$$

Deterioration Cost: Deterioration is a common characteristic of items that has an influence on a retailer's inventory. It affects both the quantity and the quality of the items. Because imperfect goods deteriorate quicker than perfect ones, the rate of decaying for imperfect objects is higher than that of perfect objects. If C_{d1} and C_{d2} are per unit time deterioration costs for perfect and imperfect items respectively. Then the deterioration Cost for perfect items is:

$$\mathrm{DC}_1 = \frac{C_{d1}}{T}0\int^T e^{-kt}\omega_1\psi(\chi)q_1(t)\mathrm{d}t$$
$$= \frac{C_{d1}D}{T}\left(\frac{\left(e^{\omega_1\psi(\chi)T}-e^{-kT}\right)}{(\omega_1\psi(\chi)+k)}+\frac{(e^{-kT}-1)}{k}\right)$$

Deterioration Cost for perfect items is:

$$\mathrm{DC}_2 = \frac{C_{d2}}{T}\int_0^{t_1} e^{-kt}\omega_2\psi(\chi)q_2(t)\mathrm{d}t$$
$$= \frac{C_{d2}D_1}{T}\left(\frac{\left(e^{\omega_2\psi(\chi)t_1}-e^{-kt_1}\right)}{(\omega_2\psi(\chi)+k)}+\frac{(e^{-kt_1}-1)}{k}\right)$$

Thus, the total deterioration cost per cycle

$$\text{D.C.} = \text{DC}_1 + \text{DC}_2 \tag{3.11}$$

Transportation Cost: Product transportation is another key problem that must be needed to manage with extra attention. Because transportation uses fuel and releases carbon dioxide, it has a direct environmental impact. When such of these factors are taken into account with some additional factors (such as the distance travelled, the number of trips made, the carbon tax, the weight of product, and capacity of the truck), the transportation cost per cycle is:

$$\text{TC} = \frac{nQF}{mT}(2u + 2v\text{d}wQ) \tag{3.12}$$

Preservation Cost per cycle is:

$$\text{PTC} = \frac{\chi T}{T}\int_0^T e^{-kt}\text{d}t = \frac{\chi T}{Tk}\left(1 - e^{-kT}\right) \tag{3.13}$$

Cost due to Carbon emission per cycle is:

$$\text{CE} = \frac{C_\text{e}}{T}\left(\left(C_f + C_v Qw\right) + \frac{2\text{d}NC_\text{g}}{m}\right) \tag{3.14}$$

As already applied by Lou et al. and Mashud et al., per unit emission of carbon can be reduced by λ percentage by investing a specific amount G where

$$\lambda = \pi\left(1 - e^{\eta G}\right)$$

The cost of investment in green per cycle is:

$$\text{GTC} = \frac{\text{GT}}{T}\int_0^T e^{-kt}\text{d}t = \frac{\text{GT}}{Tk}\left(1 - e^{-kT}\right) \tag{3.15}$$

After this investment, carbon emission cost per cycle is:

$$\text{C.E.C.} = \frac{C_\text{e}(1-\lambda)}{T}\left(\left(C_f + C_v Qw\right) + \frac{2\text{d}NC_\text{g}}{m}\right) \tag{3.16}$$

Hence the total profit function is:

$$\Pi P(p, G) = (\mathrm{SR} - \mathrm{OC} - \mathrm{PC} - \mathrm{SC} - \mathrm{HC} - \mathrm{DC} - \mathrm{TC} - \mathrm{PTC} - \mathrm{CEC} - \mathrm{GTC})$$

$$\Pi P(p, G) = \frac{1}{T}\left(\begin{array}{l} \frac{pDT}{k}\left(1 - e^{-kT}\right) + \frac{(1-r)pD_1T}{k}\left(1 - e^{-kt_1}\right) - \frac{C_o}{k}\left(1 - e^{-kT}\right) - C_pQ - C_sQ \\ -\frac{\mathrm{DC}_{h1}}{\omega_1\psi(\chi)}\left(\left(\frac{g}{(\omega_1\psi(\chi)+k)} + \frac{h}{(\omega_1\psi(\chi)+k)^2}\right)e^{\omega_1\psi(\chi)T} + \left(\frac{g+hT}{k} + \frac{h}{k^2}\right)e^{-kT}\right) \\ +\frac{\mathrm{DC}_{h1}}{\omega_1\psi(\chi)}\left(\left(\frac{g+hT}{(\omega_1\psi(\chi)+k)} + \frac{h}{(\omega_1\psi(\chi)+k)^2}\right)e^{-kT} + \left(\frac{g}{k} + \frac{h}{k^2}\right)\right) \\ -\frac{D_1C_{h2}}{\omega_2\psi(\chi)}\left(\left(\frac{g}{(\omega_2\psi(\chi)+k)} + \frac{h}{(\omega_2\psi(\chi)+k)^2}\right)e^{\omega_2\psi(\chi)t_1} + \left(\frac{g+ht_1}{k} + \frac{h}{k^2}\right)e^{-kt_1}\right) \\ +\frac{D_1C_{h2}}{\omega_2\psi(\chi)}\left(\left(\frac{g+ht_1}{(\omega_2\psi(\chi)+k)} + \frac{h_1}{(\omega_2\psi(\chi)+k)^2}\right)e^{-kt_1} + \left(\frac{g}{k} + \frac{h}{k^2}\right)\right) - C_{d1}D \\ \left(\frac{\left(e^{\omega_1\psi(\chi)T} - e^{-kT}\right)}{(\omega_1\psi(\chi)+k)} + \frac{(e^{-kT}-1)}{k}\right) - C_{d2}D_1\left(\frac{\left(e^{\omega_2\psi(\chi)t_1} - e^{-kt_1}\right)}{(\omega_2\psi(\chi)+k)} + \frac{(e^{-kt_1}-1)}{k}\right) - \\ \frac{nQF(2u + 2v\mathrm{dw}Q)}{m} - C_e(1-\lambda)\left(\left(C_f + C_vQw\right) + \frac{2\mathrm{d}NC_g}{m}\right) - \frac{(\gamma+G)T\left(1 - e^{-kT}\right)}{k} \end{array}\right) \tag{3.17}$$

3.4.2 Fuzzy Model

It is difficult to specify all parameters accurately in a fuzzy environment owing to uncertainty. Here we consider the inflation parameter k as a triangular fuzzy number

$$\text{Let}\,\tilde{k} = (k_1, k_2, k_3)$$

Therefore the total profit for fuzzy model

$$\tilde{\Pi}P = \frac{1}{T}\left(\begin{array}{l} \frac{pDT}{\tilde{k}}\left(1 - e^{-\tilde{k}T}\right) + \frac{(1-r)pD_1T}{\tilde{k}}\left(1 - e^{-\tilde{k}t_1}\right) - \frac{C_o}{\tilde{k}}\left(1 - e^{-\tilde{k}T}\right) - C_pQ - C_sQ \\ -\frac{\mathrm{DC}_{h1}}{\omega_1\psi(\chi)}\left(\left(\frac{g}{(\omega_1\psi(\chi)+\tilde{k})} + \frac{h}{(\omega_1\psi(\chi)+\tilde{k})^2}\right)e^{\omega_1\psi(\chi)T} + \left(\frac{(g+hT)}{\tilde{k}} + \frac{h}{\tilde{k}^2}\right)e^{-\tilde{k}T}\right) \\ +\frac{\mathrm{DC}_{h1}}{\omega_1\psi(\chi)}\left(\left(\frac{(g+hT)}{(\omega_1\psi(\chi)+\tilde{k})} + \frac{h}{(\omega_1\psi(\chi)+\tilde{k})^2}\right)e^{-\tilde{k}T} + \left(\frac{g}{\tilde{k}} + \frac{h}{\tilde{k}^2}\right)\right) \\ -\frac{D_1C_{h2}}{\omega_2\psi(\chi)}\left(\left(\frac{g}{(\omega_2\psi(\chi)+\tilde{k})} + \frac{h}{(\omega_2\psi(\chi)+\tilde{k})^2}\right)e^{\omega_2\psi(\chi)t_1} + \left(\frac{(g+ht_1)}{\tilde{k}} + \frac{h}{\tilde{k}^2}\right)e^{-\tilde{k}t_1}\right) + \\ \frac{D_1C_{h2}}{\omega_2\psi(\chi)}\left(\left(\frac{(g+ht_1)}{(\omega_2\psi(\chi)+\tilde{k})} + \frac{h}{(\omega_2\psi(\chi)+\tilde{k})^2}\right)e^{-\tilde{k}t_1} + \left(\frac{g}{\tilde{k}} + \frac{h}{\tilde{k}^2}\right)\right) - C_{d1}D\left(\frac{\left(e^{\omega_1\psi(\chi)T} - e^{-\tilde{k}T}\right)}{(\omega_1\psi(\chi)+\tilde{k})}\right) \\ -C_{d1}D\left(\frac{1}{\tilde{k}}\left(e^{-\tilde{k}T} - 1\right)\right) - C_{d2}D_1\left(\frac{1}{(\omega_2\psi(\chi)+\tilde{k})}\left(e^{\omega_2\psi(\chi)t_1} - e^{-\tilde{k}t_1}\right) + \frac{1}{\tilde{k}}(e^{-\tilde{k}t_1} - 1)\right) \\ -\frac{nQF}{m}(2u + 2v\mathrm{dw}Q) - C_e(1-\lambda)\left(\left(C_f + C_vQw\right) + \frac{2\mathrm{d}NC_g}{m}\right) - \frac{(\gamma+G)T\left(1 - e^{-\tilde{k}T}\right)}{\tilde{k}} \end{array}\right) \tag{3.18}$$

Now we use following methods to defuzzify the total profit function.

I. The Total Profit function using Graded Mean Integration Method is given by

$$\tilde{\Pi}P_G = \frac{(\Pi P_{G1} + 4\Pi P_{G2} + \Pi P_{G3})}{6}$$

II. The Total Profit function using Signed Distance Method is given by

$$\tilde{\Pi}P_S = \frac{(\Pi P_{S1} + 2\Pi P_{S2} + \Pi P_{S3})}{4}$$

where

$$\tilde{\Pi}P_{\alpha\beta} = \frac{1}{T}\left(\begin{array}{l} \frac{pDT}{\tilde{k}_\beta}\left(1 - e^{-\tilde{k}_\beta T}\right) + \frac{(1-r)pD_1T}{\tilde{k}_\beta}\left(1 - e^{-\tilde{k}_\beta t_1}\right) - \frac{C_o}{\tilde{k}_\beta}\left(1 - e^{-\tilde{k}_\beta T}\right) - C_pQ - C_sQ \\ -\frac{DC_{h1}}{\omega_1\psi(\chi)}\left(\left(\frac{g}{\left(\omega_1\psi(\chi) + \tilde{k}_\beta\right)} + \frac{h}{\left(\omega_1\psi(\chi) + \tilde{k}_\beta\right)^2}\right)e^{\omega_1\psi(\chi)T} + \left(\frac{(g+hT)}{\tilde{k}_\beta} + \frac{h}{\tilde{k}_\beta^2}\right)e^{-\tilde{k}_\beta T}\right) \\ +\frac{DC_{h1}}{\omega_1\psi(\chi)}\left(\left(\frac{(g+hT)}{\left(\omega_1\psi(\chi) + \tilde{k}_\beta\right)} + \frac{h}{\left(\omega_1\psi(\chi) + \tilde{k}_\beta\right)^2}\right)e^{-\tilde{k}T} + \left(\frac{g}{\tilde{k}_\beta} + \frac{h}{\tilde{k}_\beta^2}\right)\right) \\ -\frac{D_1C_{h2}}{\omega_2\psi(\chi)}\left(\left(\frac{g}{\left(\omega_2\psi(\chi) + \tilde{k}_\beta\right)} + \frac{h}{\left(\omega_2\psi(\chi) + \tilde{k}_\beta\right)^2}\right)e^{\omega_2\psi(\chi)t_1} + \left(\frac{(g+ht_1)}{\tilde{k}_\beta} + \frac{h}{\tilde{k}_\beta^2}\right)e^{-\tilde{k}_\beta t_1}\right) \\ +\frac{D_1C_{h2}}{\omega_2\psi(\chi)}\left(\left(\frac{(g+ht_1)}{\left(\omega_2\psi(\chi) + \tilde{k}_\beta\right)} + \frac{h}{\left(\omega_2\psi(\chi) + \tilde{k}_\beta\right)^2}\right)e^{-\tilde{k}_\beta t_1} + \left(\frac{g}{\tilde{k}_\beta} + \frac{h}{\tilde{k}_\beta^2}\right)\right) - C_{d1}D \\ \left(\frac{\left(e^{\omega_1\psi(\chi)T} - e^{-\tilde{k}_\beta T}\right)}{\left(\omega_1\psi(\chi) + \tilde{k}_\beta\right)} + \frac{(e^{-\tilde{k}_\beta T} - 1)}{\tilde{k}}\right) - C_{d2}D_1\left(\frac{\left(e^{\omega_2\psi(\chi)t_1} - e^{-\tilde{k}_\beta t_1}\right)}{\left(\omega_2\psi(\chi) + \tilde{k}_\beta\right)} + \frac{\left(e^{-\tilde{k}_\beta t_1} - 1\right)}{\tilde{k}_\beta}\right) - \\ \frac{nQF(2u + 2vdwQ)}{m} - C_e(1-\lambda)\left(\left(C_f + C_vQw\right) + \frac{2dNC_g}{m}\right) - \frac{(\gamma + G)T\left(1 - e^{-\tilde{k}T}\right)}{\tilde{k}} \end{array}\right) \tag{3.19}$$

where $\alpha = G, S$ and $\beta = 1, 2, 3$

3.5 Solution Methodology

Consider the case where the selling price (p) and green investment (G) are both non-zero real quantities. There are precise, unique values for p and G under these requirements that maximize the retailer's profit while also meeting the condition of first-order derivative, which are as follows:

$$\frac{\partial \Pi P}{\partial p} = 0 \tag{3.20}$$

$$\frac{\partial \Pi P}{\partial G} = 0 \tag{3.21}$$

Solving the above differential Eqs. (3.20) and (3.21), we obtain the point (*p*, *G*) and check the nature of the Hessian matrix at the point (*p*, *G*), where:

$$\Omega = \begin{bmatrix} \frac{\partial^2 \Pi P}{\partial p^2} & \frac{\partial^2 \Pi P}{\partial p \partial G} \\ \frac{\partial^2 \Pi P}{\partial G \partial p} & \frac{\partial^2 \Pi P}{\partial G^2} \end{bmatrix}$$

At (p^*, G^*), the total profit is maximized if the Hessian matrix Ω is negative definite (i.e.$\Omega_1 < 0$ and $\Omega_2 > 0$).

3.6 Numerical Illustration

In this section, a continuous review inventory system is used to demonstrate the stability and practicability of the proposed models. The mathematical model developed can be illustrated by considering numerical values for the parameters with appropriate units as follows:

$$\begin{aligned} a_1 &= 300,\ a_2 = 100,\ b = 4,\ r = 0.5,\ k = 0.015, \\ t_1 &= 0.5\,\text{years},\ q = 0.1,\ \chi = \$3,\ j = 3\ \delta = 0.3, \\ \omega_1 &= 0.4,\ \omega_2 = 0.8, \\ C_o &= \$100,\ C_p = \$80,\ C_s = \$20,\ C_{h1} = \$3,\ C_{h2} = \$7, \\ g &= 90,\ h = 30,\ C_{d1} = \$5,\ C_{d2} = \$8,\ u = \$0.3,\ v = \$0.2, \\ d &= 30,\ w = 30,\ n = 1,\ F = \$0.1,\ m = 3,\ N = 50, \\ C_{oe} &= 1.5,\ C_g = \$0.6,\ C_f = 0.8,\ C_v = 0.7,\ \pi = 0.2, \\ \eta &= 0.6,\ T = 1.6\,\text{years},\ k_1 = 0.01,\ k_2 = 0.04,\ k_3 = 0.07 \end{aligned}$$

Solution: The optimal solution for total profit and the corresponding selling price is given in Table 3.2.

Graphical Representation

Figure 3.3, 3.4 and 3.5 illustrates the concavity of the total profit function in crisp sense, while Figs. 3.6, 3.7, 3.8, 3.9, 3.10 and 3.11 depict the concavity of the overall profit function in fuzzy sense using Graded Mean Integration and the Signed Distance Method, respectively.

Table 3.2 Optimal solution [*Source* Own]

Decision variables	Crisp solution	Fuzzy solution using graded mean method	Fuzzy solution by signed distance method
Total profit	$2079.36	$2069.54	$2069.54
Selling price	$75.9673	$75.9640	$75.964
Investment in green (per unit)	$5.98495	$5.99093	$5.99093

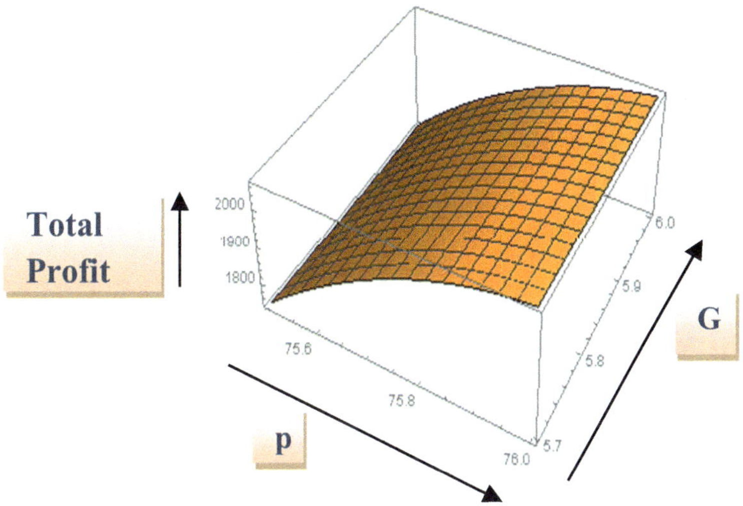

Fig. 3.3 Concavity of the ΠP in crisp sense [*Source* Own]

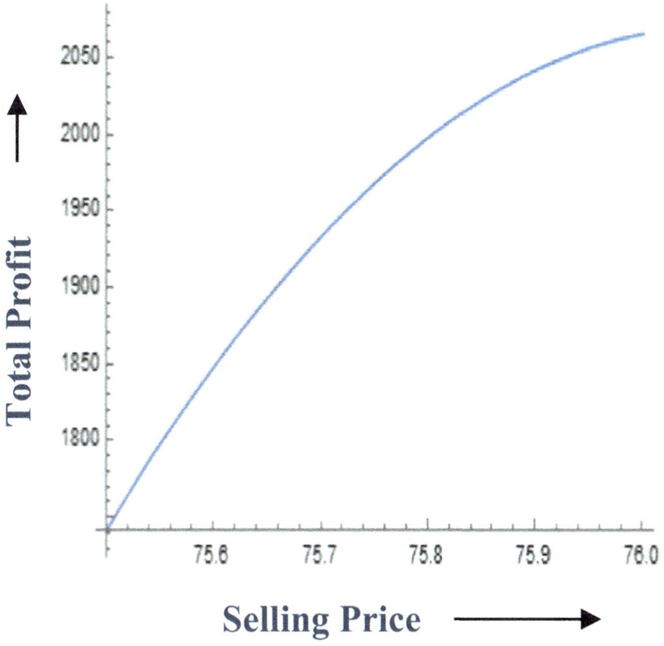

Fig. 3.4 Total profit function v/s selling price for crisp model [*Source* Own]

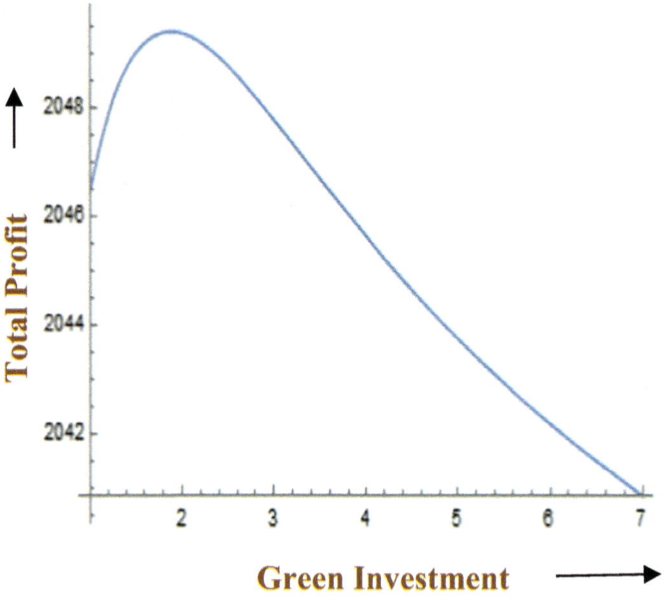

Fig. 3.5 Total profit function v/s green investment for crisp model [*Source* Own]

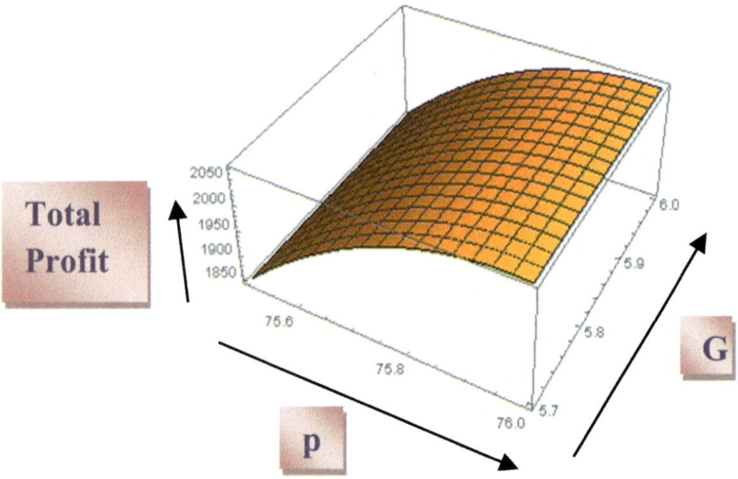

Fig. 3.6 Concavity of the ΠP in fuzzy sense using signed distance method [*Source* Own]

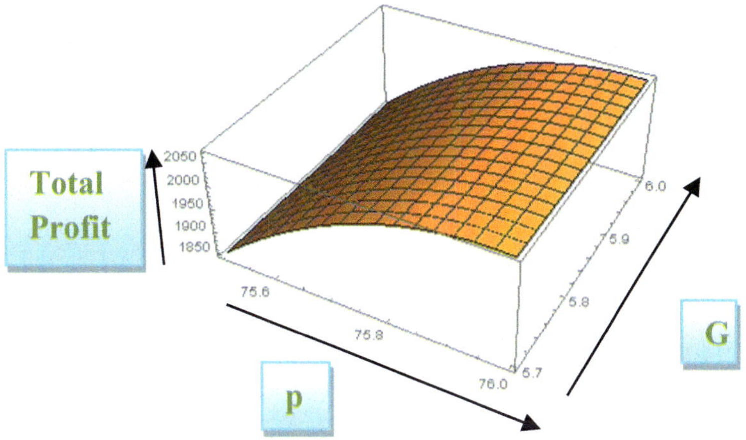

Fig. 3.7 Concavity of the ΠP in fuzzy sense using graded mean method [*Source* Own]

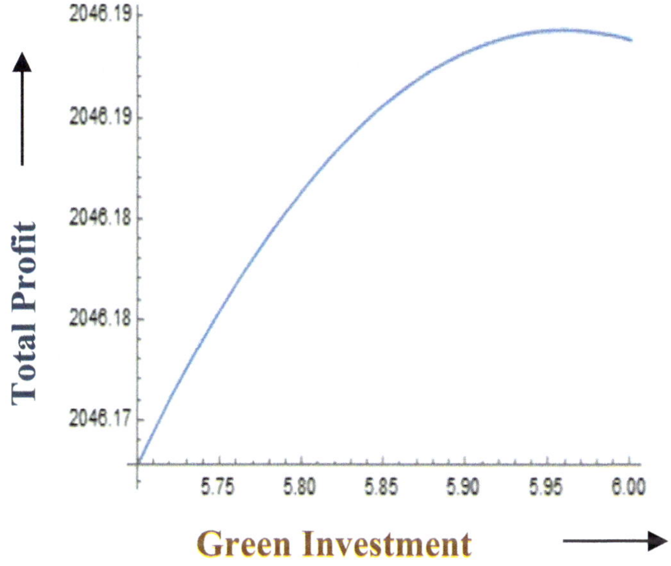

Fig. 3.8 Total profit function v/s green investment for graded mean method [*Source* Own]

3.7 Sensitivity Analysis

With regard to deterioration, purchase cost, demand parameters and the holding cost parameters etc., a sensitivity analysis is presented. This sensitivity analysis involves parameter variations ranging from − 20 to 20% (Figs. 3.12, 3.13, 3.14, 3.15, 3.16, 3.17, 3.18, 3.19 and 3.20).

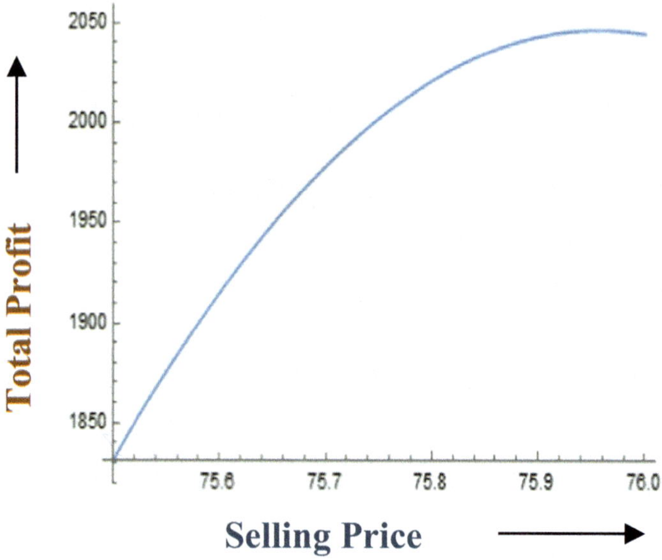

Fig. 3.9 Total profit function v/s selling price for graded mean method [*Source* Own]

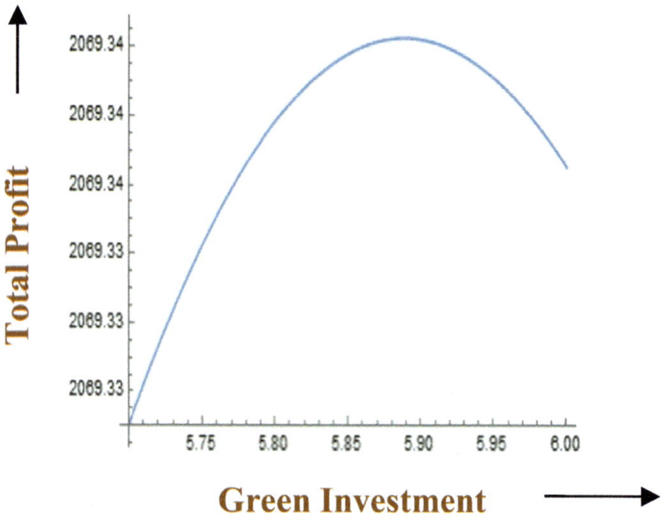

Fig. 3.10 Total profit function v/s green investment for signed distance method [*Source* Own]

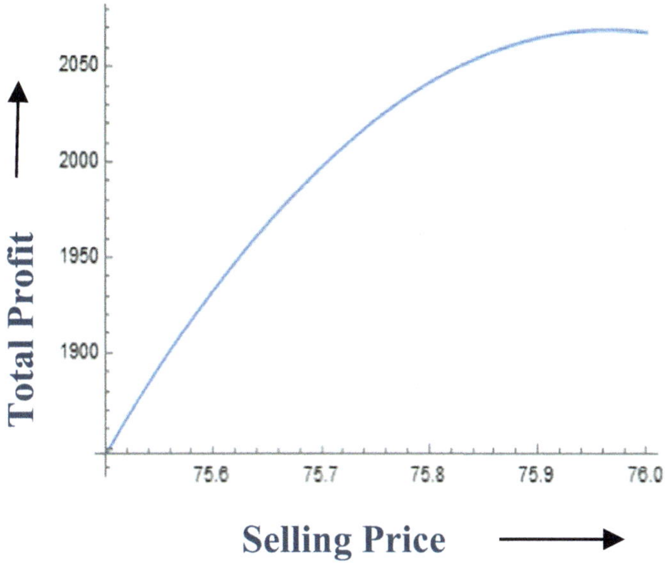

Fig. 3.11 Total profit function v/sselling price for signed distance method [*Source* Own]

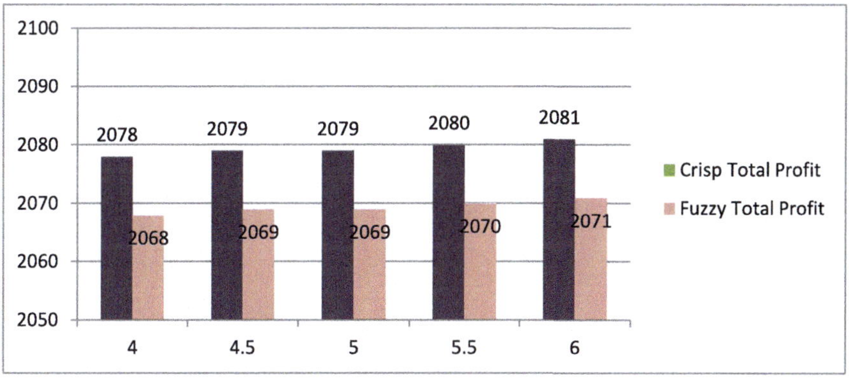

Fig. 3.12 The variation between fuzzy and crisp total profit in relation to 'C_{d1}' [*Source* Own]

3.8 Observations and Managerial Implications

3.8.1 Observations

(a) Tables 3.3 and 3.4 show that when the value of deterioration cost for perfect items (C_{d1}) increases, the total profit and selling price also increases. At the same time, the investment in green is less sensitive concerning C_{d1} for both

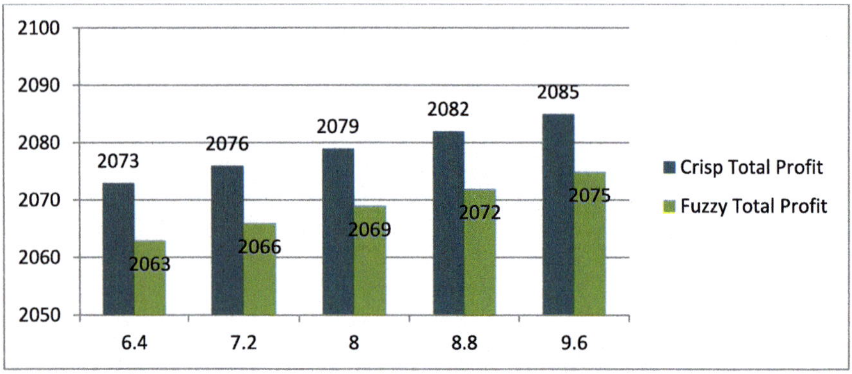

Fig. 3.13 The changes in fuzzy and crisp total profit w.r. to 'C_{d2}' [*Source* Own]

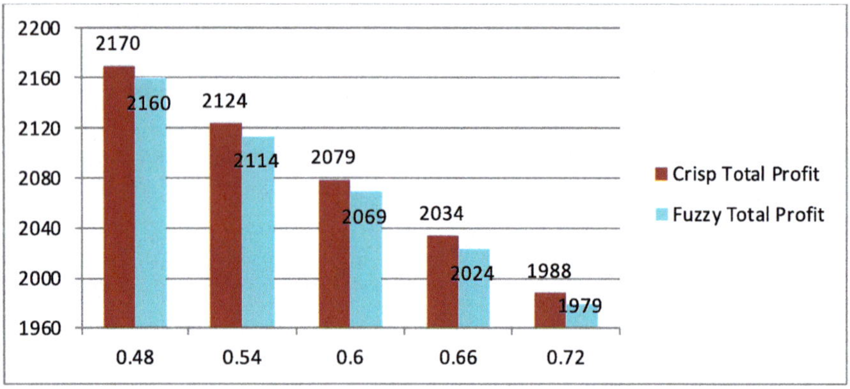

Fig. 3.14 Difference between fuzzy and crisp total profit w.r. to 'C_e' [*Source* Own]

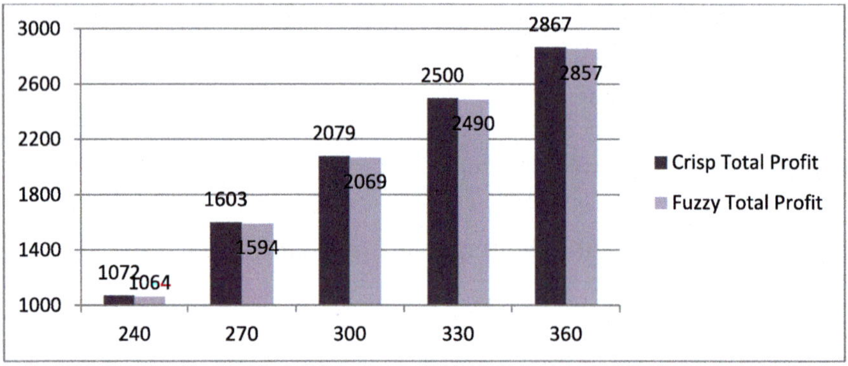

Fig. 3.15 The alteration in fuzzy and crisp total profit w.r. to 'a_1' [*Source* Own]

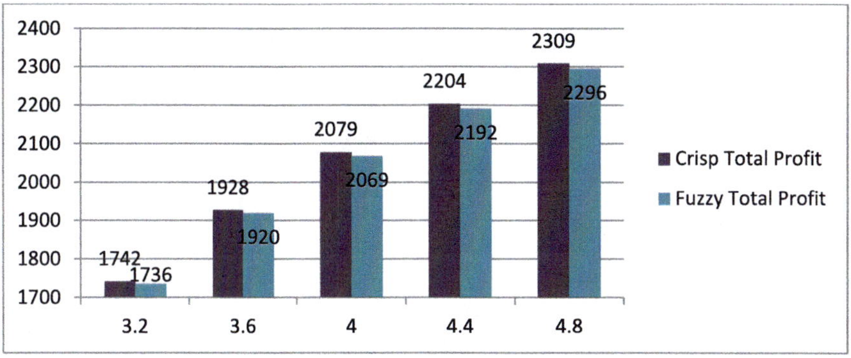

Fig. 3.16 The alteration in fuzzy and crisp total profit w.r. to 'b' [*Source* Own]

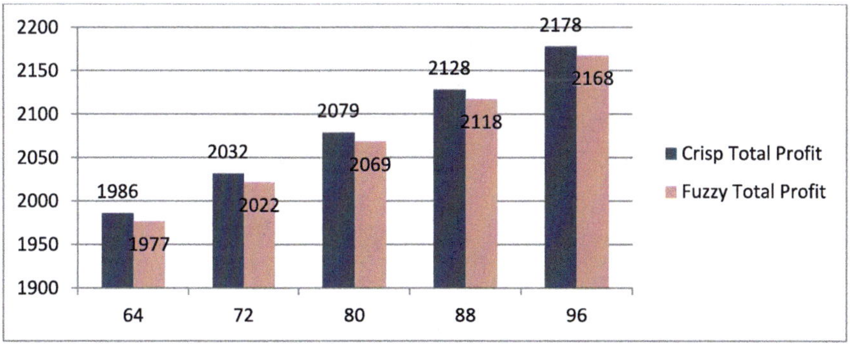

Fig. 3.17 The changes in fuzzy and crisp total profit w.r. to C_p [*Source* Own]

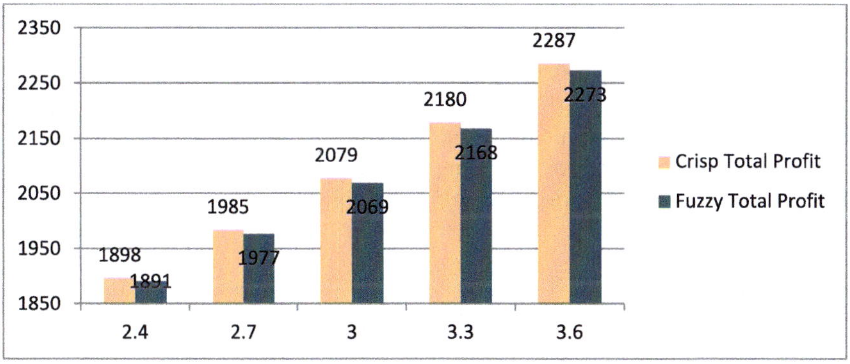

Fig. 3.18 Changes in fuzzy and crisp total profit w.r. to 'C_{h1}' [*Source* Own]

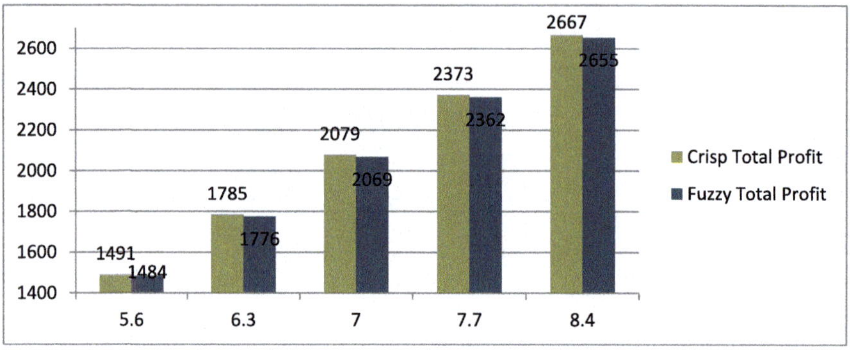

Fig. 3.19 The variance in fuzzy and crisp total profit w.r. to 'C_{h2}' [*Source* Own]

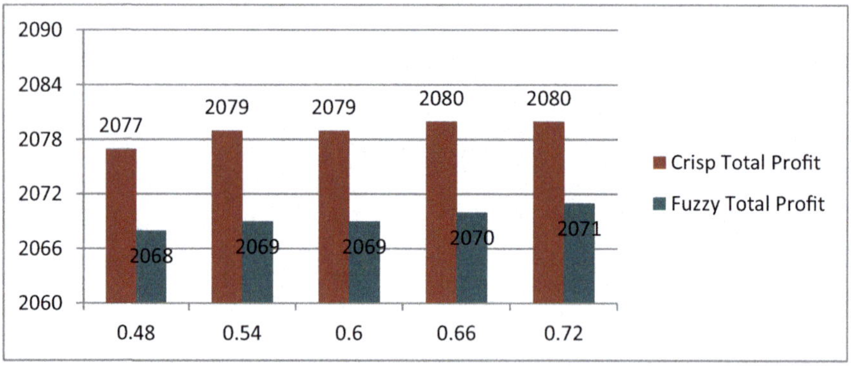

Fig. 3.20 Changes in fuzzy and crisp total profit w.r. to 'C_g' [*Source* Own]

models. Variations in the deterioration cost for defective items (C_{d2}) have a similar impact.

(b) When the value of GHG emissions of the truck fuel (C_e) increases, the total profit decreases, whereas the selling price and green investment value increase for crisp and fuzzy models, according to Table 3.5.

Table 3.3 Differences between the crisp and fuzzy models resulting from changing the perfect item's deterioration cost value [*Source* Own]

% variation	C_{d1}	For crisp sense			For fuzzy sense		
		ΠP	p	G	$\tilde{\Pi}P_G$	$\tilde{p}$	$\tilde{G}$
− 20	4.0	2078.13	75.9665	5.98589	2068.33	75.963	5.99186
− 10	4.5	2078.75	75.9669	5.98542	2068.93	75.964	5.99140
+ 10	5.5	2079.98	75.9676	5.98448	2070.14	75.964	5.99048
+ 20	6.0	2080.59	76.9680	5.98401	2070.75	75.965	5.98001

Table 3.4 Differences between the crisp and fuzzy models resulting from changing the imperfect item's deterioration cost value [*Source* Own]

% variation	C_{d2}	For crisp sense			For fuzzy sense		
		ΠP	p	G	$\tilde{\Pi} P_G$	$\tilde{p}$	$\tilde{G}$
– 20	6.4	2073.69	75.9672	5.98601	2063.89	75.964	5.99198
– 10	7.2	2076.53	75.9672	5.98548	2066.71	75.964	5.99146
+ 10	8.8	2082.20	75.9673	5.98443	2072.36	75.965	5.99042
+ 20	9.6	2085.03	76.9674	5.98390	2075.18	75.965	5.98989

Table 3.5 The variation in the crisp and fuzzy models caused by modifying the value of the GHG emissions of truck fuel [*Source* Own]

% variation	C_e	Crisp model			Fuzzy model		
		ΠP	p	G	$\tilde{\Pi} P_G$	$\tilde{p}$	$\tilde{G}$
– 20	0.48	2170.14	75.9652	5.20824	2160.31	75.962	5.21777
– 10	0.54	2124.70	75.9665	5.64151	2144.88	75.963	5.64886
+ 10	0.66	2034.08	75.9678	6.26953	2024.25	75.965	5.27457
+ 20	0.72	1988.83	76.9682	6.51250	1979.01	75.965	5.51866

(c) The observation from Table 3.6 indicates that as the scale parameter of the demand function for perfect items ($a1$) decreases, there is a corresponding decrease in total profit, selling price, and the incorporation of green technology for both models (Table 3.7).

(d) The variance in total profit, for both fuzzy and crisp sense, with respect to holding cost parameter modifications for the perfect products is shown in Table 3.8. The value of the green investment is marginally reduced with the increase in C_{h1}, but the overall profit and selling price are significantly raised. This effect has also been observed for purchasing cost parameters (C_p) and holding cost parameters for defective items (C_{h2}).

(e) Table 3.9 shows that the value of total profit and selling price is slightly increased, and the investment in green is decreasing with an increment in the value of carbon emission tax of GHG emission (C_g) (Tables 3.10 and 3.11).

Table 3.6 Variations to the value of the constant component of the demand function for perfect products result in changes to the crisp and fuzzy models [*Source* Own]

% variation	a_1	For crisp model			For fuzzy model		
		ΠP	p	G	$\tilde{\Pi} P_G$	$\tilde{p}$	$\tilde{G}$
– 20	240	1072.95	61.0203	5.91458	1064.32	61.061	5.92210
– 10	270	1603.45	68.4938	5.95014	1594.07	68.490	5.95688
+ 10	330	2500.70	83.4408	6.01906	2490.72	83.438	6.02432
+ 20	360	2867.45	90.9143	6.05248	2857.61	90.912	6.05704

Table 3.7 Variations in the price sensitivity parameter that result in changes to the total profit in crisp and fuzzy sense [*Source* Own]

% variation	b	Crisp model			Fuzzy model		
		ΠP	p	G	$\tilde{\Pi}P_G$	$\tilde{p}$	$\tilde{G}$
− 20	3.2	1742.15	94.8784	6.08674	1064.32	61.061	5.92210
− 10	3.6	1928.42	84.3762	6.03089	1594.07	68.490	5.95688
+ 10	4.4	2204.14	69.0825	5.94649	2490.72	83.438	6.02432
+ 20	4.8	2309.00	63.3420	5.91380	2857.61	90.912	6.05704

Table 3.8 Changes in the crisp and fuzzy models caused by modifying the value of the purchasing cost parameter [*Source* Own]

% variation	C_p	Crisp model			Fuzzy model		
		ΠP	p	G	$\tilde{\Pi}P_G$	$\tilde{p}$	$\tilde{G}$
− 20	64	1986.59	75.9108	6.05680	1977.15	75.907	6.06251
− 10	72	2032.15	75.9390	6.02126	2022.51	75.935	6.02711
+ 10	88	2128.23	75.9955	5.94784	2118.22	75.992	5.95398
+ 20	96	2178.76	76.0237	5.90987	2168.55	76.021	5.91615

Table 3.9 Changes in the crisp and fuzzy models caused by modifying the value of the holding cost parameter for perfect items [*Source* Own]

% variation	C_{h1}	Crisp model			Fuzzy model		
		ΠP	p	G	$\tilde{\Pi}P_G$	$\tilde{p}$	$\tilde{G}$
− 20	2.4	1898.67	75.8531	6.12711	1891.87	75.851	6.13073
− 10	2.7	1985.63	75.9102	6.05755	1977.41	75.908	6.06230
+ 10	3.3	2179.86	76.0243	5.90905	2168.25	76.020	5.91638
+ 20	3.6	2287.13	76.0814	5.82952	2273.55	76.077	5.83832

Table 3.10 Changes in the crisp and fuzzy models caused by modifying the value of the holding cost parameter for imperfect items [*Source* Own]

% variation	C_{h2}	Crisp model			Fuzzy model		
		ΠP	p	G	$\tilde{\Pi}P_G$	$\tilde{p}$	$\tilde{G}$
− 20	5.6	1491.32	75.9564	6.09069	1484.01	75.953	6.09588
− 10	6.3	1785.31	75.9618	6.03866	1776.74	75.958	6.04423
+ 10	7.7	2373.48	75.9727	5.92946	2362.40	76.969	5.93588
+ 20	8.4	2667.66	75.9781	5.87205	2655.32	76.974	5.87894

Table 3.11 Changes in the crisp and fuzzy models caused by modifying the value of the carbon emission tax of GHG emission [*Source* Own]

% variation	C_g						
		ΠP	p	G	$\tilde{\Pi}P_G$	$\tilde{p}$	$\tilde{G}$
− 20	0.48	2077.91	75.9664	7.01605	2068.09	75.963	7.02353
− 10	0.54	2078.71	75.9669	6.45474	2068.88	75.964	6.46138
+ 10	0.66	2079.91	75.9676	5.58535	2070.09	75.964	5.59078
+ 20	0.72	2088.38	76.9679	5.24080	2070.56	75.965	5.24579

3.8.2 Managerial Implications

1. Results of the present model suggest that supply chain managers must invest in preservation technologies to minimize waste and maintain the quality and freshness of their inventory. It is beneficial for improved customer satisfaction, reduced costs, and better financial performance.
2. The current study suggests that supply chain managers should focus on discount policies to encourage the sale of defective items, which is beneficial for maximizing profit.
3. The present study suggests that supply chain managers should focus on investment in green technologies as it benefits the environment and the system economically.

3.9 Conclusion

This study explores a sustainable inventory model for perishable goods with imperfect products under demand dependent on price and carbon reduction. Deterioration is a common feature of items that has an impact on the inventory of a retailer. It reduces both the quantity and the quality of the items. In the proposed model preservation investment is used to keep the products from decaying and making the business more profitable. This model is developed by assuming distinct time varying storage costs for perfect and imperfect things under inflationary and fuzzy environment. To separate the imperfect items from the perfect ones, a screening method has been implemented in this model. It is clear from the suggested structure how the screening process benefits from separating out the defective items from the perfect ones. To encourage the sale of imperfect items, a discount strategy is introduced, which was found to be quite beneficial. To validate the proposed model, numerical examples in both crisp and fuzzy environments were analyzed, with MATHEMATICA software illustrating the concavity of the objective function in both cases.

This study illustrates the influence of the green degree on environmentally conscious consumer choices when purchasing sustainable inventory. These outcomes are likely to positively impact customers' environmental awareness in their daily lives. As more customers prioritize high-green-degree items, suppliers will be compelled to produce products that minimize greenhouse gas emissions, such as CO2. This discovery highlights how a strategic investment in green practices can contribute to mitigating the escalating carbon emissions in the environment. These modifications will assist to restore the climate in the long run, as well as have other positive consequences, such as enhancing people's health.

There are a few limitations in the proposed model as well. It focused solely on transportation as a source of carbon emissions; however, future studies might look at other sources. Other carbon-reduction measures, such as cap-and-trade policies, can be used to expand the model in a variety of ways. In the future, instead of using a single inspection procedure, a continuous inspection approach might be adopted. Another possible expansion for this suggested model includes variations in demand patterns, such as probabilistic and stochastic demand. Furthermore, another interesting extension could be whether the retailer provides its customers with a multi or partial trade credit policy.

References

Ahi P, Searcy C (2013) A comparative literature analysis of definitions for green and sustainable supply chain management. J Clean Prod 52:329–341

Alamri OA, Jayaswal MK, Khan FA, Mittal M (2022) An EOQ model with carbon emissions and inflation for deteriorating imperfect quality items under learning effect. Sustainability 14(3):1365

Bierman H Jr, Thomas J (1977) Inventory decisions under inflationary conditions. Decis Sci 8(1):151–155

Buzacott JA (1975) Economic order quantities with inflation. J Oper Res Soc 26(3):553–558

Chen LH, Ouyang LY (2006) Fuzzy inventory model for deteriorating items with permissible delay in payment. Appl Math Comput 182(1):711–726

Chen W, Wei L, Li Y (2018) Fuzzy multi cycle manufacturing/remanufacturing production decisions considering inflation and the time value of money. J Clean Prod 198:1494–1502

Chaudhary R, Mittal M, Jayaswal MK (2023) A sustainable inventory model for defective items under fuzzy environment. Decis Anal J: 100207

Dissorn A (2018) Trend of green logistics model on sustainable inventory management of corporate community in agriculture and food product. PSAKU Int J Interdisc Res 7(1)

Dye CY, Hsieh TP (2012) An optimal replenishment policy for deteriorating items with effective investment in preservation technology. Eur J Oper Res 218(1):106–112

Esmaeili M, Nasrabadi M (2021) An inventory model for single-vendor multi-retailer supply chain under inflationary conditions and trade credit. J Ind Prod Eng 38(2):75–88

Gautam P, Maheshwari S, Kausar A, Jaggi CK (2023) Sustainable retail model with preservation technology investment to moderate deterioration with environmental deliberations. J Clean Prod: 136128

Hatibaruah A, Saha S (2022) A production inventory model for ameliorating and deteriorating items with price, time and advertisement frequency dependent demand under the effect of inflation. Int J Appl Comput Math 8(4):201

Hsu PH, Wee HM, Teng HM (2010) Preservation technology investment for deteriorating inventory. Int J Prod Econ 124(2):388–394

Khan M, Shaikh AA, Panda GC, Bhunia AK, Konstantaras I (2020) Non-instantaneous deterioration effect in ordering decisions for a two-warehouse inventory system under advance payment and backlogging. Ann Oper Res 289(2):243–275

Kumar S, Sami S, Agarwal S, Yadav D (2023) Sustainable fuzzy inventory model for deteriorating item with partial backordering along with social and environmental responsibility under the effect of learning. Alex Eng J 69:221–241

Lu CJ, Lee TS, Gu M, Yang CT (2020) A multistage sustainable production–inventory model with carbon emission reduction and price-dependent demand under Stackelberg game. Appl Sci 10(14):4878

Mahapatra GS, Adak S, Kaladhar K (2019) A fuzzy inventory model with three parameter Weibull deterioration with reliant holding cost and demand incorporating reliability. J Intell Fuzzy Syst 36(6):5731–5744

Mashud AHM, Roy D, Daryanto Y, Ali MH (2020) A sustainable inventory model with imperfect products, deterioration, and controllable emissions. Mathematics 8(11):2049

Mashud AHM, Roy D, Daryanto Y, Chakrabortty RK, Tseng ML (2021a) A sustainable inventory model with controllable carbon emissions, deterioration and advance payments. J Clean Prod 296:126608

Mashud AHM, Roy D, Daryanto Y, Wee HM (2021b) Joint pricing deteriorating inventory model considering product life cycle and advance payment with a discount facility. RAIRO-Oper Res 55:S1069–S1088

Mishra U, Cárdenas-Barrón LE, Tiwari S, Shaikh AA, Treviño-Garza G (2017) An inventory model under price and stock dependent demand for controllable deterioration rate with shortages and preservation technology investment. Ann Oper Res 254(1):165–190

O'Connor M (1994) Value system contests and the appropriation of ecological capital. Manchester School Econ Soc Stud 61(4):398–424

Padiyar SVS, Singh SR, Punetha N (2021) Inventory system with price dependent consumption for deteriorating items with shortages under fuzzy environment. Int J Sustain Agric Manage Inform 7(3):218–231

Poswal P, Chauhan A, Boadh R, Rajoria YK, Kumar A, Khatak N (2022) Investigation and analysis of fuzzy EOQ model for price sensitive and stock dependent demand under shortages. Mater Today Proc

Ray J, Chaudhuri KS (1997) An EOQ model with stock-dependent demand, shortage, inflation and time discounting. Int J Prod Econ 53(2):171–180

Sarkar B, Moon I (2011) An EPQ model with inflation in an imperfect production system. Appl Math Comput 217(13):6159–6167

Shah NH, Shah BJ (2014) EPQ model for time-declining demand with imperfect production process under inflationary conditions and reliability. Int J Oper Res 11(3):91–99

Singh S, Chaudhary R (2023) Effect of inflation on EOQ model with multivariate demand and partial backlogging and carbon tax policy. J Future Sustain 3(1):35–58

Singh C, Ambedkar GR (2023) Optimizing EOQ model for expiring items with stock, selling cost and lifetime dependent demand under inflation. OPSEARCH: 1–14

Singh V, Singh SR, Padiyar SVS (2024) Benefits of preservation, green and quality improvement investment for waste management in sustainable supply chain under fuzzy learning and inflation. Contemp Math 5(1):326–364

Taleizadeh AA, Aliabadi L, Thaichon P (2022) A sustainable inventory system with price-sensitive demand and carbon emissions under partial trade credit and partial backordering. Oper Res: 1–46

Tsao YC (2015) Design of a carbon-efficient supply-chain network under trade credits. Int J Syst Sci Oper Logistics 2(3):177–186

Zadeh LA (1965) Fuzzy sets. Inf Control 8(3):338–353

Chapter 4
Multi Warehouse Inventory Optimization with Varying Holding Costs, Deterioration Rates, and Carbon Tax

Anshika Singh and Abhinav Goel

Abstract Warehouses are essential for inventory management as they offer a regulated environment for storing, sorting, and controlling products. In times of low demand, the warehouse enables businesses to keep extra inventory and release it when the demand rises. Companies can position goods closer to the end customers by strategically locating multiple warehouses in various areas or close to crucial marketplaces. Therefore, the study offers a multi warehouse inventory model for perishable goods with different deterioration rates. Here, preservation technology is used in its own warehouse, resulting in a material deterioration rate that is far lower than in a rented warehouse. First, inventory is sold out of a rented warehouse, and then the products are sold from their own warehouse. The study assumes that the storage capacities of the two warehouses are equivalent. Additionally, many companies have committed to minimizing their carbon impact and pursuing environmental goals. Considering carbon expenses, inventory and warehousing strategies can be coordinated with these objectives, encouraging ecologically friendly behaviour. By implementing carbon tax into inventory management and warehouse optimization models, the research proves its dedication to upholding environmental duties and minimizing carbon footprint. By optimizing the length of the inventory model's cycle and the products price, the study aims to minimize the overall cost. Numerical examples and sensitivity tests for the crucial factors are also discussed in the study. The study suggests that retailers can reduce profit margins by optimizing the delivery routes, negotiating better terms, streamlining logistics, reducing lead times, reviewing cost structures, and implementing strict quality control procedures.

Keywords Multiple warehouses · Carbon tax · Variable holding cost · Preservation investment · Deteriorating products · Sustainable inventory model

---

A. Singh · A. Goel (✉)
Department of Mathematics, Graphic Era Deemed to be University, Dehradun 248001, India
e-mail: abhinavgoel4maths@gmail.com

A. Singh
e-mail: anshikasingh.phd@geu.ac.in

N. H. Shah and M. Mittal (eds.), *Sustainable Inventory Management*, Inventory Optimization, https://doi.org/10.1007/978-981-97-6765-6_5

4.1 Introduction

The practice of managing a firm's supply of goods, whether they are finished goods that are ready for distribution, raw materials, or corporate assets, is known as inventory management. It is essential for optimizing expenses and lowering the stress. By reducing inventory costs and levels, cutting down on resource waste, and putting in place a closed-loop system, effective inventory management is crucial for businesses looking to achieve green growth. Reconciling assets with holdings reports, confirming items on the shelf list, and enhancing the collection quality and general efficiency are all part of physical inventory in libraries. Inventory systems helps in decision making by giving information about a company's inventory data. Maintaining the proper number of supplies, lowering losses, and enhancing business operations and profitability are all made possible by effective inventory management. The industrial features of integrated inventory management and routing in road based and maritime transportation were explained by Andersson et al. (2010). The benefits of bulk purchasing for retailers include lower ordering costs and the ability to take advantage of discounts. However, efficient warehouse management is essential for smoothly handling this increased inventory. Regarding perishable goods, the warehouse management is critical since they must be adequately preserved to avoid spoiling, which could lead to a loss of sales and harm the retailer's reputation. Storage facilities must be planned with the best conditions for different kinds of products; perishables products need refrigeration units, while the temperature sensitive commodities need climate controlled spaces.

4.1.1 Literature Review

4.1.1.1 Multiple Warehouse Inventory Models

Managing inventories across many warehouses is essential to supply chain optimization. It entails effectively managing inventory across several warehouses in order to reduce expenses and increase revenue. Several publications address various facets of inventory management across several warehouses. Alberto modelled an inventory routing issue involving several products and warehouses (Alberto 2023). Paam et al. suggested establishing an operation regime by resolving an inventory control optimization problem spanning many periods, multiple items, and multiple warehouses, which stems from handling agri-fresh products (Paam et al. 2022). A multi warehouse inventory model with a quality-based discount was created by Panwar et al. (2022). For non-instantaneous decaying products in a fuzzy environment that includes multiple warehouse facilities, Chakraborty et al. designed a multi item inventory model. The model seeks to identify optimal replenishment strategies for retailers in order to optimize overall profit by permitting partial backlogs in owned warehouses (Chakraborty et al. 2020). Qiu et al. investigated a warehouse inventory problem and identified the optimal review inventory rules (Qiu et al. 2022). The advance payment two storage inventory model was developed by Khan et al. in three distinct scenarios based on the potential beginning periods of degradation in both warehouses (Khan et al. 2020). Singh and Goel established a framework for trade credit policies to address deteriorating merchandise in a retail setting, including several warehouses (Singh and Goel 2024). Considering shortages, Kumar and Mahapatra investigated a multi warehousing model with a restricted storage capacity for degrading items (Kumar and Mahapatra 2021). A computational method was created by Huang et al. to manage the sizing of inventory replenishment lots across various warehouses while taking budgetary restrictions, quantity discounts, and supplier selection into account (Huang et al. 2023). Choi et al. studied stochastic inventory models focusing on limited warehouse capacity for many items with equal and different replenishment intervals (Choi et al. 2005). For a production/distribution network where several suppliers replenish a central warehouse that distributes to various merchants, Ganeshan presented a near optimal inventory policy (Ganeshan 1999). Panda et al. investigated demand inversely affected by selling price and linearly reliant on stock in two warehouse inventory models for one vendor, many retailers (Panda et al. 2010). In order to evaluate the effects of a selling price decrease in situations where an Own Warehouse (O.W.) capacity is constrained and a Rented Warehouse (R.W.) is utilized, Sana et al. constructed a structural Economic Order Quantity (EOQ) model. The demand rate up until degradation was considered fixed in the analysis and the new demand rate was viewed as a nonlinear growing power function of the reduction rate. The model talks about related profit functions that trade-off inventory (Sana et al. 2011).

4.1.1.2 Deteriorating Goods Inventory Model

Preserving items in a warehouse to prevent deterioration is known as preservation. Certain kinds of warehouses have required the development of different preservation methods; for example, dry carbide slag storage requires a steam heat preservation system. Inventory control models have been created in order to optimize the preservation and storage of items in warehouses, considering variables such as degradation, demand, and preservation rates. Furthermore, appliances with characteristics like humidifiers, information display displays, oxygen supply tanks, and carbon dioxide supply tanks have been developed to help preserve freshness in warehouse storage. These developments aim to make warehouse preservation procedures safer and more effective. A sustainable production inventory model for low quality degrading products is developed by Sepehri et al. The model assumes that the degradation of things occurs at a consistent rate and that the pace of deterioration may be regulated by investing in preservation technologies (Sepehri et al. 2021). Chang et al. analyzed a multi-stage production-inventory model based on joint preservation technology investment for degrading products, such as raw materials and finished goods (Chang et al. 2022). Mashud et al. sought to shed light on preservation technologies to lower the pace of degradation and give shops flexible funding (Mashud et al. 2021b). The issues of pricing, frequency of advertisements, and preservation technology investment optimization have been addressed by Rapolu and Kandpal (2020). An inventory model for economic production amount with decaying goods was solved by Pervin et al. (2020). Poswal et al. created a fuzzy inventory model that included variable holding costs under allowable stock levels, a quadratic demand rate, and a Weibull degradation rate (Poswal et al. 2022). Lok et al. developed an economic order quantity model incorporating preservation (Lok et al. 2023). Bhunia and Maiti created two models for deteriorating items with linearly time-dependent demand, in which the amount of inventory on hand and demand both affect the replenishment rate linearly (Bhunia and Maiti 1998). Das et al. designed an inventory model that considered the product selling price to modify demand for non-instantaneously deteriorating items (Das et al. 2020). A two-warehouse inventory model for deteriorating items with stock and selling price-dependent demand under a partial trade credit policy was developed by Guchhait et al. (2013). An inventory model featuring two warehouses, one designated for products with defective quality and the other for deteriorating goods, was developed by Jaggi et al. (2015). With stock-dependent demand, Lee and Dye developed a degrading inventory model that took preservation technology costs and replacement policies into account. They estimated a partial shortage based on the time they had to wait for the next resupply (Lee and Dye 2012). Min et al. developed an inventory model for deteriorating items based on stock-dependent demand and a two-level trade credit policy (Min et al. 2010). Ouyang et al.'s inventory model study aimed to determine the best replenishment strategy for reducing inventory costs for non-instantaneously degrading products incorporating payment delays (Ouyang et al. 2006). Sarker et al. developed a model where demand is a composite function with a variable component proportionate to inventory levels during positive inventory buildup and a constant component. Whereas the decay rate is exponential, the production rate is finite. Four cost components from every cycle stage comprise the total cost function (Sarker et al. 1997). Sarma created a deterministic model for two warehouses storing a single product. Excess inventory beyond an owner's set warehouse capacity is stored in a rented warehouse, which has higher unit holding costs but provides superior preservation. The model matches the order level model for products with a single storage facility, and the ideal stock level is determined at the start of the period (Sarma 1987).

4.1.1.3 Carbon Emission Inventory Model

A carbon tax strategy is being explored for warehouse management to lower carbon emissions and encourage supply chains to operate sustainably. Operating expenses may increase because of the regulation of carbon taxes and other carbon-related charges. Nevertheless, the savings from the decrease in carbon emissions exceed this gain. Investing in green technology may lower emissions and increase profitability, and it is crucial for controlling carbon emissions in warehouses. Under the cap-and-trade emissions legislation, the best choices for technology investment and warehouse management may assist lower carbon emissions and enhance the financial and environmental performance of warehousing operations. Retailers stand to gain financially from investing in environmentally friendly operations and accounting for carbon taxes in their inventory models. Under the regulatory framework for the carbon tax, Konstantaras et al. address a supply chain system that integrates production, remanufacturing, and repair operations to meet a time-varying demand (Konstantaras et al. 2021). A method for inventorying production that combined cap and trade and carbon tax policies was examined by Datta et al. (2020). Yadav and Khanna address a model for goods with an expiration date under the carbon tax legislation to meet sustainability objectives (Yadav and Khanna 2021). Xu et al. presented inventory models to examine how carbon emissions affect inventory systems for degrading commodities with time-varying demand (Xu et al. 2020). These models allowed for shortages and partial backlogs of customer demand. Mahato et al. worked on a model for non-instantaneously decaying products with time-varying deterioration rates under carbon tax policies (Mahato et al. 2023). Alternative carbon control strategies, including carbon cap and trade, trade and credit policy, and carbon-emission control, should be considered. Verma et al. investigated deteriorating inventory to handle short-life inventory problems, considering trade and credit policy, carbon-emission control, and carbon cap and trade as carbon control strategies (Verma and Mishra 2024). Christata and Daryanto conducted a study on the single-echelon EOQ model, which includes carbon emissions in its operation (Christata and Daryanto 2020). Chaudhari et al. investigate the impact of carbon tax laws on company strategies for perishable goods regarding down-cash-credit payments (Chaudhari et al. 2023). Bhavani et al. presented a method for managing depository inventory with last-in-first out and first-in-first out, and they investigated a two-warehouse model for degrading goods where the demand is dependent on pricing and marketing (Bhavani et al. 2022). Chen et al. investigated optimal practices for managing warehouses and investing in technology in the context of cap-and-trade emissions policies. They also looked at the effects of transaction costs and the initial carbon emission allowance on the financial and environmental outcomes of warehousing operations that supply the external market (Chen et al. 2016). De et al. used joint inventory control and sustainable trade credit financing for degrading items under a volumetric fuzzy system to study carbon emission issues in a supplier-retailer-customer model (De et al. 2021). In a supply chain that includes warehouse, distribution centre, and retailer, Hariga et al. assessed the effects of accounting for carbon emissions from cold item transportation and storage (Hariga et al. 2017). Considering transportation logistics systems and warehouse activities as sources of emissions, Hasan et al. created three models to maximize inventory and technology investment under a carbon tax, cap and trade, and severe limit restrictions (Hasan et al. 2021). Incorporating carbon emission considerations with interval-valued time-dependent emission rates, Manna et al. constructed a model with time-dependent faulty rate, greenness of product demand (Manna et al. 2022). To prevent stock-out situations and boost corporate profitability by lowering carbon emissions during transportation, Mashud et al.'s study sought to reduce carbon emissions by putting money into green technology inside a two-warehouse system (Mashud et al. 2021a). Through investments in green technology in various scarcity scenarios, Mishra et al. created a sustainable economic production quantity (SEPQ) carbon tax and cap model to carbon emission (Mishra et al. 2020). An inventory model for green retail investments was created by Paul et al., considering variable keeping costs, selling prices, and degrees of green concern. The ideal replenishment period and green concern level were determined by analyzing the impacts of greening levels on buying and selling prices while taking profit maximization into account (Paul et al. 2022). Using interval numbers for inventory cost and carbon emission parameters, Ruidas et al. created an imperfect production inventory model for carbon emission regulatory policies. Simple tax policy, cap and purchase policy, cap and reward policy, and strictly under permitted cap policy were the four policies they discussed. Four alternative inventory models were created based on these policies (Ruidas et al. 2021). Sarker et al. proposed an integrated inventory model that uses the Stackelberg game policy to optimize the joint total cost of a vendor and buyer system. To maximize profit and reduce vendor setup costs, the model considers carbon emissions, fixed and variable transportation, and setup expenses (Sarkar et al. 2016). Tiwari et al. developed an inventory model that considered carbon emissions for decaying products of undesirable quality. This model takes into account emissions from storage, warehousing, and transportation. Fuel consumption and distance travelled are used to calculate transportation emissions, while total inventory and energy consumption per item are used to calculate warehouse emissions (Tiwari et al. 2018).

4.1.2 Comparison of Study

Table 4.1 presents the comparison of the previous literature with the current study. The remainder of the paper covers notation and assumptions in section 2, whereas Sects. 4.3 and 4.4 provide mathematical formulation and the solution methodology, respectively. Section 4.5 deals with numerical analysis, whereas Sect. 4.6 addresses sensitivity analysis. Section 4.7 concludes the study with directions for future work.

Table 4.1 Comparison of previous and current study [*Source* Own]

Author (s)	Demand type	Preservation investment	Multiple warehouses	Carbon emission
Chakraborty et al. (2020)	Stock dependent	No	Yes	No
Mahato et al. (2023)	Selling price dependent	Yes	No	Yes
Singh and Goel (2024)	Advertisement and selling price	No	Yes	No
Sepehri et al. (2021)	Price dependent	Yes	No	Yes
Xu et al. (2020)	Time-varying	No	No	Yes
This model	**Stock dependent**	**Yes**	**Yes**	**Yes**

Table 4.2 Notations [*Source* Own]

W	Capacity of O.W. and R.W. (units)
h_1	Holding cost for R.W. ($)
h_2	Holding cost for O.W. ($)
m_0	Deterioration rate before preservation
$m(\xi)$	Deterioration rate after preservation
δ	Sensitive parameter of investment to the deterioration rate
h_1'	The cost associated with energy consumption and carbon emission while holding inventory in R.W. ($)
h_2'	Cost associated with energy consumption and carbon emission while holding inventory in O.W. ($)
ξ'	The cost associated with energy consumption and carbon emission while preservation. ($)
F	Fixed transportation cost
V	Variable transportation cost

4.2 Notations and Assumptions

4.2.1 Notations

Table 4.2 illustrates the list of notations used in the study to build the mathematical model.

4.2.2 Assumptions

i. The study considers a multi-warehouse inventory model, where the retailer has its own warehouse (O.W.) and rented warehouse (R.W.).
ii. Both warehouses stock perishable products. Where demand is stock dependent i.e., $D(t) = a + bI_1(t)$.
iii. Preservation is applied in the O.W., so the rate of deterioration of both warehouses is different. O.W.'s deterioration rate is less than that of R.W.
iv. Preservation investment defines the decrease in the rate of deterioration. The original deterioration rate is m_0, and after investing in preservation ξ, the reduction in the rate of deterioration is $m(\xi) = m_0 e^{-\delta\xi}$
v. Goods are first sold from the R.W. warehouse to avoid giving additional rent for longer.
vi. Equal goods are in both warehouses, i.e., W.
vii. Carbon tax policy is incorporated and used while holding inventory, transportation, and preservation investments. Companies are encouraged to lower their carbon footprints by imposing a carbon price and reducing emissions and their

environmental impact. This frequently results in better resource consumption, decreased waste, and increased efficiency.

viii. Shortages are not permitted in the study.
ix. The model is developed for only one product.
x. O.W. has a lower holding cost than R.W.
xi. The transportation cost comprises a fixed price, F, and a variable cost, V which is determined by the quantity of the transported product.

4.3 Mathematical Formulation

Figure 4.1 illustrates the inventory level with time. Initially, both the warehouses have the same level of goods, i.e., W. The inventory in O.W. declines due to the deterioration in $[0, t_1]$. In contrast, the inventory in R.W. declines because of demand and deterioration in the R.W. All the stock in R.W. is sold by the time t_1. Then, the retailer sells the product from his O.W., which decreases because of both the demand and the deterioration throughout $[t_1, T]$.

The mathematical formation for the inventory is given below.

4.3.1 R.W.

$$\frac{dI_1(t)}{dt} = -D - m_0 I_1(t), \quad 0 \le t \le t_1 \tag{4.1}$$

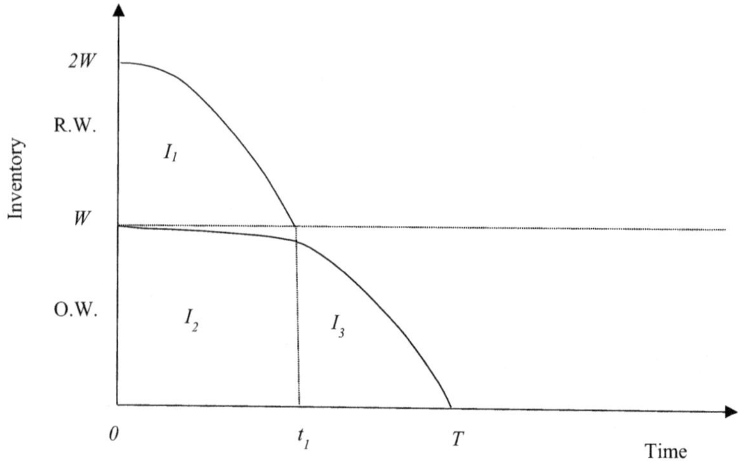

Fig. 4.1 Inventory level [*Source* Own]

Boundary conditions for the R.W. are given below

$$I_1(0) = W, I_1(t_1) = 0 \tag{4.2}$$

$$I_1(t) = \frac{-a}{(b+m_0)} + \left(W + \frac{a}{b+m_0}\right)e^{-(b+m_0)t}. \tag{4.3}$$

$$W = \frac{a}{(b+m_0)}\left(e^{(b+m_0)t_1} - 1\right). \tag{4.4}$$

4.3.2 *O.W.*

$$\frac{\mathrm{d}I_2(t)}{\mathrm{d}t} = -m(\xi)I_2(t) \quad 0 \leq t \leq t_1 \tag{4.5}$$

$$\frac{\mathrm{d}I_3(t)}{\mathrm{d}t} = -m(\xi)I_3(t) - D \quad t_1 \leq t \leq T \tag{4.6}$$

Boundary conditions for the O.W. are

$$I_2(0) = W, I_3(T) = 0 \tag{4.7}$$

$$I_2(t) = We^{-m_0 t(1-\delta\xi)}. \tag{4.8}$$

$$I_3(t) = \frac{a}{(b+m_0(1-\delta\xi))}\left(e^{(b+m_0(1-\xi\delta))(T-t)} - 1\right). \tag{4.9}$$

4.3.3 *Cost Calculation*

The retailer accounts for ordering, holding, purchasing, preservation, degradation, and transportation costs in their cost estimate.

4.3.3.1 Ordering Cost

Ordering costs are the costs associated with placing and receiving inventory orders. They are often referred to as procurement or setup costs.

$$OC = \frac{O}{T}. \tag{4.10}$$

4.3.3.2 Holding Cost

The costs associated with keeping and storing merchandise for a predetermined time are called holding costs, often called carrying costs.

$$HC = \frac{1}{T}(HC_R + HC_O). \tag{4.11}$$

Here, HC_R is the holding cost of the R.W., and HC_O represents the holding cost for the O.W.

Carbon emissions from warehouse operations, such as lighting, heating, and cooling, are caused mainly by energy use.

$$HC_R = \left(h_1 + h_1'\right)\int_0^{t_1} I_1(t)\mathrm{d}t. \tag{4.12}$$

Here, h_I is the per unit holding cost for the R.W. and h_1' is the per unit carbon emission cost while keeping inventory in the R.W.

$$HC_R = \frac{\left(h_1 + h_1'\right)}{(b + m_0)}\left(\left(1 - e^{-t_1(b+m_0)}\right)\left(W + \frac{a}{(b + m_0)}\right) - at_1\right). \tag{4.13}$$

$$HC_o = \left(h_2 + h_2'\right)\left(\int_0^{t_1} I_2(t) + \int_{t_1}^{T} I_3(t)\right). \tag{4.14}$$

Here, h_2 is the per unit carbon emission while holding inventory in O.W. and h_2' is the per unit carbon emission cost while holding inventory in O.W.

$$HC_O = \left(h_2 + h_2'\right)\left(\frac{W\left(1 - e^{-m_0(1-\delta\xi)t_1}\right)}{m_0(1 - \delta\xi)} + \frac{a}{(b + m_0(1 - \delta\xi))}\left(\frac{\left(e^{(b+m_0(1-\xi\delta))} - 1\right)}{(b + m_0(1 - \xi\delta))} - T + t_1\right)\right). \tag{4.15}$$

$$\begin{aligned} HC = {} & \frac{\left(h_1 + h_1'\right)}{T(b + m_0)}\left(\left(1 - e^{-t_1(b+m_0)}\right)\left(W + \frac{a}{(b + m_0)}\right) - at_1\right) \\ & + \frac{\left(h_2 + h_2'\right)}{T}\left(\frac{W\left(1 - e^{-m_0(1-\delta\xi)t_1}\right)}{m_0(1 - \delta\xi)} + \frac{a}{(b + m_0(1 - \delta\xi))}\left(\frac{\left(e^{(b+m_0(1-\xi\delta))} - 1\right)}{(b + m_0(1 - \xi\delta))} - T + t_1\right)\right). \end{aligned} \tag{4.16}$$

4.3.3.3 Purchasing Cost

The cost of purchasing items from suppliers to resell to clients, including different expenses associated with the procurement process, is known as the procurement cost.

$$\mathrm{PC} = \frac{p}{T}2W. \tag{4.17}$$

where p is per unit purchasing cost.

$$\mathrm{PC} = \frac{2p}{T}\frac{a}{(b+m_0)}\left(e^{(b+m_0)t_1} - 1\right). \tag{4.18}$$

4.3.3.4 Preservation Cost

Retailers incur preservation expenditures to keep their inventory in excellent condition throughout time, particularly for perishable items with short shelf life, to avoid spoiling, degradation, or obsolescence. Due to their manufacturing procedures and material sourcing, preservation-related packaging materials such as vacuum-sealed plastic and moisture-resistant coatings may have a larger carbon footprint.

$$\mathrm{PT} = \frac{(\xi+\xi')}{T}. \tag{4.19}$$

Here, ξ is the preservation cost, and ξ' is the cost associated with energy consumption and carbon emission while preservation.

4.3.3.5 Deterioration Cost

Deterioration costs are expenses retailers incur due to the decline in inventory quality over time, especially for products susceptible to deterioration, spoilage, or obsolescence.

$$\mathrm{DC} = \frac{1}{T}(\mathrm{DC}_O + \mathrm{DC}_R). \tag{4.20}$$

DC_O is the deterioration cost for the products in O.W., and DC_R is the deterioration cost for the products in R.W.

$$\mathrm{DC}_O = c_d\left(W - \int_{t_1}^{T}(a + bI_3(t))\mathrm{d}t\right). \tag{4.21}$$

$$\mathrm{DC}_O = c_d\left[W - a\left(T - t_1 - \frac{b}{b + m_0(1 - \delta\xi)}\left(T - t_1 + \frac{\left(1 - e^{(b+m_0(1-\xi\delta))(T-t_1)}\right)}{(b + m_0(1 - \xi\delta))}\right)\right)\right]. \tag{4.22}$$

$$\mathrm{DC}_R = c_d\left(W - \int_0^{t_1}(a + bI_1(t))\mathrm{d}t\right). \tag{4.23}$$

$$\mathrm{DC}_R = \frac{c_d}{(b + m_0)}\left(a\left(e^{t_1(b+m_0)} - 1 - am_0\right) + b\left(e^{-t_1(b+m_0)} - 1\right)\left(W + \frac{a}{(b + m_0)}\right)\right). \tag{4.24}$$

$$\mathrm{DC} = \frac{c_d}{T}\left(\begin{array}{l} W - a\left(T - t_1 - \dfrac{b}{b + m_0(1 - \delta\xi)}\left(T - t_1 + \dfrac{\left(1 - e^{(b+m_0(1-\xi\delta))(T-t_1)}\right)}{(b + m_0(1 - \xi\delta))}\right)\right) \\ + \dfrac{1}{(b + m_0)}\left(a\left(e^{t_1(b+m_0)} - 1 - am_0\right) + b\left(e^{-t_1(b+m_0)} - 1\right)\left(W + \dfrac{a}{(b + m_0)}\right)\right) \end{array}\right). \tag{4.25}$$

4.3.3.6 Transportation Cost

The charges involved in moving items from suppliers to the retailer's site or from the store to consumers are referred to as transportation costs for retailers.

$$\mathrm{TS} = \frac{(F + V(2W))}{T}. \tag{4.26}$$

where F is the fixed transportation cost, and V is the variable cost that depends on the number of goods.

$$\mathrm{TS} = \frac{1}{T}\left(F + \frac{2Va}{(b + m_0)}\left(e^{(b+m_0)t_1} - 1\right)\right). \tag{4.27}$$

The total cost of the retailer is given as

$$\mathrm{TC}(\xi, t_1, T) = \mathrm{OC} + \mathrm{HC} + \mathrm{PC} + \mathrm{PT} + \mathrm{DC} + \mathrm{TS} \tag{4.28}$$

4.4 Solution Methodology

This section presents the method for addressing the inventory model's optimization problems. The goal is to show that the total cost function is convex and to reduce the total cost function per unit of time. The three independent variables in the total cost equations: ξ, T, and t_1 are included in the proposed model. The following procedures are used to optimize the total cost equation and determine the values of all independent factors.

Step 1. To determine the value of decision variables, put the first order partial derivative of the total cost function T.C., with respect to ξ, t_1, and T and equate it to zero.

$$\frac{\partial \mathrm{TC}}{\partial \xi} = 0, \frac{\partial \mathrm{TC}}{\partial t_1} = 0, \text{ and } \frac{\partial \mathrm{TC}}{\partial T} = 0 \tag{4.29}$$

Step 2. Determine the second-order partial derivatives for each independent variable.
Step 3. Create a Hessian matrix as shown below.

$$H = \begin{bmatrix} \frac{\partial^2 \mathrm{TC}}{\partial \xi^2} & \frac{\partial^2 \mathrm{TC}}{\partial \xi \partial t_1} & \frac{\partial^2 \mathrm{TC}}{\partial \xi \partial T} \\ \frac{\partial^2 \mathrm{TC}}{\partial t_1 \partial \xi} & \frac{\partial^2 \mathrm{TC}}{\partial t_1^2} & \frac{\partial^2 \mathrm{TC}}{\partial t_1 \partial T} \\ \frac{\partial^2 \mathrm{TC}}{\partial T \partial \xi} & \frac{\partial^2 \mathrm{TC}}{\partial T \partial t_1} & \frac{\partial^2 \mathrm{TC}}{\partial T^2} \end{bmatrix}. \tag{4.30}$$

Step 4. H_1, H_2, and H_3 denotes the first, second and third principal minor respectively. The principal minors $|H_1| > 0$, $|H_2| > 0$, and $|H_3| > 0$ must show a positive sign to reduce the inventory management system's overall integrated cost function. At the optimal value of the decision variables, the global minimum of the total cost is reached if the condition is met.

4.5 Numerical Example

The numerical experiment is carried out in this section. Assume that the produced model's constraints have the following values: $h_1 = \$10$/unit, $h_2 = \$5$/unit, $h'_1 = \$0.75$/unit, $h'_2 = \$0.35$/unit, $m_0 = 0.07$, $\delta = 0.001$, $\xi' = \$12$, $F = \$60$, $V = \$10$, $a = 40$, $b = 1$, $c_d = \$2$/unit, $O = \$500$/order, $p = \$30$/unit. Using the above values and solving Eq. (4.29) the optimal value for preservation investment ξ is \$1092.6964, t_1 is 1.5497 weeks and cycle time T 6.5471 weeks (Table 4.3).

At \$8089.4000, the most economical approach to inventory management across several warehouses is accomplished, balancing expenses related to shipping, holding, preservation, and maybe carbon taxes. The \$1092.6964 preservation investment seeks to preserve product quality and lower deterioration costs by using techniques like better packing and climate management to increase product shelf life.

Table 4.3 Optimal solution [*Source* Own]

ξ (\$)	t_1 (weeks)	T (weeks)	T.C. (\$)
1092.6964	1.5497	6.5471	8089.4000

4.6 Sensitivity Analysis

Sensitivity analysis is a crucial tool for assessing the robustness of a supply chain, identifying key elements influencing system behaviour and providing a clear understanding of the relationship between input variables and outcomes.

The analysis from Table 4.4 yielded the following managerial insights:

i. The increase in R.W. and O.W.'s holding cost results in rise in the retailer's total price. A retailer's capacity to expand in other business areas or adjust to market changes may be restricted by higher holding costs, which reduce profit margins by devoting more resources to inventory management.
ii. With the increase in the deterioration rate of products, the total cost increases moderately. Inventory that needs to be updated or unsaleable results in more considerable losses for retailers and more expenses. Purchasing specialist storage facilities or equipment could aid in preserving perishable items.
iii. The increase in the sensitive investment parameter to the deterioration rate slightly increases the retailer's total cost. Retailers should be aware of the sensitivity of deterioration rates and monitor how they affect inventory investment. Working with suppliers and securing flexible contracts can assist in controlling costs and reducing risks associated with variable product quality.
iv. Total cost also increases with the increase in fixed and variable transportation costs. To cut costs, retailers should optimize delivery routes, combine shipments, negotiate better terms, streamline logistics, enhance inventory management, and decrease lead times. They should also assess transportation costs and identify cost-saving strategies.
v. The demand parameter significantly decreases while the shape parameter substantially increases the total cost. Retailers should review cost structures to maximize savings, minimize expenses, and reevaluate demand forecasting algorithms to anticipate future demand patterns. This could be part of renegotiating supplier agreements, reassessing pricing tactics, and implementing cost-cutting initiatives.
vi. Total cost moderately increases with the increase in per unit deterioration cost. Retailers should have strict quality control procedures to reduce product deterioration and cut expenses. These procedures should include inventory inspection, better storage conditions, and correct handling through the supply chain.
vii. Increases in ordering and purchasing costs also increase the total cost. Retailers should optimize stock, maintain correct records, monitor demand patterns, and improve inventory management methods to cut expenses. Reducing delivery costs or negotiating better terms with suppliers can also lessen the impact of rising costs (Fig. 4.2).

Table 4.4 Sensitivity analysis [*Source* Own]

Parameter	% Change	ξ ($)	t_1 (weeks)	T (weeks)	T.C. ($)
h_1	– 20	12,902.3000	0.5031	6.5791	7909.0000
	– 10	1191.5000	1.5437	6.5630	8038.9000
	10	993.9229	1.5556	6.5313	8140.0000
	20	895.1484	1.5615	6.5157	8190.7000
h_2	– 20	100.1504	1.5635	6.5608	7543.3000
	– 10	512.1680	1.5572	6.5449	7825.0000
	10	1649.2000	1.5411	6.5633	8342.1000
	20	2185.8000	1.5316	6.5911	8586.8000
m_0	– 20	3545.0000	1.4952	7.0211	7982.2000
	– 10	2195.6000	1.5159	6.7708	8023.4000
	10	167.3838	1.5795	6.3450	8173.9000
	20	105.8078	1.6085	6.1609	8273.0000
δ	– 20	3479.4000	1.4988	6.9756	8163.0000
	– 10	2153.6000	1.5243	6.7484	8114.9000
	10	223.6710	1.5746	6.3667	8079.8000
	20	151.9516	1.5988	6.2037	8001.8000
F	– 20	1096.3000	1.5495	6.5477	8087.5000
	– 10	1094.5000	1.5496	6.5474	8088.5000
	10	1090.9000	1.5498	6.5468	8090.3000
	20	1089.1000	1.5499	6.5465	8091.2000
V	– 20	1629.9000	1.5381	6.6356	7816.2000
	– 10	1361.4000	1.5439	6.5907	7952.3000
	10	824.0119	1.5555	6.5045	8227.3000
	20	555.3582	1.5614	6.4631	8366.2000
a	– 20	2749.1000	1.5012	6.9689	9679.7000
	– 10	1921.1000	1.5255	6.7454	8878.8000
	10	263.0518	1.5627	6.3692	7311.9000
	20	168.4308	1.5970	6.2083	6546.8000
b	– 20	1843.0000	1.4180	7.0224	5937.8000
	– 10	1577.5000	1.4863	6.7856	6919.3000
	10	316.1642	1.6101	6.3026	9492.8000
	20	251.6473	1.669	6.0490	11,188.0000
c_d	– 20	1595.8000	1.5432	6.5684	7892.0000
	– 10	1346.1000	1.5466	6.5567	7991.7000
	10	835.3876	1.5527	6.5399	8185.2000
	20	573.7510	1.5555	6.5353	8279.5000
O	– 20	1122.5000	1.5479	6.5519	8074.1000

(continued)

Table 4.4 (continued)

Parameter	% Change	ξ ($)	t_1 (weeks)	T (weeks)	T.C. ($)
	− 10	1107.6000	1.5488	6.5495	8081.7000
	10	1077.8000	1.5506	6.5447	8097.0000
	20	1062.8000	1.5515	6.5423	8104.7000
p	− 20	2701.9000	1.5153	6.8272	7281.1000
	− 10	1898.3000	1.5323	6.6816	7681.0000
	10	286.7915	1.5672	6.4227	8505.9000
	20	N517.8712	1.5846	6.3074	8930.2000

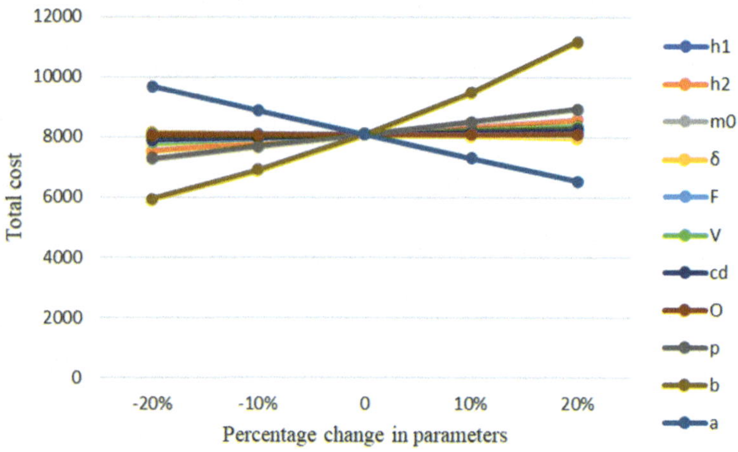

Fig. 4.2 Effects of several factors on the total cost [*Source* Own]

4.7 Conclusion

The study highlights the importance of warehouses in effective inventory management, introducing a multi-warehouse inventory model for perishable goods with varying deterioration rates. It also highlights the growing need for environmental sustainability in business practices, integrating carbon expenses into inventory management and warehousing strategies. The research provides insights into the impact of critical factors on the system's ideal total cost. The sensitivity analysis of the study suggests that higher holding costs can limit a retailer's ability to expand or adapt to market changes, reducing profit margins. To cut costs, retailers should optimize delivery routes, negotiate better terms, streamline logistics, and reduce lead times. They should also review cost structures, reevaluate demand forecasting algorithms, and implement strict quality control procedures to minimize product deterioration and costs. The study can be further extended by considering the trade credit policy or inflation concept.

Declaration of Competing Interests No funding from public or commercial sources was provided for this study. The authors disclose no conflicts of interest.

References

Alberto G (2023) Model Matematis untuk Multi-product multi-warehouse inventory routing problem. Jurnal Rekayasa Sistem Industri 12(1):27–34

Andersson H, Hoff A, Christiansen M, Hasle G, Løkketangen A (2010) Industrial aspects and literature survey: combined inventory management and routing. Comput Oper Res 37(9):1515–1536

Bhavani GD, Meidute-Kavaliauskiene I, Mahapatra GS, Činčikaitė R (2022) Pythagorean fuzzy storage capacity with controllable carbon emission incorporating green technology investment on a two-depository system. Energies 15(23):9087

Bhunia AK, Maiti M (1998) Deterministic inventory model for deteriorating items with a finite replenishment rate dependent on inventory level. Comput Oper Res 25(11):997–1006

Chakraborty D, Jana DK, Roy TK (2020) Multi-warehouse partial backlogging inventory system with inflation for non-instantaneous deteriorating multi-item under an imprecise environment. Soft Comput 24:14471–14490

Chang CC, Lu CJ, Yang CT (2022) Multi-stage supply chain production-inventory model with collaborative preservation technology investment. Scientia Iranica 29(4):2099–2114

Chaudhari U, Bhadoriya A, Jani MY, Sarkar B (2023) A generalized payment policy for deteriorating items when demand depends on price, stock, and advertisement under carbon tax regulations. Math Comput Simul 207:556–574

Chen X, Wang X, Kumar V, Kumar N (2016) Low carbon warehouse management under cap-and-trade policy. J Clean Prod 139:894–904

Choi J, Cao JJ, Romeijn HE, Geunes J, Bai SX (2005) A stochastic multi-item inventory model with unequal replenishment intervals and limited warehouse capacity. IIE Trans 37(12):1129–1141

Christata BR, Daryanto Y (2020) A systematical review on the economic order quantity model with carbon emission: 2010–2020. Adv Industr Eng Manage (AIEM) 9(2):20–26

Das SC, Zidan AM, Manna AK, Shaikh AA, Bhunia AK (2020) An application of preservation technology in an inventory control system with price-dependent demand and partial backlogging. Alex Eng J 59(3):1359–1369

Datta TK, Nath P, Dutta Choudhury K (2020) A hybrid carbon policy inventory model with emission source-based green investments. Opsearch 57:202–220

De SK, Mahata GC, Maity S (2021) Carbon emission sensitive deteriorating inventory model with trade credit under the volumetric fuzzy system. Int J Intell Syst 36(12):7563–7590

Ganeshan R (1999) Managing supply chain inventories: a multiple retailer, one warehouse, multiple supplier model. Int J Prod Econ 59(1–3):341–354

Guchhait P, Maiti MK, Maiti M (2013) Two storage inventory model of a deteriorating item with variable demand under partial credit period. Appl Soft Comput 13(1):428–448

Hariga M, As'ad R, Shamayleh A (2017) Integrated economic and environmental models for a multi-stage cold supply chain under carbon tax regulation. J Clean Prod 166:1357–1371

Hasan MR, Roy TC, Daryanto Y, Wee HM (2021) Optimizing inventory level and technology investment under a carbon tax, cap-and-trade and strict carbon limit regulations. Sustain Prod Consumpt 25:604–621

Huang Y-D, Chen T-H, Chih M, Chang W-J, Lien C-C (2023) An adaptive GLNPSO method for inventory replenishment supply chain problem with multiple-warehouse policy and budget consideration. Eng Appl Artif Intell 126:107124

Jaggi CK, Tiwari S, Shafi A (2015) Effect of deterioration on two-warehouse inventory model with imperfect quality. Comput Ind Eng 88:378–385

Khan MAA, Shaikh AA, Panda GC, Bhunia AK, Konstantaras I (2020) Non-instantaneous deterioration affects ordering decisions for a two-warehouse inventory system under advance payment and backlogging. Ann Oper Res 289:243–275

Konstantaras I, Skouri K, Benkherouf L (2021) Optimizing inventory decisions for a closed–loop supply chain model under a carbon tax regulatory mechanism. Int J Prod Econ 239:108185

Kumar S, Mahapatra RP (2021) Design of multi-warehouse inventory model for an optimal replenishment policy using a rain optimization algorithm. Knowl-Based Syst 231:107406

Lee YP, Dye CY (2012) An inventory model for deteriorating items under stock-dependent demand and controllable deterioration rate. Comput Ind Eng 63(2):474–482

Lok YW, Supadi SS, Wong KB (2023) Optimal investment in preservation technology for non-instantaneous deteriorating items under carbon emissions consideration. Comput Ind Eng 183:109446

Mahato C, Mahato F, Mahata GC (2023) Bi-level trade credit policy under pricing and preservation technology in inventory models for non-instantaneous deteriorating items under carbon tax policy. Sādhanā 48(3):103

Manna AK, Rahman MS, Shaikh AA, Bhunia AK, Konstantaras I (2022) Modeling of a carbon emitted production inventory system with interval uncertainty via meta-heuristic algorithms. Appl Math Model 106:343–368

Mashud AHM, Pervin M, Mishra U, Daryanto Y, Tseng ML, Lim MK (2021a) A sustainable inventory model with controllable carbon emissions in green-warehouse farms. J Clean Prod 298:126777

Mashud AHM, Wee HM, Huang CV (2021b) Preservation technology investment, trade credit and partial backordering model for a non-instantaneous deteriorating inventory. RAIRO-Oper Res 55:S51–S77

Min J, Zhou YW, Zhao J (2010) An inventory model for deteriorating items under stock-dependent demand and two-level trade credit. Appl Math Model 34(11):3273–3285

Mishra U, Wu JZ, Sarkar B (2020) A sustainable production-inventory model for a controllable carbon emissions rate under shortages. J Clean Prod 256:120268

Ouyang LY, Wu KS, Yang CT (2006) A study on an inventory model for non-instantaneous deteriorating items with permissible delay in payments. Comput Ind Eng 51(4):637–651

Paam P, Berretta R, García-Flores R, Paul SK (2022) Multi-warehouse, multi-product inventory control model for agri-fresh products—a case study. Comput Electron Agric 194:106783

Panda D, Maiti MK, Maiti M (2010) Two warehouse inventory models for single vendor multiple retailers with price and stock dependent demand. Appl Math Model 34(11):3571–3585

Panwar A, Pareek S, Dhaka V, Mittal M (2022) An imperfect inventory model for multi-warehouses under different discount policies with shortages. Int J Decis Support Syst Technol (IJDSST) 14(1):1–15

Paul A, Pervin M, Roy SK, Maculan N, Weber GW (2022) A green inventory model with the effect of carbon taxation. Ann Oper Res 309(1):233–248

Pervin M, Roy SK, Weber GW (2020) Deteriorating inventory with preservation technology under price-and stock-sensitive demand. J Industr Manage Optim 16(4):1585–1612

Poswal P, Chauhan A, Rajoria YK, Boadh R, Goel A (2022) Fuzzy optimization model of two parameter weibull deteriorating rate with quadratic demand and variable holding cost under allowable shortages. Yugoslav J Oper Res 32(4):453–470

Qiu R, Sun Y, Sun M (2022) A robust optimization approach for multi-product inventory management in a dual-channel warehouse under demand uncertainties. Omega 109:102591

Rapolu CN, Kandpal DH (2020) Joint pricing, advertisement, preservation technology investment and inventory policies for non-instantaneous deteriorating items under trade credit. Opsearch 57(2):274–300

Ruidas S, Seikh MR, Nayak PK (2021) A production inventory model with interval-valued carbon emission parameters under price-sensitive demand. Comput Ind Eng 154:107154

Sana SS, Mondal SK, Sarkar BK, Chaudhuri K (2011) Two-warehouse inventory model on pricing decision. Int J Manage Sci Eng Manage 6(6):467–480

Sarkar B, Saren S, Sarkar M, Seo YW (2016) A Stackelberg game approach in an integrated inventory model with carbon-emission and setup cost reduction. Sustainability 8(12):1244

Sarker BR, Mukherjee S, Balan CV (1997) An order-level lot size inventory model with inventory-level dependent demand and deterioration. Int J Prod Econ 48(3):227–236

Sarma KVS (1987) A deterministic order level inventory model for deteriorating items with two storage facilities. Eur J Oper Res 29(1):70–73

Sepehri A, Mishra U, Sarkar B (2021) A sustainable production-inventory model with imperfect quality under preservation technology and quality improvement investment. J Clean Prod 310:127332

Singh A, Goel A (2024) Warehouse inventory model for perishable items with hybrid demand and trade credit policy. Process Integr Optim Sustain: 1–15

Tiwari S, Daryanto Y, Wee HM (2018) Sustainable inventory management with deteriorating and imperfect quality items considering carbon emission. J Clean Prod 192:281–292

Verma P, Mishra VK (2024) Inventory optimization of deteriorating items: a comprehensive review of carbon-control policies and their impact on shelf life, greening effects, and rework policies. WPOM-Work Pap Oper Manage 15(1):39–56

Xu C, Liu X, Wu C, Yuan B (2020) Optimal inventory control strategies for deteriorating items with a general time-varying demand under carbon emission regulations. Energies 13(4):999

Yadav S, Khanna A (2021) Sustainable inventory model for perishable products with expiration date and price reliant demand under carbon tax policy. Process Integr Optim Sustain 5:475–486

Chapter 5
Green Logistics Optimization for Sustainable Supply Chains in the Textile Industry: A Carbon Emissions and Water Footprint Perspective

Divya Bharti, Alka Chaudhary, S. R. Singh, and Surbhi Singhal

Abstract The textile industry, which contributes significantly to global manufacturing, is under increasing pressure to align its operations with environmentally friendly methods. This study proposes a complete methodology for optimizing green logistics in the textile supply chain, with a dual emphasis on lowering carbon emissions and reducing water footprints. The study incorporates environmental concerns into logistics decision-making processes in order to promote a more sustainable and environmentally responsible industry. The proposed model employs life cycle assessment (LCA) methods to calculate the carbon footprint and water footprint associated with each stage of the textile supply chain. It investigates important logistical components such as transportation, warehousing, and distribution in order to discover potential for efficiency gains and emissions reductions. The suggested model provides a comprehensive view of sustainability by taking into account both carbon emissions and water footprints. Finally, the research hopes to steer the textile sector toward a more ecologically conscious and economically viable future by encouraging a paradigm shift toward greener logistics techniques. The goal of this research is to optimize production quantity, total expenses per production cycle, and waste emissions. Data from the pulp and paper mill industry was used to validate and test the model. The model's effectiveness was determined by comparing the costs generated in two (2) scenarios: (1) an EPQ model that takes into account the costs of greenhouse gas (GHG) emissions; (2) an EPQ model that takes shortages.

D. Bharti (✉)
Department of Statistics, Meerut College, Meerut 250001, India
e-mail: divya.statistics14@gmail.com

A. Chaudhary
KLPG College, Meerut 250002, India

S. R. Singh
Department of Mathematics, C.C.S. University, Meerut 250001, India

S. Singhal
Department of Statistics, Vardhaman College, Bijnor 246701, India

N. H. Shah and M. Mittal (eds.), *Sustainable Inventory Management*, Inventory Optimization, https://doi.org/10.1007/978-981-97-6765-6_6

Keywords Sustainability · Carbon emission · Paper and pulp mills · Supply chain · Wastewater · Greenhouse gas

5.1 Introduction

The worldwide textile sector, which is essential to contemporary economic activity and consumerism, is faced with both revolutionary possibilities and previously unheard-of obstacles. Green logistics optimization entails incorporating environmentally friendly methods into logistics operations to reduce negative environmental impacts while preserving efficiency and profitability. This method takes into account carbon emissions and water footprint reduction across the whole supply chain, from raw material procurement to manufacture, distribution, and end-of-life disposal. In the textile sector, green logistics optimization tries to solve important environmental concerns such as greenhouse gas emissions from transportation and manufacturing processes, as well as water pollution and depletion caused by dyeing and finishing operations. Textile companies can reduce environmental impacts by applying sustainable logistical methods while increasing competitiveness, meeting regulatory standards, and meeting consumer demand for eco-friendly products. Although the textile industry is important to worldwide trade, its activities frequently have severe environmental consequences, particularly in terms of carbon emissions and water use. In response to growing concerns about sustainability, there is a greater emphasis on implementing green logistics optimization solutions to enhance sustainable supply chains in the textile sector. This article investigates the concept of green logistics optimization for sustainable supply chains in the textile sector, specifically in terms of carbon emissions and water footprint. It investigates strategies and approaches for lowering carbon emissions and water consumption throughout the textile supply chain, such as adopting cleaner production technologies, optimizing transportation routes, and implementing reverse logistics and recycling programmes.

The textile sector faces a pressing challenge in balancing the growing demand for its products with the pressing need for sustainable practices. The textile industry is forced to negotiate the challenging landscape of supply chain dynamics while pursuing ecological responsibility in response to environmental concerns, regulatory demands, and the changing expectations of eco-conscious consumers. EPQ model with partial and phase-dependent backordering rate was developed by Wee and Wang (2012). The present introduction establishes the framework for an in-depth investigation into the complex field of "Green Logistics Optimization for Sustainable Supply Chains in the Textile Industry: A Carbon Emissions and Water Footprint Perspective." The textile business is located where industrial production, consumer demand, and environmental effect converge in today's global marketplace. Further Singhal and Singh (2013) focused on volume flexible multi-items inventory systems. The textile industry must strike a balance between environmental responsibility and operational efficiency as the focus on sustainable practices grows.

This paper aims to provide insights and recommendations for textile companies looking to improve their environmental performance and contribute to the transition to a more sustainable and resilient textile industry by conducting a thorough analysis of carbon emissions and water footprint reduction strategies. Textile firms that embrace green logistics optimization can not only minimize their environmental impact, but also improve their reputation, establish customer loyalty, and create long-term value for stakeholders in a fast-changing business climate. The textile sector stands out in the huge tapestry of global commerce, weaving together economies, cultures, and lifestyles through its delicate threads of production and consumption. As the backbone of the world's manufacturing sector, the paper and pulp industry has long been a vital source of economic activity, supplying the raw materials for an enormous range of goods that affect almost every area of everyday life. carbon emission and energy effects on manufacturing and re-manufacturing inventory model by Bazan (2015). Singhal (2017) proposed a machine breakdown inventory system with partial backlogging. The difficulties related to this sector's environmental impact have changed along with the industrial techniques used to suit the needs of an expanding population. Shankar (2017) studied on analyzing sustainable manufacturing practices case study in Indian context. This introduction lays the groundwork for a thorough investigation into the complex dynamics surrounding "Paper and Pulp Mills, Supply Chain, Wastewater, and Greenhouse Gas Emissions"; this is a multifaceted study of the intricate relationships among industrial production, the complexities of the supply chain, wastewater management, and the need to cut greenhouse gas emissions. Singhal (2018) proposed multiple market demand models; after that, Vishnoi and Singh (2018) created SCIM with an expiration date in the inflationary environment. The textile sector, which is well-known for playing a crucial part in global manufacturing, is currently facing a paradigm shift that is being driven by increased consumer demands and environmental consciousness. Taleizadeh (2018) created a sustainable model with shortages, and Daryanto (2018) created a sustainable model toward cleaner production. The industry is defined by intricately linked supply chains that span from the production of raw materials to the stages of manufacturing, distribution, and sale. Despite its significant contributions to human civilization, the textile industry has left an unmistakable mark on the earth, including environmental deterioration and resource depletion. The textile supply chain has numerous issues, ranging from wide cotton fields to bustling garment factories, the most notable of which are the considerable carbon emissions and water consumption connected with its activities. In response to growing concerns about sustainability and environmental stewardship, there has been a clear call for revolutionary change in the textile sector. This call to arms has ushered in a period of innovation and reform, marked by a rising realization of the need to incorporate environmental considerations into all aspects of the textile supply chain. At the vanguard of this movement is the concept of green logistics optimization, a paradigm change that tries to balance commercial and environmental imperatives. Green logistics optimization is a comprehensive approach to supply chain management that goes beyond standard concepts of efficiency and cost minimization to incorporate principles of environmental responsibility and social equality. Green logistics optimization is fundamentally the deliberate integration of environmentally friendly techniques into logistics operations, with the goal of lowering carbon emissions and water consumption while preserving or improving total supply chain performance. In the context of the textile sector, green logistics optimization has enormous potential as a change agent.

The creation, manufacturing, distribution, and sale of textiles, along with other aspects of this complex ecosystem, all contribute significantly to the worldwide fabric of commerce. However, the industry's sustainability standards have come under intense scrutiny due to its historical reliance on resource-intensive procedures and worries about environmental deterioration. Mashud (2020) and Bai (2020) produced an EOQ model with different types of demands and effects of sustainability under carbon tax policy respectively. The need for innovation and change has been sparked by the ecological impact of the textile supply chain, which spans from cotton farming to the manufacture of clothing. The foundation of the larger forest products sector, the paper and pulp industry makes a substantial contribution to employment and global economic growth. A flexible inventory model with a reliability process was developed by Singhal (2021); after that, Shah (2021) developed an upper lower bound inventory model underpriced stock life time-dependent demand. The environmental impact of the paper industry has come under more scrutiny as demand for paper-based products has expanded over the years. In order to maintain ecological sustainability while promoting economic growth, modern paper and pulp mills must evaluate and improve their operational procedures from an integrated standpoint. The complex supply chain of the paper and pulp industries is the foundation of their sustainability journey. The industry's supply chain is a complicated web that includes many parties, extending from forestry and raw material extraction to production procedures and product distribution. Effective and sustainable supply chain management is essential for reducing environmental impact as well as maintaining economic viability. Chaudhary et al. (2022) proposed a stock and price-dependent demand with inflation and partial backlogging. The industry is looking at creative ways to guarantee the sustainability of its supply chain, from ethical raw material sourcing to efficient transport.

Paper and pulp mill production operations always produce large amounts of wastewater that are loaded with different kinds of chemicals and organic materials. Reducing the negative effects of these activities on the environment requires effective wastewater management. To reduce the number of pollutants discharged into water bodies, mills are forced to use closed-loop systems, apply cutting-edge treatment technology, and investigate sustainable practices as a result of tightening regulations and increased public awareness of water pollution. Similar to many other manufacturing sectors, the paper and pulp business primarily contributes to greenhouse gas emissions through energy-intensive processes. Chaudhary et al. (2023) proposed sustainable EOQ models for expiring goods addressing carbon emissions. As mills become more aware of the need to address climate change, demand to lower their carbon footprint grows. Bharti et al. (2024) discussed green supply chain with reliability. This includes using more energy-efficient production techniques, switching to greener energy sources, and investigating cutting-edge technology to capture and mitigate greenhouse gas emissions. The textile supply chain, with its vast network of suppliers, manufacturers, and distributors around the world, provides an ideal environment for sustainability innovation and experimentation. Textile firms that adopt a carbon emissions and water footprint viewpoint can acquire a better understanding of the environmental consequences of their operations and find possibilities for improvement at every stage of the supply chain. This study investigates the multidimensional environment of green logistics optimization for sustainable supply chains in the textile sector, with a particular emphasis on solving carbon emissions and water footprint issues. This article intends to highlight the obstacles and opportunities inherent in greening the textile supply chain by conducting a thorough assessment of existing research, case studies, and best practices, as well as providing insights and advice for organizations looking to embark on this transformative journey.

By delving into the complexities of carbon emissions and water footprint reduction measures, this article aims to give a roadmap for textile companies seeking to navigate the the complicated landscape of sustainability. From the adoption of cleaner production technologies to the optimization of transportation routes, from the implementation of reverse logistics programmes to the promotion of recycling and circular economy principles, the path to a greener textile industry is fraught with challenges but also ripe with opportunities. The textile industry is forced to reconsider established operational frameworks and adopt sustainability at every stage of the supply chain as environmental issues grow more pressing. The strategic response of green logistics optimization presents a comprehensive way to strike a compromise between decreased carbon emissions and water footprint and operational efficiency. The textile industry is going through a paradigm shift in the way it approaches operations in response to the growing awareness of environmental deterioration and the pressing need to combat climate change. The need for green logistics optimization emerges as a tactical reaction to this evolving environment. Acknowledging the interdependence of logistics operations and supply chain components, the sector aims to develop innovative solutions that improve operational effectiveness while minimizing environmental impact. This study explores the two main components of environmental impact carbon emissions and water footprint realizing how important they are to the conversation about sustainability. Climate change is a result of carbon emissions, and pollution and water use present serious ecological problems.

Examining these elements from the perspective of logistics optimization offers a thorough understanding of the environmental impact of the sector. Two key areas of focus for sustainable transformation are water footprint and carbon emissions. Climate change is mostly caused by carbon emissions, which come from energy-intensive industries, transportation, and manufacturing. In addition, the textile industry's water footprint which includes pollution and consumption presents complex difficulties for aquatic ecosystems. This study acknowledges the importance of taking a comprehensive approach that addresses both carbon emissions and water footprint within the context of logistics optimization. It places itself at the intersection of these crucial environmental factors. As we enter a new era in textile production, marked by increased awareness of environmental concerns and a renewed dedication to sustainability, the need to embrace green logistical optimization has never been clearer. Textile firms who heed this call and chart a route for a more sustainable future can not only reduce their environmental footprint, but also improve their resilience, competitiveness, and long-term sustainability in an ever-changing global marketplace. The purpose of this project is to investigate and suggest methods for streamlining logistical procedures in the textile sector, with a focus on environmentally friendly methods that reduce water and carbon emissions. Through an examination of the interdependencies between supply chain components and logistics processes, the study aims to provide practical guidance to companies who are pursuing sustainability objectives. Best practices will be identified, frameworks for green logistics optimization will be developed, and stakeholders in the textile industry will receive useful suggestions as a result of this research. The study's ultimate goal is to further the conversation on sustainable business practices by demonstrating how green logistics may significantly reduce environmental effect while maintaining operational effectiveness in the textile supply chain. The goal of this study is to clarify the difficulties that come with optimizing green logistics for long-term, sustainable supply chains in the textile sector. Through a dual lens of carbon emissions and water footprint analysis, the study aims to identify game-changing tactics capable of revolutionizing supply chain operations. The reasoning is based on the belief that the textile sector can both lead the way in novel ways toward a future that is both ecologically conscious and more robust, while also being in line with changing sustainability standards through systematic logistics optimization.

This study's main goal is to investigate, evaluate, and suggest methods for streamlining logistics procedures in the textile sector, with an emphasis on cutting carbon emissions and minimizing water impact. Through an examination of the intricacies involved in supply chain operations and logistics, the research hopes to provide practical insights that surpass theoretical frameworks and concrete suggestions for industry participants. The expected consequence is the possible conversion of the textile supply chain into a more robust, sustainable, and environmentally friendly model that strikes a compromise between the demands of environmental stewardship and operational effectiveness. As we set out on our investigation, the voyage into the domains of green logistics optimization in the textile sector promises to reveal obstacles as well as creative solutions that have the potential to completely transform one of the most significant industries in the world. This in-depth investigation seeks to analyze the complex interplay between pulp and paper mills, the dynamics of their supply chains, the difficulties associated with managing wastewater, and the necessity of lowering greenhouse gas emissions. By exploring the complexities of these interrelated aspects, the study aims to reveal prospects for long-term change in the sector. Offering insights that not only address environmental issues but also support the long-term viability and resilience of paper and pulp plants is the main objective. The expected results of this investigation include a comprehensive comprehension of the potential and difficulties present in the paper and pulp industry's transition to sustainability. This research aims to provide actionable insights by deciphering the intricacies of wastewater management, greenhouse gas emissions reduction, and supply chain dynamics. In the context of paper and pulp mills, it is intended that these insights would direct industry stakeholders, legislators, and environmental advocates toward cooperative efforts that strike a balance between economic imperatives and ecological responsibility.

5.2 Assumptions and Notations

5.2.1 Notations

P	Production rate.
A	Reliability.
Q	Demanded quantity.
θ	Deterioration rate.
Q_1	Stock at the end of first phase.
D	Demand rate.
C_O	Setup cost.
$(C_{\mathrm{M}} + C_{\mathrm{Me}})$	Manufacturing cost with carbon emission.
$(C_{\mathrm{W}} + C_{\mathrm{We}})$	Waste Dispose Cost with Carbon Emission.
$(C_{\mathrm{D}} + C_{\mathrm{De}})$	Deterioration cost with carbon emission.
$(C_{\mathrm{H}} + C_{\mathrm{He}})$	Holding cost with carbon emission.
$(C_{\mathrm{S}} + C_{\mathrm{Se}})$	Shortage cost with carbon emission.
$(C_{\mathrm{L}} + C_{\mathrm{Le}})$	Lost sale cost with shortages.
λ	Backordering rate.
T	Total replenishment time cycle.
T_1	Time when inventory is at its highest in manufacturing cycle.
T_2	Initial time when inventory reaches zero in manufacturing cycle.
T_3	Shortage time period.
$\prod_1$	Total cost without shortages.
$\prod_2$	Total cost with shortages.

5.2.2 Assumptions

- Demand is taken as a quadratic function of time $d = b_1 + b_2 t + b_3 t^2$
- Deterioration rate is taken as a constant
- Sustainability and carbon emission are also considered in this model
- Shortages are permitted and partially backlogged
- Transport activities can generate carbon emission, so maintaining an eco-friendly environment carbon tax policy is also considered.

5.3 Mathematical Model

5.3.1 Sustainable EPQ Model

Differential equations for sustainable EPQ models without shortages are given below; Eq. (5.1) defined as the inventory of excellent things rises throughout the manufacturing stage as a result of production, but it falls as a result of demand and item loss (Fig. 5.1).

$$\frac{dI_1(t)}{dt} = -\theta I_1(t) + PA - \left(b_1 + b_2 t + b_3 t^2\right); \quad 0 \leq \mathrm{t} \leq \mathrm{T}_1 \tag{5.1}$$

The following equations describes the consuming phase during which there is no production and the consequent reduction in inventory level as a result of item rate:

$$\frac{dI_2(t)}{dt} = -\theta I_2(t) - \left(b_1 + b_2 t + b_3 t^2\right); \quad T_1 \leq t \leq T \tag{5.2}$$

Solutions of the above differential equations with the following boundary conditions:

$$I(t) = 0, t = 0 \quad I(t) = 0, t = T$$

$$I_1(t) = \left[\left(\frac{AP}{\theta} - \frac{b_1}{\theta} + \frac{b_2}{\theta^2} - \frac{2b_3}{\theta^3}\right)\left(1 - e^{-\theta t}\right) - \frac{t}{\theta}\left(b_2 + b_3 t - \frac{2b_3}{\theta}\right)\right] \tag{5.3}$$

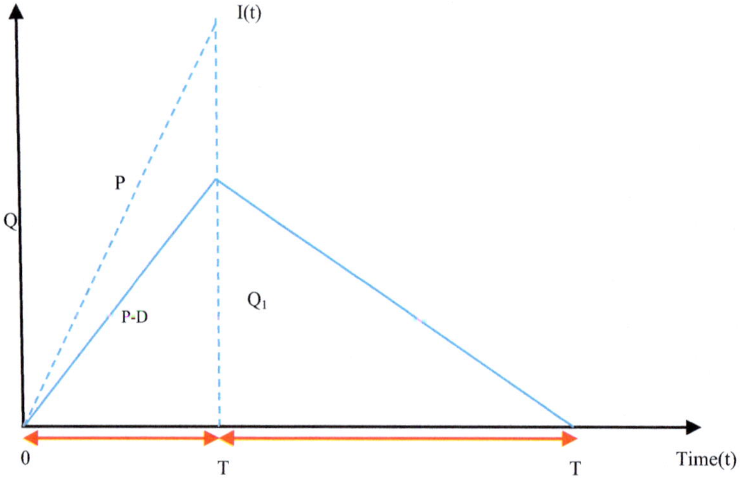

Fig. 5.1 Production inventory cycle without shortages [*Source* Own]

$$I_2(t) = \left[\left(\frac{b_2}{\theta^2} - \frac{b_1}{\theta} - \frac{2b_3}{\theta^3}\right)\left(1 - e^{\theta(T-t)}\right) + \left(\frac{2b_3}{\theta^2} - \frac{b_2}{\theta}\right)\left(t - Te^{\theta(T-t)}\right) - \frac{b_3}{\theta}\left(t^2 - T^2e^{\theta(T-t)}\right)\right] \tag{5.4}$$

To find the demanded quantity from Eq. (5.4)

$I(t) = Q, t = 0$

$$Q = \left[\left(\frac{b_2}{\theta^2} - \frac{b_1}{\theta} - \frac{2b_3}{\theta^3}\right)\left(1 - e^{\theta T}\right) + \left(\frac{2b_3}{\theta^2} - \frac{b_2}{\theta}\right)\left(-Te^{\theta T}\right) - \frac{b_3}{\theta}\left(-T^2e^{\theta T}\right)\right] \tag{5.5}$$

To find the value of T_1 and Q_1, we equate Eqs. (5.3) and (5.4) as $t = T_1$:

$$T_1 = \frac{b_1T + \frac{2b_2T}{\theta} + b_2T^2 - \frac{4b_3t}{\theta^2} - \frac{b_3T^2}{\theta} + b_3T^3}{AP - 2b_1 + \frac{2b_2}{\theta} - \frac{4b_3}{\theta^2} + b_2T - \frac{2b_3T}{\theta} + b_3T^2} \tag{5.6}$$

With boundary condition $I(t) = Q_1, t = T_1$, Eq. (5.3) becomes

$$Q_1 = \left(AP - b_1 - \frac{b_3T_1}{\theta}\right)T_1 \tag{5.7}$$

The sustainable EPQ model with carbon emission includes different costs like setup cost, manufacturing cost, holding cost, deterioration cost, and waste disposal cost. The proposed EPQ model has the following Total cost (Π_1):

$$\text{TC}\left(\prod_1\right) = \text{SC} + \text{MC} + \text{HC} + \text{DC} + \text{WDC} \tag{5.8}$$

5.3.2 Setup Cost

Expense of setting up the machinery using the conventional EPQ model prior to production starts:

$$\text{SC} = C_O \tag{5.9}$$

5.3.3 Manufacturing Cost

All of the expenditures related to the actual production process are included in manufacturing costs. These expenses consist of labor, raw material, machine operation, and other costs directly related to the product's manufacture. Expenses associated with manufacturing are sometimes seen as variable expenses per unit produced. The cost of manufacturing for the inventory system is denoted by C_M, while the cost of carbon emissions C_{Me} is included. Consequently, the following may be used to represent the entire manufacturing cost:

$$\mathrm{MC} = \left[(C_M + C_{Me})\left(\int_0^{T_1} (\mathrm{d}PA)\mathrm{d}t\right)\right]$$

$$\mathrm{MC} = \left[(C_M + C_{Me})\mathrm{PAT}_1\left(b_1 + \frac{b_2T_1}{2} + \frac{b_3T_1^2}{3}\right)\right] \tag{5.10}$$

5.3.4 Holding Cost

One important expense in the cooperative supply chain is the holding cost. Following production, the producer must keep the products in a warehouse for storage. It may be a warehouse attached to their company or a rented home. The holding cost in this case is divided into two components: the product holding component, denoted as C_H, and the carbon emission component, designated as C_{He}. Consequently, the entire holding cost may be expressed as follows:

$$\mathrm{HC} = \left[(C_H + C_{He})\left(\int_0^{T_1} I_1(t)\mathrm{d}t + \int_{T_1}^{T} I_2(t)\mathrm{d}t\right)\right]$$

$$\mathrm{HC} = \left[(C_H + C_{He})\left(\frac{APT_1^2}{2} - \frac{2T_1^3b_3}{3\theta} + \frac{b_1T^2}{2} + \frac{b_2T^3}{2} - T^3\left(\frac{b_2}{2} - \frac{b_3}{3\theta}\right) + \frac{T^4b_3}{2}\right.\right.$$
$$\left.\left. - b_1TT_1 - T^2T_1\left(b_2 + \frac{b_3}{\theta}\right) - T^3T_1b_3 + TT_1^2\left(\frac{b_2}{2} - \frac{b_3}{\theta}\right) + \frac{b_3T^2T_1^2}{2}\right)\right] \tag{5.11}$$

5.3.5 Deterioration Cost

For items that have deteriorated inside the system between $[0, T_1]$ and $[T_1, T]$, the cost of degradation is taken into account. The cost of degradation during production is represented by the following relationship:

$$\mathrm{DC} = \left[(C_{\mathrm{D}} + C_{\mathrm{De}})\theta\left(\int_0^{T_1} I_1(t)\mathrm{d}t + \int_{T_1}^{T} I_2(t)\mathrm{d}t\right)\right]$$

$$\mathrm{DC} = \left[(C_{\mathrm{D}} + C_{\mathrm{De}})\theta\left(\frac{APT_1^2}{2} - \frac{2T_1^3 b_3}{3\theta} + \frac{b_1 T^2}{2} + \frac{b_2 T^3}{2} - T^3\left(\frac{b_2}{2} - \frac{b_3}{3\theta}\right) + \frac{T^4 b_3}{2}\right.\right.$$
$$\left.\left.-b_1 T T_1 - T^2 T_1\left(b_2 + \frac{b_3}{\theta}\right) - T^3 T_1 b_3 + TT_1^2\left(\frac{b_2}{2} - \frac{b_3}{\theta}\right) + \frac{b_3 T^2 T_1^2}{2}\right)\right] \quad (5.12)$$

5.3.6 Waste Disposal Cost

A certain quantity of solid waste is produced during manufacturing, and this leads to the emission of certain gases that are extremely detrimental to the environment. So, each company needs to dispose of this solid waste in order to safeguard the environment. The production waste disposal cost may be expressed as follows:

$$\mathrm{WDC} = \left[\left(C_{\mathrm{M}} + \left(C_{\mathrm{Me}}\left(\int_0^{T_1} (\mathrm{d}PA)\right)\mathrm{d}t\right)\right)\right]$$

$$\mathrm{WDC} = \left[\left(C_{\mathrm{W}} + \left(C_{\mathrm{We}} PAT_1\left(b_1 + \frac{b_2 T_1}{2} + \frac{b_3 T_1^2}{3}\right)\right)\right)\right] \quad (5.13)$$

5.3.7 Sustainable EPQ Model with Shortages

Inventory levels are managed while taking shortages and partial backordering into account in an Economic Production Quantity (EPQ) model with shortages. Differential equations are frequently used to depict the EPQ with shortages and explain the dynamic behavior of the system (Fig. 5.6.2).

$$\frac{\mathrm{d}I_3(t)}{\mathrm{d}t} = -\lambda\left(b_1 + b_2 t + b_3 t^2\right); \quad T_2 \le t \le T_3 \quad (5.14)$$

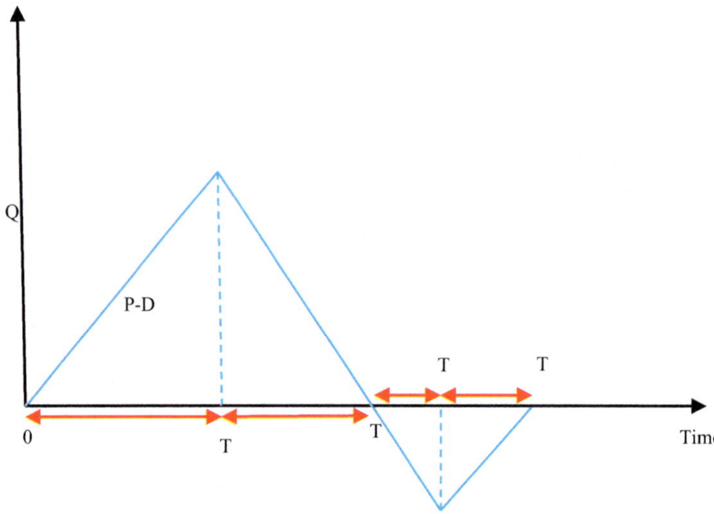

Fig. 5.2 Production inventory cycle with shortages [*Source* Own]

$$\frac{dI_4(t)}{dt} = PA - \left(b_1 + b_2t + b_3t^2\right); \quad T_3 \leq t \leq T \tag{5.15}$$

Here are the solutions of the above differential equations with boundary conditions $I(t) = 0, t = T_2$ and $I(t) = 0, t = T$:

$$I_3(t) = \lambda b_1(T_2 - t) + \frac{\lambda b_2}{2}\left(T_2^2 - t^2\right) + \frac{\lambda b_3}{3}\left(T_2^3 - t^3\right) \tag{5.16}$$

$$I_4(t) = (AP - b_1)(t - T) - \frac{b_2}{2}\left(t^2 - T^2\right) - \frac{b_3}{3}\left(t^3 - T^3\right) \tag{5.17}$$

The sustainable EPQ model with shortages and carbon emission includes different costs like setup cost, manufacturing cost, holding cost, deterioration cost, shortage cost, lost sale cost, and waste disposal cost. The proposed EPQ model has the following Total cost (Π_2):

$$\mathrm{TC}\left(\prod_2\right) = \frac{1}{T}[\mathrm{SC} + \mathrm{MC} + \mathrm{MC}_1 + \mathrm{HC} + \mathrm{DC} + \mathrm{WDC} + \mathrm{WDC}_1 + S_oC + \mathrm{LSC}] \tag{5.18}$$

Here SC, MC, HC, DC, and WDC are given by Eqs. 5.9, 5.10, 5.11, 5.12, and 5.13.

5.3.8 Manufacturing Cost for Shortages

The cost of manufacturing for the inventory system is denoted by C_{M1}, while the cost of carbon emissions C_{M1e} is included. Consequently, the following may be used to represent the entire manufacturing cost:

$$\mathrm{MC}_1 = \left[(C_{M1} + C_{M1e}) \left(\int_{T_3}^{T} (\mathrm{d}PA)\mathrm{d}t \right) \right]$$

$$\mathrm{MC}_1 = \left[(C_{M1} + C_{M1e}) \left[PA \left(b_1(T - T_3) + b_2\left(\frac{T^2}{2} - \frac{T_3^2}{2} \right) + b_3\left(\frac{T^3}{3} - \frac{T_3^3}{3} \right) \right) \right] \right] \tag{5.19}$$

5.3.9 Waste Disposal Cost for Shortages

The production waste disposal cost with shortages may be expressed as follows:

$$\mathrm{MC}_1 = \left[\left(C_{M1} + \left(C_{M1e} \left(\int_{T_3}^{T} (\mathrm{d}PA)\mathrm{d}t \right) \right) \right) \right]$$

$$\mathrm{WDC}_1 = C_{W1} + \left(C_{W1e} \left[PA \left(b_1(T - T_3) + b_2\left(\frac{T^2}{2} - \frac{T_3^2}{2} \right) + b_3\left(\frac{T^3}{3} - \frac{T_3^3}{3} \right) \right) \right] \right) \tag{5.20}$$

5.3.10 Shortage Cost

A shortfall or stock–out cost arises when there are insufficient supplies to meet client demand during a stock-out situation. The shortage cost of the system is computed as follows:

$$S_o C = \left[(C_S + C_{Se}) \left(-\int_{T_2}^{T_3} I_3(t)\mathrm{d}t - \int_{T_4}^{T} I_4(t)\mathrm{d}t \right) \right]$$

$$\begin{aligned} S_o C = [(C_S + C_{Se}) \\ \left[\left((PA - b_1)\left(\frac{T^2}{2} - T_3 T + \frac{T_3^2}{2} \right) - b_2\left(\frac{T^3}{6} - \frac{T_3 T^2}{2} + \frac{T_3^3}{6} - \frac{\lambda T_2^3}{3} - \frac{\lambda T_3 T_2^2}{2} - \frac{\lambda T_3^3}{6} \right) \right. \right. \\ \left. \left. -b_3\left(\frac{T^4}{4} - \frac{T_3 T^3}{3} + \frac{\lambda T_2^4}{4} + \frac{T_3^4}{12} + \frac{\lambda T_3 T_2^3}{3} - \frac{\lambda T_2^3}{12} \right) + \lambda b_1\left(\frac{T_2^2}{2} - T_2 T_3 + \frac{T_3^2}{2} \right) \right) \right] \right] \end{aligned} \tag{5.21}$$

5.3.11 Lost Sale Cost

When clients find other ways to satisfy their needs during a stock-out situation, missed sale costs are recorded in the inventory system. The following formula is used to get the lost sale cost:

$$\mathrm{LSC} = \left[(C_{\mathrm{L}} + C_{\mathrm{Le}})\left(\int_{T_2}^{T_3} \mathrm{d}(1-\lambda)\mathrm{d}t\right)\right]$$

$$\mathrm{LSC} = \left[(C_{\mathrm{L}} + C_{\mathrm{Le}})\left[(1-\lambda)\left(b_1(T_3 - T_2) + b_2\left(\frac{T_3^2}{2} - \frac{T_2^2}{2}\right) + b_3\left(\frac{T_3^3}{3} - \frac{T_2^3}{3}\right)\right)\right]\right] \tag{5.22}$$

5.4 Solution Procedure

Four independent variables P, T_1, T_2, and T become a function of total cost. This is the objective function, hence

$$\frac{\partial \Pi_1}{\partial P} = 0 \text{ and } \frac{\partial \Pi_1}{\partial \mathrm{T}} = 0 \tag{5.23}$$

provided, they satisfy the following conditions:

$$\left.\begin{array}{r} \frac{\partial^2 \Pi_1}{\partial^2 P} > 0 \text{ and } \frac{\partial^2 \Pi_1}{\partial^2 T} > 0 \\ \text{and} \left(\frac{\partial^2 \Pi_1}{\partial^2 P}\right)\left(\frac{\partial^2 \Pi_1}{\partial^2 T}\right) - \left(\frac{\partial \Pi_1}{\partial P \partial T}\right)^2 > 0 \end{array}\right\} \tag{5.24}$$

and

$$\frac{\partial E[\Pi_2]}{\partial P} = 0, \frac{\partial E[\Pi_2]}{\partial T} = 0, \frac{\partial E[\Pi_2]}{\partial T_1} = 0$$
$$\text{and } \frac{\partial E[\Pi_2]}{\partial T_2} = 0 \tag{5.25}$$

provided, they satisfy the following conditions:

$$\left.\begin{array}{r} \frac{\partial^2 \Pi_2}{\partial^2 P} > 0, \frac{\partial^2 \Pi_2}{\partial^2 T} > 0, \frac{\partial^2 \Pi_2}{\partial^2 T_1} > 0, \frac{\partial^2 \Pi_2}{\partial^2 T_2} > 0 \\ \text{and} \left(\frac{\partial^2 \Pi_2}{\partial^2 P}\right)\left(\frac{\partial^2 \Pi_2}{\partial^2 T}\right)\left(\frac{\partial^2 \Pi_2}{\partial^2 T_1}\right)\left(\frac{\partial^2 \Pi_2}{\partial^2 T_2}\right) - \left(\frac{\partial \Pi_2}{\partial P \partial T \partial T_1 \partial T_2}\right)^2 > 0 \end{array}\right\} \tag{5.26}$$

5.5 Algorithm

The objective functions generated by Eqs. (5.8) and (5.18) are functions of P, T, T_2, and T_3. The methods outlined below were used to determine the ideal answer.

Step 1: Assign hypothetical values to the starting parameters in the objective functions in Eqs. (5.8) and (5.18).
Step 2: Use Mathematica 12.0 to solve simultaneous Eqs. (5.23) and (5.25).
Step 3: Verify the necessary conditions defined in Eqs. (5.24) and (5.26).
Step 4: Calculate the average manufacturing cost for the integrated inventory system using Eqs. (5.8) and (5.18).

5.6 Numerical Example and Sensitivity Analysis

Next, let's look at a numerical example of the EPQ model with waste disposal costs and analyze the impact of a few important factors. The fundamental EPQ model equation takes into account all expenses. For the numerical example, let's use the following parameter values.

Example 1 for Sustainable EPQ Model without shortages

$A = 0.5$, $b_2 = 0.02$, $b_1 = 0.03$, $b_3 = 0.02$, $\theta = 0.09$, $C_O = 100$, $C_{\mathrm{M}} = 3$, $C_{\mathrm{Me}} = 5$, $C_{\mathrm{H}} = 0.2$, $C_{\mathrm{He}} = 2$, $C_{\mathrm{D}} = 7$, $C_{\mathrm{De}} = 8$, $C_{\mathrm{W}} = 0.2$, $C_{\mathrm{We}} = 0.5$, $t = 0.8$.

By using the Mathematica 12.0 software, we obtained the optimal solution as follows:

Total Cost $(\Pi_1) = 25.3533$.
$P = 11.1911$.
$T = 5.49608$.

Example 2 for Sustainable EPQ Model with shortages

$A = 0.6$, $b_2 = 0.03$, $b_1 = 0.02$, $b_3 = 0.07$, $\theta = 0.05$, $C_O = 110$, $C_{\mathrm{M}} = 2$, $C_{\mathrm{Me}} = 3$, $C_{\mathrm{H}} = 0.6$, $C_{\mathrm{He}} = 2$, $C_{\mathrm{D}} = 2$, $C_{\mathrm{De}} = 2$, $C_{\mathrm{W}} = 0.5$, $C_{\mathrm{We}} = 0.5$, $C_{\mathrm{S}} = 5$, $C_{\mathrm{Se}} = 2$, $C_{\mathrm{L}} = 4$, $C_{\mathrm{Le}} = 3$, $t = 0.8$, $\lambda = 0.7$.

By using the Mathematica 12.0 software, we obtained the optimal solution as follows (Figs. 5.3 and 5.4).

Total Cost $(\Pi_2) = 25.7122$.
$P = 15.4577$.
$T_2 = 0.748123$.
$T_3 = 6.38402$.
$T = 6.73782$.

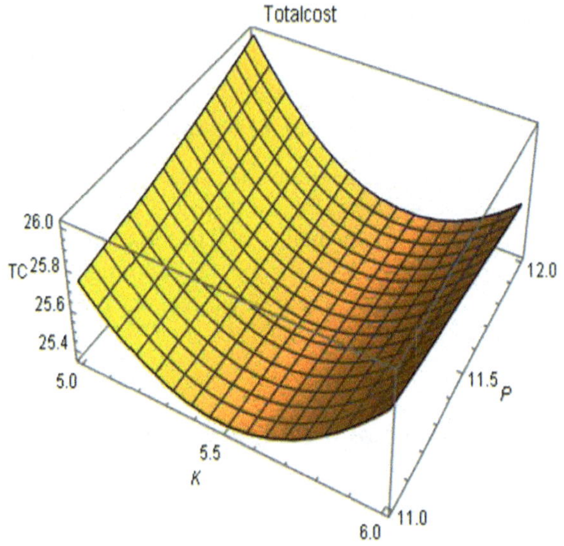

Fig. 5.3 Convexity for total cost (Π_1) (case 1) [*Source* Own]

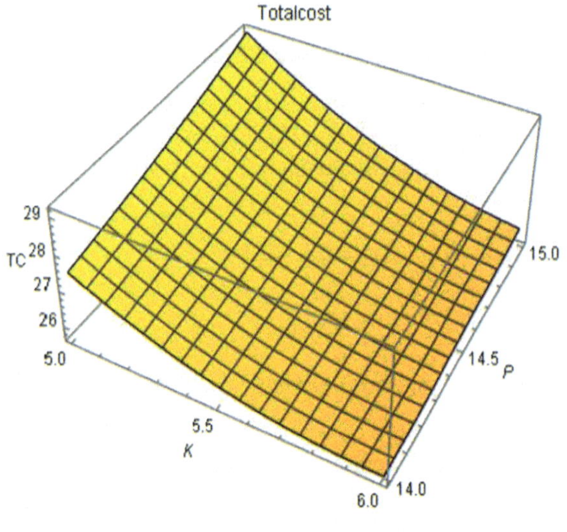

Fig. 5.4 Convexity for total cost (Π_2) (case 2) [*Source* Own]

5.6.1 Sensitivity Analysis

- The study found that the manufacturing cost, holding cost, and deteriorating rate significantly impact the overall cost of the inventory system. When modeling, decision-makers should account for flexibility in manufacturing processes.
- Allowing for flexible production rates can reduce carbon emissions, energy usage, and faults, thus lowering overall costs.

- From Table 5.1, and Figs. 5.5, 5.6 and 5.7, production rate, total time, and total cost increase whenever the rate of change in reliability, ordering cost, deterioration cost, demand parameters, and waste disposal cost decreases and production rate, total time, and total cost decrease whenever manufacturing cost and holding cost increase.

- From Table 5.2, and Figs. 5.8, 5.9, 5.10, 5.11 and 5.12, production rate, total replenishment time, T_3, T_2 increase and total cost decreases whenever the rate of change in reliability, ordering cost, demand parameters, and holding costs decreases and vice versa for manufacturing cost and deterioration cost.
- Production rate, total replenishment time, T_3, T_2, and total cost always decrease whenever waste disposal cost changes and vice versa for backordering rate.
- Changes in the backlogging rate parameter considerably affect the overall cost T.C. for Case 2. Table 5.2 shows that increasing the backlogging rate parameter leads to a drop in TC.

5.7 Conclusion

The textile industry is at a turning point in its history, straddling the boundaries of sustainability, responsibility, and innovation. The investigation "Green Logistics Optimization for Sustainable Supply Chains in the Textile Industry: A Carbon Emissions and Water Footprint Perspective" has explored the nuances of a revolutionary path aimed at balancing environmental stewardship with operational efficiency. Upon the conclusion of this investigation, a number of significant observations and revelations become apparent, indicating a direction that is in line with the requirements of a responsible and sustainable future. Therefore, shortages are permitted with partial backlogging, and backlogging rate is taken as probabilistic and follows a beta distribution of the first kind.

Holistic Integration of Green Logistics

The study emphasizes how crucial it is for the textile sector to adopt green logistics as a key element of sustainable supply chain strategies. Businesses may greatly cut their water and carbon footprints while simultaneously improving operational efficiency by streamlining their inventory, distribution, and transportation processes. A symbiotic relationship between economic success and environmental responsibility is fostered by the full integration of green logistics, which emerges as a strategic priority.

Balancing Carbon Emissions and Water Footprints

There are several opportunities and challenges associated with the textile supply chain's twin focus on carbon emissions and water impact. According to the research, certain tactics including adopting eco-friendly production methods, sustainable sourcing, and technology innovation can help attain equilibrium. Through the careful

Table 5.1 Sustainable EPQ model without shortages [*Source* Own]

Parameter	Change in %	P	T	TC (Π_1)
A	+ 20	8.7262	5.35129	25.6897
	+ 10	9.45029	5.43961	25.7171
	− 10	12.4346	5.59608	25.9533
	− 20	13.9889	5.80528	24.6981
θ	+ 20	11.0052	5.88025	24.5537
	+ 10	11.2147	5.66748	24.9789
	− 10	10.65	5.34214	25.6947
	− 20	9.05731	5.19125	26.0087
C_O	+ 20	12.5258	5.8521	28.8772
	+ 10	11.8941	5.67905	27.1429
	− 10	10.4001	5.30135	23.5012
	− 20	9.49831	5.09242	21.5772
C_M	+ 20	10.9957	5.47631	25.4033
	+ 10	11.0931	5.48607	25.3786
	− 10	11.29	5.50635	25.3275
	− 20	11.3896	5.51689	25.3014
b_1	+ 20	11.024	5.46987	25.4826
	+ 10	11.1083	5.48296	25.4182
	− 10	11.2725	5.50925	25.2879
	− 20	11.3526	5.52247	25.2219
C_H	+ 20	11.1387	5.47815	25.4251
	+ 10	11.1649	5.48709	25.3893
	− 10	11.2174	5.50513	25.3172
	− 20	11.2438	5.51424	25.2809
C_W	+ 20	11.1941	5.49684	25.3606
	+ 10	11.1926	5.49646	25.357
	− 10	11.1896	5.49571	25.3497
	− 20	11.1882	5.49533	25.346
b_2	+ 20	11.5611	5.46602	25.5409
	+ 10	11.2009	5.50116	25.3224
	− 10	11.0131	5.51127	25.2596
	− 20	10.8396	5.52655	25.1659
b_3	+ 20	11.0025	5.1648	26.4955
	+ 10	11.1408	5.31957	25.9502
	− 10	11.1438	5.70079	24.6955
	− 20	10.987	5.94348	23.9641

(continued)

Table 5.1 (continued)

Parameter	Change in %	P	T	TC (Π_1)
C_{Me}	+ 20	10.8669	5.46364	25.4354
	+ 10	11.0281	5.47954	25.3951
	– 10	11.3563	5.51335	25.31
	– 20	11.5238	5.53139	25.2652
C_{He}	+ 20	10.6773	5.32586	26.0455
	+ 10	10.9319	5.4085	25.7065
	– 10	11.4568	5.58914	24.985
	– 20	11.7281	5.68827	24.6
C_D	+ 20	11.0268	5.4403	25.5775
	+ 10	11.1087	5.46793	25.4661
	– 10	11.2744	5.52478	25.239
	– 20	11.3578	5.55404	25.1231
C_{De}	+ 20	11.0035	5.4325	25.609
	+ 10	11.0969	5.46395	25.4821
	– 10	11.2861	5.52892	25.2225
	– 20	11.3818	5.5625	25.0897
C_{We}	+ 20	11.1584	5.49272	25.3618
	+ 10	11.1747	5.4944	25.3576
	– 10	11.2076	5.49778	25.3491
	– 20	11.224	5.49948	25.3448

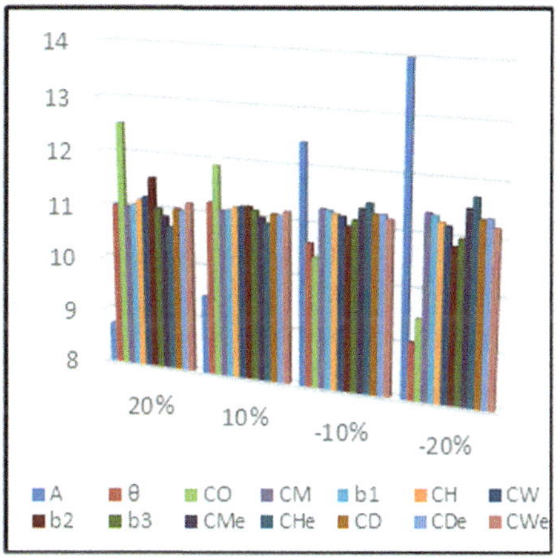

Fig. 5.5 Sensitivity analysis for P (case 1) [*Source* Own]

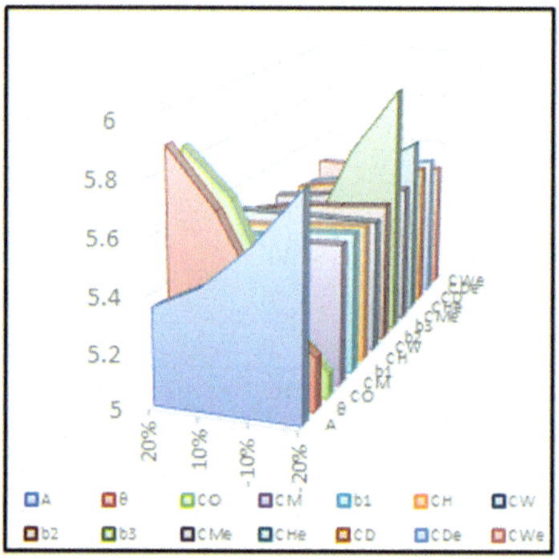

Fig. 5.6 Sensitivity analysis for T (case 1) [*Source* Own]

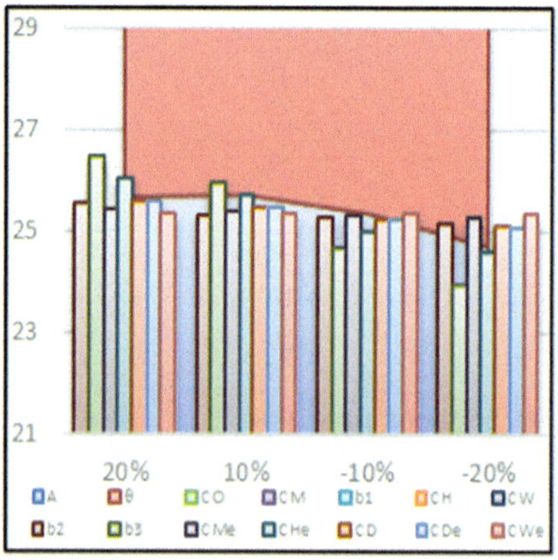

Fig. 5.7 Sensitivity analysis for TC (Π_1) (case 1) [*Source* Own]

consideration of these factors, the manufacturing sector may effectively manage the complex trade-offs associated with water-intensive operations, all the while reducing the environmental damage caused by carbon emissions.

Technological Innovation as a Catalyst

Within the textile business, technological innovation emerges as a catalyst for transformation. Adopting creative solutions is essential to reducing environmental effect, from improved water treatment technology in manufacturing processes to precision agriculture in cotton production. Incorporating Internet of Things (IoT), data analytics, and other Industry 4.0 technologies improves operational efficiency and offers insightful information for sustainable decision-making throughout the supply chain.

Table 5.2 Sustainable EPQ model with shortages [*Source* Own]

Parameter	Change in %	P	T_2	T_3	T	TC (Π_2)
b_2	+ 20	15.3131	0.604357	6.30573	6.67426	26.1006
	+ 10	15.3834	0.667072	6.34435	6.70536	25.9084
	– 10	15.5364	0.859883	6.43514	6.77173	25.9117
	– 20	1,536,198	1.03505	6.46775	6.80729	25.3057
Θ	+ 20	14.8621	0.748488	6.42575	6.78004	25.4169
	+ 10	14.6167	0.749042	6.48656	6.84494	25.4003
	– 10	15.8676	0.740376	6.2014	6.54078	26.1765
	– 20	16.5414	0.745807	6.14154	6.77866	26.4802
C_O	+ 20	16.7532	0.751965	6.80359	7.20405	29.0478
	+ 10	16.1438	0.750145	6.59982	6.97735	27.4065
	– 10	14.7143	0.745957	6.16478	6.49497	24.0389
	– 20	13.8619	0.743502	5.93	6.23539	22.3028
C_{M}	+ 20	15.6076	0.748831	6.82014	6.82014	25.6374
	+ 10	15.5301	0.74847	6.40376	6.77791	25.6763
	– 10	15.3905	0.747792	6.36578	6.69972	25.7454
	– 20	15.3434	0.747551	6.35301	6.67239	25.7685
C_{Me}	+ 20	15.6906	0.749208	6.44809	6.86468	25.5955
	+ 10	15.5682	0.748646	6.41421	6.79874	25.6572
	– 10	15.3588	0.747631	6.35718	6.68139	25.7610
	– 20	15.285	0.747242	6.33716	6.6375	25.7970
b_1	+ 20	15.4191	0.9001	6.36723	6.72051	25.822
	+ 10	15.4384	0.823819	6.37559	6.72911	25.7676
	– 10	15.4771	0.672887	6.39252	6.74661	25.6561
	– 20	15.4964	0.597991	6.40109	6.7555	25.599
b_3	+ 20	15.7489	0.7895	6.19615	6.59468	26.4233
	+ 10	15.5495	0.766094	6.28995	6.66436	26.054
	– 10	15.4581	0.732015	6.49056	6.82411	25.339
	– 20	15.5822	0.717443	6.61113	6.92486	24.9344
C_{H}	+ 20	15.2413	0.747457	6.31527	6.66167	25.9433
	+ 10	15.3489	0.747788	6.34926	6.69931	25.8285
	– 10	15.5676	0.748463	6.41959	6.77722	25.5945
	– 20	15.6787	0.748808	6.45599	6.81757	25.4751
C_{He}	+ 20	14.7527	0.745972	6.16598	6.49648	26.461
	+ 10	15.0994	0.747022	6.27109	6.61277	26.0942
	– 10	15.8098	0.749218	6.49956	6.86588	25.3339
	– 20	16.2135	0.750492	6.63805	7.0196	24.8964

(continued)

Table 5.2 (continued)

Parameter	Change in %	P	T_2	T_3	T	TC (Π_2)
C_W	+ 20	15.463	0.748141	6.38564	6.73961	25.7248
	+ 10	15.4604	0.748132	6.38483	6.73871	25.7185
	− 10	15.4551	0.748116	6.38321	6.73692	25.706
	− 20	15.4539	0.74811	6.38261	6.73625	25.7013
C_{We}	+ 20	15.4932	0.748295	6.3937	6.7576	25.6946
	+ 10	15.4753	0.748209	6.38881	6.74765	25.7035
	− 10	15.4424	0.748047	6.37979	6.72908	25.7199
	− 20	15.4235	0.747956	6.37472	6.71853	25.7292
λ	+ 20	15.3574	0.685063	6.35425	6.69896	25.7807
	+ 10	15.4092	0.713753	6.36957	6.71895	25.7455
	− 10	15.5065	0.79364	6.39862	6.75686	25.6784
	− 20	15.5540	0.857318	6.41334	6.77605	25.644
C_S	+ 20	14.9508	0.73164	6.25254	6.53594	26.1743
	+ 10	15.0712	0.735388	6.28316	6.58202	26.063
	− 10	15.7421	0.758138	6.46103	6.86073	25.4605
	− 20	15.9901	0.767267	6.53033	6.97410	25.2455
C_L	+ 20	15.4223	0.760715	6.37353	6.72356	25.7652
	+ 10	15.4379	0.755126	6.37814	6.72982	25.7419
	− 10	15.4767	0.741562	6.38965	6.74545	25.6839
	− 20	15.4956	0.735105	6.3953	6.75311	25.6555
C_{Le}	+ 20	15.4294	0.758165	6.37562	6.7264	25.7546
	+ 10	15.4435	0.753114	6.37982	6.7321	25.7334
	− 10	15.4696	0.744012	6.38754	6.74259	25.6945
	− 20	15.4838	0.739129	6.39176	6.74832	25.6733
C_D	+ 20	15.4168	0.747997	6.3709	6.72327	25.756
	+ 10	15.435	0.748053	6.37672	6.72972	25.7366
	− 10	15.476	0.74818	6.38989	6.74432	25.6927
	− 20	15.4942	0.748236	6.39579	6.75085	25.6731

Collaborative Stakeholder Engagement

One important lesson to be learned from this investigation is the value of cooperative stakeholder participation. The intricate dynamics of the textile supply chain require collaboration between producers, suppliers, governments, and consumers. Stakeholders can work together to push the adoption of sustainable practices, impact legislative frameworks, and sway consumer behavior toward more environmentally friendly decisions by cultivating a culture of shared responsibility and understanding.

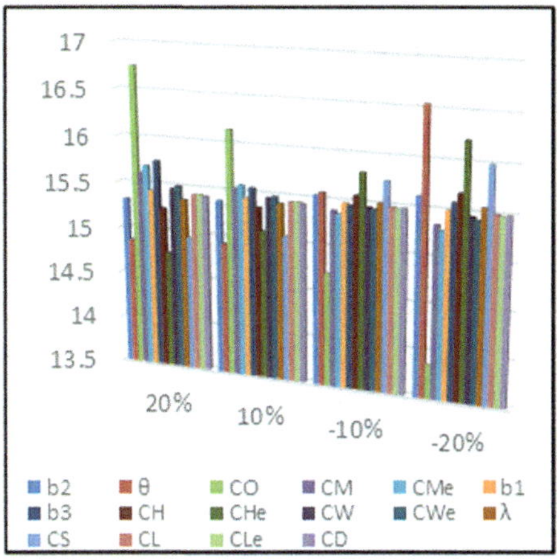

Fig. 5.8 Sensitivity analysis for P (case 2) [*Source* Own]

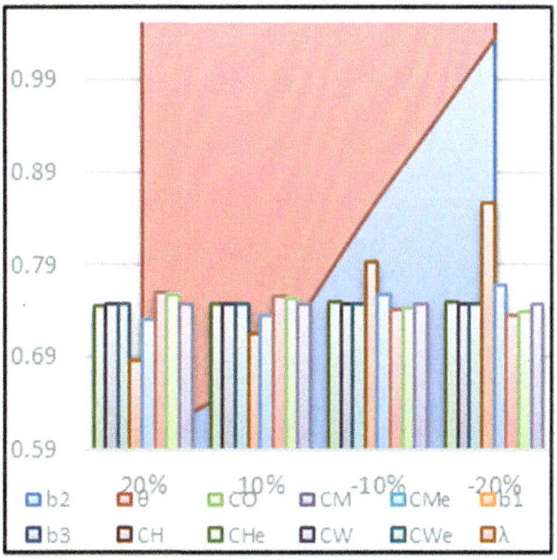

Fig. 5.9 Sensitivity analysis for T_2 (case 2) [*Source* Own]

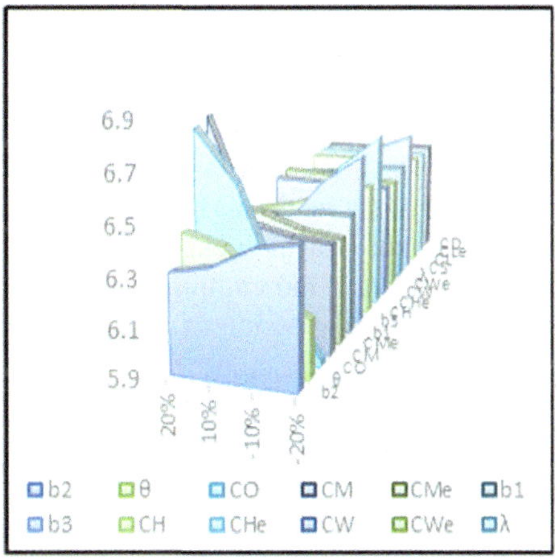

Fig. 5.10 Sensitivity analysis for T_3 (case 2) [*Source* Own]

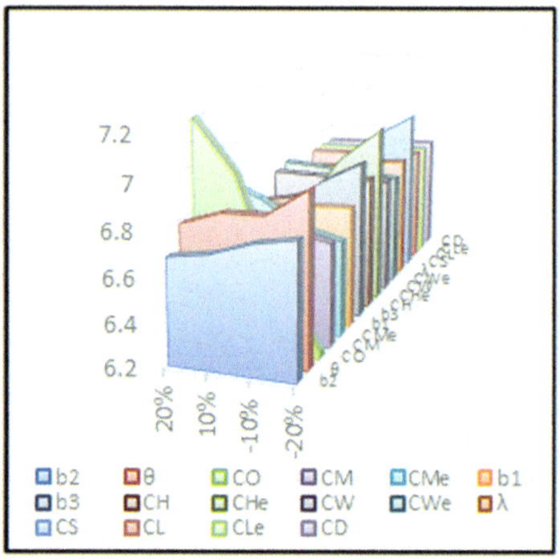

Fig. 5.11 Sensitivity analysis for *T* (case 2) [*Source* Own]

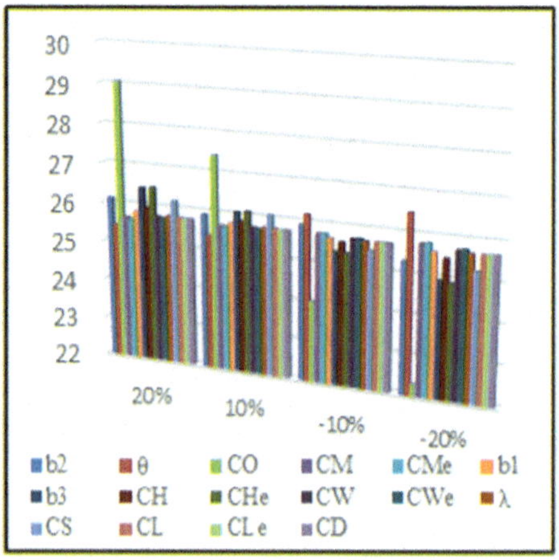

Fig. 5.12 Sensitivity analysis for TC (Π_2) (case 2) [*Source* Own]

The Road Ahead

The textile sector must remain committed to innovation and ongoing improvement as it steers toward a more sustainable future. Through the use of green logistics optimization insights, the sector may create a new model in which environmental stewardship and economic growth coexist harmoniously. The textile sector is set to undergo a transformation in the coming years due to the incorporation of circular economy concepts, the progression of sustainable fashion trends, and the development of a wider ecological consciousness.

Finally, "Green Logistics Optimization for Sustainable Supply Chains in the Textile Industry: A Carbon Emissions and Water Footprint Perspective" highlights how ethical supply chain methods have the capacity to change the world. The textile sector can reduce its environmental effect and pave the way for resilience, innovation, and long-term success in a global marketplace that places a growing emphasis on moral and environmentally responsible business practices by adopting sustainability as a strategic objective.

References

Bai Q, Xu J, Chauhan SS (2020) Effect of sustainability investment and risk aversion on a two-stage supply chain coordination under a carbon tax policy. Comput Ind Eng 142:306–324

Bazan E, Jaber MY, El Saadany AMA (2015) Carbon emissions and energy effects on a manufacturing-remanufacturing inventory models. Comput Ind Eng 88:307–316

Bharti D, Chaudhary A, Singh SR, Singhal S (2024) Green supply chain management model on reliability and demand dependent on time with carbon tax. AIP Conf Proc 3081:090002-1–090002-12

Chaudhary A, Singh SR, Bharti D, Singhal S (2022) An inventory model displayed stock and price dependent demand under non-instantaneous deterioration with inflation for partially backlogged shortages. IJICM 11:35–57

Chaudhary A, Singh SR, Bharti D, Singhal S (2023) Sustainable EOQ models for expiring goods: addressing carbon emissions and demand fluctuations. Stochastic Model Comput Sci 3:50–61

Daryanto Y, Wee HM (2018) Sustainable economic production quantity models: an approach toward a cleaner production. J Adv Manag Sci 6:206–212

Mashud AHM (2020) An EOQ deteriorating inventory model with different types of demand and fully backlogged shortages. Int J Logist Syst Manag 36(1):16–45

Shah NH, Patel E, Rabari K (2021) Upper–lower bounds for the profit of an inventory system under price-stock life time dependent demand. Int J Manag Decis Making: 1–16

Shankar KM, Kannan D, Kumar PU (2017) Analyzing sustainable manufacturing practices—a case study in Indian context. J Clean Prod 164:1332–1343

Singhal S, Vishnoi M (2021) Flexible production inventory model with time dependent holding cost and reliability process. RT&A 16:123–131

Singhal S, Gupta PK, Singh SR (2017) Machine breakdown inventory system with multi-items and partial backlogging. Int J Eng Manage Res 7:758–764

Singhal S, Singh SR (2013) Volume flexible multi-items inventory systems with imprecise environment. Int J Indus Eng Comput 4:457–468

Singhal S, Singh SR (2018) Supply chain system for time and quality dependent decaying items with multiple market demand and volume flexibility. Int J Oper Res 31:245–261

Taleizadeh AA, Soleymanfar VR, Govindan K (2018) Sustainable economic production quantity models for inventory systems with shortage. J Clean Prod 174:1011–1020

Vishnoi M, Singh SR, Singhal S (2018) A supply chain inventory model with expiration date, variable holding cost in an inflationary environment. Int J Pure Appl Math 118:1353–1360

Wee H-M, Wang WT (2012) A supplement to the EPQ with partial backordering and phase-dependent backordering rate. Omega 40:264–266

Chapter 6
Optimization of a Sustainable Integrated Inventory Model for Decaying Items with Multi-variate Demand and Controllable Emission

Monika Vishnoi, Surbhi Singhal, and S. R. Singh

Abstract By embracing sustainability, we can address the social and environmental challenges of the manufacturing industry without compromising productivity in today's manufacturing landscape, two major concerns are maintaining high product quality and mitigating environmental impact. This chapter introduces a comprehensive model designed to create an eco-friendly manufacturing ecosystem and significantly reduce carbon emissions throughout the supply chain. The proposed model employs a multifaceted approach to cost minimization, incorporating various strategic elements. It considers market price fluctuations, enabling manufacturers to make cost-effective procurement decisions. Additionally, it takes into account stock-dependent demand, allowing for more accurate demand forecasting and inventory management. The chapter also delves into the role of pricing dynamics in capturing and retaining customer interest. Dynamics pricing strategies, which adjust prices based on various factors such as demand and competition, are explored for their potential to boost sales and customer satisfaction. A key aspect of this model is the emphasis on volume flexibility within flexible manufacturing systems. In flexibility systems, the model ensures that production can be adjusted based on current demand, reducing waste and overproduction. Furthermore, efficient replenishment strategies are included to maintain optimal inventory levels, thus minimizing holding costs and resource use. Transportation costs are another significant focus of the model. The chapter examines how transportation logistics, including fuel consumption, emissions, and distance covered, impact overall sustainability. By optimizing transportation routes and methods, manufacturers can reduce their carbon footprint and operational costs. To validate the practicality and effectiveness of the proposed

M. Vishnoi
Symbiosis Statistical Institute, Symbiosis International (Deemed University), Pune, India

S. Singhal (✉)
Department of Statistics, Vardhaman College, Bijnor 246701, India
e-mail: singhalsurbhi2006@gmail.com

S. R. Singh
Department of Mathematics, C.C.S. University, Meerut 250001, India

N. H. Shah and M. Mittal (eds.), *Sustainable Inventory Management*, Inventory Optimization, https://doi.org/10.1007/978-981-97-6765-6_7

model, the chapter presents a detailed numerical example. This example, along with a sensitivity analysis, demonstrates how the model can be applied in real-world scenarios to solve complex manufacturing problems. The sensitivity analysis further highlights the model's robustness and its ability to adapt to different conditions and variables. Overall, the integration of sustainable practices into the manufacturing system, as outlined in this chapter, provides a pathway to address environmental and social issues while maintaining high productivity and quality standards. By adopting this model, manufacturers can achieve a balanced approach to sustainability and economic viability.

Keywords Integrated model · Stock and selling price demand · Volume flexibility · Controllable emission

6.1 Introduction

A link between clients, vendors, granaries, plants, raw material sellers, and distribution owners is known as a supply chain. Administrators of the supply chain aim to diminish the costs that are directly and indirectly involved in the supply chain as production costs, inventory carrying costs, purchase costs, sales revenue etc. The area of exploration of the supply chain has been highly energetic for previous epochs. It is observed that it will be more effective if we deal with the enhancement of the entire supply chain through optimization efforts instead of it in pieces like plants, distribution etc. But optimization of the complete supply chain requires the greatest coordination of members of the constituency, like plant managers and distributor providers, etc., in terms of revealing precise information between them, like production costs and distribution costs, etc. This scenario is only possible if all the commitments linked to the manufacturing and distribution departments are taken by the same individual.

To run the manufacturing company smoothly, inventory is a leading feature and an essential component from production to sales. To fulfill the requirements of the market and customers, inventory is an unavoidable part of the company. Companies should be able to work together to maintain their position in global markets. For that reason, successful inventory management is rudimentary to worldwide manufacturing supply chain policy. Many organizations and business groups have to balance cost and service constantly. They spend enough time and money managing their supplier or customer base to accomplish this aim, but oftentimes outcomes are incompatible and uncertain. Inventory management becomes compassionate and labor-intensive, which resonates across the supply chain, causing: unplanned production downtime, too much inventory carrying costs, speed-up shipments and premium freight bills, raised administrative costs, inability to perform customer service demand, etc. Currently, manufacturers have turned to the combined inventory policy to meet these provocations. Inventory collaboration policies require mechanization of an organization's replenishment procedures as well as the relationship of the customer and distributor bodies with real-time prediction, inventory available, optimal lot sizing, quality advancement and inspections and shipment details to reduce inventory and eliminate dispensable charges. These policies have been broadly accepted in industries such as general manufacturing, medical gadgets, telecommunications manufacturing, automotive, etc. Jointly, vendors and buyers must improve their working efficiency and get immediate responses to customer demands. It helps to diminish inventory expenses and increase revenues in extremely competitive situations.

Nowadays, sustainability is an international concern and a sustainable integrated model is favourable and leads to financial sustainability. Sustainable models always attract more customers to the business provide more or less relaxation to the leaders and make the environment friendly. To grow the ecological integrated model to meet with the expected tendency of control of carbon emission. The manufacturing industries have produced outsized amounts of carbon dioxide. The issues of gases discharged from industry earlier were not major. Carbon emissions are the main causes of greenhouse gases in industries such as construction, commerce, and conveyance. In 2010, Sundarakani and co-authors formulated a vendor–buyer strategy aimed at understanding how carbon emissions reduction affected inventory levels and increased reflectivity during the delivery process. Jaber et al. (2013) introduced a seller-buyer collaboration approach with the consideration of emissions in the trade processes, which reduces the total cost without some modification regarding the environmental impact and associated fines. Battini et al. (2014) developed the price of emissions from transportation, warehouses, and discarding the waste material. Ghovelaque and Bironneau (2015) deal with an order-level model as the emission from the storeroom and carriage. An inventory model where carbon emissions come from holding inventory, freight, and items deteriorates by Hua et al. (2016). Bouchery et al. (2017) explored a two-tiered supply chain model, examining the impact of carbon emission pricing in both non-collaborative and collaborative settings. Wangsa (2017) considered emission costs with the government's penalty and incentive plans for industrial and transport activities. Taleizadeh et al. (2018) formulated an economic quantity model that takes into account environmental considerations and permissible shortages. A model of the supply chain has been discussed by Vishnoi et al. (2018) for decomposing items with the concept of expiration date in the situation of inflation. Aljazzar et al. (2018) deal with the impression of trade credit and the reduction in carbon emissions. A sustainable inventory model with both types of items, i.e., perfect and imperfect, considering controllable emissions and deterioration, was proposed by Mashud et al. (2020). Pan et al. (2020) introduced a manufacturing stock system aimed at mitigating carbon emissions by incorporating sustainability measures alongside investments. Singh et al. (2021) studied an inventory system using the implementation of the Just in Time concept for the duration of the lockdown. Barman et al. (2022) analyzed the supply chain model with pricing policies for allowing and not allowing shortages, using both concepts to represent the view of business tactics in different zones of the market. Singh et al. (2023) devised a sustainability-oriented model utilizing passive RFID tags amid the pandemic.

In the realm of economic production quantity models, the conventional approach often assumes a static, unchanging production environment. However, reality seldom adheres strictly to this model. With market dynamics in constant flux, the recognition of flexibility as a pivotal attribute in manufacturing has gained considerable traction, particularly in the realm of volume flexibility. Volume flexibility stands out as a crucial capability within manufacturing systems, enabling them to seamlessly adjust production levels within expansive parameters prior to commencing a production cycle.

Flexibility, in essence, embodies an organization's capacity to adeptly accommodate a broadening spectrum of customer demands without succumbing to excessive costs, time constraints, organizational upheavals, or performance setbacks. Within the context of manufacturing, a particularly noteworthy facet of this flexibility is the ability to tailor production rates in response to fluctuations in market demand, aptly termed volume flexibility. Singhal et al. (2014) devised a probabilistic inventory framework tailored for Weibull deteriorating goods, incorporating considerations of adaptability and dependability amidst the influence of inflationary forces. Singhal and Singh (2014) proposed a manufacturing reprocessing setup designed for stochastic diminishing items within a context of adaptable production surroundings.

In an economy, demand typically declines as the costs for goods rise, which impacts overall profitability. Since the pandemic outbreak, the prices of fruits, vegetables, grains, medicines, and other essential items have been steadily increasing. This study examines the principle of future price increases, where a supplier announces an impending price hike for a product, which has a measurable effect at a specific point in time. Product pricing directly influences customer demand, as higher prices tend to deter purchases. This study focuses on the effect of future price increases for products with expiry dates and price-sensitive demand under various payment policies. Price-sensitive demand is a crucial factor in selling any product and is a central theme in this model. In economics, demand represents the customers' need and desire to purchase products and services. It is a key driver of global growth and expansion. No firm would invest in production without the assurance of demand.

The revised paragraph is more concise, uses active voice, and employs transitions to improve the flow of ideas. It also incorporates more specific examples and clarifies the main points. The language is more precise and engaging, making it easier for the reader to grasp the key concepts.

This study spreads out the proposed model by integrating the optimistic consequences of emissions with the decline in customer demand. To grasp the customer's devotion, the selling price is an essential feature of the trade business. Usually, demand and price have a negative correlation, as the higher the item's price, the lower the product's market need or consumer interest. However, the vendor may adjust the market price to stabilize the influence of expenditures and the adverse influence of cost rises in response to customer needs. In the significance of market price, here we have taken the sales trend with stock and price-dependent and controllable emissions.

In today's world, technology is indispensable in both domestic and industrial settings. However, its widespread use has led to increased carbon emissions, contributing to environmental degradation. From homes to factories, every sector releases carbon into the atmosphere. This can be mitigated by adopting advanced manufacturing technologies that enhance product quality while reducing emissions. Consequently, many businesses are actively striving to minimize their carbon footprint. Recent studies indicate that reducing carbon emission has become a primary goal for industries, alongside profitability.

We undertook this research to optimize the most effective replenishment cycle, investment in environmentally sustainable technology, and market pricing when a company seeks to maximize revenue with a commitment to addressing environmental concerns.

To appeal to consumers, stock and price-dependent demand play a vital role in inventory management. In 1972, Levin et al. proposed that the presence of inventory has motivational significance for both consumers and the demand for stock levels. Silver and Peterson (1985) explore an inventory model wherein retail-level sales are typically linked proportionally to the amount of inventory showcased. Several authors have attempted to analyze inventory models that consider the current on-hand inventory level. Gupta and Vrat (1986) introduced a technique for minimizing costs in an inventory system that is dependent on demand and involves replenishing stock based on the initial quantity.

In addition, some researchers jointly considered both stock level and demand as price- dependent. Lau and Lau (1988) simultaneously considered the work on price dependence and the newsboy problem.

Over the past two decades, numerous researchers have contributed extensively to the exploration of topics such as on-hand inventory levels, deterioration, pricing strategies, inflation, production variability, holding costs, two warehouse systems, and other relevant subjects. Pal et al. (1993), Giri et al. (1996), Giri and Chaudhary (1998), Datta and Pal (1990, 1998), Datta and Paul (2001), Ouyang et al. (2003), Alfares (2007), and Dutta Choudhury and Datta (2010) have all delved into these areas. In 1999, Wee concentrated specifically on a model in which the demand is described as a convex, decreasing function of the selling price.

The idea of utilizing advanced payment to establish the optimal ordering strategy in the presence of stochastic lead times and demand influenced by price variations is shown by Maiti et al. (2009). Singhal et al. (2010) presented a model involving the supply chain and integrating probabilistic lead times. In 2011, Liang and Zhou investigated two inventory models for warehouses that involve items prone to deterioration, considering realistic demand patterns specifically influenced by pricing. Singh and Vishnoi (2013) introduced a supply chain inventory framework integrating a consumption rate contingent upon price variations, encompassing both ameliorating and deteriorating items, and featuring dual storage tiers. Shaikh et al. (2017) explored a model incorporating fully backlogged shortages, demand dependent on stock levels, and non-instantaneous deterioration, all within an inflationary context. Singhal et al. (2019) elucidated a model that incorporates the impact of preservation technology for sustainable inventory model with the concept of fuzzification. They took into account demand dependency on both pricing and inventory levels. In 2021, Singhal and Vishnoi investigated the factors of flexibility, price variations, and reliability, taking into account the influence of inflation. Gautam et al. (2022) employed a methodology for an imperfect production model that accounts for both price and advertising-induced demand. Chaudhary et al. (2022) implemented a tactic in the context of a model related to inventory incorporating displayed supply and market requirements influenced by pricing, all within an inflationary environment. In 2024, Bharti et al. expanded a model with green supply chain management on reliability and demand depend on time with carbon tax.

This recently developed unified inventory model for a system involving a sole vendor and buyer accommodates deterioration as well as carbon emissions simultaneously. The study investigates the extent to which this integrated inventory model contributes to the reduction of carbon emissions. We have considered a demand scenario involving multiple variables, coupled with a production rate that varies, emphasizing volume flexibility. Carbon emissions play a crucial role in warehousing, transportation, and the deterioration of items.

During the age of ecological responsibility, the impact of carbonaceous emissions is a significant worldwide concern. This impact can be influenced by adopting sustainable practices or selecting unprocessed materials and items for sale that result in minimal emissions. The model is exemplified using numerical instances accompanied by a parameter variation. The results of the impact assessment are visually depicted through graphical representations.

Many researchers in the field typically refer to demand rates as either constant or dependent on a single parameter. However, it's evident that such classifications only capture a limited scope of real-world business scenarios. In reality, customer demand is influenced by multiple factors, making it pragmatic to consider a demand rate that accounts for both selling price and stock levels. Surprisingly, none of the existing studies have employed an integrated model that incorporates volume flexibility alongside demand dependent on stock and selling price, all while addressing controllable emissions concurrently.

6.2 Assumptions and Notations

A subsequent set of assumptions and symbols is employed in the models involving vendors and buyers.

6.2.1 Notations

θ	Deterioration rate
q	Order quantity
P	Production rate
a	The fixed component of the demand function
c	Indicator of price responsiveness
j	Factor representing the preference of customers for environmentally friendly options
λ	The proportion of emissions decreased per unit of products
S	Selling price per unit
t_f	Fixed transportation cost ($/trip)
t_v	The expenses accrued by the vendor for transporting every individual unit per unit distance, ($/unit/km)
L	Distance travelled from vendor to buyer
t_r	The cost incurred by the vendor for a round-trip per unit distance travelled, expressed as a variable cost ($/km)
v_e	The mean cost associated with carbon emissions from the vehicle ($/km)
UPC	Cost per unit of producing an item and UPC = M + E/P + DP, where M is material cost, E is energy and labour cost and D is a tool or die cost

6.2.2 Assumptions

- The rate of demand is presumed to be selling and inventory dependent with controllable emissions i.e. $d_r = a + bI(t) - cS + \lambda j$ where, a, b and $c > 0$, j is the coefficient of customer choice for low carbon, and the demand is easily influenced by j when λ is high.
- The deterioration in the inventory of both the vendor and buyer takes place at a consistent or steady pace.
- The rate of production is regarded as a variable, meaning it is subject to change or adjustment.
- The replenishment is instantaneous.
- The shortage is not endorsed.
- Carbon emissions arise as a consequence of the transportation, warehousing, and storage of deteriorating items.
- The known factor is the distance covered in transit from the vendor to the buyer.

6.3 Mathematical Modelling

The two-echelon mathematical inventory model of the decaying product with controllable emissions is exemplified.

6.3.1 *The Cumulative Cost Function Model for the Buyer*

The representation of the inventory owned by the purchaser model is illustrated in Fig. 6.1. Initially, the purchaser acquires 'q' units of the product from a vendor, denoted by $I(0)$, and transports the stock to their warehouse via truck, emitting carbon dioxide in the process. The order submission and receipt, i.e., lead time, are considered negligible. Throughout the period [0, Tb], the buyer's stock level gradually diminishes as a result of both demand and deterioration until it reaches zero. The overall cost incurred by the buyer per unit of time (TC_b) is assessed during this period.

$$\begin{aligned}\text{Buyer's Total Cost } (TC_b) &= \text{Buyer's Ordering cost}\\ &\quad + \text{Buyer's holding cost}\\ &\quad + \text{Buyer's deterioration cost}\end{aligned}$$

The equation below represents the buyer's inventory level while undergoing replenishment, considering both demand and item deterioration:

$$I_b'(t) + \theta I(t) = -(a + bI_b(t) - cS + \lambda j)0 \leq t \leq T_b \tag{6.1}$$

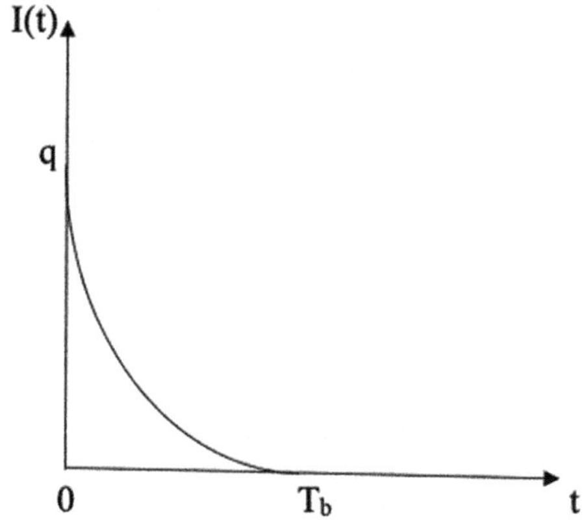

Fig. 6.1 Buyer's model [*Source* Own]

Under initial condition $I(T_b) = 0$, the derived solution indicates that the stock level of the buyer is

$$I_b(t) = \frac{(a - cS + \lambda j)}{(\theta + b)}\left(e^{(\theta+b)(T_b-t)} - 1\right)0 \le t \le T_b. \tag{6.2}$$

The quantity ordered by the buyer, denoted as q, equals the initial inventory level $I(0)$ at time $t = 0$.

$$T_b = \frac{1}{(\theta + b)}\log\left(\frac{(\theta + b)q}{(a - cS + \lambda j)} + 1\right). \tag{6.3}$$

The overall cost incurred by the buyer in each replenishment cycle:

(a)

$$\text{The cost is borne by the buyer for placing an order in each replenishment cycle} = O_c \tag{6.4}$$

(b) The cost incurred by the buyer for holding inventory during each replenishment cycle $= h_b \int_0^{T_b} I_b(t)\mathrm{d}t$

$$= h_b\left[\frac{q}{(\theta + b)} - \frac{(a - cS + \lambda j)}{(\theta + b)^2}\log\left(\frac{q(\theta + b)}{(a - cS + \lambda j)} + 1\right)\right] \tag{6.5}$$

(c) The cost to the buyer associated with product deterioration during each replenishment cycle $= d_{cb} \int_0^{T_b} \theta I_b(t)\mathrm{d}t$

$$= d_{cb}\left[\frac{q\theta}{(\theta + b)} - \frac{(a - cS + \lambda j)\theta}{(\theta + b)^2}\log\left(\frac{q(\theta + b)}{(a - cS + \lambda j)} + 1\right)\right] \tag{6.6}$$

The Total cost incurred by the buyer, encompassing ordering cost, holding cost, and deterioration cost (BTC) = Buyer's Ordering cost + Buyer's holding cost+ Buyer's deterioration cost

$$= \mathrm{Oc} + h_b\left[\frac{q}{(\theta + b)} - \frac{(a - cS + \lambda j)}{(\theta + b)^2}\log\left(\frac{q(\theta + b)}{(a - cS + \lambda j)} + 1\right)\right] + d_{cb}[\frac{q\theta}{(\theta + b)} - \frac{(a - cS + \lambda j)\theta}{(\theta + b)^2}\log\left(\frac{q(\theta + b)}{(a - cS + \lambda j)} + 1\right)] \tag{6.7}$$

6.3.2 The Overall Cost Function for the Vendor, Covering Various Elements Such as Production, Transportation, and Other Associated Costs.

Products manufactured within the timeframe of T_S are promptly delivered to the buyer upon completion of the shipment. Equation (6.19) delineates the total cost incurred by the vendor per unit of time, denoted as TC_v. It is determined by the vendor's setup cost, transport cost, holding cost, and per-unit time-deteriorating cost (Fig. 6.2).

$$I'_{v1}(t) + \theta I_{v1}(t) = P - (a + bI_{v1}(t) - cS + \lambda j), 0 \le t \le T_S. \quad (6.8)$$

$$I'_{v2}(t) + \theta I_{v2}(t) = -(a + bI_{v2}(t) - cS + \lambda j), 0 \le t \le T_v \quad (6.9)$$

With initial condition: $I_{v1}(0) = 0$ and $I_{v2}(T_v) = 0$. Here solution found that the inventory level of vendor are:

$$I_{v1}(t) = \frac{(P - (a - cS + \lambda j))}{(\theta + b)}\left(1 - e^{-(\theta+b)t}\right) \quad 0 \le t \le T_S. \quad (6.10)$$

$$I_{v2}(t) = \frac{(a - cS + \lambda j)}{(\theta + b)}\left(e^{(\theta+b)(T_v - t)} - 1\right) \quad ,0 \le t \le T_v. \quad (6.11)$$

From Eqs. (6.10) and (6.11), the value of

$$T_S = \frac{(a - cS + \lambda j)}{(P - (a - cS + \lambda j))} T_v \left(\frac{(\theta + b)T_v}{2} + 1\right). \quad (6.12)$$

Since $T = T_S + T_v$

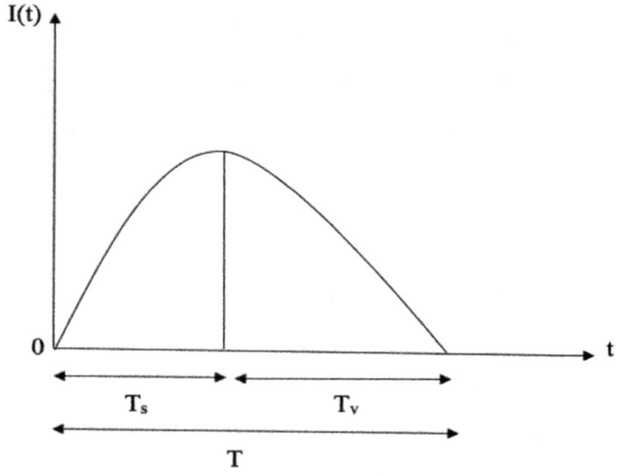

Fig. 6.2 Vendor's model [*Source* Own]

$$= \frac{T_{\mathrm{v}}}{(P-(a-cS+\lambda j))}\left(P+\frac{(a-cS+\lambda j)(\theta+b)T_{\mathrm{v}}}{2}\right). \tag{6.13}$$

(a)

$$\text{Vendor's cost incurred for each production cycle's setup} = C_{\mathrm{sp}} \tag{6.14}$$

(b) Vendor's production cost $= \int_0^{T_{\mathrm{S}}}\left(M+\frac{E}{P}+DP\right)P\mathrm{d}t$

$$= \left(M+\frac{E}{P}+DP\right)PT_{\mathrm{S}}$$

$$= \left(M+\frac{E}{P}+DP\right)\frac{(a-cS+\lambda j)}{(P-(a-cS+\lambda j))}T_{\mathrm{v}}\left(\frac{(\theta+b)T_{\mathrm{v}}}{2}+1\right) \tag{6.15}$$

(c) Vendor's holding cost $= h_v\left[\int_0^{T_S} I_{v1}(t)dt + \int_0^{T_v} I_{v2}(t)dt - \int_0^{T_b} I_b(t)dt\right]$

$$\begin{aligned} &= h_{\mathrm{v}}\left[\frac{(P-(a-cS+\lambda j))}{(\theta+b)}\left(T_{\mathrm{S}}+\frac{e^{-(\theta+b)T_{\mathrm{S}}}}{(\theta+b)}-\frac{1}{(\theta+b)}\right)\right. \\ &\quad+\frac{(a-cS+\lambda j)}{(\theta+b)}\left(\frac{e^{(\theta+b)T_{\mathrm{v}}}}{(\theta+b)}-\frac{1}{(\theta+b)}-T_{\mathrm{v}}\right)-\frac{q}{(\theta+b)} \\ &\quad\left.+\frac{(a-cS+\lambda j)}{(\theta+b)^2}\log\left(\frac{q(\theta+b)}{(a-cS+\lambda j)}+1\right)\right] \end{aligned} \tag{6.16}$$

(d) Vendor's deterioration cost $= d_v\left[\int_0^{T_{\mathrm{S}}}\theta I_{v1}(t)\mathrm{d}t + \int_0^{T_{\mathrm{v}}}\theta I_{v2}(t)\mathrm{d}t\right]$

$$= d_{\mathrm{v}}\left[\begin{array}{l}\frac{(P-(a-cS+\lambda j))\theta}{(\theta+b)}\left(T_{\mathrm{S}}+\frac{e^{-(\theta+b)T_{\mathrm{S}}}}{(\theta+b)}-\frac{1}{(\theta+b)}\right) \\ +\frac{(a-cS+\lambda j)\theta}{(\theta+b)}\left(\frac{e^{(\theta+b)T_{\mathrm{v}}}}{(\theta+b)}-\frac{1}{(\theta+b)}-T_{\mathrm{v}}\right)\end{array}\right] \tag{6.17}$$

(e)

$$\text{Vendor's transportation Cost} = t_{\mathrm{f}} + t_{\mathrm{v}}I_{\mathrm{b}}(0)L + t_{\mathrm{r}}L + 2Lv_{\mathrm{e}} \tag{6.18}$$

$$\begin{aligned}\text{Vendor's Total Cost (VTC)} = {} & \text{Vendor's Set up cost} \\ & + \text{Vendor's production cost} \\ & + \text{Vendor's holding cost} \\ & + \text{Vendor's deterioration cost} \\ & + \text{Vendor's Transportation cost}\end{aligned}$$

$$= \text{Csp} + \left(M + \frac{E}{P} + DP\right)\frac{(a - cS + \lambda j)}{(P - (a - cS + \lambda j))}T_v\left(\frac{(\theta + b)T_v}{2} + 1\right)$$
$$+ h_v\left[\frac{(P - (a - cS + \lambda j))}{(\theta + b)}\left(T_S + \frac{e^{-(\theta+b)T_S}}{(\theta + b)} - \frac{1}{(\theta + b)}\right)\right.$$
$$+ \frac{(a - cS + \lambda j)}{(\theta + b)}\left(\frac{e^{(\theta+b)T_v}}{(\theta + b)} - \frac{1}{(\theta + b)} - T_v\right)$$
$$\left. - \frac{q}{(\theta + b)} + \frac{(a - cS + \lambda j)}{(\theta + b)^2}\log\left(\frac{q(\theta + b)}{(a - cS + \lambda j)} + 1\right)\right]$$
$$+ t_f + t_v I_b(0)L + t_r L + 2Lv_e \tag{6.19}$$

6.3.3 *The All-Encompassing Cost Function that Combines and Considers Various Components Within the Integrated System*

The combined system's overall cost function arises from adding together the total expenses incurred by both the buyer and the vendor

$$\text{TIC} = \text{BTC} + \text{VTC} \tag{6.20}$$

BTC and VTC are represented by the Eqs. (6.7) and (6.19) respectively.

6.4 Solution Procedure

The total integrated cost (TIC) is expressed as a function dependent on four distinct variables: S, q, λ and T_v.

For finding an optimal solution, we consider

$$\frac{\partial TIC}{\partial S} = 0, \frac{\partial TIC}{\partial q} = 0, \frac{\partial TIC}{\partial \lambda} = 0 \text{ and}$$
$$\frac{\partial TIC}{\partial \text{Tv}} = 0 \tag{6.21}$$

Put, the values of S, q, λ and T_v which satisfy the following conditions:

$$\frac{\partial^2 TIC}{\partial S^2} > 0, \frac{\partial^2 TIC}{\partial q^2} > 0, \frac{\partial^2 TIC}{\partial \lambda^2} > 0 \text{ and}$$
$$\frac{\partial^2 TIC}{\partial \text{Tv}^2} > 0 \tag{6.22}$$

6.5 Illustrative Instance and Analysis of Sensitivity

Data related to different costs, emissions, demand patterns, deterioration, and investments within the stock management system are compiled from a manufacturing company (as based on the previous studies) and presented in appropriate units as outlined below:

6.5.1 Numerical Example

Next, let's look at a numerical example of the EPQ model with waste disposal costs and analyze the impact of a few important factors. The fundamental EPQ model equation takes into account all expenses. For the numerical example, let's use the following parameter values:

$$\begin{aligned} C_{sp} &= 10{,}000/\text{Setup},\ M = 150,\ E = 2000, \\ D &= 0.01,\ P = 20{,}000\ \text{units/year}, \\ h_v &= \$40/\text{unit/year},\ h_b = \$60/\text{unit/year}, \\ \theta &= 0.1,\ a = 60,\ b = 40,\ c = 0.1, \\ O_c &= \$2000/\text{units/order},\ d_{cb} = 600/\text{unit}, \\ d_v &= 200/\text{unit},\ t_f = \$500/\text{trip},\ t_v = \$0.50/\text{litre}, \\ L &= 100\ \text{km},\ t_r = \$20/\text{km},\ v_e = 0.048/\text{km}. \end{aligned}$$

- Upon implementing the proposed action plan, optimal values for S, q, λ and T_v are determined to minimize the expected combined total cost TIC across varying values of j^* from 0 to 14. According to Table 6.1, the optimal order delivery

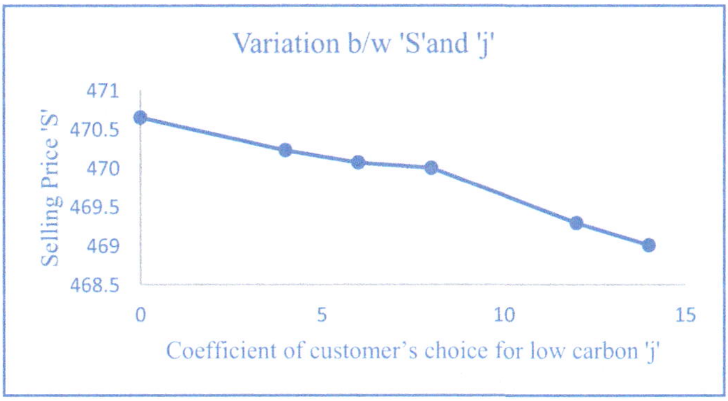

Fig. 6.3 Variation b/w S and 'j' [*Source* Own]

Table 6.1 Optimal solution [*Source* Own]

J	*S*	'*q*'	λ	T_V (10^{-5})	TIC
0	470.657	56,477	1.02294	1.00431	105,510
4	470.235	78,166	1.06831	3.58396	105,222
6	470.077	83,414	1.14682	5.69163	105,189
8	**470.008**	**86,563**	**1.24962**	**8.8458**	**105,027**
12	469.297	59,788	1.30276	5.03856	105,105
14	469.012	30,564	1.32163	6.60517	105,471

Fig. 6.4 Variation b/w 'TIC' and '*j*' [*Source* Own]

size q^* is found to be 86,563 units. The optimal selling price is 470.008 units. The optimal emission reduction rate (λ) per unit product is 1.24962, and the total time taken by vendor T_v is 8.8458×10^{-5}. Considering all the most favourable values for the decision variables, the lowest possible expected integrated cost is determined to be 105,027.

6.5.2 *Sensitivity Analysis*

The analysis of sensitivity is implemented by varying some parameters at − 20, − 10, 10, 20% and these variations shown graphically with Figs. 6.5, 6.6, 6.7, 6.8, 6.9, 6.10, 6.11, 6.12, 6.13 and 6.14.

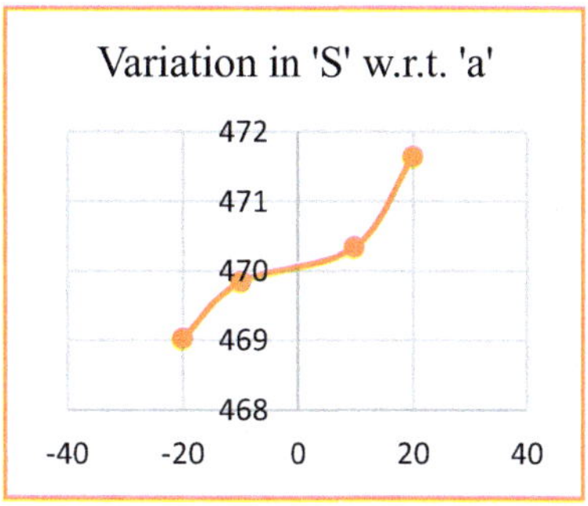

Fig. 6.5 Variation in S w.r.t. 'a' [*Source* Own]

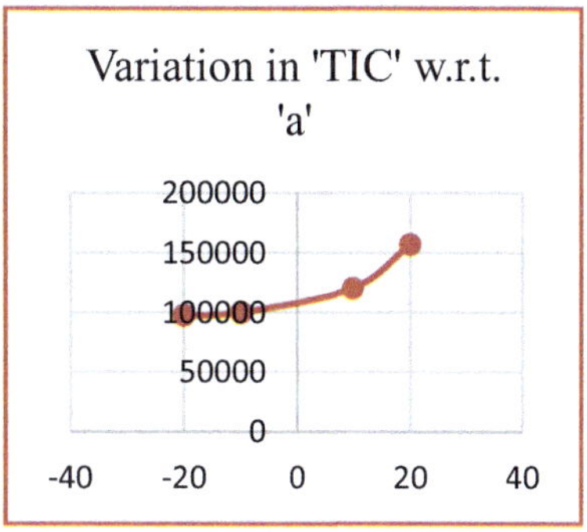

Fig. 6.6 Variation in TIC w.r.t. 'a' [*Source* Own]

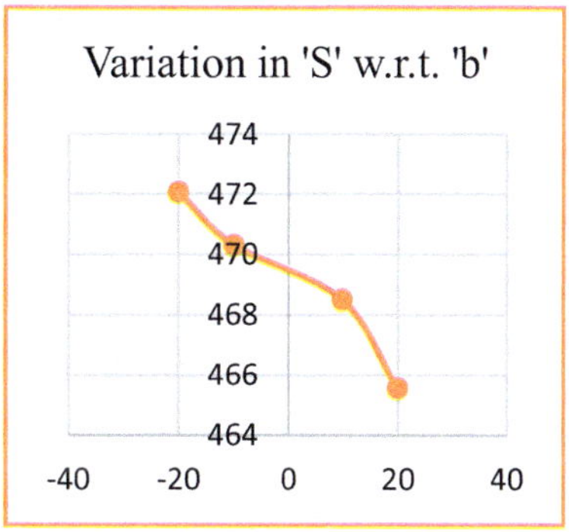

Fig. 6.7 Variation in S w.r.t. 'b' [*Source* Own]

6.6 Observations

From the provided table, we have identified and examined several sensitivity aspects.

1. An augmentation in the consumption rate factor 'a' corresponds to a simultaneous escalation in the market price 'S' of the products, the emission reduction per unit product 'λ', the time taken by the vendor 'T_V', and the overall integrated cost.

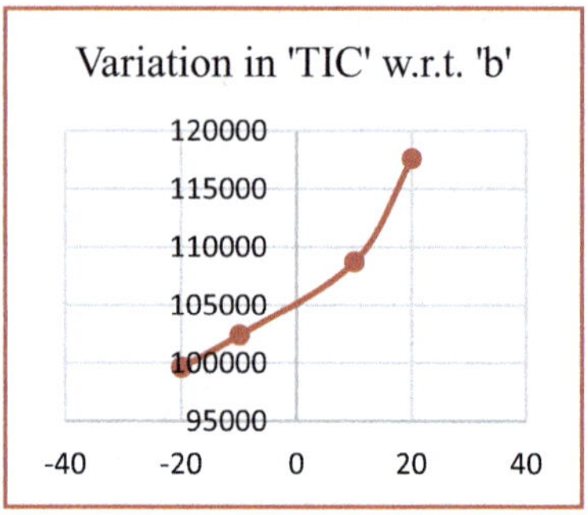

Fig. 6.8 Variation in TIC w.r.t. 'b' [*Source* Own]

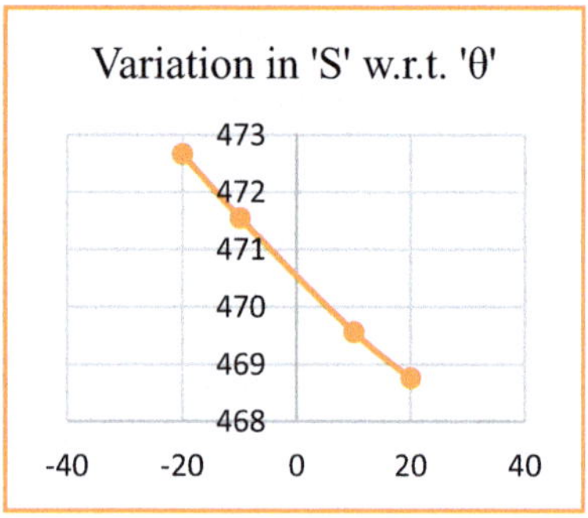

Fig. 6.9 Variation in S w.r.t. 'θ' [*Source* Own]

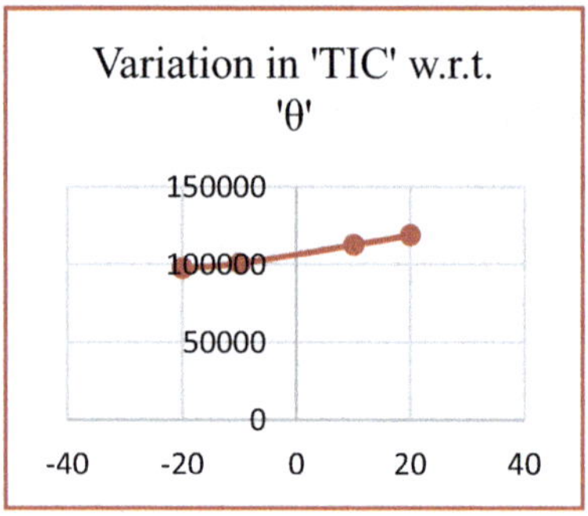

Fig. 6.10 Variation in TIC w.r.t. 'θ' [*Source* Own]

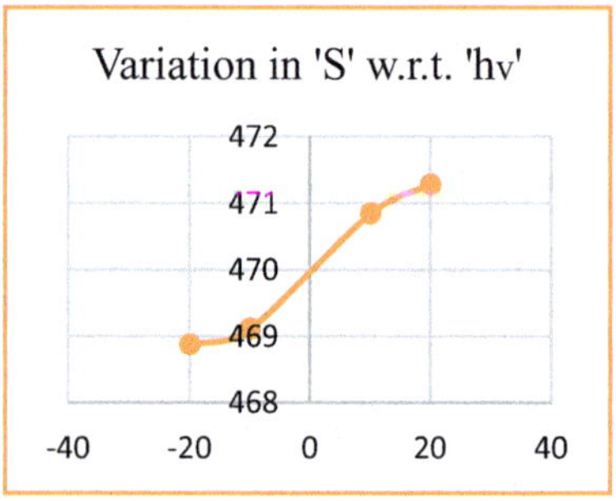

Fig. 6.11 Variation in S w.r.t. 'h_V' [*Source* Own]

Fig. 6.12 Variation in TIC w.r.t. 'h_v' [*Source* Own]

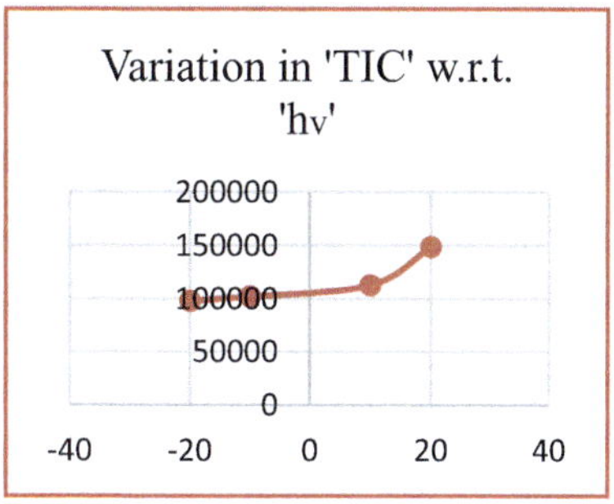

Fig. 6.13 Variation in *S* w.r.t. 'h_b' [*Source* Own]

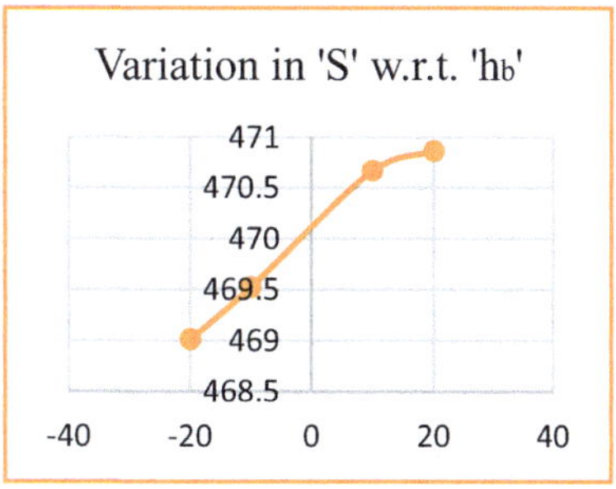

Fig. 6.14 Variation in TIC w.r.t. 'h_b' [*Source* Own]

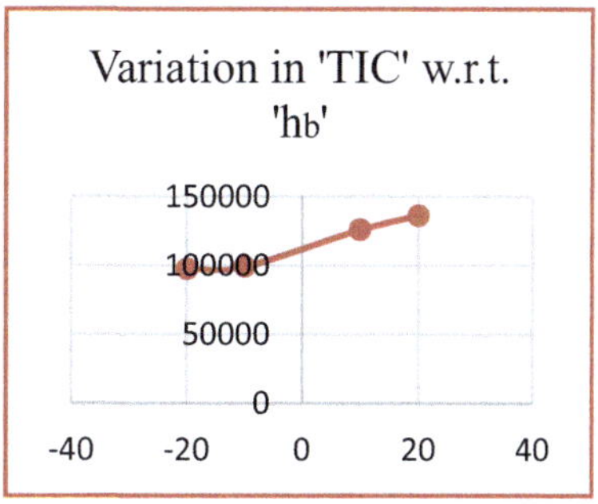

2. When the demand rate stock dependent parameter 'b' increases, the market price 'S' of the products decreases, while emission reduction per unit product 'λ', time is taken by vendor 'T_v' and the comprehensive cost encompassing various elements within an integrated system.
3. The overall integrated cost experiences a reduction with a decrease in the production rate 'P'. In real life, when production increases, it increases the selling price 'S' as per the Table 6.2 observations. When the production rate increases, emission reduction per unit product 'λ', time is taken by vendor 'T_v', and the total integrated cost increases. The Vendor needs to invest more effort in reducing carbon emissions to decrease the total cost.

Table. 6.2 Analysis of sensitivity for different parameters [*Source* Own]

Parameter	% change	S	'λ'	T_v	TC
a	− 20	469.047	1.22291	7.3588	98,761
	− 10	469.875	1.24678	8.6345	101,289
	10	470.367	1.25898	9.9926	121,256
	20	471.665	1.26498	10.006	157,872
b	− 20	472.123	1.19889	7.1256	99,678
	− 10	470.368	1.20887	8.3564	102,451
	10	468.561	1.28788	9.1022	108,757
	20	465.612	1.30378	9.3873	117,652
P	− 20	469.356	1.16287	4.6769	62,352
	− 10	469.987	1.18293	6.4799	81,276
	10	470.324	1.26834	11.378	131,979
	20	470.687	1.28123	15.988	161,205
θ	− 20	472.688	1.22082	7.0288	98,124
	− 10	471.564	1.23367	8.3499	101,278
	10	469.576	1.25132	9.2742	113,426
	20	468.779	1.26765	9.9882	119,668
h_v	− 20	468.887	1.18561	5.7763	98,754
	− 10	469.127	1.20467	7.7975	102,855
	10	470.856	1.27478	9.3657	113,346
	20	471.288	1.30272	11.875	149,123
h_b	− 20	469.025	1.17467	6.8944	97,875
	− 10	469.534	1.22577	7.1679	99,657
	10	470.679	1.26236	8.9834	126,542
	20	470.875	1.28679	9.4782	136,757

4. When the perishable rate parameter 'θ' increases, this will decrease the selling price 'S' of the products, while the emission reduction per unit product 'λ' is moderately constant. The rising rate of deterioration contributes to an escalation in both the overall cost and the time required by the vendor 'T_v' due to increasing product loss. Due to unavoidable deterioration, the buyer opts to lower the selling price, facilitating the swift sale of items.
5. An escalation in the carrying cost parameters for the vendor 'h_v' and buyer 'h_b' leads to a corresponding increase in the selling price 'S' of the products. This adjustment is made to offset the total cost of the products. Additionally, the emission reduction per unit product 'λ' and time taken by vendor 'T_v' exhibit a certain level of sensitivity about the holding cost parameters.

6.7 Managerial Insights

A comprehensive sustainable vendor-buyer inventory model has been meticulously developed to tackle the growing significance of carbon emission reduction and its impact on customer demand. This model empowers administrators to determine the optimal selling price, ensuring not only a secure profit margin but also an increase in customer demand. By integrating multiple key factors, the model takes into account both selling price and stock-dependent demand.

The primary focus of this model is on reducing carbon emissions through improved inventory management and strategic pricing. It recognizes that customer demand is influenced by both the cost of goods and the environmental impact of their production and storage. By aligning these considerations, the model aims to create a balance between economic goals and environmental responsibility. This approach ensures that businesses can achieve profitability while contributing to the reduction of their carbon footprint.

Through this innovative model, administrators are equipped with the tools needed to make informed decisions that drive both customer satisfaction and sustainability. The integration of these elements highlights the model's ability to adapt to the changing market dynamics and environmental standards, making it a crucial tool for modern business operations.

The model is particularly relevant for grocery items such as pulses, various grains, rice, and packaged fruit drinks. These items require specific storage conditions that can contribute significantly to carbon emissions. By managing the storage and handling of these products more efficiently, emissions can be reduced. Furthermore, the model suggests that offering discounted prices during festive seasons or sales can lead to increased customer purchases. This strategy is directly influenced by the selling price of the items and has the potential to decrease the overall carbon footprint by encouraging bulk buying and reducing the frequency of shopping trips.

The importance of considering carbon emissions in conjunction with stock-dependent and selling-price-dependent consumption cannot be overstated. By incorporating these factors into inventory management, businesses can not only improve their profitability but also contribute to environmental sustainability. This approach demonstrates that economic objectives and environmental responsibilities can be aligned, fostering a more sustainable and profitable business model.

6.8 Conclusion

To establish a sustainable model, our focus is on fostering a collaborative approach between vendors and buyers, which aligns with the critical trend of carbon emission control. This collaborative effort is essential for creating a unified strategy that integrates the impact of emission reductions on customer demand.

Within this comprehensive framework, the consumption rate is influenced by multiple factors, primarily the retail price of products and the customers' preference for low-carbon options. By considering these variables, the model seeks to understand how price adjustments and environmentally friendly practices can drive consumer behaviour towards more sustainable choices.

This approach involves detailed analysis and strategic planning to balance economic objectives with environmental goals. By integrating the impact of carbon emission reductions into the decision-making process, businesses can not only meet regulatory requirements and societal expectations but also tap into the growing market of environmentally conscious consumers. This dual focus on profitability and sustainability ensures that the model is robust, adaptable, and aligned with the long-term goals of reducing carbon footprints while maintaining competitive advantage.

To establish a sustainable model, our focus is on a collaborative approach between vendors and buyers, aligning with the critical trend of carbon emission control. This approach involves integrating the impact of emission reductions on customer demand. Within this framework, the consumption rate depends on both the retail price and the customer's preference for low-carbon options.

The primary goal of this investigation is to determine the most efficient strategies for production levels, shipping, and technology investments that minimize carbon emissions for all participants in the supply network. By doing so, we aim to reduce the total expenditure of the entire supply chain system.

Our model incorporates a variable production rate, which emphasizes flexibility in production volume to efficiently meet fluctuating demand. To illustrate the practical application of our model, we provide a detailed real-world example. This example demonstrates the resolution methodology in action and is supported by an in-depth impact analysis of key parameters. The analysis is presented visually to enhance understanding and provide clear insights into how different factors influence the model's performance. This comprehensive approach ensures that users can grasp the full potential and practical benefits of implementing the model in various scenarios.

This model has the potential for expansion into various domains, including considerations for reliability, operations in fuzzy environments, and allowances for shortages. By addressing these factors, the model can be adapted to a wide range of applications, ensuring its relevance and effectiveness in promoting sustainable practices across different industries.

References

Alfares HK (2007) Inventory model with stock-level dependent demand rate and variable holding cost. Int J Prod Econ 108(1–2):259–265

Aljazzar SM, Gurtu A, Jaber MY (2018) Delay-in-payments e a strategy to reduce carbon emissions from supply chains. J Clean Prod 170:636–644

Barman A, Das R, De Kanti P (2022) An analysis of optimal pricing strategy and inventory scheduling policy for a non-instantaneous deteriorating item in a two-layer supply chain. Appl Intell 52:4626–4650

Battini D, Persona A, Sgarbossa F (2014) A sustainable EOQ model: theoretical formulation and applications. Int J Prod Econ 149(1):145–153

Bharti D, Chaudhary A, Singh SR, Singhal S (2024) Green Supply chain management model on reliability and demand dependent on time with carbon tax. AIP Conf Proc 3081(1):090002-1–090002-12

Bouchery Y, Ghaffari A, Jemai Z, Tan T (2017) Impact of coordination on cost and carbon emissions for a two echelon serial economic order quantity problem. Eur J Oper Res 260(2):520–533

Chaudhary A, Singh SR, Bharti D, Singhal S (2022) An inventory model displayed stock and price dependent demand under non-instantaneous deterioration with inflation for partially backlogged shortages. Int J Invent Con Manag 11(1):35–57

Datta TK, Pal AK (1990) A note on an inventory model with inventory-level-dependent demand rate. J Oper Res Soc 41(10):971–975

Datta TK, Paul K, Pal AK (1998) Demand promotion by upgradation under stock-dependent demand situation a model. Int J Prod Econ 55(1):31–38

Datta TK, Paul K (2001) An inventory system with stock-dependent, price-sensitive demand Rate. Prod Plan Control 12(1):13–20

Dutta Choudhury K, Datta TK (2010) An inventory model with stock-dependent demand rate and dual storage facility. Assam Univ J Sci Technol 5(11):53–63

Gautam P, Maheshwari S, Hasan A, Kausar A, Jaggi CK (2022) Optimal inventory strategies for an imperfect production system with advertisement and price reliant demand under rework option for defectives. RAIRO Oper Res 56:183–197

Giri BC, Chaudhuari KS (1998) Deterministic models of perishable inventory with stock-dependent demand rate and nonlinear holding cost. Eur J Oper Res 105:467–474

Giri BC, Pal S, Goswami A, Chaudhuri KS (1996) An inventory model for deteriorating items with stock-dependent demand rate. Eur J Oper Res 95(3):604–610

Gupta R, Vrat P (1986) Inventory model for stock-dependent consumption rate. OPSEARCH 23(1):19–24

Ghovelaque V, Bironneau L (2015) The carbon-constrained EOQ model with carbon emission dependent demand. Int J Prod Econ 164(1):285–291

Hua GW, Cheng TCE, Zhang Y, Zhang JL, Wang SY (2016) Carbon-constrained perishable inventory management with freshness-dependent demand. Int J Simul Model 15(3):542–552

Jaber MY, Glock CH, El-Saadany AMA (2013) Supply chain coordination with emissions reduction incentives. Int J Prod Res 51(1):69–82

Lau AHL, Lau HS (1988) The Newsboy problem with price dependent demand distributions. IIE Trans 20:168–175

Levin RI, McLaughlin CP, Lamone RP, Kottas JF (1972) Production/operations management: contemporary policy for managing operating system, vol 373. McGraw-Hill, New York

Liang Y, Zhou F (2011) A two-warehouse inventory model for deteriorating items under conditionally permissible delay in payment. Appl Math Model 35:2221–2231

Maiti AK, Maiti MK, Maiti M (2009) Inventory model with stochastic lead time and price dependent demand incorporating advance payment. Appl Math 33:2433–2443

Mashud AHM, Roy D, Daryanto Y, Ali MH (2020) A sustainable inventory model with imperfect products, deterioration, and controllable emissions. Mathematics 8(2049):1–23

Ouyang LY, Hsieh TP, Dye CY, Chang HC (2003) An inventory model for deteriorating items with stock-dependent demand under the conditions of inflation and time-value of money. Eng Econ 48(1):52–68

Pal S, Goswami A, Chaudhuri KS (1993) A deterministic inventory model for deteriorating items with stock-dependent demand rate. Int J Prod Econ 32(3):291–299

Pan JL, Chiu CY, Wu KS, Yen HF, Wang YW (2020) Sustainable production-inventory model in technical cooperation on investment to reduce carbon emissions. Processes 8(1438):1–17

Shaikh AA, Mashud AHM, Uddin MS, Khan MAA (2017) Non-instantaneous deterioration inventory model with price and stock dependent demand for fully backlogged shortages under inflation. Int J Bus Forecast Market Intell 3(2):152–164

Silver EA, Peterson R (1985) Decision systems for inventory management and production planning, 2nd edn. Wiley, New York

Singh SR, Rastogi A, Singhal S (2021) JIT: the best approach after lockdown in country. Int J Serv Oper Inf 11(1):75–86

Singhal S, Rastogi A, Singh SR, Singh RB (2019) Preservation technology for sustainable fuzzified inventory model for a stock and price-dependent demand. Int J Invent Control Manage 8(1):01–15

Singhal S, Singh SR, Singh D (2014) A probability inventory model for Weibull deteriorating items with flexibility and reliability under the effect of inflation. Proceedings of 1st international science & technology congress. Elsevier, pp 504–514

Singhal S, Singh SR (2014) A production remanufacturing system for probabilistic decaying items with volume flexible environment. Proceedings of 3rd international conference on recent trends in engineering & technology (ICRTET'2014). Elsevier, pp 431–437

Singh SR, Singh RB, Rastogi A, Singhal S (2023) A sustainable approach to manage the inventory during pandemic through passive RFID tags. Novel developments in futuristic AI-based technologies, pp 37–46

Singhal S, Singh SR, Gupta PK (2010) Volume flexible supply chain system with uncertain lead time and stochastic deterioration. International Transaction in Mathematical Sciences and Computers 3(1):181–193

Singhal S, Vishnoi M (2021) Flexible production inventory model with time dependent holding cost and reliability process. Reliabil Theor Appl 16(2(64)):123–131

Singh SR, Vishnoi M (2013) Supply chain inventory model with price-dependent consumption rate with ameliorating and deteriorating items and two levels of storage. Int J Procurement Management 6(2):129–151

Sundarakani B, de Souza R, Goh M, Wagner SM, Manikandan S (2010) Modeling carbon footprints across the supply chain. Int J Prod Econ 128(1):43–50

Taleizadeh AA, Soleymanfar VR, Govindan K (2018) Sustainable economic production quantity models for inventory systems with shortages. J Clean Prod 174:1011–1020

Vishnoi M, Singh SR, Singhal S (2018) A supply chain inventory model with expiration date, variable holding cost in an inflationary environment. Int J Pure Appl Math 118(22):1353–1360

Wangsa ID (2017) Greenhouse gas penalty and incentive policies for a joint economic lot size model with industrial and transport emissions. Int J Industr Eng Comput 8(4):453–480

Wee HM (1999) Deteriorating inventory model with quantity discount, pricing and partial back ordering. Int J Prod Econ 59:511–518

Chapter 7
A Sustainable Production Inventory Model for Perishable Products Under the Markdown Approach and Carbon Emission Reduction Investments

Dharmesh K. Katariya and Kunal Tarunkumar Shukla

Abstract In the proposed chapter, we developed an environmentally conscious inventory model for a producer who produces and marketplaces fresh products using the markdown strategy. Products whose condition progressively deteriorates at a constant pace over time and products whose freshness quality deteriorates over time are two different types of product deterioration to take into account. The demand for a product is influenced by factors such as its selling price, level of freshness, and advertising campaigns. The markdown strategy was implemented to enhance demand and maximize profit by releasing stocks at the end of their useful lives. On other hand, the carbon emissions from industries due to different activities and controlling carbon emission is one of the parts of inventory management. The study aims to determine the optimal period for replenishment cycles, the optimal value for green investments, and the optimum markdown percentages that will maximize the producer's total profit. Three cases are discussed as, (i) producer's total profit under markdown approach, (ii) producer's total profit under markdown approach and carbon emissions from production set up, from production process, from deterioration of products and during holing inventory with carbon tax, and (iii) producer's total profit under markdown approach with carbon emissions and green investments. A mathematical formulation that represents real-world situations is validated through the use of numerical examples. To ascertain the reliability of the model, a sensitivity analysis of the parameters has been carried out. After presenting some noteworthy managerial findings, the chapter considers the future directions of this field of study.

Keywords Inventory · EPQ model · Freshness level · Carbon emission · Green investment · Deterioration · Markdown · Perishable products

---

D. K. Katariya (✉)
Shantilal Shah Engineering College, Bhavnagar, Gujarat 364060, India
e-mail: dkkatariya99@gmail.com

K. T. Shukla
Vishwakarma Government Engineering College, Ahmedabad, Gujarat 382424, India

N. H. Shah and M. Mittal (eds.), *Sustainable Inventory Management*, Inventory Optimization, https://doi.org/10.1007/978-981-97-6765-6_8

MSC 90B05

7.1 Introduction

Nowadays, people buy perishable goods like fruits, vegetables, meat, dairy products, various beverages, etc. based on factors including cost, freshness, and selling price of product. From the business activities the emissions of carbon; businesses such as manufacturers and retailers who are committed to becoming environmentally friendly have taken a variety of steps. Green marketing techniques will save costs, attract new clients, and protect the natural world. Green-packaged fruit juices and green-packaged plain drinking water are environmentally friendly drinks that lose some of their freshness over time. Eco-friendly technologies are used by the dairy and beverage industries to reduce their greenhouse gas emissions. For instance, they package their dairy and beverage products in environmentally friendly ways. They have also implemented a number of other initiatives, such as planting trees, using solar power, and electric vehicles to lessen the impact of carbon emissions. Customers like to buy things based on how fresh they are, so the degree of freshness, price of product and popularity of product have a big influence on demand. At the beginning of their shelf life, perishable goods might not be more susceptible to deterioration, and their freshness doesn't vary during this period. The quality of the item decline with time due to deterioration effect. To compensate for losses due to deterioration, the producer used a markdown strategy. In order to increase profits and get rid of inventory, manufacturers occasionally use the markdown policy for clearing at the end of the season or to sell off outdated goods during the product's life. Advertisement is one of the best ways to market a product extensively. Effectively planning and executing advertising campaigns might lead to unexpected rises in demand for the product. All of these variables are taken into consideration while designing a sustainable production inventory model for perishable goods, in which the selling price, freshness level, and advertising effort determine the demand rate.

7.1.1 Significance of the Study

A manufacturer uses a variety of business techniques to boost their earnings. The work we do revolves around dealing with the perishable goods that firm produce and trade. Key elements influencing consumer demand are the perishable product quality and rate of degradation. For perishable products, the deterioration effect is minimal in the beginning of its manufacturing time frame, and the product's quality does not decline as much throughout this time. That is, the product is absolutely in its natural state. The impact of deterioration begins when production ends. After a period of deterioration, policymakers implement a markdown schedule to increase demand since the effect of deterioration causes the product to gradually lose its freshness, which affects market demand. Product demand also depends on advertising strategy, and investment in advertisement increases demand. In the industry, carbon emission generated due to the set up process of production, manufacturing process, holding operations and deterioration process. Green investments are a way to promote environmental sustainability and reduce the negative effects of greenhouse gases on the environment. Considering all of these aspects, the selling price, the product's age (freshness), and advertising campaigns determine the demand for perishable products. The following are the major challenges associated with the suggested problem: (i) what is the optimal replenishment time, green investments, and percentage of markdown, so that the producer's net profit is optimized? (ii) At what point should production originate and finish? The markdown offer is applied when by the decision-maker. (iii) What impact does the quality of the product have on total profit? (iv) What impact does green investing have on the quantity of orders and revenue? (v) How does the markdown policy help? Before now, no literature integrated a markdown strategy with product freshness, green investment, and advertising activities. To maximize the profit of the producer within the EPQ framework, using marking down this study seeks to determine the optimal cycle length as well as the investment needed for greening and markdown percentage. This model is validated using a sensitivity assessment and a numerical illustration.

The remaining portion of the chapter follows this format. In Sect. 7.2, a review of the literature and an analysis of research gaps are presented. Section 7.3 describes the model's notations and underlying assumptions. Mathematical formulations and solution methodology are discussed in Sect. 7.4. Section 7.5 numerical examples and graphical representation of concavity for profit function. In Sect. 7.6, the sensitivity of the parameters is determined, along with some managerial insights. Lastly, conclusions are drawn and future study directions are indicated.

7.2 Literature Study

To accurately reflect product demand regarding freshness and selling price with an advertisement, we created a sustainable production quantity model for perishable products. Fujiwara and Perera (1993) conducted the initial research to examine how a product's freshness affects demand. Chen et al. (2016) investigated this idea in an EOQ model for fresh products, whereby demand affects the freshness expiry date and quantity of stock. Demand rate decline linearly due to product freshness is investigated by Dobson et al. (2017). Product quality base degradation in perishable product and physical deterioration of product and optimized the total profit with demand depends on product freshness in the study of Agi and Soni (2020). Recently, Katariya and Shukla (2023) developed an EPQ model for delay deterioration products whose demand depends on product freshness, selling price and greening level.

Manufacturers attempt to find a satisfactory equilibrium between the desire to maximize profits and the necessity to get clear of end-of-life stock along the life cycle. To maximize profit per unit of time, Urban and Baker (1997) examined the amount of a selling price discount that may be implemented during the deterioration period as well as the potential effects of a pre-deterioration markdown on unit profit. Wee and Widyadana (2007) constructed an inventory model with demand as a nonlinear function of selling price while considering a markdown strategy to increase the total revenue for deteriorating products. Srivastava and Gupta (2014) developed a production quantity model with selling price and time sensitive demand by applying markdown strategy to clear stock at end of inventory cycle and increase profit. Kamaruzaman and Omar (2020) established an inventory framework for a fresh product where demand is determined by its selling price, quantity of stock, freshness and expiry date in the setting of a markdown plan. A flawed production system that has declining products, price-dependent demand work in progress, and lead times in a markdown strategy were studied by Shee and Chakrabarti (2022) together an EPQ model.

Recently, producers and retailers have undertaken several initiatives to demonstrate their commitment to lowering carbon emissions brought on by their operations. Green investment and carbon tax policies adopted by industries are effective initiatives to reduce carbon emissions. According to Plambeck (2007), who reviewed Walmart's green programs, "being a good steward of the environment and being profitable are the same." Because of sustainability issues, one of the largest beverage manufacturers in the world, Coca-Cola, has begun to recycle and reprocess discarded bottles in developing nations like India through incentives. Bouchery et al. (2012) developed a sustainable inventory model with a carbon tax policy. Benjaafar et al. (2012) looked into the relationship between emission reductions and emissions costs. Swami and Shah (2013) suggested channel coordination in a supply chain with greening investments. An inventory model with various carbon reduction policies and green investment concepts was examined by Toptal et al. (2014). Shi et al. (2020) design an inventory model taking various payment system and carbon tax policy under product's expiration dates. To determine the highest profits from investing in green technology to reduce emissions under carbon tax policy, Lou et al. (2015) employed a couple of ecological inventory models. Bhattacharyya and Sana (2019) determined the impact of investing in green technologies on sustainable production techniques. The SEPQ model that has continuous demand and shortages as well as without shortages was invented by Mishra et al. (2020). They employed a carbon cap and tax mechanism in conjunction with green investment to reduce carbon emissions. Hasan et al. (2021) developed EOQ model with green investments and promotion dependent demand under carbon tax, cap-trade and carbon limit policy. Ji et al. (2022) conducted research on how a discounted rate of green credit financing incentivizes suppliers to enhance their efforts towards reducing carbon emissions. Mashud et al. (2021) developed a sustainable deteriorating inventory model with green investment and advance payment. Shah et al. (2022) made pricing decisions based on advertising and greening initiatives for the greengrocer. Jain et al. (2023) optimized the supply chain strategies included carbon emissions for deteriorating products.

Since the start of the inventory process, deterioration has been a major source of concern for companies. Deterioration was first conceptualized in relation to inventory systems by Ghare and Schrader (1963). Based on whether the deterioration is instantaneous or non-instantaneous, current research studies can be categorized into two distinct categories. Goyal and Giri (2001) examined numerous articles that examined declining inventory dating back to the turn of the twentieth century. The authors (Shah and Vaghela 2018) developed an Economic Production Quantity (EPQ) model for deteriorating products, considering price-dependent demand and two-level trade credit finance. The selling price of a product represents one of several crucial elements that decide its level of demand. Many studies have examined the effect of pricing on demand. Sundararajan et al. (2021) talked about an EOQ model that included pricing, time-dependent demand, backlogs, and non-instantaneous deteriorating products. Soni (2021) design an inventory model with price and freshness sensitive demand with a discount on product selling price. Shaikh et al. (2022) studied inventory system with product demand is price dependent quadratic form under the advance-cash-credit payment. Katariya and Shukla (2022) designed a sustainable production model, considering green investment and pricing sensitive demand.

One of the most effective methods for widely promoting a product is advertisement. Establishing and carrying out advertising campaigns well can result in unanticipated increases in product demand. Khan et al. (2020), Shah et al. (2021) and Udayakumar et al. (2021) provided a model with demand that is affected by advertisement and pricing of products, as well as the optimal pricing methods for various circumstances. Marketing or advertising contributes to an enhanced quantity of sales and higher profit margins as per the study of Shah et al. (2022). After examining the sustainable supply chain with advertising, Zeng et al. (2022) concluded that consumers are encouraged to purchase green products for a low-carbon supply chain by advertisement.

Research Gap and Our Contribution

A number of strategies that have been discussed in the subject of green inventory management have received a lot of attention in the previous literature. Price, advertisements, and product freshness all have an enormous effect on perishable demand for products. Demand for perishable commodities such as organic agricultural products, packaged beverages, and dairy products were influenced by advertising practices in addition to product quality and pricing. It has been noted that perishable commodities should be presumed to be 100% fresh during production and should not either quantitatively or qualitatively deteriorate more rapidly. As a result, demand at the beginning of the inventory cycle depends primarily on price and advertising activities because $g(t) \to 1$ and $\theta \to 0$. Products impacted by deterioration of both type and product value deteriorate frequently after production ends; during this time, demand patterns are determined by freshness, price, and advertisement based; as a result of freshness deterioration, a markdown strategy is implemented to increase demand following a period of product deterioration. Another novel idea introduced in this study is carbon emissions during cycle time and the green investing concept in the EPQ model with a freshness and markdown approach. By considering every aspect, the current study seeks to maximize the producer's total profit. These set the current study apart from analogous earlier research studies. In Table 7.1 (Source: Own), the key aspects of the research gap are addressed.

Table 7.1 Literatures related to proposed model and analysis of research gap (*Source* Own)

References	Demand modelling	Deterioration	Markdown approach	Carbon emissions	Green investments
Urban and Baker (1997)	PD, SD, TD	No	Yes	No	No
Wee and Widyadana (2007)	PD	Yes	Yes	No	No
Srivastava and Gupta (2014)	SP, TD	Yes	Yes	No	No
Lou et al. (2015)	PD	Yes	No	Yes	Yes
Chen et al. (2016)	FD, SD	No	No	No	No
Dobson et al. (2017)	FD	No	No	No	No
Mishra et al. (2020)	CD	Yes	No	Yes	Yes
Agi and Soni (2020)	PD, FD, SD	Yes	No	No	No
Kamaruzaman and Omar (2020)	PD, FD, SD	No	Yes	No	No
Khan et al. (2020)	PD, AD	Yes	No	No	No
Soni (2021)	PD, FD	Yes	No	No	No
Udayakumar et al. (2021)	PD, AD	Yes	No	No	No
Shah et al. (2022)	PD, AD, GE	Yes	No	No	Yes
Katariya and Shukla (2023)	PD, FD, GE	Yes	Yes	No	Yes
Proposed model	PD, FD, AD	Yes	Yes	Yes	Yes

Note *PD* Price dependent, *FD* Freshness dependent, *SD* Stock dependent, *TD* Time dependent, *CD* Constant demand, *AD* Advertisement dependent, *GE* Greening efforts

7.3 Notations and Assumptions

7.3.1 Notations

See Table 7.2.

Table 7.2 Notations for proposed model (*Source* Own)

Parameters	
A	Cost of set up per cycle (in \$/order)
h_c	Constant holding operations cost (\$/unit/unit time)
p	Original price of product (\$/unit)
m_r	The markdown rate is defined as the percentage decrease of the original price of a product
P	Production rate proportional to demand (unit/year)
κ	Production cost per unit per cycle (\$/unit)
δ	Production percentage
τ	Maximum life-time of the product beyond which no consumer will buy the product $0 < L \leq \tau$
θ	Rate of deterioration of product $0 < \theta < 1$
d_c	Deterioration cost (unit/year)
e_{sp}	Carbon emission due to set up production (in kg)
e_m	Carbon emission during manufacturing process (in kg)
e_{dp}	Carbon emission from deterioration of products (in kg)
e_h	Carbon emission from holding operations (in kg)
ρ	Carbon tax (in \$/kg)
ℓ_1	Production span (in years)
$\ell_1 + \ell_2$	Markdown offering from (in years)
ℓ_3	Markdown offered period (in years)
l	Proportional factor of production rate and demand, $l \geq 1$
A_d	Advertisement cost per cycle (in \$/unit)
Decision variables	
L	Replenishment cycle time; (in years); where $\ell_1 + \ell_2 + \ell_3 = L$
g	Green investment cost per cycle (in \$/unit)
v	Markdown percentage
Expressions and functions	
$\pi_1(L, v)$	Producer's total profit per cycle for Case 1 (in \$)
$\pi_2(L, v)$	Producer's total profit per cycle for Case 2 (in \$)
$\pi_3(L, g, v)$	Producer's total profit per cycle for Case 3 (in \$)
$R(p, t, A_d)$	Demand function at time t
$y_1(t)$	Inventory level at time t during $0 \leq t \leq \ell_1$
$y_2(t)$	Inventory level at time t during $0 \leq t \leq \ell_2$, 0 indicated inventory $y_2(t)$ initiated time after $t = \ell_1$
$y_3(t)$	Inventory level at time t during $0 \leq t \leq \ell_3$, 0 indicated inventory $y_3(t)$ initiated time after $t = \ell_1 + \ell_2$
Q_1	Inventory level (total production) at time ℓ_1 (units)
Q_2	Total quantity under markdown offered after time ℓ_2 (units). $Q_2 \leq Q_1$

7.3.2 Assumptions

- A single type of perishable goods is taken into account during cycle time.
- The production rate is proportional to market demand i.e. $P = l \cdot R(p, t, A_d),\ 0 \leq t \leq \ell_1$ and production stops at time ℓ_1. After a product unit has been produced, it must be sold.
- The production time is directly proportional to the cycle time, which is the same as $\ell_1 = \delta L$.
- After production is stopped, a product begins to deteriorate, and after a while, a markdown is offered. Products might deteriorate physically at a constant rate and they also deteriorate in terms of their freshness quality.
- Products that are deteriorated are unusable and cannot be repaired or replaced.
- Markdown pricing is applied only once during the inventory cycle.
- The markdown price is known, in advance.
- Numerous factors, such as the product's length of time in stock, heating rate, humidity, and storage, can affect how fresh it is. Acquiring the precise freshness rating of a product appears to be unattainable. Hence, we can infer that the freshness index starts at 1 at time 0 and progressively diminishes until it ultimately reaches 0 as the product approaches its expiration date (i.e., rendering it unsellable). The freshness level is defines as $g(t) = \frac{\tau - t}{\tau},\ 0 \leq t \leq \tau$.
- The product has a longer lifespan than the time it takes to replenish i.e. $L \leq \tau$.
- The set-up production system, the manufacturing process, the deterioration of the product, and holding operations are sources of carbon emissions considered.
- Investment in green technologies should be taken into consideration to lessen the impact of carbon emissions. The fraction of reduction of average emission is $f(g) = \xi(1 - e^{-\eta g})$; where, $0 < \xi < 1$ is the fraction of carbon emission after investing in green technology, $\eta > 0$ efficiency of greener technology in reducing emission and $g > 0$ is the green investment cost.
- The producer's greening effort requires a capital investment in greening efforts over a certain time frame rather than raising the unit price of the product. The producer uses green investments to produce or maintain organic or green products.
- The product demand rate is depending on selling price, freshness index, i.e. age of product as well as advertisement efforts. Demand rate function defined as, $R(p, t, A_\mathrm{d}) = \begin{cases} r(p) + \gamma A_d, & 0 \leq t \leq \ell_1 \\ r(p)g(t) + \gamma A_d, & 0 \leq t \leq \ell_2 \\ r(p_r)g(t) + \gamma A_d, & 0 \leq t \leq \ell_3 \end{cases}$ in this expression $r(p) = \alpha - \beta p$ and $r(p_\mathrm{r}) = \alpha - \beta p(1 - m_\mathrm{r})$, are any non-negative, continuous, convex decreasing functions of selling price, and $\alpha > 0$ represent the constant market demand, $\beta > 0$ is the price elasticity and $\gamma > 0$, $\ell_1 + \ell_2 + \ell_3 = L$.
- The lead time is zero and the replenishment rate infinite and shortages are not allowed.

7.4 Mathematical Modelling of Inventory System

Figure 7.1 (Source: Own) shows the behaviour of the inventory system based on the notations and hypotheses

From Fig. 7.1 (Source: Own), the stock level is zero at time $t = 0$. Production operations and supply of the fresh product begin simultaneously, and production stops at time $t = \ell_1$ at which highest inventory level Q_1 is accomplished. In the time interval $0 \leq t \leq \ell_1$, the physical and quality based deterioration of product is not affected and index of freshness for the product is $g(t) \to 1$, i.e. product is fully fresh. The stock during $0 \leq t \leq \ell_1$ can be written by the differential equation,

$$\frac{\mathrm{d}y_1(t)}{\mathrm{d}t} = P - (r(p) + \gamma A_\mathrm{d}) = (l - 1)(r(p) + \gamma A_\mathrm{d}), \quad 0 \leq t \leq \ell_1 \tag{7.1}$$

The initial condition $I_1(0) = 0$, the solution of Eq. (7.1) is,

$$y_1(t) = (l - 1)(r(p) + \gamma A_\mathrm{d})t \tag{7.2}$$

The stock level of fresh product at time $t = \ell_1$ is i.e. $y_1(\ell_1) = Q_1$;

$$Q_1 = (l - 1)(r(p) + \gamma A_\mathrm{d})\ell_1 \tag{7.3}$$

After time $t = \ell_1$, inventory level decline by the joint effect of demand and physical deterioration as well as freshness degradation of product. Level of inventory after $t = \ell_1$, during the period $0 \leq t \leq \ell_2$ is,

$$\frac{\mathrm{d}y_2(t)}{\mathrm{d}t} + \theta y_2(t) = -(r(p)g(t) + \gamma A_\mathrm{d}), \quad 0 \leq t \leq \ell_2 \tag{7.4}$$

In the condition $0 \leq t \leq \ell_2$, 0 is indicated inventory $y_2(t)$ initiated time after $t = \ell_1$, according to condition $y_2(0) = Q_1$, the solution of Eq. (7.4) is;

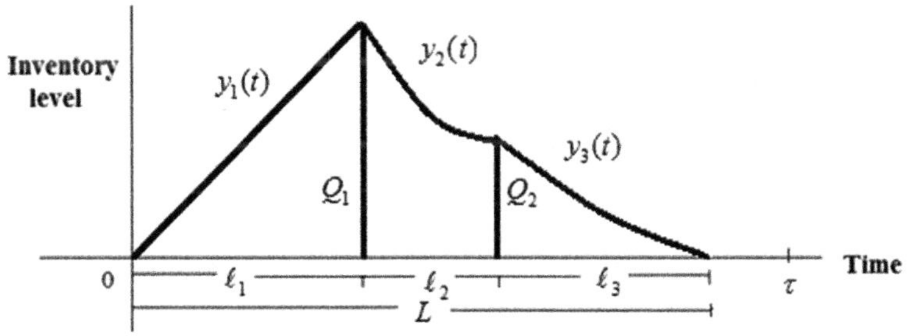

Fig. 7.1 Behaviour of inventory system with markdown approach (*Source* Own)

$$y_2(t) = Q_1 e^{-\theta t} + \left(e^{-\theta t} - 1\right)\left(\frac{\gamma A_d}{\theta} + \frac{r(p)}{\theta} + \frac{r(p)}{\tau\theta^2}\right) + \frac{r(p)t}{\tau\theta} \tag{7.5}$$

Likewise, during $0 \le t \le \ell_3$, stock level reduces due to joint effect of demand and deterioration. The demand is also decrease with time. Markdown strategy is applied during this span to increase the demand through depletion in the original selling price. The inventory level with markdown policy after $t = \ell_1 + \ell_2$ can be derive as,

$$\frac{dy_3(t)}{dt} + \theta y_3(t) = -(r(p_r)g(t) + \gamma A_d), \quad 0 \le t \le \ell_3 \tag{7.6}$$

In Eq. (7.6), $0 \le t \le \ell_3$, 0 indicated inventory $y_3(t)$ initiated time after $t = \ell_1 + \ell_2$. Finally, using boundary condition $y_3(0) = Q_2$, the solution of Eq. (7.6),

$$y_3(t) = Q_2 e^{-\theta t} + \left(e^{-\theta t} - 1\right)\left(\frac{\gamma A_d}{\theta} + \frac{r(p_r)}{\theta} + \frac{r(p_r)}{\tau\theta^2}\right) + \frac{r(p_r)t}{\tau\theta} \tag{7.7}$$

But $y_3(\ell_3) = 0$; the inventory level at $t = \ell_2$ is,

$$Q_2 = \left(e^{\theta\ell_3} - 1\right)\left(\frac{\gamma A_d}{\theta} + \frac{r(p_r)}{\theta} + \frac{r(p_r)}{\tau\theta^2}\right) - \frac{r(p_r)\ell_3}{\tau\theta} e^{\theta\ell_3} \tag{7.8}$$

Now, calculate the different inventory costs and sales revenue, to find the total profit of producer.

$$\text{Production fixed setup cost is,} \quad \text{SC} = \frac{A}{L} \tag{7.9}$$

Production cost per unit time is,

$$P_c = \frac{\kappa}{L}\int_0^{\ell_1} l \cdot (r(p) + \gamma A_d)dt \tag{7.10}$$

The cost incurred for storing inventory over a specific period of time is referred to as the holding cost per unit time,

$$H_c = \frac{h_c}{L}\left[\int_0^{\ell_1} y_1(t)dt + \int_0^{\ell_2} y_2(t)dt + \int_0^{\ell_3} y_3(t)dt\right] \tag{7.11}$$

Deterioration cost per cycle time be,

$$D_c = \frac{d_c}{L}\left[\left(Q_1 - \int_0^{\ell_2} y_2(t)dt\right) + \left(Q_2 - \int_0^{\ell_3} y_3(t)dt\right)\right] \tag{7.12}$$

The revenue before markdown and the revenue after markdown are combined to form the total revenue. Hence, the total sales revenue generated by each cycle is given as,

$$T_{\mathrm{SR}} = \frac{p}{L}\left(\int\limits_0^{\ell_1} (r(p) + \gamma A_{\mathrm{d}})\mathrm{d}t + \int\limits_0^{\ell_2} (r(p)g(t) + \gamma A_{\mathrm{d}})\mathrm{d}t\right) + \frac{p(1-m_{\mathrm{r}})}{L}\int\limits_0^{\ell_3} (r(p_{\mathrm{r}})g(t) + \gamma A_{\mathrm{d}}))\mathrm{d}t \quad (7.13)$$

Carbon emissions resulting from industrial and commercial activities play a crucial role in inventory management. Implementing a carbon tax policy and increasing green investment are effective measures to mitigate the negative effects of carbon emissions.

The carbon emissions due to setup production is

$$E_{\mathrm{sp}} = \frac{e_{\mathrm{sp}}}{L} \quad (7.14)$$

The carbon emissions from manufacturing process is,

$$E_{\mathrm{m}} = \frac{e_{\mathrm{m}}}{L}\left(\int\limits_0^{\ell_1} l \cdot (r(p) + \gamma A_{\mathrm{d}})\mathrm{d}t\right). \quad (7.15)$$

The carbon emissions due to deterioration of products per cycle time is,

$$E_{\mathrm{dp}} = \frac{e_{\mathrm{dp}}}{L}\left[\left(Q_1 - \int\limits_0^{\ell_2} y_2(t)\mathrm{d}t\right) + \left(Q_2 - \int\limits_0^{\ell_3} y_3(t)\mathrm{d}t\right)\right] \quad (7.16)$$

The carbon emission due to holding operations is,

$$E_{\mathrm{h}} = \frac{e_{\mathrm{h}}}{L}\left[\int\limits_0^{\ell_1} y_1(t)\mathrm{d}t + \int\limits_0^{\ell_2} y_2(t)\mathrm{d}t + \int\limits_0^{\ell_3} y_3(t)\mathrm{d}t\right] \quad (7.17)$$

Total carbon emissions as per Eqs. (7.14)–(7.17) is,

$$\widehat{C} = E_{\mathrm{sp}} + E_{\mathrm{m}} + E_{\mathrm{dp}} + E_{\mathrm{h}} \quad (7.18)$$

The carbon reduction fraction is determined based on the study conducted by Lou et al. (2015). It represents the proportion of carbon emissions that are reduced after implementing green technology investments is,

$$\widehat{C}_g = \widehat{C}(1 - f(g)) = \widehat{C}(1 - \xi(1 - e^{-\eta g})) \tag{7.19}$$

Producer's total profit under carbon tax and green investment can be deduced as,

$$\pi(\ell_1, \ell_2, \ell_3, g, v) = T_{SR} - (S_c + P_c + H_c + D_c + \rho\widehat{C}_g) \tag{7.20}$$

$$\begin{aligned}
&\pi(\ell_1, \ell_2, \ell_3, g, v) \\
&= \frac{p}{L}\left(\int_0^{\ell_1} (r(p) + \gamma A_d)dt + \int_0^{\ell_2} (r(p)g(t) + \gamma A_d)dt\right) \\
&+ \frac{p(1 - m_r)}{L}\int_0^{\ell_3} (r(p_r)g(t) + \gamma A_d))dt \\
&- \left(\begin{aligned}
&\frac{A}{L} + \frac{\kappa}{L}\int_0^{\ell_1} l \cdot (r(p) + \gamma A_d)dt \\
&+ \frac{h_c}{L}\left[\int_0^{\ell_1} y_1(t)dt + \int_0^{\ell_2} y_2(t)dt + \int_0^{\ell_3} y_3(t)dt\right] \\
&+ \frac{d_c}{L}\left[\left(Q_1 - \int_0^{\ell_2} y_2(t)dt\right) + \left(Q_2 - \int_0^{\ell_3} y_3(t)dt\right)\right] \\
&+ \rho\left[\frac{e_m}{L}\left(\int_0^{\ell_1} l \cdot (r(p) + \gamma A_d)dt\right)\right. \\
&+ \frac{e_{dp}}{L}\left[\left(Q_1 - \int_0^{\ell_2} y_2(t)dt\right) + \left(Q_2 - \int_0^{\ell_3} y_3(t)dt\right)\right] \\
&\frac{e_h}{L}\left[\int_0^{\ell_1} y_1(t)dt + \int_0^{\ell_2} y_2(t)dt + \int_0^{\ell_3} y_3(t)dt\right] \\
&\left. + \frac{e_{sp}}{L}\right](1 - \xi(1 - e^{-\eta g}))
\end{aligned}\right)
\end{aligned}$$

The Eq. (7.20) is the form of ℓ_1, ℓ_2 and ℓ_3, using the relations of ℓ_1, ℓ_2 and ℓ_3 with δ, v and L defined by Srivastava and Gupta (2014) are $\ell_1 = \delta L$, $\ell_2 = v(L - \ell_1) = v(1 - \delta)L$ and $\ell_3 = L - (\ell_1 + \ell_2) = (1 - \delta)(1 - v)L$.

After substitute the relations defined above, the new form of total profit function of L, g, v as below in Case 1, Case 2 and Case 3.We discuss three cases regarding carbon tax and green investments.

Case 1 If carbon tax $\rho = 0$ and green investment $g = 0$.

Producer's total profit from Eq. (7.20) in form of L, g, v for without considering carbon emissions, carbon tax and green investment is,

$$\pi_1(L, v) = T_{\mathrm{SR}} - (S_{\mathrm{c}} + P_{\mathrm{c}} + H_{\mathrm{c}} + D_{\mathrm{c}}) \tag{7.21}$$

Case 2 If carbon tax $\rho \neq 0$ and green investment $g = 0$.

Producer's total profit from Eq. (7.20) in form of L, g, v for considering carbon emissions, carbon tax and without invest in green technology is,

$$\pi_2(L, v) = T_{\mathrm{SR}} - (S_{\mathrm{c}} + P_{\mathrm{c}} + H_{\mathrm{c}} + D_{\mathrm{c}} + \rho\widehat{C}) \tag{7.22}$$

Case 3 If carbon tax $\rho \neq 0$ and green investment $g \neq 0$.

Producer's total profit from Eq. (7.20) in form of L, g, v for considering carbon emissions, carbon tax and invest in green technology is,

$$\pi_3(L, g, v) = T_{SR} - (S_c + P_c + H_c + D_c + \rho\widehat{C}_g) \tag{7.23}$$

Equations (7.21), (7.22), and (7.23) exhibit a high degree of nonlinearity, making direct solution challenging. To overcome this, we employed the following solution procedure to determine the values of decision variables and the total profit of the producer.

7.4.1 Solution Procedures to Find the Optimal Solution and Concavity for Case 1 and Case 2

In this section, for **Case 1** and **Case 2**, we determine the optimal value of decision variables L^*, v^* which maximize the total profit $\pi_i(L^*, v^*)$, $i = 1, 2$ per cycle. The necessary conditions for maximize of the total profit function given by (8.21) and (8.22) are,

$$\frac{\partial \pi_i}{\partial L} = 0, i = 1, 2 \tag{7.24}$$

$$\frac{\partial \pi_i}{\partial v} = 0, i = 1, 2 \tag{7.25}$$

The sufficient conditions for profit function $\pi_i(L^*, v^*)$,$i = 1, 2$ to be maximize are,

$$\begin{gathered}\frac{\partial^2 \pi_i(L^*, v^*)}{\partial L^2} < 0, \quad \frac{\partial^2 \pi_i(L^*, v^*)}{\partial v^2} < 0 \text{ and} \\ \frac{\partial^2 \pi_i(L^*, v^*)}{\partial L^2}\frac{\partial^2 \pi_i(L^*, v^*)}{\partial v^2} - \left(\frac{\partial^2 \pi_i(L^*, v^*)}{\partial L \partial v}\right)^2 > 0\end{gathered} \tag{7.26}$$

To achieve an optimal solution for decision variables and the optimal profit function, follow the steps outlined below:

Step 1: First assigned parameters value with proper unit other than decision variables in Eqs. (7.21) and (7.22).
Step 2: Using mathematical software like Maple 18 or mathematica, solve Eq. (7.24) and (7.25) simultaneously and find to find T^* and v^*.
Step 3: Verify the sufficient conditions stated in Eq. (7.26) at T^* and v^* obtained in Step-2, if not satisfied go to step 1 and choose other value of parameters in step 1, repeat process till Eq. (7.26) satisfied.
Step 4: From Eqs. (7.21) and (7.22), find total profit $\pi_1(L^*, v^*)$ and $\pi_2(L^*, v^*)$ respectively.
Step 5: From Eqs. (7.3) and (7.8), find Q_1^* and Q_2^* value.
Step 6: Using Eq. (7.18), find total carbon emission for Case 2.
Step 7: Stop.

7.4.2 Solution Procedures to Find the Optimal Solution and Concavity for Case 3

To find optimal value of L,g and v for Case 3 and to prove the concavity of Eq. (7.23) with respected to L, g and v, the following methodology to be adopted.

Step 1: Assigned value of parameters with proper unit in Eq. (7.23).
Step 2: At initial stage, to set $g = 0$.
Step 3: Evaluate L and v from $\frac{\partial \pi_3}{\partial L} = 0$ and $\frac{\partial \pi_3}{\partial v} = 0$ by solving simultaneously.
Step 4: Verify the sufficient conditions $\frac{\partial^2 \pi_3}{\partial L^2} < 0$, $\frac{\partial^2 \pi_3}{\partial v^2} < 0$ and $\frac{\partial^2 \pi_3}{\partial L^2}\frac{\partial^2 \pi_3}{\partial v^2} - \left(\frac{\partial^2 \pi_3}{\partial L \partial v}\right)^2 > 0$ at value of L and v obtained in Step 3. If not satisfied, choose different parametric value in Step 1.
Step 5: Increase the value of g from 0 and repeat Step 3 and Step 4 until to get maximum value of $\pi_3(L, g, v)$.
Step 6: Evaluate total carbon emission from Eq. (7.19), from Eqs. (7.3) and (7.8), find Q_1^* and Q_2^* value.

Step 7: Obtain manufacturer's total profit using Eq. (7.23).
Step 8: Stop.

7.5 Numerical Analysis

To illustrate the result of the model that was proposed to demonstrate the payoff of the proposed model, the following parameter values are employed for numerical demonstrations.

Example 8.1 For a Case 1, consider a inventory system under markdown approaches, where $\alpha = 450$ units, $\beta = 3.3$, $\gamma = 0.5$, $l = 2$, $A = \$200$/setup, $d_c = \$10$/unit, $h_c = \$3$/unit, $\kappa = \$2$/unit, $\delta = 0.4$, $m_r = 5\%$, $\tau = \frac{180}{365}$ year, $p = \$100$/unit, $\lambda = 5$, $\theta = 0.08$, $A_d = \$2$/unit. As per the solution process described in Sect. 4.1 and for $i = 1$, the optimal results are found (Table 7.3).

Further, the optimal production duration $\ell_1^* = 0.1144$ year, markdown policy offered from $\ell_1^* + \ell_2^* = 0.2045$ year and markdown period $\ell_3^* = 0.0814$ year.

The sufficient conditions for $\frac{\partial^2 \pi_1(L^*, v^*)}{\partial L^2} = -17280 < 0$, $\frac{\partial^2 \pi_1(L^*, v^*)}{\partial v^2} = -5466.91 < 0$ and $\frac{\partial^2 \pi_1(L^*, v^*)}{\partial L^2} \frac{\partial^2 \pi_1(L^*, v^*)}{\partial v^2} - \left(\frac{\partial^2 \pi_1(L^*, v^*)}{\partial L \partial v}\right)^2 = 9.4177 \times 10^7 > 0$ satisfied for the total profit function $\pi_1(L^*, v^*)$ is maximize.

Example 8.2 For a Case 2, consider a inventory system under markdown approaches with carbon emission and carbon tax, in addition to those parameters in Example 7.1, we assume $e_{\text{sp}} = 0.6$ kg, $e_{\text{m}} = 0.44$ kg, $e_{\text{dp}} = 0.3$ kg, $e_{\text{h}} = 0.33$ kg and carbon tax per cycle $\rho = \$5$/kg. As per the solution process described in Sect. 4.1 and for $i = 2$, the optimal results are found (Table 7.4).

The optimal production span $\ell_1^* = 0.1136$ year, markdown policy offered from $\ell_1^* + \ell_2^* = 0.2061$ year and markdown offering duration $\ell_3^* = 0.0778$ year.

The sufficient conditions for $\frac{\partial^2 \pi_2(L^*, v^*)}{\partial L^2} = -17905.5 < 0$, $\frac{\partial^2 \pi_2(L^*, v^*)}{\partial v^2} = -5467.95 < 0$ and $\frac{\partial^2 \pi_2(L^*, v^*)}{\partial L^2} \frac{\partial^2 \pi_2(L^*, v^*)}{\partial v^2} - \left(\frac{\partial^2 \pi_2(L^*, v^*)}{\partial L \partial v}\right)^2 = 9.7031 \times 10^7 > 0$ satisfied for the total profit function $\pi_2(L^*, v^*)$ is maximize.

Table 7.3 Output optimal results for Case 1 (*Source* Own)

L^* (year)	v^* (%)	(in $)	Q_1^* (units)	Q_2^* (units)
0.2859	0.5254	10,664.42	14	10

Table 7.4 Output optimal results for Case 2 (*Source* Own)

L^*(year)	v^*(%)	$\pi_1(L^*, v^*)$(in $)	$\overset{\frown}{C}{}^*$ (in kg)	Q_1^*(units)	Q_2^*(units)
0.2839	0.5430	10,409.66	50.78	14	10

Example 8.3 In a Case 3, consider an inventory system that uses markdown methods using carbon emissions carbon tax, carbon emission and green investments. In addition to the parameters mentioned from Examples 7.1 and 7.2. We take into account the carbon emissions that are generated after investing in green technology $\xi = 0.2$ and the efficiency of green technology in reducing emissions $\eta = 0.8$.

According to the solution procedures mentioned in Sect. 4.2, the results obtained (Table 7.5).

The optimal production period $\ell_1^* = 0.1137$ year, markdown policy offered from $\ell_1^* + \ell_2^* = 0.2058$ year and markdown offering period $\ell_3^* = 0.0778$ year. At the optimal value of decision variables $L^* = 0.284331$ year, $g^* = \$4.64$ and $v^* = 0.539597$, the sufficient conditions $\frac{\partial^2 \pi_3(L^*, g^*, v^*)}{\partial L^2} = -17776.30 < 0, \frac{\partial^2 \pi_3(L^*, g^*, v^*)}{\partial v^2} = -5468.26 < 0$ and $\frac{\partial^2 \pi_3}{\partial L^2} \cdot \frac{\partial^2 \pi_3}{\partial v^2} - \left(\frac{\partial^2 \pi_3}{\partial L \partial v}\right)^2 = 9.6469 \times 10^7 > 0$.

The concave nature of the total profit function $\pi_1(L, v)$ is illustrated through two-dimensional graphs in Fig. 7.2 (Source: Own) and Fig. 7.3 (Source: Own).

The concavity nature of total profit function $\pi_2(L, v)$ is demonstrated as two dimensional graphs in Fig. 7.4 (Source: Own) and Fig. 7.5 (Source: Own).

The concavity of total profit function $\pi_3(L, g, v)$ is demonstrated as three dimensional graphs in Fig. 7.6 (Source: Own), Fig. 7.7 (Source: Own) and Fig. 7.8 (Source: Own).

Table 7.5 Output results for Case 3 (*Source* Own)

g^*	L^*	v^*	$\pi_3(L^*, g^*, v^*)$	$\widehat{C}_g^*$	Q_1^*	Q_2^*
0	0.283917	0.543047	10,409.66	50.7803	14	10
1	0.284152	0.541099	10,436.63	45.22129	14	10
2	0.284256	0.540224	10,448.2	42.72135	14	10
3	0.284303	0.539831	10,452.86	41.59696	14	10
4	0.284324	0.539654	10,454.40	41.09197	14	10
4.64 ←	**0.284331** ←	**0.539597** ←	**10,454.59** ←	**40.92768** ←	**14** ←	**10** ←
5	0.284333	0.539575	10,454.53	40.86498	14	10
6	0.284337	0.539539	10,454.05	40.76249	14	10
7	0.284339	0.539523	10,453.28	40.71681	14	10

← The most advantageous solution; the bold value signifies the best possible outcomes

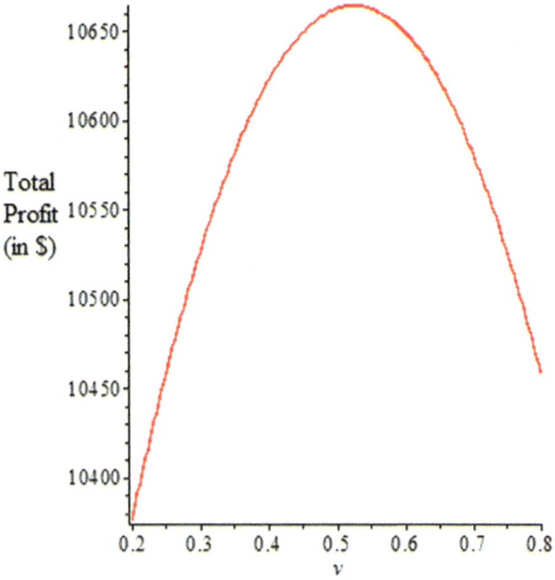

Fig. 7.2 Concavity of $\pi_1(L, v)$ with respect to markdown percentage (*Source* Own)

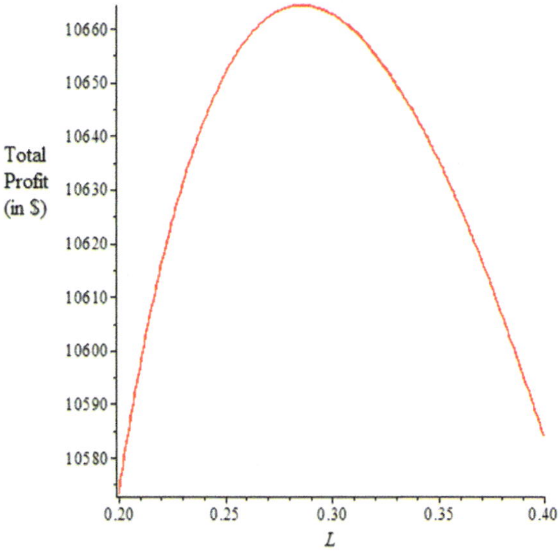

Fig. 7.3 Concavity of $\pi_1(L, v)$ with respect to cycle time (*Source* Own)

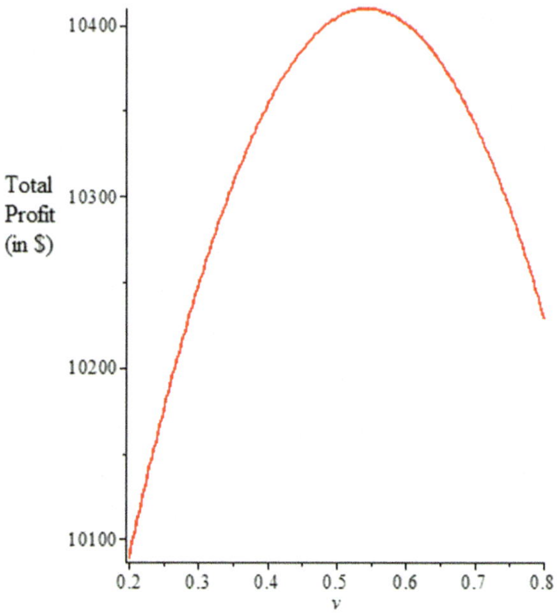

Fig. 7.4 Concavity of $\pi_2(L, v)$ with respect to markdown percentage (*Source* Own)

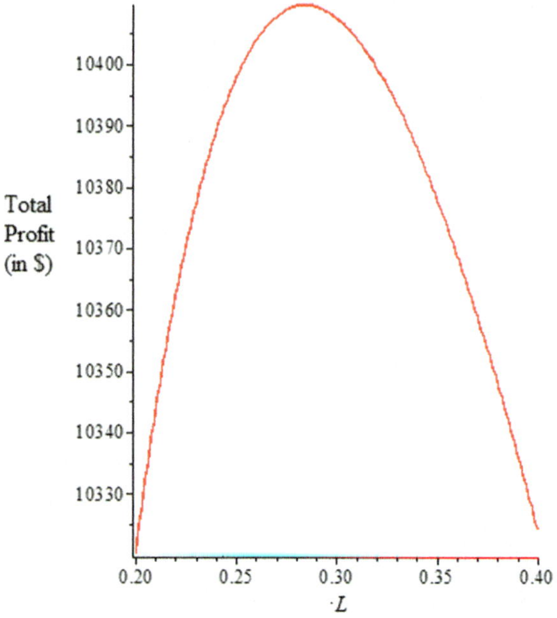

Fig. 7.5 Concavity of $\pi_2(L, v)$ with respect to cycle time (*Source* Own)

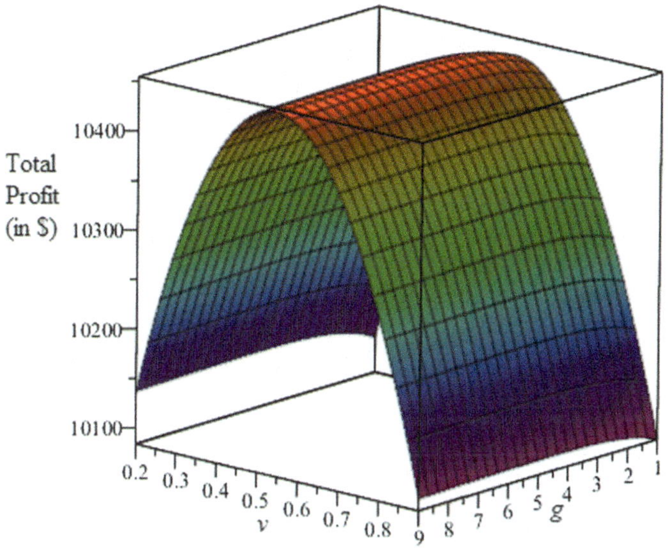

Fig. 7.6 Concavity of $\pi_3(L, g, v)$ with respect to markdown percentage and green investment (*Source* Own)

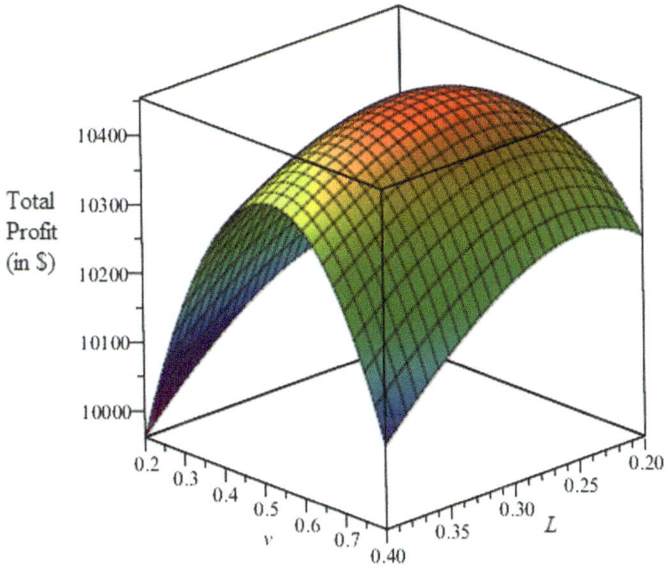

Fig. 7.7 Concavity of $\pi_3(L, g, v)$ with respect to markdown percentage and cycle time (*Source* Own)

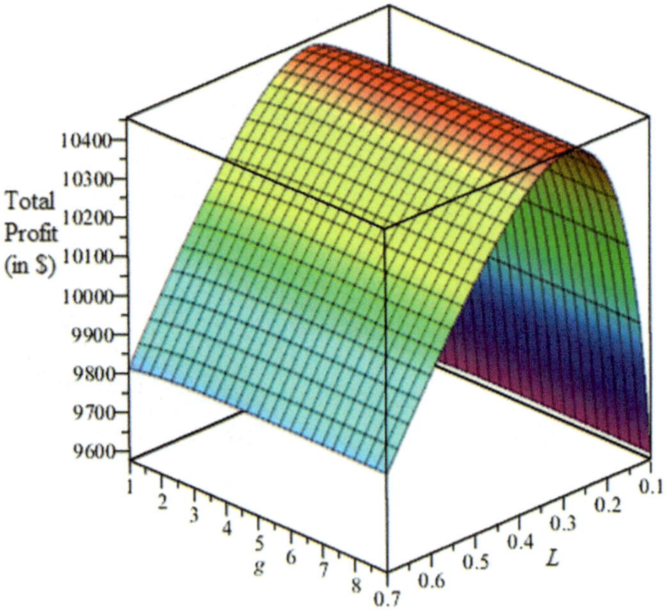

Fig. 7.8 Concavity of $\pi_3(L, g, v)$ with respect to green investment and cycle time (*Source* Own)

7.6 Sensitivity Analyses and Discussion

A sensitivity analysis is used in this section for the Case 3 to show the effects of key parameters on total profit, carbon emission, and decision variables, which are varies sequentially from − 20% to + 20% while leaving the remaining parameters unchanged.

- **Impact of demand related parameters α, price elasticity factor β, and advertisement scale γ:**

It is observed from Table 7.6 (Source: Own) the constant demand increases from − 20% to + 20% resulted profit highly increases, on other side cycle time L^* and production time t_3^* decreases. Total carbon emission increases, green investment cost, markdown percentage will be increases if increases in constant demand. There is a positive impact on production quantity and markdown quantity of constant demand.

According to Table 7.7 (Source: Own) the higher value of β indicated the, increases markdown period and profit of producer's is negative related to β. Replenishment cycle will be increases with β but green investment cost, markdown percentage decreases, production quantity and markdown quantity decreases slightly.

Table 7.8 (Source: Own), indicated that γ increases by − 20% to − 20% then total profit increases slightly. Q_1^* and Q_2^* also increases slightly with increases γ. Total cycle time and markdown offer period and total cycle time with total cycle

Table 7.6 Sensitivity impact of α (*Source* Own)

α	L^*	g^*	v^*	π_3^*	$\widehat{C}_g^*$	Q_1^*	Q_2^*	t_3^*
360	0.4842	3.13	0.3401	2647.03	12.52	6.00	7.43	0.1917
405	0.3537	4.12	0.4680	6486.86	27.19	10.75	9.30	0.1129
450	0.2843	4.63	0.5396	10,454.59	40.93	13.76	9.98	0.0785
495	0.2400	4.98	0.5960	14,491.11	53.96	15.94	10.02	0.0582
540	0.2082	5.24	0.6460	18,574.85	66.38	17.57	9.63	0.0442

Table 7.7 Sensitivity impact of β (*Source* Own)

β	L^*	g^*	v^*	π_3^*	$\widehat{C}_g^*$	Q_1^*	Q_2^*	t_3^*
2.64	0.2211	5.09	0.6479	16,278.64	69.08	16.54	10.18	0.0536
2.97	0.2493	4.89	0.5958	13,373.28	50.27	15.36	9.61	0.0605
3.3	0.2843	4.63	0.5396	10,454.59	40.93	13.76	9.98	0.0785
3.63	0.3295	4.29	0.4738	7579.68	31.11	11.60	9.93	0.1240
3.96	0.3892	3.78	0.3819	4767.76	20.78	8.56	9.29	0.1444

time reduces as γ increases. Green investment cost almost remains unchanged due to change in γ.

- **Impact of markdown rate** m_r**:**

From Table 7.9 (Source: Own), observed that, total profit increases 1% to 2% if increase the markdown rate by − 20% to + 20% and markdown percentage and production quantity reduces decreases slightly. Markdown period t_3^* slightly increases with number of markdown quantities increases.

- **Impact of production percentage** δ**:**

Table 7.10 (Source: Own) shown that, production quantity, cycle time and green investment cost is increases with increases the production percentage δ. Total profit and markdown offering quantity decreases with increase in δ.

Table 7.8 Sensitivity impact of γ (*Source* Own)

γ	L^*	g^*	v^*	π_3^*	$\widehat{C}_g^*$	Q_1^*	Q_2^*	t_3^*
0.4	0.2844	4.63	0.5392	10,435.69	40.87	13.74	9.97	0.0786
0.45	0.2843	4.63	0.5394	10,445.14	40.90	13.75	9.97	0.0786
0.5	0.2843	4.63	0.5396	10,454.59	40.93	13.76	9.98	0.0785
0.55	0.2843	4.63	0.5398	10,464.04	40.96	13.77	9.98	0.0785
0.6	0.2843	4.63	0.5400	10,473.49	40.99	13.78	9.98	0.0785

Table 7.9 Sensitivity impact of m_r (*Source* Own)

m_r	L^*	g^*	v^*	π_3^*	$\widehat{C}_g^*$	Q_1^*	Q_2^*	t_3^*
0.04	0.2841	4.62	0.5562	10,409.94	40.67	13.75	9.41	0.0757
0.045	0.2843	4.63	0.5478	10,432.30	40.80	13.76	9.69	0.0771
0.05	0.2843	4.63	0.5396	10,454.59	40.93	13.76	9.98	0.0785
0.055	0.2843	4.64	0.5317	10,476.84	41.05	13.76	10.25	0.0799
0.06	0.2844	4.65	0.5234	10,458.99	40.15	13.76	10.53	0.0812

Table 7.10 Sensitivity impact of τ (*Source* Own)

δ	L^*	g^*	v^*	π_3^*	$\widehat{C}_g^*$	Q_1^*	Q_2^*	t_3^*
0.32	0.2529	4.25	0.5412	10,551.59	30.29	9.79	10.02	0.0789
0.36	0.2677	4.46	0.5404	10,503.34	35.60	11.66	10.00	0.0787
0.4	0.2843	4.63	0.5396	10,454.59	40.93	13.76	9.98	0.0785
0.44	0.3030	4.79	0.5387	10,405.24	46.30	16.13	9.95	0.0783
0.48	0.3241	4.93	0.5376	10,355.15	51.70	18.82	9.90	0.0779

- **Impact of maximum product life time** τ:

  Table 7.11 (Source: Own) depicted that producers profit increases if we increase the life of product. The production quantity and markdown offering quantity increases with increases the life of product. Green investment cost decreases and carbon emission increases with increases in $\tau_.$

- **Effect of cost parameters** A, A_d, κ, h_c, d_c:

  As per the Table 7.12 (Source: Own) and Table 7.13 (Source: Own), observed that the total profit slightly decreases with cost parameters A decreases but increases advertisement cost then total profit moves upward. The cycle time L^* and green investment cost increases slightly with increases in A and A_d. Production quantity and markdown offering quantity increases corresponding to cost parameters A, A_d, κ, h_c, d_c. If the increases in κ, h_c, d_c then total profit of producer's decreases.

Table 7.11 Sensitivity impact of τ (*Source* Own)

τ	L^*	g^*	v^*	π_3^*	$\widehat{C}_g^*$	Q_1^*	Q_2^*	t_3^*
0.3945	0.2556	4.64	0.5340	10,291.85	41.12	12.37	8.97	0.0715
0.4438	0.2704	4.63	0.5368	10,380.08	41.02	13.09	9.49	0.0752
0.4932	0.2843	4.63	0.5396	10,454.59	40.93	13.76	9.98	0.0785
0.5425	0.2974	4.63	0.5423	10,518.59	40.86	14.40	10.43	0.0817
0.5918	0.3099	4.63	0.5448	10,574.33	40.79	15.00	10.85	0.0846

Table 7.12 Sensitivity impact of A (*Source* Own)

A	L^*	g^*	v^*	π_3^*	$\widehat{C}_g^*$	Q_1^*	Q_2^*	t_3^*
160	0.2548	4.63	0.5448	10,602.99	40.77	12.33	8.92	0.0696
180	0.2699	4.63	0.5420	10,526.76	40.84	13.07	9.47	0.0742
200	0.2843	4.63	0.5396	10,454.59	40.93	13.76	9.98	0.0785
220	0.2980	4.63	0.5375	10,385.9	41.01	14.42	10.46	0.0827
240	0.3111	4.64	0.5357	10,320.24	41.09	15.06	10.91	0.0867

Table 7.13 Sensitivity impact of A_d (*Source* Own)

A_d	L^*	g^*	v^*	π_3^*	$\widehat{C}_g^*$	Q_1^*	Q_2^*	t_3^*
1.6	0.2841	4.6303	0.5393	10,437.09	40.87	13.7266	9.96	0.0785
1.8	0.2842	4.6312	0.5394	10,445.85	40.90	13.7441	9.97	0.0785
2	0.2843	4.6321	0.5396	10,454.59	40.93	13.7616	9.98	0.0785
2.2	0.2845	4.6330	0.5398	10,463.34	40.96	13.7791	9.99	0.0786
2.4	0.2846	4.6339	0.5399	10,472.08	40.99	13.7966	9.99	0.0786

Effect of Carbon Emission and Green Investments Parameters

Noticed from Fig. 7.9 (Source: Own), the total profit of producer decreases due to the high value e_m, e_{dp}, e_h and e_{sp}. Higher carbon tax resulted to lower profit, on other side higher value of ξ and η have a positive impact on total profit of producer. Figure 7.10 (Source: Own) indicated that total carbon emission highly increases with increases in e_m, e_{dp}, e_h and e_{sp} but emission reduction parameters ξ, η and carbon tax ρ increases then total carbon emission highly decreases.

As per Fig. 7.11 (Source: Own) cycle time decreases due to the increases nature of e_m, e_{dp}, e_h,e_{sp} and ρ but cycle time increase with the improve the value of parameters ξ and η. Green investment cost and carbon tax are positive proportional. If the η increases then green investment cost highly decreases as per Fig. 7.12 (Source: Own).

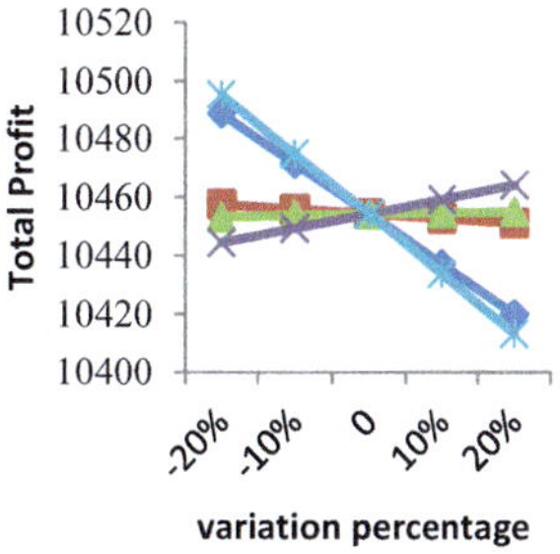

Fig. 7.9 Sensitivity of total profit with respect to change in carbon emission related parameters (*Source* Own)

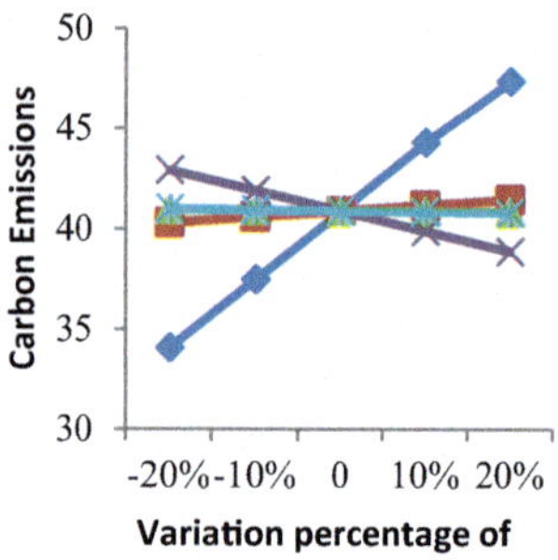

Fig. 7.10 Sensitivity of total carbon emissions with respect to change in carbon emission related parameters (*Source* Own)

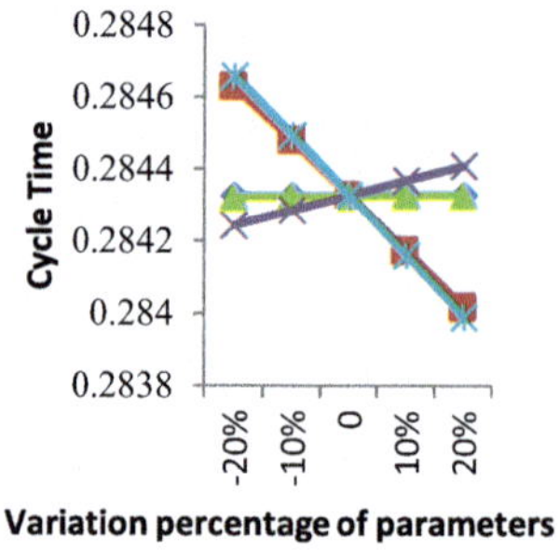

Fig. 7.11 Sensitivity of cycle time with respect to change in carbon emission related parameters (*Source* Own)

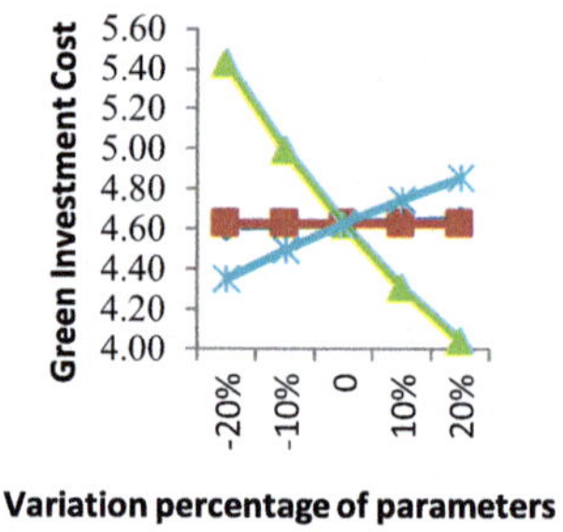

Fig. 7.12 Sensitivity of green investment cost with respect to change in carbon emission related parameters (*Source* Own)

7.6.1 Results and Managerial Insights

The managerial insights that follow are summarized based on the mathematical and sensitivity analysis shown above:

- The optimal value of cycle time is useful to the producer for deciding when to initiate production and end production, when to apply the markdown policy, and how much time to markdown.
- The optimal value of production quantity of fresh product; and optimal product quantity with markdown offered, indicates to the producer how much quantity should be produce and replenish per cycle such that profit is maximized.

- Profit increases with a larger markdown rate. To increase profit, a producer ought to accept a higher markdown rate. Markdown approaches helps to clear the stock at end of inventory cycle.
- The producer should maintain scale demand by advertising efforts for the product, higher value of scale demand gives a higher profit with the minimum cycle time and maximum product quantity.
- Product freshness is the key determinant of market demand; our investigation revealed that if a product has a longer shelf life, the producer will make more revenue by selling more of it.
- Deterioration has no effect at the beginning life of the product; its degree of freshness is determined by how quickly it deteriorates. When there is a longer non-deterioration time (i.e. the markdown offered late), the products are fresher. Thus, the producer makes more profit from a product with a longer non-deterioration span. A significant factor is the product's rate of physical degradation, whereby a higher rate of degradation results in a slight drop in profit.
- The optimal markdown percentage enables the producer to determine the most advantageous time to implement price reductions in the markdown approach and span of the markdown policy so that producer profit is maximized.
- Higher carbon emissions which are decrease total profit and harmful to the environment. The higher green investment resulted minimize the carbon emissions. This is measured by the success of greening green operations. This study indicated that more investments in green technology result in the highest profits, which are increased by greater product volumes and higher markdown percentages.
- The entire cost of the system rises and profit is decreased due to higher production setup, deterioration, carrying, and manufacturing costs. The producer should make an effort to lower the expenses associated with various inventory items, guarantee system functionality, and boost overall profit. If we consider carbon emission and carbon tax in inventory system which reduces the producers total profit but higher carbon tax helps to minimize the carbon emission.
- Due to advertising efforts the selling of products increases with increased production quantity, hence profit increases continuously.

Figure 7.13 (Source: Own) indicated that the producer total profit is highest if a carbon emission not taken in to account, but profit reduces due to carbon emissions and investing in green technology, the profit increases as per Fig. 7.13 (Source: Own) and Fig. 7.14 (Source: Own).

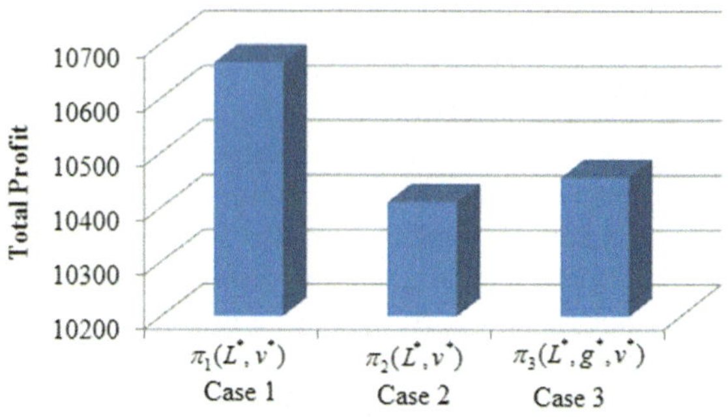

Fig. 7.13 Total profit for Case 1, Case 2, and Case 3 (*Source* Own)

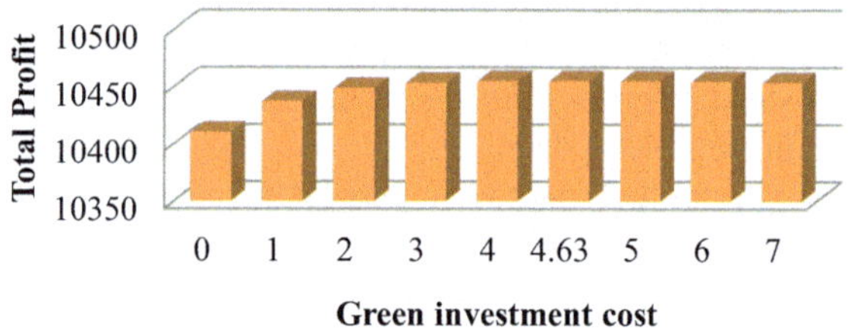

Fig. 7.14 Relation of total profit and green investment for Case 3 (*Source* Own)

7.7 Conclusion

This chapter presents a model called the EPQ model for delay deteriorating products. The model takes into account factors such as price, freshness index, and advertising efforts to determine demand. The model is built based on the markdown principle. Perishable products' freshness and greening level can be considered the major elements that influence a buyer's purchasing behaviour. The novelty of the proposed model is the concept of advertisement efforts with freshness and price-related demand; controlling carbon emissions is considered. Price, advertising, and product freshness all affect consumer demand for perishable commodities like dairy products, beverages, and perishable agricultural products. The idea that perishable commodities shouldn't physically or quantitatively deteriorate more quickly throughout the production period and freshness index $g(t) \to 1$. Demand is therefore based on price and advertising efforts at the start of the inventory cycle. After a stop of production, product quality declines continuously due to physical deterioration, and qualitative degradation of the product. During this time, demand patterns are influenced by factors such as freshness, price, and advertising efforts. As a result, a markdown strategy is implemented to increase demand during a period of product deterioration. Another novel aspect of this study is the inclusion of green investments and carbon tax policy in the EPQ model along with product freshness and markdown approach. The findings indicate that the timing of the markdown offering and the markdown rate are significant factors in maximizing the total profit. Therefore, decision-makers need to be extremely careful when determining the timing of the markdown providing and the markdown rate because the markdown offering should not be made too soon or too late to maximize the total profit. One important strategy for eliminating products before they reach their maximum life is the markdown approach. To maximize profit, decision-makers can better determine the markdown duration with the help of markdown percentage optimization. The analysis shows that higher green investments reduce carbon emissions; higher investment in green technology boosts the profit and also increases total profit with the increase in advertising efforts under a markdown strategy. For framework explanation, the problem has been transformed into a mathematical model, and examples and a procedure for solving it have been given. Sensitivity analysis is used to highlight the analytical findings and provide important managerial implications as a conclusion.

By including preservation strategies that prevent deterioration, this chapter might be expanded. In the future, the model may include other payment schemes and concepts for carbon policies, such as cap and trade, and carbon limit regulations. Additionally, the proposed model can be made more accessible by incorporating shortages.

References

Agi MA, Soni HN (2020) Joint pricing and inventory decisions for perishable products with age-, stock-, and price-dependent demand rate. J Oper Res Soc 71(1):85–99

Benjaafar S, Li Y, Daskin M (2012) Carbon footprint and the management of supply chains: Insights from simple models. IEEE Trans Autom Sci Eng 10(1):99–116

Bhattacharyya M, Sana SS (2019) A mathematical model on eco-friendly manufacturing system under probabilistic demand. RAIRO-Oper Res 53(5):1899–1913

Bouchery Y, Ghaffari A, Jemai Z, Dallery Y (2012) Including sustainability criteria into inventory models. Eur J Oper Res 222(2):229–240

Chen S-C, Min J, Teng J-T, Li F (2016) Inventory and shelf-space optimization for fresh produce with expiration date under freshness-and-stock-dependent demand rate. J Oper Res Soc 67(6):884–896

Dobson G, Pinker EJ, Yildiz O (2017) An EOQ model for perishable goods with age-dependent demand rate. Eur J Oper Res 257(1):84–88

Fujiwara O, Perera U (1993) EOQ models for continuously deteriorating products using linear and exponential penalty costs. Eur J Oper Res 70(1):104–114

Ghare P, Schrader G (1963) An inventory model for exponentially deteriorating items. J Ind Eng 14(2):238–243

Goyal SK, Giri BC (2001) Recent trends in modeling of deteriorating inventory. Eur J Oper Res 134(1):1–16

Hasan MR, Roy TC, Daryanto Y, Wee H-M (2021) Optimizing inventory level and technology investment under a carbon tax, cap-and-trade and strict carbon limit regulations. Sustain Prod Consump 25:604–621

Jain R, Mittal M, Mangla SK, Baraiya R (2023) Optimizing supply chain strategies for deteriorating items and imperfect manufacturing under carbon emission regulations. Comput Indus Eng 182:109350

Ji J, Tang D, Huang J (2022) Green credit financing and emission reduction decisions in a retailer-dominated supply chain with capital constraint. Sustainability 14(17):10553

Kamaruzaman NA, Omar M (2020) Inventory model for a fresh product when demand depends on freshness, price, inventory level and expiration date under markdown policy. J Intell Fuzzy Syst 39(3):3453–3461

Katariya D, Shukla K (2022) Sustainable economic production quantity (SEPQ) model for inventory having green technology investments-price sensitive demand with expiration dates. Econ Comput Econ Cybern Stud Res 56(3)
Katariya DK, Shukla KT (2023) An EPQ Model for delay deteriorating products with price, freshness and greening efforts dependent demand under markdown strategy. Yugoslav J Oper Res
Khan MA-A, Shaikh AA, Konstantaras I, Bhunia AK, Cárdenas-Barrón LE (2020) Inventory models for perishable items with advanced payment, linearly time-dependent holding cost and demand dependent on advertisement and selling price. Int J Prod Econ 230:107804
Lou GX, Xia HY, Zhang JQ, Fan TJ (2015) Investment strategy of emission-reduction technology in a supply chain. Sustainability 7(8):10684–10708
Mashud AHM, Roy D, Daryanto Y, Chakrabortty RK, Tseng M-L (2021) A sustainable inventory model with controllable carbon emissions, deterioration and advance payments. J Clean Prod 296:126608
Mishra U, Wu J-Z, Sarkar B (2020) A sustainable production-inventory model for a controllable carbon emissions rate under shortages. J Clean Prod 256:120268
Plambeck EL (2007) The greening of Wal-Mart's supply chain. Supply Chain Manage Rev 11(5)
Shah NH, Vaghela CR (2018) An EPQ model for deteriorating items with price dependent demand and two level trade credit financing. Investig Oper 39(2)
Shah NH, Shah PH, Patel MB (2021) Retailer's inventory decisions with promotional efforts and preservation technology investments when supplier offers quantity discounts. Opsearch 58(4):1116–1132
Shah N, Shah P, Patel M (2022) Pricing decisions with effect of advertisement and greening efforts for a greengocer. Sustainability 14(21):13807
Shah NH, Shah PH, Patel MB (2022) Retailer's inventory decisions with exchange scheme under the effect of advertisement efforts. J Indus Prod Eng 39(2):158–165
Shaikh A, Mishra P, Talati I (2022) Optimal ordering and pricing decision for items following price sensitive quadratic demand under combined payment scheme. Yugoslav J Oper Res 33(1):41–58
Shee S, Chakrabarti T (2022) An EPQ model for imperfect production system with deteriorating items, price-dependent demand, rework and lead time under markdown policy. In: Data analytics and artificial intelligence for inventory and supply chain management. Springer, pp 81–96
Shi Y, Zhang Z, Chen S-C, Cárdenas-Barrón LE, Skouri K (2020) Optimal replenishment decisions for perishable products under cash, advance, and credit payments considering carbon tax regulations. Int J Prod Econ 223:107514
Soni HN (2021) Joint pricing and inventory policies for perishable items with price discount based on freshness index. Turk J Comput Math Educ (TURCOMAT) 12(11):1954–1963
Srivastava M, Gupta R (2014) An EPQ model for deteriorating items with time and price dependent demand under markdown policy. Opsearch 51:148–158
Sundararajan R, Palanivel M, Uthayakumar R (2021) An EOQ model of non-instantaneous deteriorating items with price, time-dependent demand and backlogging. J Control Decis 8(2):135–154
Swami S, Shah J (2013) Channel coordination in green supply chain management. J Oper Res Soc 64:336–351
Toptal A, Özlü H, Konur D (2014) Joint decisions on inventory replenishment and emission reduction investment under different emission regulations. Int J Prod Res 52(1):243–269
Udayakumar R, Geetha K, Sana SS (2021) Economic ordering policy for non-instantaneous deteriorating items with price and advertisement dependent demand and permissible delay in payment under inflation. Math Methods Appl Sci 44(9):7697–7721
Urban TL, Baker R (1997) Optimal ordering and pricing policies in a single-period environment with multivariate demand and markdowns. Eur J Oper Res 103(3):573–583

Wee HM, Widyadana GA (2007) A replenishment policy for item with price dependent demand and deteriorating under markdown policy. J Teknik Industri 9(2):75–84

Zeng H, Jiang D, Li Y (2022) Cooperative and non-cooperative green advertising in the low-carbon supply chain under monopoly or competitive market. Sustainability 14(15):9190

Chapter 8
Deteriorating Inventory Model for Stock- and Advertisement-Sensitive Demand with a Prepayment Scheme Under Permitted Shortage and Backordering Rate

Nita H. Shah and Kavita Rabari

Abstract This research paper proposes a novel deteriorating inventory model tailored to address the complexities arising from stock- and advertisement-sensitive demand dynamics within the framework of a prepayment scheme. The model integrates considerations for product deterioration, fluctuating demand patterns influenced by advertising efforts, and prepayment arrangements. Additionally, the model accommodates permissible shortage and backordering rates, reflecting realistic scenarios encountered in supply chain management. By employing mathematical formulations and optimization techniques, the study aims to provide decision-makers with a comprehensive framework for managing inventory levels, pricing strategies, and advertising investments to optimize profit margins while ensuring customer satisfaction. The proposed model contributes to the existing literature by offering insights into the intricate interplay between inventory management, demand dynamics, and marketing strategies in a competitive business environment. The proposed model's effectiveness and robustness are demonstrated through numerical experiments and sensitivity analyses, providing valuable implications for practitioners aiming to improve operational efficiency and profitability in inventory management systems.

Keywords Stock- and advertisement-sensitive demand · Constant deterioration · Shortages · Backordering · Prepayment scheme

---

N. H. Shah (✉) · K. Rabari
Department of Mathematics, School of Emerging Science and Technology, Gujarat University, Ahmedabad, Gujarat 380009, India
e-mail: nitahshah@gmail.com

N. H. Shah and M. Mittal (eds.), *Sustainable Inventory Management*, Inventory Optimization, https://doi.org/10.1007/978-981-97-6765-6_9

8.1 Introduction

Running a business requires a lot of inventory management. In addition, it keeps track of all the purchases to ensure that enough inventory is available for customers and also handling the purchasing of new inventory when current items are close to being completely used up. In the conventional economy, inventory management was a relatively straightforward process. The owner of a small retail store, for example, would keep a close eye on the items that were on the shelves, making sure that enough of each product was available to satisfy demand. Whereas, in today's retail environment, where the pace of online sales is constantly accelerating, the inventory function has become even more important.

In several business operations, it can be seen that by having many items on display, you can attract an increased number of customers as compared to a small shopkeeper with fewer items on display. According to the observed trend, there appears to be a positive relationship between the amount of stock in the warehouse and the amount of demand. Since a company's price tag and inventory levels can have a significant impact on the demand for its products from buyers, an organization should carefully assess its price points and order tactics in such a situation in order to maintain a competitive price. One way to boost sales at a company is to provide seasonal cuisine during that period. As a matter of fact, the reality of the modern world is that dealers of all ages are using assets to provide customers with a way to acquire a sale at stock levels. The "stock-induced method" has been the subject of many studies showing that the number of items in stock at the retailer affects the popularity rate of the retailer. There is no doubt that an additional inventory in a storage facility attracts buyers in general. It is vital that companies thoroughly evaluate pricing strategies for the purpose of maximizing income and earnings, while also considering facets such as competitor behaviour, consumer behaviour, or the perceived value of the goods they are selling. There is no doubt that advertisements are one of the most effective tools for raising consumer awareness of and desire for goods. Having proper advertising for a product can have a number of beneficial effects that are capable of leading to an increase in demand for the product that is being advertised. A good advertisement can explain to the audience in question what the benefits and drawbacks of a particular product are, and can also give the audience insight into how the product can meet their requirements and goals. Additionally, a skilfully written commercial has the ability to arouse emotions in the viewer, which can have a positive impact on the choice of the customer to buy the product in question. It is also important to keep in mind that product publicity might set a product apart from the competition, thus giving it an edge over the competition, and thus increasing sales and revenues. Throughout the universe, whether it is a living organism or a non-living organism, decay is an inevitable phenomenon. Almost all goods decay as they age due to the fact that they are exposed to the environment. It is called degradation when something is degraded as a result of being ruined in terms of efficiency, standard, or quality. Listed below are a few examples of how the environment is deteriorating: (1) limestone, which gets progressively poorer over time as a result of saltwater precipitation; (2) the atmosphere, which is becoming increasingly polluted due to an increase in pollution. Special attention must be taken while managing deteriorating products, particularly when dealing with quantity and trading based on price fluctuations. Often, however, inventory management involves managing deteriorating items, such as fresh produce and meat. This means that it's important to identify when items need to be purchased so that they're on hand when needed. Due to the perishable nature of inventory, it's often necessary to have a method for paying for items as they're used up. One of the most common ways to accomplish this is to have a method for prepaying for items that are expected to be used up within a specific time. In the information age, people are expecting a high level of knowledge about the products they want to buy. Thus, the key to a successful inventory management strategy is to closely monitor advertisements and reviews and then act accordingly. It is no longer enough to simply order enough of the right products; a savvy business owner must also order enough of the products that are being heavily demanded. This allows the business to maintain a high level of customer satisfaction while ensuring that the most popular products are always readily available. Business owners who are looking to implement a new inventory management strategy should begin by creating a payment scheme that rewards customers for preordering desired products. The question arises—why does a buyer purchase goods from a company that is asking for prepayment in a highly competitive global marketplace, while other vendors or producers are able to supply the goods at no cost or perhaps are even offering extra advantages? There are several different types of alluring incentives available to customers if they choose to pay in advance, depending on the quantity ordered. The most popular incentive is the cumulative discount offered to the customer. Furthermore, the deposit amount reduces as the amount of goods ordered rises, and clients have the option to settle their prepayment in one or more instalments, at their discretion. These features encourage customers to conduct business with prepayment policies. As a result, vendors and producers simultaneously lower the risk of terminating or delaying an order.

This allows the business to build up a large reserve of inventory, which can then be used to satisfy high-demand products. The stock level can then be adjusted based on actual customer demand, allowing the business to react quickly to changing market conditions. In order to guarantee that their preferred products are delivered on time, buyers can also choose to contribute the full amount or a portion of the purchase price. Also, due to high demand, the model faces shortages. To overcome the loss, the owner permits backordering.

In current work, the demand depends on both stock and number of advertisements. The products deteriorate over time. The problem allows prepayment schemes under shortages and backordering.

Section 8.2 deliberates the review of the literature. The model presents assumptions and notations in Sect. 8.3, which are used to assess the given issue. The mathematical formulation is performed in Sect. 8.4. A methodology is created in Sect. 8.5 to determine the best values for the choice factors and the profit margin for the retailer. In Sect. 8.6, the model is modified through an example together with some managerial insights, representing the variation in decision variables for different inventory parameters. At last, Sect. 8.7 concludes the article.

8.2 Literature Review

A few investigators used advanced payment mechanisms within the stock model for degrading products. In the inventory model for deteriorating products, a small number of researchers worked with advanced payment schemes. In the prepayment scheme, a customer pays off a little portion of the maker's buying price within equal segments and the remaining amount is paid during delivery time. To overcome the problems faced by the manufacturer due to cancellation, the model considers a certain percentage of cost price to be paid under a fixed time interval. The concept was first studied by Zhang (1996). The model presents an optimal payment policy under fixed cost. The mathematical framework accounts for the variance between the fixed payment price and the interest rate that vanishes once the financial deposit is made. It applies renewal theory to determine future payments using past historical data. The model devises optimal deposit amounts and numerical methods for strategy development.

Maiti et al. (2009) introduced a random lead time model in a plan for upfront payments. The framework's projected average earnings are calculated through a mathematical equation, taking into account various factors. This concept is illustrated through numerical examples, comparing the outcomes of two different models based on distinct strategies in different scenarios. Additionally, sensitivity analysis and parametric evaluations were conducted to showcase the functionality of the proposed framework. It is acknowledged that the initial pay-out is advantageous for the overall system. Rahman et al. (2021) investigated a model under discount facility together with demand function changes with stock and hybrid price. In order to enhance customer satisfaction and ensure the long-term financial stability, this system integrates a prepayment policy. Taleizadeh (2017) proposed a model where disruption in source takes place. The problem emphasizes advance payment along with backordering issues. For retailers dealing with disruptions, a lot-sizing model is introduced in this research article. According to the model, part of the purchase price should be paid for in advance of delivery, with the possibility of a partial backorder in the event of shortages. The total cost function accounts for a number of variables, including capital, holding, backordering, and lost sale expenses. The most suitable options can be determined by demonstrating the anticipated total expense function's convexity. A solution algorithm is also provided, along with a number of numerical examples and analysis, to show how the model and the findings it derives can be applied to actual inventory management issues. Rad et al. (2018) primarily concentrated on a dual-phase framework of the supply chain concerning distribution strategies and the efficient manufacturing of flawed products. Their objective was to assess the most favourable advertising approach, backorder rate, and pricing, considering that consumer demand is influenced by both price and advertising efforts. Chawdhary et al. (2014) established a model under advertisement-sensitive demand. It is assumed that there is a quadratic pattern in the link between salesmen's labour and the cost of advertising. The study expands an inventory model to cover fixed and endless time periods. The "Euler–Lagrangian method" is employed to tackle the question of revenue maximization. Shaikh et al. (2020) discussed a problem, considering non-instantaneous declining goods. The demand function is depending on price and advertisements with trade credit varying according to the quantity. Besides, a marketing and budget-flexible demand is simulated; this form of consumption is perfect for the commodities for whom the demand is impacted by the marketing and budget. Khan et al. (2021) studied a credit policy with permissible all-unit quantity discount under an applied hybrid partial advance payment. The model estimates optimum renewal and ordering policies. Shaikh et al. (2019) advanced a two storage facilities model for intermediate storage cost and advance payment. The problem is solved with the help of swarm techniques using interval relations. Giri and Dash (2021) examined a production model that was not flawless. The consumption rate varies according to greening level, advertisement frequency, and retail price. The orders are being placed in unequal-sized batches. Geetha and Udayankumar (2016) proposed an optimal lot-sizing system. The system permits partial backlogging under a slow-moving degradation ratio. Mandal et al. (2021) worked on a sustainable inventory model for variable demand. The methodology is developed to find global optimal cycle time and credit periods. Tavakoli and Taleizadeh (2017) studied limited savings and advance payment. The traditional economic model is constructed under the assumption that costs are paid immediately upon delivery. In practice, however, numerous vendors offer customers the option to pay a portion of the total cost after the goods have been delivered. The study examines two models: one without shortages and another with full backordering and permissible shortages. To demonstrate the findings, numerical analysis is conducted along with providing managerial insights. Chaudhari et al. (2020) discussed preservation technology to reduce decay rate, having quadratic demand function. The company introduces an advance payment plan to evade moderating danger that happens due to cancellation. Shah and Naik (2018) created a decreasing EOQ model with a cost-conscious demand parameter and full advance payment. Wee (1997) introduced a replenishment policy for the time-varying damage rate. Chen et al. (2019) studied an algorithm to evaluate optimal replenishment policy and optimal pricing while dealing with decay goods. Banerjee and Agrawal (2017) documented the importance of freshness. The manuscript is solved for net profit function where sales costs and quality determine the interest level. Sarkar and Sarkar (2013) introduced a time-fluctuating deterioration inventory model.

8.3 Notations and Assumptions

The paper uses the following notations and assumptions. The notations are introduced in Table 8.1.

Notations

Assumptions

Table. 8.1 List of notations

C	Purchase price (\$/unit)
C_o	Opportunity price (\$/unit)
C_s	Scarcity price (\$/unit)
P	Selling price (\$/unit)
k	Set up cost (\$)
h	Holding cost (\$/unit time/unit)
θ	Rate of deterioration
α	Fixed scale demand, $\alpha > 0$
β	Stock-sensitive variable
$R(A, I(t))$	Stock and Advertisement-sensitive demand
S_i	Initial stock
ψ	Backlogging parameter
B_q	Backordering quantity
Q	Order quantity
δ	Advertisement scale parameter
A	Number of advertisement
η	Cost per advertisement
t_1	Physical stock time
T	Cycle period (years)
$I_1(t)$	Inventory for time $[0, t_1]$
$I_2(t)$	Inventory for time $[t_1, T]$
TP	Total revenue (in \$/week)

- The model is formulated for a single decay product.
- The demand pattern is assumed as an exponential function of the number of advertisements and a linear function of stock level, given by $R(I(t), A) = (\alpha + \beta I(t))A^{\delta}$, where $\alpha > 0$ and $\beta > 0$, $\beta \ll \alpha$.
- The decay rate is supposed to be constant.
- Replacement of the products is not permissible below acceptable shortages and backlogging rates.
- Prepayment is approved for n identical divisions, taking Ω the percentage of procurement cost in ε time units.

8.4 Mathematical Model

A perishable inventory model is established where the practitioners created $Q = (S_i + B_q)$ units of products, before the time provided to the supplier by giving Ω the percentage of manufacturing cost ε time units. The prepayment scheme is used with n equal intervals. The pending expanse, i.e., $(1 - \Omega)$ the fraction of manufacturing cost is salaried when the order is received. Because of the simultaneous effect of damage rate and consumer's demand, the inventory level reaches down and turns into zero at times $t = t_1$. In the interim $[t_1, T]$, shortages are factored in for the subsequent delivery window.

The differential equations governing inventory stock of the time period $[0, T]$ are in this way:

$$\frac{dI_1(t)}{dt} + \theta I_1(t) = -(\alpha + \beta I_1(t))A^{\delta}, t \in [0, t_1] \tag{8.1}$$

$$\frac{dI_2(t)}{dt} = -\psi \alpha A^{\delta}, t \in [t_1, T] \tag{8.2}$$

Under complementary conditions, $I_1(t) = 0$ at $t = t_1$, $I_1(t) = S_i$ at $t = 0$, and $I_2(t) = -B_q$ at $I_2(t) = -B_q$. With these boundary conditions, the resultant product amounts are

$$I_1(t) = \frac{\alpha A^{\delta}}{\left(\theta + \beta A^{\delta}\right)}\left(e^{\left(\theta+\beta A^{\delta}\right)(t_1-t)} - 1\right), t \in [0, t_1] \tag{8.3}$$

$$I_2(t) = \psi \alpha A^{\delta}(t_1 - t), t \in [t_1, T] \tag{8.4}$$

Applying condition $I_1(0) = S_i$ at $t = 0$, we have

$$S_i = \frac{\alpha A^{\delta}}{\left(\theta + \beta A^{\delta}\right)}\left(e^{\left(\theta+\beta A^{\delta}\right)t_1} - 1\right) \tag{8.5}$$

The backorder amount is

$$B_q = \Psi \alpha A^{\delta}(T - t_1) \tag{8.6}$$

Hence, the order quantity is

$$Q = S_i + B_q \tag{8.7}$$

The purchase cost relevant to the available order quantity is

$$\text{PC} = CQ \tag{8.8}$$

The storage cost to hold the stock during period $[0, t_1]$ is

$$\text{HC} = h\int_0^{t_1} I_1(t)dt \tag{8.9}$$

The set up cost is

$$\mathrm{OC} = k \tag{8.10}$$

The cost associated per advertisement is η; the advertisement cost is

$$\mathrm{AC} = \eta A \tag{8.11}$$

The capital cost is

$$\mathrm{CC} = \frac{(n+1)}{2n}\varepsilon I_c \Omega C Q \tag{8.12}$$

For the time interval $[t_1, T]$, the shortages are being collected as the storage becomes zero for period $t = t_1$, depending on the new arrival of the stock. The associated shortage cost and loss on sales cost are as follows:

$$\mathrm{SC} = C_S \int_{t_1}^{T} -I_2(t)\mathrm{d}t \tag{8.13}$$

$$\mathrm{LSC} = C_o \alpha A^{\delta}(1-\psi)(T-t_1) \tag{8.14}$$

The sales revenue is

$$\mathrm{SR} = P \int_{0}^{t_1} (\alpha + \beta I_1(t))A^{\delta}\mathrm{d}t + \mathrm{PB}_q \tag{8.15}$$

The profit function is

$$\mathrm{TP} = \frac{1}{T}(\mathrm{SR} - \mathrm{PC} - \mathrm{OC} - \mathrm{HC} - \mathrm{AC} - \mathrm{SC} - \mathrm{LSC} - \mathrm{CC}) \tag{8.16}$$

The goal is to assess the realistic values of A, t_1, T so that the profit margin attains its highest possible value.

8.5 Computational Algorithm

The algorithm to estimate the optimum value of practitioner's profit function is described as

Step 1: Allocate numerical values to parameters: $\alpha, \beta, \theta, \delta, \psi, C, P, h, k, \eta, C_s, \sigma, C_o, \Omega, \eta, \varepsilon, I_c$.

Step 2: Find the first-order partial derivative of total revenue function related to A, t_1, T and equate the respective differential terms equal to zero to calculate feasible value of decision variables given as follows:

$$\frac{\partial \mathrm{TP}}{\partial T}=0, \frac{\partial \mathrm{TP}}{\partial A}=0, \frac{\partial \mathrm{TP}}{\partial t_1}=0 \tag{8.17}$$

Step 3: Solve Eq. (8.17) simultaneously.By solving we get Eq. (8.17), the values of A, t_1, T. The decision variable gives the values of the total revenue function.

8.6 Numerical Validation and Sensitivity Analysis

Example 1 For $\alpha = 10$, $\beta = 0.005$, $\theta = 0.1$, $\delta = 0.2$, $\psi = 0.8$, $C =$ \$20/unit, $P =$ \$50/unit, $h =$ \$1.5/unit/year, $k=$ \$10/order, $\eta = 7$, $C_s =$ \$5/unit, $\sigma = 10$, $C_o =$ \$8/unit, $\Omega = 0.2$, $n = 20$, $\varepsilon = 0.2$, and $I_c = 0.12$, by putting these parametric values in Eq. (8.17), we have $A = 60$, $T = 3.864$ weeks, and $t_1 = 2.973$ weeks and yield the profit value, i.e., TP $=$ 426.975 \$/week. The concavity of the retailer's total profit function for Case 1 is shown in Fig. 8.1.

With reference to the above-mentioned example, a sensitivity analysis is carried out, to analyse the fluctuation of the physical stock time, cycle time, and the number of advertisements together with retailer's profit value, while changing the input parameters by − 20, − 10, 10, and 20%. Table 8.2 represents the sensitivity analysis.

- The cycle time is less sensitive related to β and C_s. It is moderately sensitive to α, h, I_c. The model is developed under prepayment schemes that implement better output, as this strategy is one of the best riskless and secure trading. Prepayment initiatives that integrate improved production can help buyers and sellers optimize profits by decreasing uncertainties.
- The operations and profitability of the company may be significantly impacted by this increase in cycle time. Longer cycle durations could make it difficult for the business to satisfy consumer demand, which would result in product shortages. Customers may become disgruntled and sales may decline as a result. The organization may be required to make lesser orders to refill inventory more often as an outcome of such shortfalls. Small orders from suppliers come with high charges, resulting in increased expenses. This, in turn, decreases the level of profit, which has an impact on the overall turnover of the company. In order to sustain profitability from small orders, it is necessary to raise the selling price of the products, thereby exerting pressure on individuals or customers. This can be done by putting effective project management techniques into practice, simplifying procedures, investing in technology and automation, and regularly assessing and enhancing the supply chain.

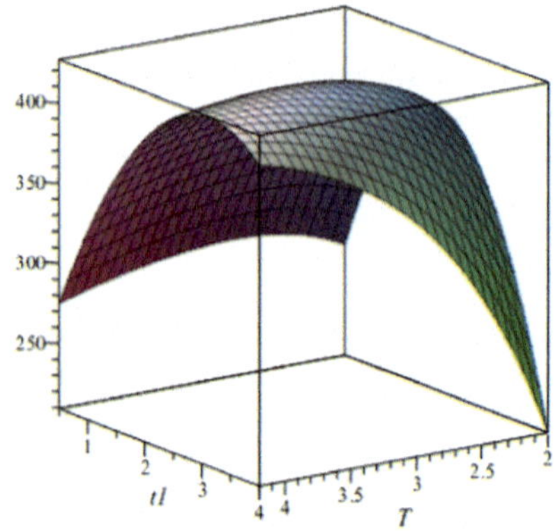

Graph between t_1 and T

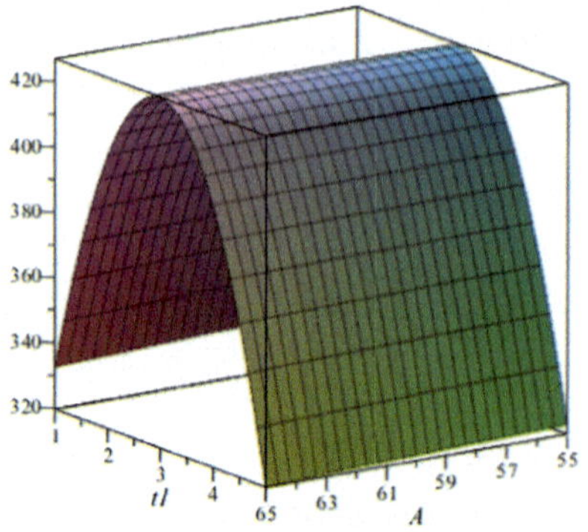

Graph between t_1 and A

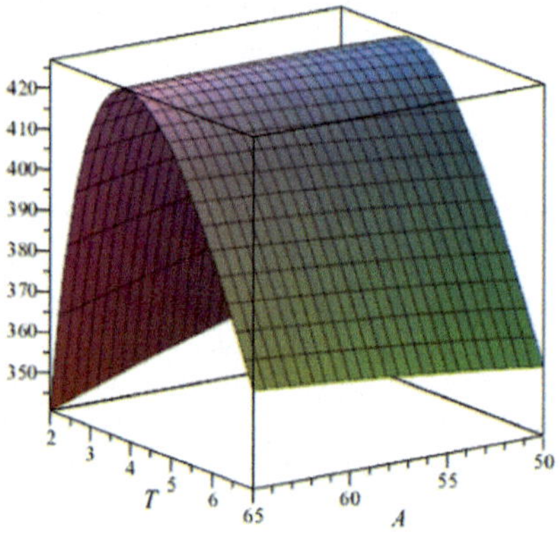

Graph between T and A

Fig. 8.1 Concavity of total profit function for T, A and t_1

- The physical stock time period (t_1) is moderately sensitive to fixed scale demand (α) and opportunity cost (C_o). It is not sensitive to backlogging rate (ψ) and advertisement scale parameter (δ).
- When I_c and ε increase, t_1 fluctuates faster. Therefore, one should be very careful while selecting such values to find the optimal solution.
- Increase in δ refers to the positive effect of advertisement. One should increase the initial stock level because of the high demand resulting in a shortage level. Also, due to deterioration factor, profit value, initial storage quantity, it is essential to take into account the possibility of a spike in demand whenever thinking about enhancing the starting inventory level. Companies are able to prepare over arising orders from clients and avoid shortfalls that could lead to diminished revenue and unhappy clients by improving the holding level. For the purpose of establishing the

Table. 8.2 Sensitivity table [*Source* Own]

Parameters	A	T	t_1	Q	S	TP
α	⇈	↓	↓	↑	↑	⇈
β	↑	↓	↓	↑	↑	↑
θ	↓	↓	↓	↓	↓	↓
δ	↑	↑	↑	↑	↑	↑
h	↓	↓	↓	↑	↓	↓
ψ	–	–	–	–	–	–
η	↓	↑	↑	↓	↑	↓
C_s	↓	↓	↑	↑	↓	↓
k	–	–	–	–	–	–
C_o	↑	↑	↑	↑	↑	↓
Ω	↓	↑	↓	↓	↑	↓
n	↓	↓	–	↑	↓	↑
ε	↓	↓	↑	↑	↓	↑
I_c	↓	↑	↓	↓	↑	↓

right inventory threshold, variables including commodity degradation, earnings margin, and the amount of beginning retention should be taken into account in addition to variations in demand. It might be needed to preserve consumable goods at bigger quantities in order to prepare for eventual degradation or expiry.

- The cycle duration refers to the time it takes for the company to transform raw goods into sellable products. It can be challenging for the company to maintain inventory for an extended period as this leads to higher holding costs. To address this, the company can effectively manage its cycle time by placing frequent orders for smaller quantities. Cycle duration and profit value typically decline as holding costs rise. Hence, to lessen the harm that takes place due to high carrying costs, the company orders less quantity at a time. To satisfy client demand, the business must, therefore, combine cutting expenses associated with inventory management with maintaining sufficient stock levels.
- The diminutive order not only diminishes the rate of deterioration but also disregards insufficiencies. Furthermore, the rate of harm escalates, leading to a decline in the amount of profit. The value of profit is exceedingly responsive to the inventory on hand and the quantity of advertisements. Failure to monitor short orders may lead to a decrease in corporate performance due to lost sales. Total profit is insensitive with respect to k and ψ.

8.7 Conclusion

This model introduces perishable products for stock and advertisement-dependent demand rates. The problem permits a prepayment strategy where the seller observes shortages and permits backordering. A computational method is proposed to find the optimal value of decision variables and the profit function of the retailer.

The sensitivity analysis conducted on the given example provides valuable insights into the impact of varying the decision variables. By adjusting the variation of the decision variables by − 20, − 10, 10, and 20%, the retailer can assess the robustness of their profit function and make informed decisions based on different scenarios. The research findings highlight the importance of offering a wide range of perishable products to consumers. By providing variety, the retailer can cater to different consumer preferences and increase their chances of making a sale. Additionally, the inclusion of high-quality products ensures customer satisfaction and loyalty, further contributing to increased profit levels. Advertising strategies are proven to be highly effective in boosting consumption rates. By implementing targeted marketing campaigns, the retailer can reach a larger audience and increase awareness of their perishable products. This, in turn, leads to higher demand and increased profits. The prepayment strategy introduced in this model is a valuable tool for mitigating the cash flow risk associated with perishable products. By allowing backordering, the retailer can observe shortages and adjust their inventory accordingly. This helps prevent spoilage and ensures a steady cash flow for the retailer. In the future, the model can be enhanced by incorporating a demand function that takes into account factors such as quality, timing, and sustainability efforts. By considering these variables, the retailer can better understand consumer preferences and tailor their offerings accordingly. This can lead to increased customer satisfaction and higher profit levels. Furthermore, implementing preventive measures to slow down the depreciation process can be beneficial for the retailer. By investing in proper storage and handling techniques, the retailer can extend the shelf life of their perishable products and reduce the risk of spoilage. This not only helps maintain product quality but also contributes to cost savings and increased profits. Overall, this model provides valuable insights into optimizing decision variables and maximizing profit levels for retailers selling perishable products. By incorporating additional factors and conducting sensitivity analyses, retailers can make informed decisions and adapt their strategies to changing market conditions.

References

Banerjee S, Agrawal S (2017) Inventory model for deteriorating items with freshness and price dependent demand: optimal discounting and ordering policies. Appl Math Model 52:53–64

Chaudhari U, Shah NH, Jani MY (2020) Inventory modelling of deteriorating item and preservation technology with advance payment scheme under quadratic demand. In: Optimization and inventory management. Springer, Singapore, pp 69–79

Chen L, Chen X, Keblis MF, Li G (2019) Optimal pricing and replenishment policy for deteriorating inventory under stock-level-dependent, time-varying and price-dependent demand. Comput Ind Eng 135:1294–1299
Chowdhury RR, Ghosh SK, Chaudhuri KS (2014) An inventory model for perishable items with stock and advertisement-sensitive demand. Int J Manage Sci Eng Manage 9(3):169–177
Duary A, Das S, Arif MG, Abualnaja KM, Khan MAA, Zakarya M, Shaikh AA (2022) Advance and delay in payments with the price-discount inventory model for deteriorating items under capacity constraint and partially backlogged shortages. Alex Eng J 61(2):1735–1745
Geetha KV, Udayakumar R (2016) Optimal lot sizing policy for non-instantaneous deteriorating items with price and advertisement-dependent demand under partial backlogging. Int J Appl Comput Math 2(2):171–193
Giri BC, Dash A (2021) Optimal batch shipment policy for an imperfect production system under price-, advertisement- and green-sensitive demand. J Manage Anal: 1–34
Khan MAA, Shaikh AA, Cárdenas-Barrón LE (2021) An inventory model under linked-to-order hybrid partial advance payment, partial credit policy, all-units discount and partial backlogging with capacity constraint. Omega 103:102418
Khan MAA, Shaikh AA, Cárdenas-Barrón LE, Mashud AHM, Treviño-Garza G, Céspedes-Mota A (2022) An inventory model for non-instantaneously deteriorating items with nonlinear stock-dependent demand, hybrid payment scheme and partially backlogged shortages. Mathematics 10(3):434
Maiti AK, Maiti MK, Maiti M (2009) Inventory model with stochastic lead-time and price-dependent demand incorporating advance payment. Appl Math Model 33(5):2433–2443
Mandal B, Dey BK, Khanra S, Sarkar B (2021) Advance sustainable inventory management through advertisement and trade-credit policy. RAIRO-Oper Res 55(1):261–284
Rad MA, Khoshalhan F, Glock CH (2018) Optimal production and distribution policies for a two-stage supply chain with imperfect items and price-and advertisement-sensitive demand: a note. Appl Math Model 57:625–632
Rahman MS, Khan MAA, Halim MA, Nofal TA, Shaikh AA, Mahmoud EE (2021) Hybrid price and stock dependent inventory model for perishable goods with advance payment related discount facilities under preservation technology. Alex Eng J 60(3):3455–3465
Sarkar B, Sarkar S (2013) An improved inventory model with partial backlogging, time-varying deterioration and stock-dependent demand. Econ Model 30:924–932
Shah NH, Naik MK (2018) EOQ model for deteriorating items under full advance payment availing of discount when demand is price-sensitive. Int J Supply Chain Oper Resilience 3(2):163–197
Shaikh AA, Cárdenas-Barrón LE (2020) An EOQ inventory model for non-instantaneous deteriorating products with advertisement and price-sensitive demand under order quantity dependent trade credit. Investigación Oper 41(2):168–187
Shaikh AA, Das SC, Bhunia AK, Panda GC, Khan MAA (2019) A two-warehouse EOQ model with interval-valued inventory cost and advance payment for deteriorating item under particle swarm optimization. Soft Comput 23(24):13531–13546
Taleizadeh AA (2017) Lot-sizing model with advance payment pricing and disruption in supply under planned partial backordering. Int Trans Oper Res 24(4):783–800
Tavakoli S, Taleizadeh AA (2017) An EOQ model for decaying item with full advanced payment and conditional discount. Ann Oper Res 259(1):415–436
Wee HM (1997) A replenishment policy for items with a price-dependent demand and a varying rate of deterioration. Production Plann Control 8(5):494–499
Zhang AX (1996) Optimal advance payment scheme involving fixed per-payment costs. Omega 24(5):577–582

Chapter 9
A Sustainable Inventory Model for Online B to C Business with JIT Implementation Considering Kanban Cost for Exponential Demand

Akshika Rastogi, Surbhi Singhal, and S. R. Singh

Abstract Dealing with online business is a very challenging job for an enterprise. Online demands are very unpredictable in practical situation, and fulfilling the demand on time is another typical job to handle. In this study, an inventory model has been developed for online B to C (Business to Customer) business with just in time (JIT) deliveries. Kanban system is also being considered which is a critical part of JIT implementation which helps in managing proper work flow in an organization. A mathematical model has been developed in this study considering a single enterpriser with online B to C business. In the present model, Kanban cost is also introduced which increased the efficiency of model. The Kanban system maintains the flow of the inventory, and with the help of the visible cards information is shared which shows what work is in progress, what is required and what task have been done. It raises the level of sustainability, and there is no chance of excess inventory. A single product has been considered with JIT implementation which is one the sustainable approach. Demand is considered to be exponential with no shortages. Carbon emission cost is considered in the model. A model is analyzed, and an optimum solution has been found out in the numerical section through Mathematica 12 software. Numerical exemplification and lemma are carried out to validate the model. Different and influential parameters have been validated with the help of the Sensitivity Analysis technique. Pictorial depiction has been examined with respect to influential parameters of the model through Origin 2019.

Keywords Sustainable · Enterpriser · Business to customer · JIT · Kanban system · Origin 2019 · Exponential demand · Carbon emission

A. Rastogi (✉)
Department of Applied Sciences, MIT College, Meerut 250001, India
e-mail: akshikastats@gmail.com

S. Singhal
Department of Statistics, Vardhaman College, Bijnor 246701, India

S. R. Singh
Department of Mathematics, C.C.S. University, Meerut 250001, India

N. H. Shah and M. Mittal (eds.), *Sustainable Inventory Management*, Inventory Optimization, https://doi.org/10.1007/978-981-97-6765-6_10

9.1 Introduction

Technology has changed many things so far and influenced the business sectors as well. But still sustainability is the major concern with all the laws and regulations made by the government. Industrialization has put pressure all over the globe to reduce the waste and introduce the innovative techniques to protect the environment with optimum cost. The basic idea of green supply management is to minimize the environmental pollution and production cost. It helps in economic growth also. Green supply chain management is a win–win situation where carbon footprints can be cut back and optimize the total cost and profit of a product. Stages of production like sourcing, transportation and packaging have a direct effect on the environment. With the help of Green supply management, these stages can be improved using the commercial production techniques.

Many organizations have switched to GSCM due to its benefits. Nowadays, every organization and customer understands that harming natural resources cannot benefit anyone. There are techniques like JIT and RFID which are very sustainable and give optimal results.

Any business, whether it is business to business, business to customer or both, has to deal with uncertainty of demand. Online model of business has changed the attitude of customers' behaviors and preferences. If an enterprise has an online mode of business, then it is very necessary to fulfill the demand of customers on time. Basically, the time of deliveries is already mentioned in an online mode while you're shopping. So it is very challenging to deliver the items at a specific date and time. Online orders are needed to be delivered on time, otherwise it affects the goodwill in the market and the producer has to face the shortage cost. Many companies like Toyota, Apple and McDonald's have implemented the newest technology to accomplish the demand of a purchaser. The most advanced technology that all these leading companies are implementing is JIT, i.e. "just in time". JIT technique is also known as Lean production model which is associated with the producer during the world war second. Inventory is the major concern of any supply chain. With the advancement of this technology, they are able to reduce the wastage and deliver the items as they are ordered. So we can say that one of the trending techniques of any business organization these days is JIT. More items can be manufactured with the help of this technique. Items can be waiting for other processess to complete before manufacturing can go forward. The manufacturers do not need to keep excess inventory in hand, so it lesser the extra amount of storage and management. Inefficient processing results in unnecessary products and with the help of this technique, this can be avoided smartly. If an organization keeps surplus inventory, it somewhere will increase the chances that waste product will increase. With the help of this technique, such a situation can be avoided. So reliability of the product will also get increased with the help of JIT. For example, McDonald's delivers burgers just in time as they are ordered by the purchaser. Although they do not keep the burgers ready, they only make the burger on time as they are ordered and the same happens with Toyota. Toyota is the first company to implement JIT. They do not make cars in advance.

They only assemble the parts when they are ordered by the purchasers. In this way, they reduce the waste and carbon emissions and are able to deliver the items on time as all the assembled parts are already readied by them. JIT helps to reduce the inventory waste by reducing the cost involved in keeping inventory like holding cost. JIT means just in time which was first introduced by the Japanese company named Toyota manufacturing company by Taiichi Ohno specialized for consumer demands with minimum delays. The aim of JIT is to provide the right products at the right place at the right time. JIT is a part of inventory management which provides the products to the supplier whenever it is needed and also doesn't allow excess inventory. Keeping excessive inventory can increase various costs to the warehouses like rent, holding cost and many more. By implementing JIT, producers can save time and money, both. JIT not only cuts the inventory cost but also improves the efficiency and reduces the flow time.

Following are the additional benefits of implementing JIT:

- While JIT implementation local sources are more used, it enable the time of deliveries and eliminate the want for safety stock.
- JIT implementation ensures fast and short production.
- JIT implementation allows managers to focus on the optimization of high-quality products.
- Labor cost is optimized in JIT as full time production is not required.
- As production volumes are less, it would be easier to detect defective items.

One of the unique elements is Kanban. Kanban is a Japanese word which is KAN + BAN. KAN means visualization and BAN means cards. It helps to implement the JIT by providing the visual of an entire workflow and the action to be taken. Kanban controls the inventory on its own and makes the work done smoothly. It indicates the system of the organization what to produce, and of what quantity to be produced. It gives signals to the entire supply chain immediately. Kanban pulls the demand of a system and schedules the customers' needs rather than estimate as done in traditional methods. For example, there are 50 semi nuts in a crib; the person assembling the widgets takes a card that was attached to the crib and sends it to the semi nut manufacturing area. Another crib of semi nuts is then manufactured and sent to the widget assembler. Kanban system is used for a flow of operations throughout the process. Whenever any item is running low at any operational channel, there will be a visual of that item, so that one can know how much to order from the supply channel. The person using the parts orders the indicated quantity by the Kanban and gets the exact supply of the amount. The Kanban system is used within a warehouse and is also be used for the purchase of inventory from external suppliers. It provides real-time visibility to both supplier and buyer. One of the sustainable points that it carries is sustainability because it limits in the buildup of excess inventory at any point of the production line. It also limits the number of items on the waiting line at the supply zone and identifies the inefficient items so that producers can separate the inefficient items. Whenever there is an excess of inventory, it indicates it. The Kanban system reduces the carbon footprints as there will be no excess inventory by incorporating it in the system. In manual Kanban, everything depends on the manual Kanban and if anyhow the card is misplaced or lost then, it disturbs the whole inventory management and the message will be incorrectly read and the card reached the incorrect point. It raises the level of confusion and overlaps the things. So to avoid such a situation, an electronic Kanban system is introduced where this situation can be skipped. In this system, all the cards are electronically designed, and printed copies of the Kanban card are shared centrally. Bar-coded cards are scanned. Whenever it becomes empty, it triggers an immediate message to the supplier so that it can be shipped right away without any delay. There is no waiting for the physical bin to reach. Because of the centralized system, everyone both buyer and supplier can have real-time visibility and information is shared continuously without any physical efforts. Carbon footprints can be minimized in terms of keeping the inventory for a long time.

The visualization on Kanban boards are all tasks that represent a real picture of progress and identify the blockages in the supply chain. With the help of "work in progress", organizations can allocate the resources and balance the proper workflow. Kanban works with distinct types of quality control charts and cumulative flow diagrams, so that an organization can work effortlessly.

Electronic Kanban fastens the delivery cycle as it removes the chaos of the process which increases the market demand. In addition, Kanban system makes the whole system so transparent, and adaptability and regular improvement increase the overall potential. In case of supermarkets, stocks are just enough as to meet consumer demand as inventory levels match consumption patterns. The past patterns of supermarket flow of inventory and customer behavior are able to keep the inventory records. Supermarkets are significantly able to manage an inventory by decreasing the excess inventory they must hold at any given time and decrease the total cost by cutting down on holding cost and ensuring that products which are necessary are always in stock.

When the Japanese company named Toyota applied the same rule in their organization's factory floors, the objective was to better put in order its inventory levels with the actual utilization of materials. To have a real-time visibility on the factory floor, workers would pass a card, or "Kanban," between teams.

Whenever the crate is empty during the production process, information is passed to the center and whatever the material is and how much the quantity needed is will be visible to the factory floor. In Kanban system, this information is passed to the supplier. The stated process is updated from time to time since a long time; the same "just in time" (pull system) manufacturing process remains the soul of the Kanban methodology.

The electronic Kanban card managed tabs on a single page for setup, summary information, execution and transactions, and planning. The electronic Kanban card have ability to scan and perform Kanban cards transactions. Kanban with an electronic scanner has the capability to create temporary Kanban cards to handle demand fluctuation during replenishment spikes and provide options to generate additional cards without canceling existing cards, and it supports both physical and logical Kanban replenishment. It also supports multiple suppliers for Source Type of Supplier, and the ability to define the appropriate percentage of sourcing.

Countless studies have been done in the field of inventory. To minimize the cost of the model is the second main concern and in the same line EOQ model has been developed. Banerjee (1986) developed the model for a single vendor and a single customer and estimated the joint optimum total relevant cost for both buyer and vendor. Lehtonen and Holmstrom (1998) describe the various scopes of JIT in industry and business sectors. In the same direction, Pan and Liao (1989) evolved an EOQ model for use with multiple deliveries. Wee (1993) developed an EOQ model for deteriorating items with partial backlogging. Many research have been done in the field of JIT over the last the two decades. Hemamalini and Rajendran (2000) developed different kinds of Kanban and also proposed a sequence of containers to minimize several parameters. Goyal and Giri (2001) presented a review paper for deteriorating inventory of the paper in early 1990. Azadeh et al. (2005) developed a JIT model with dynamic approach and examined its dynamic behavior. Kanban is the necessary part of JIT. Ramnat et al. (2010) through a case study described the benefits of lean manufacturing and described value stream mapping for the current manufacturing line. Chung and Wee (2011) developed a green supply mathematical model for the items having shortlife deteriorating items considering remanufacturing items. Shah (2011) proposed an integrated model for single supplier, single vendor and single product with JIT deliveries and optimized the total cost. Kootanaee et al. (2013) described the overall concept of JIT and explained different parameters, principles and implementation. Ghasimi et al. (2014) developed a model for JIT logistics for supply chain using genetic algorithm. Kanchan et al. (2016) took the case of Valve Company to present a framework to implement JIT. Ezema et al. (2017) proposed the necessary algorithms of JIT. They further explained the future approach of the model. Riza and Purba (2018) conducted a survey on the fastest growing automobile Japanese company in Indonesia and further found out that the product used in manufacturing must be replaced in order to optimize the cost in the same year. Perez and Torres (2019) developed a multiple delivery model implementing JIT for deteriorating items by considering the time value of money (TVM) effect. Applying green approach in the model can increase the profitability and revenue. Perishable items need special attention to avoid the cost of deterioration and for such situation, preservation is the best technique, Singhal et al. (2019). Singh, Rastogi and Singhal (2021) described JIT to be the foremost attitude after lockdown, through a mathematical model and further added various strategies to implement JIT to raise economy of the country. Mullisa et al. (2022) developed a model using simulation technique to find the optimum number of Kanbans. A case study has been done in the study and 76.7% reduction in inventory has been found. Many policies have been made to drop the level of carbon in the atmosphere. Chaudhari et al. (2023) demonstrated a model to investigate the impact of down-cash-credit payments for perishable items in the context of the most commonly utilized carbon tax legislation. Alike JIT, there are other techniques also which are in the line of sustainability. RFID is one of the supportive techniques to handle inventory that can handle both shopping styles whether it's online or offline. This technique has been proved a great support during pandemic when social distancing is on the priority Singh et al. (2023). Keeping in mind the ease of availability and affordable price, Singh et al. (2024) demonstrated a

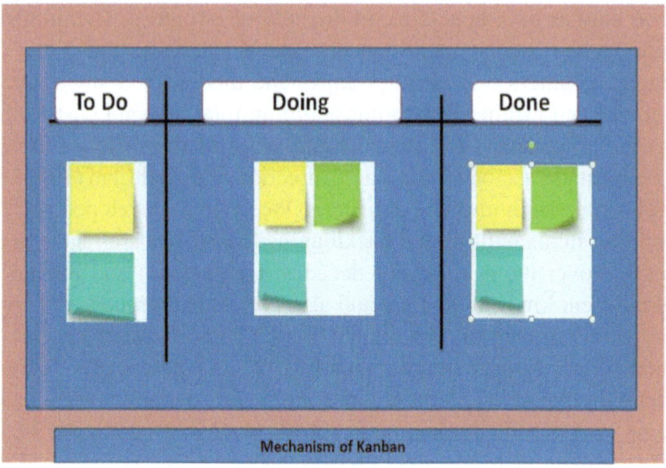

Fig. 9.1 Mechanism of Kanban (Source own)

model with smart biodiesel production system with energy utilization and less carbon emissions to produce pure biodiesel (Fig. 9.1).

In Kanban system, the case of success and failure depends upon on our choice to adapt the signal.

Kanban system mainly focuses only on the consumption of the product and not on the whole supply chain. In case of Toyoto, the Kanban system does not have to focus on the production of the car when it has been sold, and Dealers scramble for fresh items that haven't been sold yet. Kanban system has to make their focus on the processing whether the orders have been forwarded into centralized production slot and accordingly further items are scheduled or not which makes the process smooth. The Kanban system controls the overall resurrection of the components. Kanban system is never used for forecasting or projections of items, but it forecasts the replenishment of items according to the demand in near future. Many logistic companies used to have a centralized center near the plants and they use their Kanban system to pass their information to the local dealers. Kanban system does not deal with whole supply chain but supports in the processing and takes into account the issues that are involved in the supply chain. Through Kanban system, local dealers and plants, including centralized plants, share their information that is a compliment to the supply chain.

Kanban system is basically a way that balances alertness to the replenishment cycle. For the betterment of the quality of items, it is important to have a regular check on the process of production and that influences the actual demand of customers. It is just a part of agreements that provides actual orders in the form of Kanbans. For example, in any automobile company demand depends on many factors. Kanban system makes a supply chain module work well both internally and externally.

In early times, many automobile companies puzzle out devilishly difficult transmission issues. Many years back, Japan used to have a recognition of items with the help of specific colors and shapes. They use to have some color, shape, and other visually prominent means and orderliness; management of inventories was organized and maintained. For instance, they use different colors in any shape like triangle, squares or rectangles or they use to show a big circle with many subcircles with different colors. With the help of different shapes like rectangle, square or triangle, "work in progress", "work done", etc. can be monitored easily and further signify where the things should be delivered or located.

In the present study, we formulated an integrated mathematical business model for business which is business to customer and which deals with the customer online. Demand is considered to be exponential for deteriorating items. As the demand arises, the dealer has to fulfill the demand on time. Many research have been done in the line of sustainability and keeping the inventory most efficiently. Just in time is one of the techniques which minimizes the load of inventory on both purchaser and enterpriser. Recent studies show that JIT delivers the model more efficiently and maintains the cost of the system. In our model, Kanban mechanism has been explained which best supports the JIT model. Kanban cost is included in the model. It maintains the flow of inventory and cuts the extra cost borne by the producer. The updated Kanban system is also introduced by the markets which can be a bridge between the buyer and enterpriser. In the centralized system, the information is shared on the common platform and without any delays the work can be efficiently handled. Considering this situation, JIT deliveries under Kanban environment have been implemented, and further the model is validated by sensitivity analysis. In this study, Kanban cost is also being introduced which increases the efficiency of the model. Graphical interpretation of the model is done with Origin 2019 software.

9.2 Postulations and Symbols

9.2.1 Symbols

N	Number of deliveries
θ	Deterioration rate
h_p	Holding cost per unit time for purchaser
A_p	Kanban cost for purchaser
D	Exponential Demand rate
Q_p	Unit procured per delivery
a, b	Demand parameters
T_p	Delivery cycle time for the buyers in years
C_{pd}	Unit deterioration cost for purchaser
C_p	Carbon emission cost per unit time for purchaser

(continued)

(continued)

K	Fixed transportation cost per shipment for purchaser
F_p	Cost of less flexibility per unit time for purchaser
A_e	Kanban cost for enterpriser
Q_e	Production lot size per cycle
h_e	Holding cost per unit time for enterpriser
λ	Production rate
T_1	Production time in years
T_2	Non-production time in years
Cd_e	Unit deterioration cost for enterpriser
F_e	Cost of less flexibility per unit time for enterpriser
C_{if}	Fixed inspection cost per cycle time
C_{io}	Variable inspection cost per cycle time for enterpriser
C_{ins}	Unit inspection cost
V	Variable transportation cost per unit for handling and receiving items
C_e	Carbon emission cost per unit time for enterpriser

9.2.2 Postulations

- The model is constituted for business to customer (B to C) supply chain with JIT implementation and considering Kanban cost.
- The demand is exponential for the model.
- Shortages are not allowed for both purchaser and enterpriser.
- Both purchaser and enterpriser share their information completely.
- Lead time is considered to be zero.
- Enterpriser's shipment is an integer value.
- Deterioration is considered for both purchaser and enterpriser with constant rate.

9.3 Mathematical Model

In the following division, a mathematical module for total cost of an integrated inventory system for single enterpriser, single purchaser and single product under JIT deliver. During the interval $(0, T)$, enterpriser's inventory production period varies, non-production period occurs during the interval $(0, T_2)$ and purchaser's end is during $(0, T_b)$.

Following are the governing equations:

$$\frac{dI_p(t)}{dt} = -ae^{bt} - \theta I_p(t) \quad 0 < t < T_p \tag{9.1}$$

$$\frac{dI_{e_1}(t_1)}{dt_1} = P - \theta I_{e_1}(t_1) \quad 0 < t_1 < T_1 \tag{9.2}$$

and

$$\frac{dI_{e_2}(t_2)}{dt_2} = -\theta I_{e_2}(t_2) \quad 0 < t_2 < T_2 \tag{9.3}$$

Boundary conditions for the above system of equations:

$$I_{e_1}(0) = 0, I_{e_2}(T_2) = Q_e = NQ_p \text{ and } I_p(T_p) = 0$$

The solutions for the above equations are as follows:

$$I_p(t) = \frac{a}{\theta + b}\left[e^{\theta(T_b - t) + bT_b} - e^{bt}\right] \quad 0 < t < T_p \tag{9.4}$$

$$I_{e_1}(t_1) = \frac{\lambda a}{b + \theta}\left(e^{bt_1} - e^{-\theta t_1}\right) \quad 0 < t_1 < T_1 \tag{9.5}$$

$$I_{e_2}(t_2) = Q_e e^{\theta(T_2 - t_2)} \quad 0 < t_2 < T_2 \tag{9.6}$$

From Eq. (9.4), the procurement quantity, Q_p of the purchaser, is

$$Q_p = \frac{a}{\theta + b}\left(e^{(\theta + b)T_p} - 1\right) \tag{9.7}$$

and

$$\begin{aligned} Q_e &= NQ_p \\ &= \text{Na}\,T_p\left[1 + \frac{1}{2}(\theta + b)T_p\right] \end{aligned}$$

Here time t is a continuous function for any stature of inventory; we have

$$I_{e_1}(T_1) = I_{e_1}(0)$$

$$\frac{\lambda a}{b + \theta}\left(e^{bT_1} - e^{-\theta T_1}\right) = Q_e e^{\theta T_2}$$

Here it is assumed that $\theta \ll 1$ and T_1 and $T_2 \ll 1$. So we can replace

$$e^{bT_1} = \left[1 + bT_1 + \frac{(bT_1)^2}{2} + \cdots\cdots\right]$$

$$e^{-\theta T_1} = \left[1 - \theta T_1 + \frac{(\theta T_1)^2}{2} + \cdots\ldots\right]$$

$$e^{\theta T_2} = \left[1 + \theta T_2 + \frac{(\theta T_2)^2}{2} + \cdots\ldots\right]$$

Ignoring higher powers,

$$\frac{\lambda a}{b+\theta}(1 + bT_1 - 1 + \theta T_1) = Q_e(1 + \theta T_2) \tag{9.8}$$

On equating, both sides

$$T_1 = \frac{Q_e(1 + \theta T_2)}{\lambda a} \tag{9.9}$$

Substituting these values in equation $T_1 + T_2 = (N-1)T_p + \frac{Q_p}{\lambda a}$ will give.

$$T_2 = \frac{(N-1)T_p}{\left(1 + \frac{NQ_p\theta}{\lambda a}\right)} + \frac{\frac{Q_p}{\lambda a}(1-N)}{\left(1 + \frac{NQ_p\theta}{\lambda a}\right)} \quad \textbf{see Appendix 1} \tag{9.10}$$

Hence Eq. (9.9) gives

$$T_1 = \frac{NaT_p}{\lambda a}\left[1 + \theta\left(\frac{\lambda(N-1)T_p + (1-N)T_p}{\left(\lambda + NT_p\theta\right)}\right)\right] \quad \textbf{see Appendix 2} \tag{9.11}$$

During cycle time of T units, purchaser gets N deliveries each time of T_p units so $T = NT_p$.

9.3.1 Purchaser's Applicable Cost

Ordering Cost per order

$$O_{cp} = \frac{N}{T}A_p \tag{9.12}$$

Kanban Cost

$$A_p = \frac{D}{Q_p} \tag{9.13}$$

Holding Cost per unit time

$$\begin{aligned} h_{C_p} &= \frac{Nh_p}{T}\int_0^{T_p} I_p(t)\mathrm{d}t \\ &= \frac{Nh_p}{T}\int_0^{T_p} \frac{a}{\theta+b}\left[e^{\theta(T_p-t)+bT_p} - e^{bt}\right]\mathrm{d}t \end{aligned} \quad (9.14)$$

Carbon Emission Cost per unit time

$$\begin{aligned} C_{C_p} &= \frac{Nc_p}{T}\int_0^{T_p} I_p(t)\mathrm{d}t \\ &= \frac{NC_{cp}}{T}\int_0^{T_p} \frac{a}{\theta+b}\left[e^{\theta(T_p-t)+bT_p} - e^{bt}\right]\mathrm{d}t \end{aligned} \quad (9.15)$$

Deterioration Cost per unit time

$$\begin{aligned} D_{C_p} &= \frac{NC_{pd}}{T}\left(Q_p - ae^{bT_p}T_p\right) \\ &= \frac{NC_{pd}}{T}\left[\frac{a}{\theta+b}\left(e^{(\theta+b)T_p} - 1\right) - ae^{bT_p}T_p\right] \end{aligned} \quad (9.16)$$

Transportation cost per unit time

$$T_{rcp} = \frac{N\left(k + VQ_p\right)}{T} \quad (9.17)$$

Cost of Less Flexibility of Implementing JIT delivery per unit time

$$CL_{FP} = \frac{NF_p}{T} \quad (9.18)$$

Purchasers' applicable cost per unit time from Eqs. 9.12–9.18 is

$$TC_p\left(T_p, N\right) = O_{cp} + A_p + h_{c_p} + c_{c_p} + D_{C_p} + T_{rcp} + CL_{FP} \quad (9.19)$$

9.3.2 Enterpriser's Applicable Cost

Setup Cost per unit time

$$O_{ce} = \frac{A_e}{T} \tag{9.20}$$

Kanban Cost

$$A_e = \frac{D}{Q_e} \tag{9.21}$$

Holding Cost per unit time

$$\begin{aligned} h_{C_e} &= \frac{h_e}{T}\left[\int_0^{T_1} I_{e_1}(t_1)\mathrm{d}t_1 + \int_0^{T_1} I_{e_2}(t_2)\mathrm{d}t_2 - T_p\{Q_p + 2Q_p + \cdots + (N-1)Q_p\}\right] \\ &= \frac{h_e}{T}\left[\int_0^{T_1} I_{e_1}(t_1)\mathrm{d}t_1 + \int_0^{T_1} I_{e_2}(t_2)\mathrm{d}t_2 - \frac{1}{2}N(N-1)Q_pT_p\right] \end{aligned} \tag{9.22}$$

Carbon Emission Cost per unit time

$$\begin{aligned} C_{C_e} &= \frac{C_e}{T}\left[\int_0^{T_1} I_{e_1}(t_1)\mathrm{d}t_1 + \int_0^{T_1} I_{e_2}(t_2)\mathrm{d}t_2 - T_p\{Q_p + 2Q_p + \cdots + (N-1)Q_p\}\right] \\ &= \frac{C_e}{T}\left[\int_0^{T_1} I_{e_1}(t_1)\mathrm{d}t_1 + \int_0^{T_1} I_{e_2}(t_2)\mathrm{d}t_2 - \frac{1}{2}N(N-1)Q_pT_p\right] \end{aligned} \tag{9.23}$$

Deterioration Cost per unit time

$$\begin{aligned} D_{C_e} &= \frac{C_{de}}{T}\left[PI_{e_1}(t_1) - Q_e\right] \\ &= \frac{C_{de}}{T}\left[\lambda a(1 + bT_1)T_1 - NaT_p\left\{1 + \frac{1}{2}(\theta + b)T_p\right\}\right] \end{aligned} \tag{9.24}$$

Cost of Less Flexibility of Implementing JIT delivery per unit time

$$CLF_s = \frac{NF_s}{T} \tag{9.25}$$

Inspection Cost per unit time

$$\mathrm{INC}_e = \frac{1}{T}\left[NC_{i0} + \frac{C_{if}}{N} + C_{\mathrm{ins}}Q_p\right] \tag{9.26}$$

Enterprisers' applicable cost per unit time from Eqs. 9.20–9.26

$$TC_s\big(T_1, T_2, T_p, N\big) = O_{ce} + A_e + h_{c_e} + C_{C_e} + D_{C_e} + C_L F_S + \mathrm{INC}_e \tag{9.27}$$

Adding Eq. (9.19) and (9.27) gives the total cost function of the purchaser and enterpriser as.

$$\text{Total Cost Function}\,(T_1, T_2, T_b, N) = TC_s\big(T_1, T_2, T_p, N\big)TC_p\big(T_p, N\big) \tag{9.28}$$

where $T = NT_p$ and T_1, and T_2 are given in Eqs. (9.10) and (9.11). Therefore, the objective function reduces to three decision variables, i.e. N, T_p and Q_e. Here, both T_p, Q_e are continuous variables.

9.4 Theorem

Statement If the value of θ and $\beta \to 0$, for every value of $N > 1$, then values of T_1 and T_2 is a classical EOQ model.

Proof For fixed N, $N > 1$.

$$\lim_{\theta,\beta\to 0} T_1 = \lim_{\theta,\beta\to 0}\left[\left\{\frac{NaT_p}{\lambda a}\left(1 + \theta\left(\frac{\lambda(N-1)T_p + (1-N)T_p}{\big(\lambda + NT_p\theta\big)}\right)\right)\right\}\right]$$

$$\lim_{\theta,\beta\to 0} T_1 = \frac{NT_p}{\lambda}$$

Also,

$$\lim_{\theta,\beta\to 0} T_2 = \left[\left\{\frac{(N-1)T_p}{\left(1 + \frac{NQ_p\theta}{\lambda a}\right)} + \frac{\frac{Q_p}{\lambda a}(1-N)}{\left(1 + \frac{NQ_p\theta}{\lambda a}\right)}\right\}\right]$$

$$\lim_{\theta,\beta\to 0} T_2 = (N-1)T_p\big(1 - \tfrac{1}{\lambda}\big)$$

which is a classical EOQ model.

Therefore, values of T_1 and T_2 is a classical EOQ model.

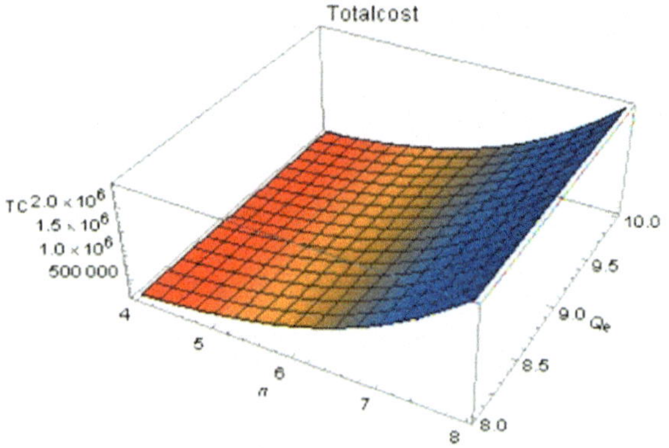

Fig. 9.2 Graphical depiction for convexity of n and T_p [source own]

9.5 Numerical Example and Sensitivity Analysis

Let the assume parameters to be $\theta = 0.255$, $h_p = 1.5$, $A_p = 100$, $D = 0.2$, $c_p = 4$, $C_{ins} = 1.5$, $C_e = 1.5$, $k = 140$, $F_p = 130$, $A_e = 15{,}000$, $h_e = 1.5$, $\lambda = 1.5$, $C_{de} = 0.005$, $F_e = 130$, $C_{if} = 2800$, $C_{i0} = 150$, $V = 0.5$, $C_{pd} = 4$, a $= 1000$ and $b = 0.5$.

With the help of Mathematica 12.1, optimum solution has been obtained.

9.5.1 Optimum solution [source own]

N	T_p	Q_e	Total cost (TC)
1.67	0.91	1.90	15,909.4

9.5.2 Sensitivity Analysis

Sensitivity is performed on various influential parameters at the change of 10%, – 5%, 5% and 10% (Figs. 9.2, 9.3, 9.4, 9.5, 9.6, 9.7, 9.8 and Table 9.1).

9.6 Practical Utility of Model and Future Implementation

JIT is the most trending technique that can fulfill the demand of the customers on a regular basis, and it can minimize the level of carbon footprints from the environment. Kanban system is the supported technique for the continuous flow of work. In the

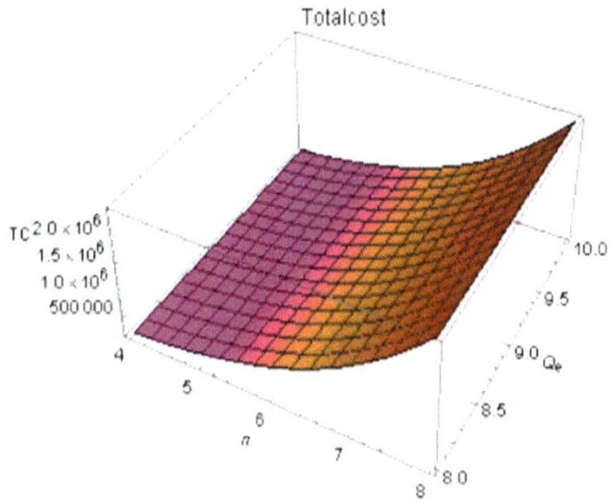

Fig. 9.3 Graphical depiction for convexity of n and Q_e [source own]

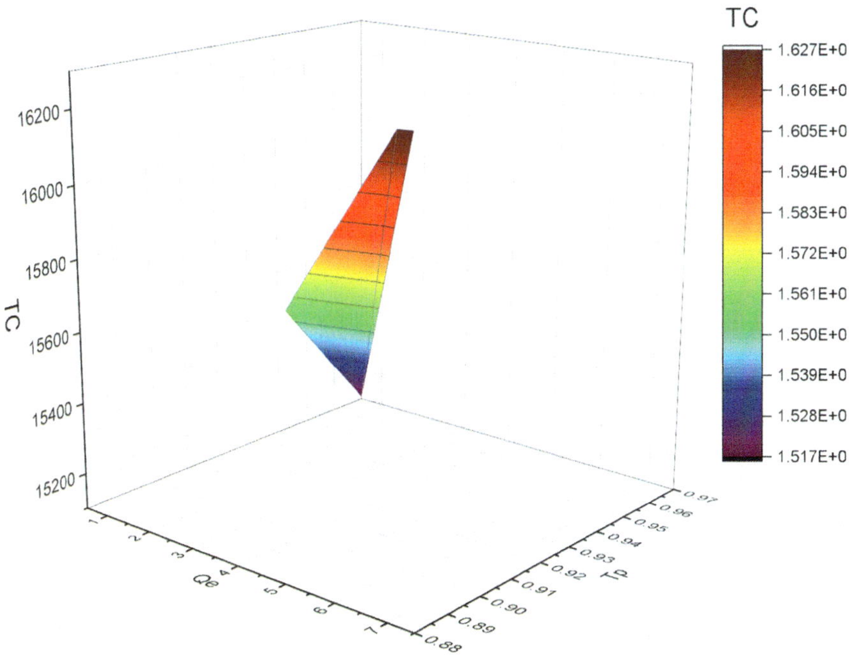

Fig. 9.4 Graphical depiction of variation in T_p, Q_e and total cost w.r.t 'θ' [source own]

present comprehensive study, JIT technique is implemented. In the present model, we consider the Kanban cost along with their other cost. Business has to compete and render all the environment laws and regulations. Keeping the inventory for long can increase the carbon footprint in the environment and on the other hand meeting the demand of customer's as when it is ordered is a challenge. JIT handles the inventory

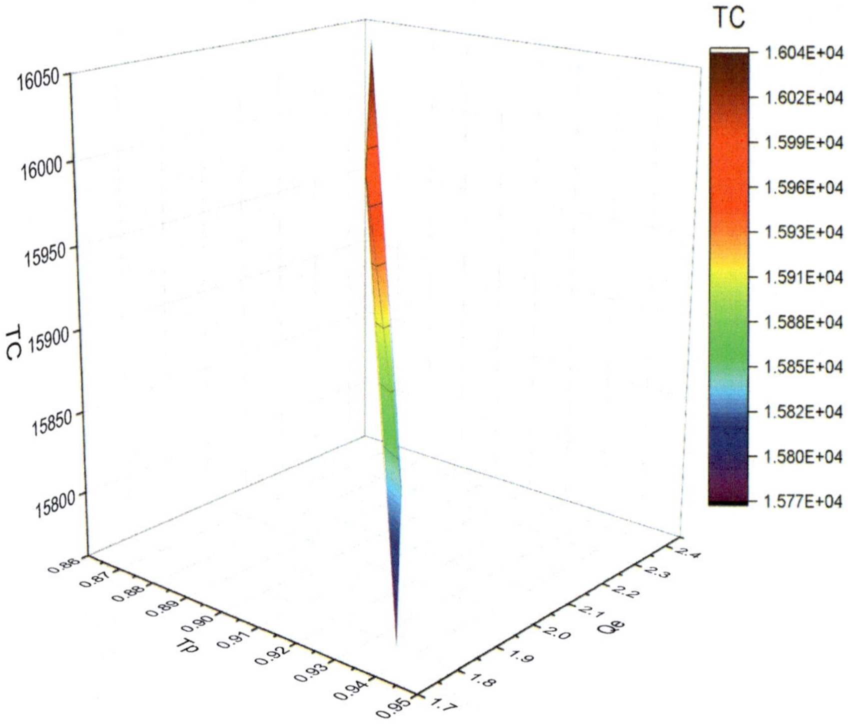

Fig. 9.5 Graphical depiction of variation in T_p, Q_e and total cost w.r.t 'h_p' [source own]

with low carbon footprints and when Kanban is incorporated in the model, then it handles the operational flow.

Kanban is a manufacturing control tool which will intercept the overproduction. Basically, there should be zero Kanban. Kanban is used in different forms. For instance, if you go to a hotel for dinner, they use tokens as Kanban. Advanced bill would be paid at the counter, and you get the token with some number. The same information (order of the food) is processed to the kitchen which starts preparing the food. If there is no token for production kitchen will not produce. Similarly, in an automobile company, we have used vehicle as a Kanban for some of the processes. In some of the manufacturing houses, parts preparation staff continuously keep track of vehicles in assembly line through their camera and start the parts preparation on the basis of real-time visibility. The vehicle reaches a certain station in the conveyor. The calculation of the number of Kanban depends on certain parameters like order cycle, lead time and delivery cycle. In case, if we decrease the time of order cycle, then it will increase the ordering frequency which is proportionate to the delivery cycle of the number of Kanbans. Lead time will have no impact on Kanban; it only influences the order which is in the pipeline.

In the line of sustainability and keeping the inventory with most efficiency, our model is developed on the just in time technique which is one of the techniques

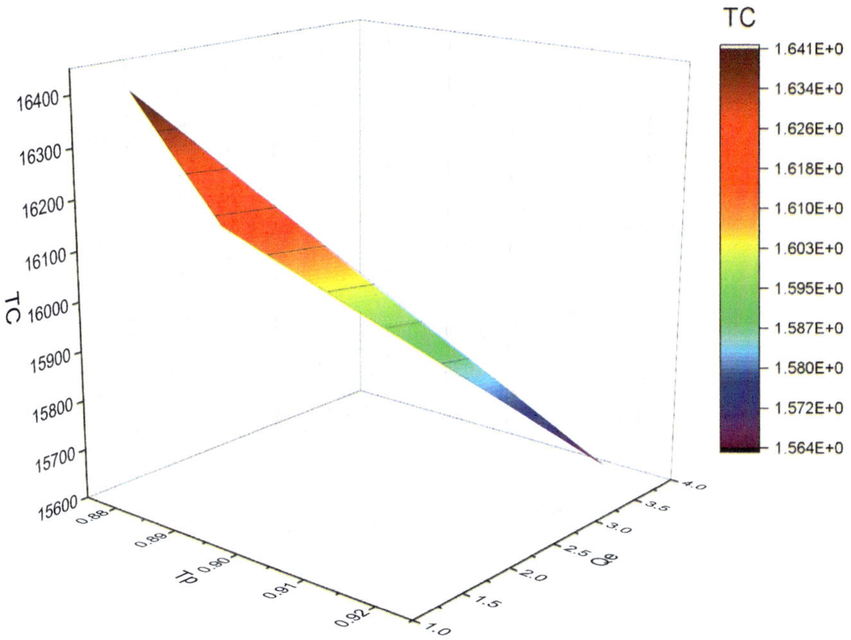

Fig. 9.6 Graphical depiction of variation in T_p, Q_e and total cost w.r.t 'h_e'

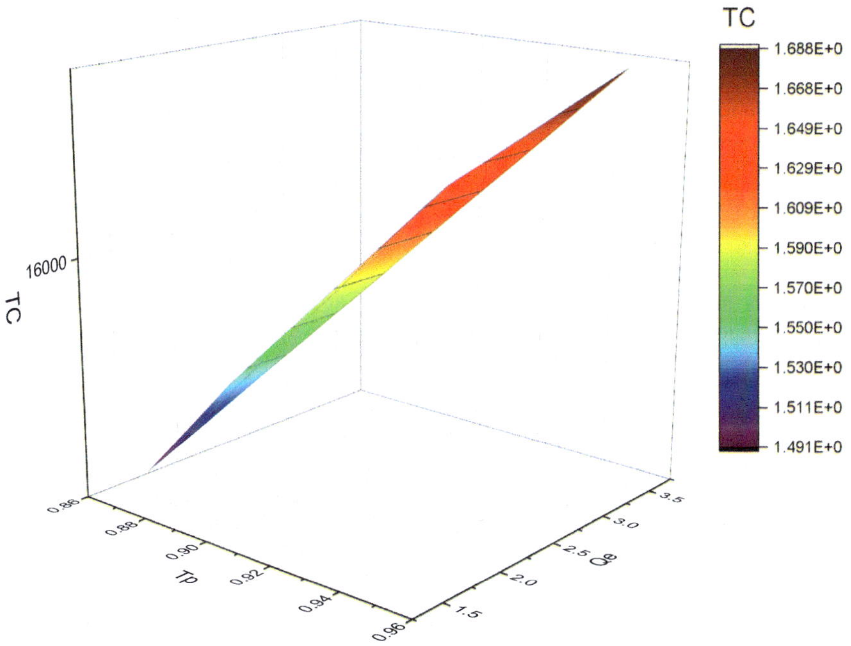

Fig. 9.7 Graphical depiction of variation in T_p, Q_e and total cost w.r.t 'A_e' [Source own]

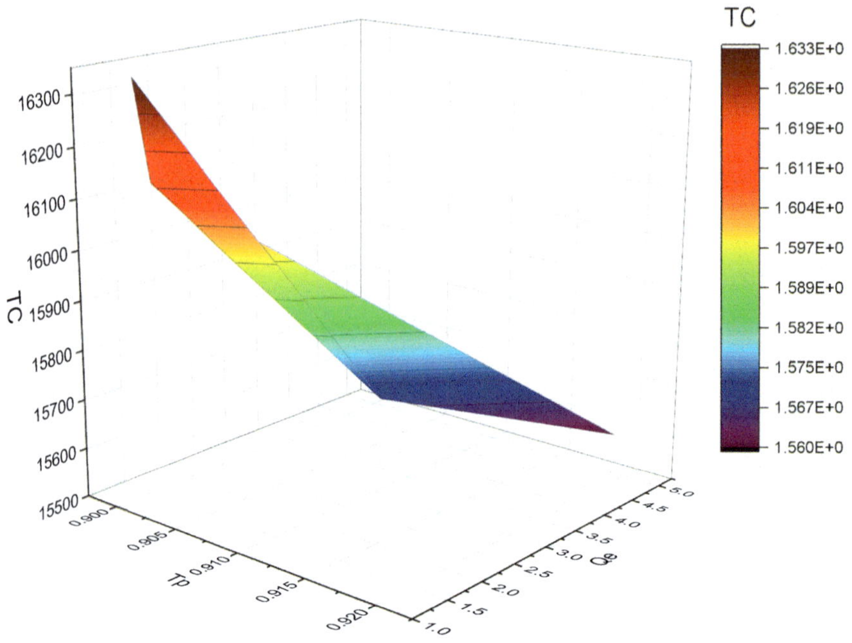

Fig. 9.8 Graphical depiction of variation in T_p, Q_e and total cost w.r.t 'a' [Source own]

which minimizes inventory extra cost for both the purchaser and enterpriser. Recent studies show that JIT models are more coherent and maintain the cost of the system. In our model, Kanban mechanism has been explained which best supports the JIT model. Kanban cost is included in the model. It balances an inventory and cuts the extra cost borne by the producer. The updated Kanban system is also introduced by the markets which share the same level of information with buyer and enterpriser. In the centralized system, the information is shared on the common platform and work can be efficiently handled.

An integrated model has been developed and analysis has been done. Numerical exemplification has been done to validate the model by sensitivity analysis through Mathematica 12. Graphs for the parameters have been interpreted by Original 2019 software with 4-dimensional graphs.

The model has future projections in other sectors also like medical, defense or banking. In the stated model, JIT technology has been adopted but the model can be extended to other technologies like RFID and Artificial Intelligence or Machine Learning. The model can be further expanded with fuzzy environment or AI with fuzzy environment. The updated model can be considered by taking E Kanban (Electronic Kanban) in the model. The bar-coded unit cost can be included. To save the time and for real-time visibility, this system can be proven very fruitful and flawless. Both buyer and purchaser are continuously updated by the centralized system, and

Table 9.1 Optimal solution w.r.t. n, T_p and Q_e and total cost using sensitivity technique [source own]

%	N	T_p	Q_e	Total cost (TC)
Variation in parameter 'θ'				
− 10%	1.69	0.96	1.17	15,167.5
− 5%	1.68	0.93	1.43	15,542.5
0%	1.67	0.91	1.90	15,909.4
+ 5	1.67	0.89	6.5	16,260.6
+ 10%	1.67	0.88	6.8	16,263.3
Variation in parameter 'h_p'				
− 10%	1.62	0.94	1.75	15,769.8
− 5%	1.65	0.93	1.86	15,840.3
0%	1.67	0.91	1.90	15,909.4
+ 5	1.70	0.89	2.16	15,977.2
+ 10%	1.73	0.87	2.37	16,043.8
Variation in parameter 'h_e'				
− 10%	1.67	0.93	4.03	15,617.5
− 5%	1.67	0.92	3.57	15,644.6
0%	1.67	0.91	1.90	15,909.4
+ 5	1.68	0.89	1.52	16,164.5
+ 10%	1.68	0.88	1.26	16,410.7
Variation in parameter 'A_e'				
− 10%	1.71	0.87	1.51	14,918.6
− 5%	1.69	0.89	1.71	15,417.0
0%	1.67	0.91	1.90	15,909.4
+ 5	1.66	0.93	2.46	16,396.3
+ 10%	1.64	0.95	3.50	16,877.9
Variation in parameter 'a'				
− 10%	1.68	0.92	4.80	15,599.6
− 5%	1.68	0.91	3.08	15,689.3
0%	1.67	0.91	1.90	15,909.4
+ 5	1.67	0.90	1.60	16,123.9
+ 10%	1.66	0.90	1.39	16,333.2
Variation in parameter 'b'				
− 10%	1.80	0.84	5.70	16,042.4
− 5%	1.70	0.87	2.66	15,978.8
0%	1.67	0.91	1.90	15,909.4
+ 5	1.61	0.95	1.66	15,833.8
+ 10%	1.55	0.99	1.45	15,751.7

items are shipped as per the requirement. The integrated model can be developed by considering the E Kanban environment with JIT deliveries.

Many big organizations like TP Synergy incoporate an electronic version of the Kanban system that makes their work flawless. First, they recognize a few key items that are used on a regular basis and being supplied by the supplier that is located near to them. When lead time is minimum, it builds the best Kanban system. Inventory will be more regular. The merits of Kanban system can be seen with immediate effects as it decreases the time and efforts. Electronic Kanban cards can be used as the requirement of your business. E Kanbans have a bigger picture in the future and are a fine example of emerging technology. They can be used in other sectors as well such as education sector where the inventory of the books can be managed with the help of information shared through an E Kanban system.

Appendix 1

From Eq. (9.9)

$$T_1 = \frac{Q_e(1+\theta T_2)}{\lambda a}$$

Now,

$$T_1 + T_2 = (N-1)T_p + \frac{Q_p}{\lambda a}$$

$$T_2 = (N-1)T_p + \frac{Q_p}{\lambda a} - T_1$$

$$T_2 = (N-1)T_p + \frac{Q_p}{\lambda a} - \frac{Q_e(1+\theta T_2)}{\lambda a}$$

$$T_2 = (N-1)T_p + \frac{Q_p}{\lambda a} - \frac{NQ_p(1+\theta T_2)}{\lambda a}$$

$$T_2 = (N-1)T_p + \frac{Q_p}{\lambda a} - \frac{NQ_p}{\lambda a} - \frac{NQ_p\theta T_2}{\lambda a}$$

$$T_2 + \frac{NQ_p\theta T_2}{\lambda a} = (N-1)T_p + \frac{Q_p}{\lambda a} - \frac{NQ_p}{\lambda a}$$

$$T_2\left(1 + \frac{NQ_p\theta}{\lambda a}\right) = (N-1)T_p + \frac{Q_p}{\lambda a} - \frac{NQ_p}{\lambda a}$$

$$T_2\left(1 + \frac{NQ_p\theta}{\lambda a}\right) = (N-1)T_p + \frac{Q_p}{\lambda a}(1-N)$$

$$T_2 = \frac{(N-1)T_p}{\left(1+\frac{NQ_p\theta}{\lambda a}\right)} + \frac{\frac{Q_p}{\lambda a}(1-N)}{\left(1+\frac{NQ_p\theta}{\lambda a}\right)}$$

Appendix 2

$$T_1 = \frac{Q_e(1+\theta T_2)}{\lambda a}$$

$$T_1 = \frac{NQ_p(1+\theta T_2)}{\lambda a}$$

$$T_1 = \frac{N\left\{\frac{a}{\theta+b}\left(e^{(\theta+b)T_p}-1\right)\right\}(1+\theta T_2)}{\lambda a}$$

$$T_1 = \frac{N\left\{\frac{a}{\theta+b}\left(e^{(\theta+b)T_p}-1\right)\right\}\left\{1+\theta\left(\frac{(N-1)T_p}{\left(1+\frac{NQp\theta}{\lambda a}\right)}+\frac{\frac{Qp}{\lambda a}(1-N)}{\left(1+\frac{NQp\theta}{\lambda a}\right)}\right)\right\}}{\lambda a}$$

$$T_1 = \frac{NaT_p\left[1+\theta\left(\frac{(N-1)T_p}{\left(1+\frac{NQp\theta}{\lambda a}\right)}+\frac{\frac{Qp}{\lambda a}(1-N)}{\left(1+\frac{NQp\theta}{\lambda a}\right)}\right)\right]}{\lambda a}$$

$$T_1 = \frac{NaT_p\left[1+\theta\left(\frac{(N-1)T_p}{\left(1+\frac{NaTp\theta}{\lambda a}\right)}+\frac{\frac{Qp}{\lambda a}(1-N)}{\left(1+\frac{NaT_p\theta}{\lambda a}\right)}\right)\right]}{\lambda a}$$

$$T_1 = \frac{NaT_p}{\lambda a}\left[1+\theta\left(\frac{(N-1)T_p}{\left(1+\frac{NTp\theta}{\lambda}\right)}+\frac{\frac{aT_p}{\lambda a}(1-N)}{\left(1+\frac{NT_p\theta}{\lambda}\right)}\right)\right]$$

$$T_1 = \frac{NaT_p}{\lambda a}\left[1+\theta\left(\frac{\lambda(N-1)T_p+(1-N)T_p}{\left(\lambda+NT_p\theta\right)}\right)\right]$$

References

Azadeh A, Bidokhti B, Sakkaki SMR (2005) Design of practical optimum JIT systems by integration of computer simulation and analysis of variance. Comput Indus Eng 49(4): 504–519

Banerjee A (1986) A joint economic-lot-size model for purchaser and vendor. Decis Sci 17(3): 292–311

Chaudhari U, Bhadoriya A, Jani MY, Sarkar B (2023) A generalized payment policy for deteriorating items when demand depends on price, stock, and advertisement under carbon tax regulations. Math Comput Simul 207: 556–574

Chung CJ, Wee HM (2011) Short life-cycle deteriorating product remanufacturing in a green supply chain inventory control system. Int J Prod Econ 129(1): 195–203

Ezema CN, Okafor EC, Hyacinth IC (2017) A review of the implementation of JIT algorithms and models in production systems. J Appl Adv Res 2(3): 122–138

Ghasimi SA, Ramli R, Saibani N (2014) A genetic algorithm for optimizing defective goods supply chain costs using JIT logistics and each-cycle lengths. Appl Math Modell 38(4): 1534–1547

Goyal SK, Giri BC (2001) Recent trends in modeling of deteriorating inventory. Eur J Oper Res 134(1): 1–16

Hemamalini B, Rajendran C (2000) Determination of the number of containers, production kanbans and withdrawal kanbans; and scheduling in kanbanflowshops-Part 2. Int J Prod Res 38(11):2549–2572

Kanchan BK, Chandan GK, Rajenthirakumar D (2016) A framework for implementing just in time in a valve manufacturing industry. Int J Eng Res 5(4):303–307

Kootanaee AJ, Nagendra Babu K, Talari HF (2013) Just-in-time manufacturing system: from introduction to implement. Int J Econ Bus Finance 1(2): 07–25

Lehtonen JM, Holmström J (1998) Is just-in-time applicable in paper industry logistics? Supply Chain Manage Int J 3(1):21–32

Mullisa AG, Abdul-Kader W (2022) Optimal Kanban number: an integrated lean and simulation modelling approach. Int J Indus Manuf Syst Eng 7(1): 17

Pan AC, Liao CJ (1989) An inventory model under just-in-time purchasing agreement. Prod Invent Manage J 30(1):49–52

Perez F, Torres F (2019) An integrated production-inventory model for deteriorating items to evaluate JIT purchasing alliances. Int J Indus Eng Comput 10(1): 51–66

Ramnath BV, Elanchezhian C, Kesavan R (2010) Application of Kanban system for implementing lean manufacturing (a case study). J Eng Res Stud I (I) 13

Riza M, Purba HH (2018) The implementation of economic order quantity for reducing inventory cost. Res Logist Prod 8

Shah NH (2011) Single supplier–buyer integrated inventory model under multiple JIT delivery and stock-dependent demand. J Math Modell Algo 10(3):293–305

Singh SR, Rastogi A, Singhal S (2021) JIT: the best approach after lockdown in country. Int J Serv Oper Inf 11(1):75–86

Singh SR, Singh RB, Rastogi A, Singhal S (2023) A sustainable approach to manage the inventory during pandemic through passive RFID tags. In: Sahni M, Merigó JM, Hussain W (eds) Novel developments in futuristic AI-based technologies, algorithms for intelligent systems. Springer Nature, Singapore, pp 37–46

Singh SK, Chauhan A, Sarkar B (2024) Resilience of sustainability for a smart production system to produce biodiesel from waste animal fat. J Clean Prod 452: 142047

Singhal S, Rastogi A, Singh SR, Singh RB (2019) Preservation technology for sustainable fuzzified inventory model for a stock and price-dependent demand. Int J Invent Control Manage 08: 01–15

Wee HM (1993) Economic production lot size model for deteriorating items with partial backordering. Comput Ind Eng 24(3):449–458

Chapter 10
Safeguarding of Inventories with Green and Preservation Investment and Key Approach to Two-Level Trade Credit Policy

Ummeferva Zaidi, Shiv Raj Singh, and Surendra Vikram Singh Padiyar

Abstract At present, people all over the world are very concerned about the environment, are trying to protect it from pollution, and are also continuously using green technologies in the field of business to produce eco-friendly products. As a result, it has been seen that by determining the price of the item capturing the market within a particular economy is very challenging for managing a business. Every item has a specific shelf life, but to keep the inventory safe for a longer period, it is necessary to use some special techniques, i.e. preservation technology. Therefore, in this research study, an inventory model has been prepared in which trade-credit policy and price dependent demand have been taken for the convenience of customers along with the use of preservation technology for the safety of inventory. Maximum profit is obtained when the producer's credit period is greater than the cycle time. This model shows that, a more sensible approach is to invest in preservation to regulate the deterioration and invest in green technology to mitigate the emission. Further a comparative analysis validates the effectiveness of preservation and green investment with obtaining a maximum profit and less emission. Seven numerical illustration is shown to validate the proposed model and concavity is shown with help of the hessian matrix. Finally, a sensitivity table is performed to find the effect different parameters.

Keywords Deterioration · Preservation investment · Carbon tax policy · Green investment · Price dependent demand

U. Zaidi · S. R. Singh
Department of Mathematics, C.C.S. University Meerut, Meerut, Uttar Pradesh, India

S. V. S. Padiyar (✉)
H.N.B. Government Post Graduate College., Khatima, Uttarakhand, India
e-mail: surendrapadiyar1991@gmail.com

N. H. Shah and M. Mittal (eds.), *Sustainable Inventory Management*, Inventory Optimization, https://doi.org/10.1007/978-981-97-6765-6_11

10.1 Introduction and Literature Review

One of the most important factors for gaining profit in business is that every retailer should get discount in payment while taking inventory, due to which he can freely demand the inventory at his level. Therefore, trade credit policy in the inventory model acquires its own importance which provides a new direction.

In the traditional model it is prevalent that the retailer will make payment only at the time of purchasing the product. But this is not always possible in practice. To upsurge sales and market share, it is necessary for the manufacturer to give a discount to the retailer for delay in payment. According to the rules for this, Teng et al. (2013) introduced the inventory model to account for increasing demand, at two levels of trade credit related to the demand order of inventory. Teng et al. (2012) developed a new and unique model for economic consolidation by giving importance to trade credit for non-decreasing demand. Tiwari et al. (2018) facilitated backlogging of perishable goods by availing partial trade credit from two different levels in the supply chain. Singh et al. (2020) formulated trade credit to account for the impact of inflation and replenishment policy for perishable goods in an environment of acceptable shortages. Tayal et al. (2021) prepared a study in which credit facility was provided to the volume dependent business for partial backlogging. Mohanta et al. (2022) investigated a model applying neuron sophisticated logic for time-dependent demand for perishable products with a two-tier fractional trade. Moradi et al. (2023) modelled partial trade credit policy using learning effects. Shah et al. (2024) incorporates the impact of bi-level trade credit financing to the inventory model with multi variate demand and preservation investment.

In last few years, there has been a growing interest among researchers in exploring sustainable supply chains, particularly in response to the complex challenges posed by environmental concerns and evolving policies. Hua et al. (2011) [highlights the need for integrating sustainability considerations into inventory management. Toptal et al. (2014) delved into the economic order quantity model while considering investments in carbon emissions reduction under various carbon policies, demonstrating the complex relationship between inventory policy and carbon emissions mitigation. Tiwari (2019) assessed the effects of carbon tax policies on non-instantaneous deteriorating items under multiple trade credit policies, highlighting the intricate interplay between sustainability and inventory management. Padiyar et al. (2022) find use of green technology in the manufacturing process to maintain reliability strengthens the supply chain and also increases customer trust in manufacturers. Sarkar et al. (2023) proposed a study by employing a cap-trade service and devising strategies and also described the impact of information asymmetry. Singh and Chaudhary (2023) considered the effects of inflation on an inventory model with a carbon tax policy while accounting for product expiration dates, further emphasizing the need to adapt inventory strategies to evolving sustainability concerns. Kumar et al. (2024) finds the impact of learning and inflation on a multi-product manufacturing system under different carbon policies and green investment.

While developing the inventory model to save the environment, working on several important problems is necessary. A significant problem is the lack of resources to dispose of all perishable products after production or when supplying finished goods or raw inventory. To prevent wastage of material, it is necessary to use some important techniques so that the inventory can be preserved for a long time. Hsieh and Dye (2013) developed a model considering time-dependent demand, and introduces preservation investments a decision variable. This approach integrates the preservation technology cost with the production policy for a more comprehensive analysis. Ullah et al. (2019) developed two different ecological models for perishable products using conservation technology. Padiyar et al. (2022) addressed the ambiguities arising from imperfect production processes by modelling them in an integrated inventory model while providing preservation facilities under inflationary environments. Huo et al. (2023) makes every possible effort to eliminate any defective items, minimizes inventory drawdown, and keeps the quality of good products at a consistently high level. Saha et al. (2021) focused on protecting the environment as well as customer needs, using various techniques to preserve inventory, and providing a supply chain by continuously supplying fresh goods. Singh et al. (2024) finds the effect of preservation and inflation on a sustainable supply chain with demand depends on price and energy. The whole study is done in fuzzy environment.

10.1.1 Research Gap

At present, everyone is very concerned about the environment, and is making every possible effort to save the pollution caused by humans. Therefore, to save the environment in the business sector, special importance is being given to green production. Many authors have created many inventory models for different conditions but not all previous research has combined trade credit strategies with preservation technology for inventory, and balancing demand and production. The differences between the previous work and this research work can be understood through Table 10.1.

10.1.2 Contribution

Investing in conservation technology, including a smart production system, long-term storage of inventory, providing trade credit facilities to supply chain members with customers, and accurately balancing customer demand and production volumes. This is the first study on the inventory model. And along with this, providing solutions for environmental safety issues, properly holding the deteriorating inventory and delivering it to the consumer, makes it conducive for more profits in business.

The main contributions of this model that make it different from others are as follows:

Table. 10.1 Literature review

Research article	Type of credit period	Preservation technology investment	Demand type	Deterioration	Carbon policy	Green technology investment
Ma et. al. (2014)	No	No	Inventory dependent	No	Cap and trade	No
Shah (2015)	Two level	No	Price sensitive credit linked	Yes	No	No
Yadav et al. (2016)	Single-level	Yes	Multi variable	Yes	No	No
Datta (2017)	No	No	Price sensitive	No	Carbon tax	Yes
Sarkar et. al. (2020)	Single level	No	Selling-price and credit-period dependent	Yes	No	No
Shah et al. (2021)	No	Yes	Price-sensitive time dependent	Yes	No	No
Handa et. al (2022)	Two level	No	Constant	Yes	Carbon tax	No
Singh et al. (2022)	No	Yes	Stock dependent	Yes	No	No
Ummeferva et al. (2023)	Two-level	No	Price and greening degree dependent	Yes	Hybrid carbon policy	Yes
This paper	Two-level	Yes	Price dependent	Yes	Carbon tax	Yes

Source Own

- The present study in which preservation technology has been used for perishable products and this type of production system has been considered. So that protected products can be used for a longer period of time with less waste.
- Trade credit always helps in taking the business to a bigger level by giving relaxation in certain rules. Apart from this, business credit insurance rules also provide different levels of assistance to the consumer, such as taking a loan as per his need. Unlike other bad-debt reserves, if a business is not the destination of the loan, then in that case only the rules for payment become different. Therefore, trade credit policy has been used in this model.

After the above literature review, it has come to light that various researchers have made every possible effort to reduce costs and maximize profits by preparing different models at their own level. And in this proposed research, preservation technology has been used to maintain the quality of the product so that the inventory can be preserved for a long time. Along with this, discounts for payment have been provided by the manufacturers to all types of customers, so that harmony can be created between the consumer and the supplier. From the above discussion, one can conclude that the keywords taken for this research. There is a large research gap in the existing literature. Therefore, consideration has been given to bridge this research gap and provide a new model

10.2 Notations and Assumptions

Important notations and assumptions for developing the inventory model are as follows.

10.2.1 Notations

See Table 10.2.

10.2.2 Assumptions

(1) A three-echelon supply chain with single supplier, single manufacturer and single buyer is considered.
(2) The dynamics between price and demand is crucial for policymakers as they analyse market behavior and make decisions related to pricing strategies and other economic policies. Therefore, the demand is assumed as price dependent i.e. $D(x) = c - xd$ where $c > 0, d > 0$.
(3) This model considered constant deterioration rate and for reduce to deterioration preservation technology is used and $p(y) = \left(1 - e^{-ay}\right)$ be the preservation technology function which is an increasing function with $p''(y) < 0$
(4) For better relationship in a supply chain supplier provide a trade credit period of u years to the producer and in return, the manufacturer offers trade credit of v to credit-risk customers, who are required to make a payment of a $\mu\%$ of the total purchase cost at the time when order is placed (Das et al. 2021).
(5) The carbon emission costs for setup, storage and deterioration activities will be charged using the carbon tax policy (Hariga et al. 2017).
(6) Green investment is used to curb the emission and fraction $\rho\left(1 - e^{-\eta R}\right)$ is used

Table 10.2 Notations

Notations	Descriptions	Notations	Descriptions
A	Ordering cost ($/unit)	ϑ	Deterioration rate (constant)
C_H	Holding cost($/unit)	P	Manufacturing rate (units)
C_D	Deterioration cost ($/unit)	ε	Purchasing cost ($/unit)
x	Selling price ($/unit)	c	Market capacity (constant)
u	Producer's credit period provided by the supplier (year)	v	Customers' credit period given by the manufacturer (year)
d	Scale parameter of demand sensitivity with selling price (constant)	μ	Customers need to pay μ portion of the purchase price to the producer (%)
l_e	Rate of interest earned by the producer (%)	l_p	Rate of interest paid by the manufacturer (%)
F	Unit carbon emissions associated with setup (ton CO_2/unit)	η	Green investment parameter
C_{HE}	Unit carbon emission associated with holding cost (ton CO_2/unit)	λ	Tax for carbon emission
ρ	Fraction of carbon emission after green technology investment, $0 < \rho < 1$	C_{DE}	Unit carbon emission associated with deterioration cost (ton CO_2/ unit)
Decision variables			
R	Green technology investment ($)	y	Preservation technology cost per unit time ($)
t_p	Manufacturing time (year)	T	Cycle length (year)
Functions			
$I(t)$	Inventory level at any time t (units)		
$TP_i(t)$	Total profit		

Source Own

10.3 Mathematical Formulation

In this problem, the production begins at $t = 0$. The model experiences both production and concurrent demand and deterioration in the time duration 0 to t_p. At t_p manufacturing process stop. Throughout the interval $\left[t_p, T\right]$ the produced items are decreased by demand and deterioration, reaching zero at T. Consequently, the associated equations of the proposed model are defined as follows:

$$I_1'(t) = P - D(x) - \vartheta(1 - p(y))I_1(t), 0 < t < t_p \tag{10.1}$$

$$I_2'(t) = -D(x) - \vartheta(1 - p(y))I_2(t), t_p < t < T \tag{10.2}$$

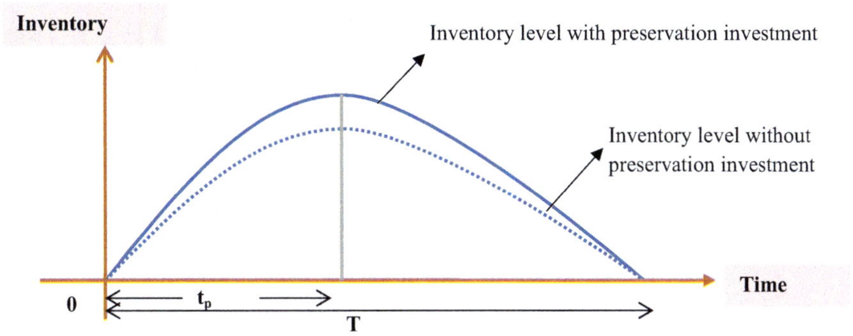

Fig. 10.1 Graphical representation for manufacturer inventory model. *Source* Own

With boundary condition $I_1(t) = 0$ at $t = 0$ and $I_2(t) = 0$ at $t = T$.

Equations (10.3) and (10.4) define the solution for the Eq. (10.1) and Eq. (10.2) respectively

$$I_1(t) = \frac{P - D(x)}{\vartheta(1 - p(y))}\left(1 - e^{-\vartheta(1-p(y))t}\right) \tag{10.3}$$

$$I_2(t) = \frac{D(x)}{\vartheta(1 - p(y))}\left(e^{\vartheta(1-p(y))(T-t)} - 1\right) \tag{10.4}$$

Total revenue generated by the manufacturer

$$\mathrm{TR} = xD(x)T \tag{10.5}$$

The computation of the system cost per unit cycle time involves the following cost components (Fig. 10.1).

(a) **Setup Cost**:

$$\mathrm{SC} = A \tag{10.6}$$

(b) **Holding Cost**:

$$\mathrm{HC} = C_H\left[\int_0^{t_p} I_1(t)\mathrm{d}t + \int_{t_p}^{T} I_2(t)\mathrm{d}t\right]$$

$$HC = C_H\left[\frac{P - D(x)}{\vartheta(1 - p(y))}\left(t_p + \frac{e^{-\vartheta(1-p(y))t_p} - 1}{\vartheta(1 - p(y))}\right)\right.$$

$$-\frac{D(x)}{\vartheta(1-p(y))}\left(T-t_p+\frac{1-e^{\vartheta(1-p(y))(T-t_p)}}{\vartheta(1-p(y))}\right)\Bigg] \tag{10.7}$$

(c) **Deterioration Cost**:

$$\mathrm{DC}=C_D\vartheta(1-p(y))\left[\int_0^{t_p} I_1(t)\mathrm{d}t+\int_{t_p}^{T} I_2(t)\mathrm{d}t\right]$$

$$\mathrm{DC}=C_D\Bigg[P-D(x)\left(t_p+\frac{e^{-\vartheta(1-p(y))t_p}-1}{\vartheta(1-p(y))}\right)$$
$$-D(x)\left(T-t_p+\frac{1-e^{\vartheta(1-p(y))(T-t_p)}}{\vartheta(1-p(y))}\right)\Bigg] \tag{10.8}$$

(d) **Preservation Technology Cost**:

$$\mathrm{PTC}=\int_0^T y\mathrm{d}t=yT \tag{10.9}$$

(e) **Emission Due to Setup**:

$$\mathrm{SC}=F \tag{10.10}$$

(f) **Emission Due to Storage**:

$$\mathrm{HC}_E=C_{\mathrm{HE}}\Bigg[\frac{P-D(x)}{\vartheta(1-p(y))}\left(t_p+\frac{e^{-\vartheta(1-p(y))t_p}-1}{\vartheta(1-p(y))}\right)$$
$$-\frac{D(x)}{\vartheta(1-p(y))}\left(T-t_p+\frac{1-e^{\vartheta(1-p(y))(T-t_p)}}{\vartheta(1-p(y))}\right)\Bigg] \tag{10.11}$$

(g) **Emission Due to Deterioration**:

$$\mathrm{DC}_E=C_{\mathrm{DE}}\Bigg[P-D(x)\left(t_p+\frac{e^{-\vartheta(1-p(y))t_p}-1}{\vartheta(1-p(y))}\right)$$
$$-D(x)\left(T-t_p+\frac{1-e^{\vartheta(1-p(y))(T-t_p)}}{\vartheta(1-p(y))}\right)\Bigg] \tag{10.12}$$

(h) **Green Technology Investment Cost**:

$$\mathrm{GTC}=\mathrm{RT} \tag{10.13}$$

(i) **Total Carbon Emission Cost**:

$$\text{Total carbon emission} = \text{Emission due to setup} + \text{Emission due to storage} + \text{Emission due to deterioration}$$

$$\text{TCE} = F + \left(\frac{C_{\text{HE}}}{\vartheta(1-p(y))} + C_{\text{DE}}\right)\left[P - D(x)\left(t_p + \frac{e^{-\vartheta(1-p(y))t_p} - 1}{\vartheta(1-p(y))}\right) - D(x)\left(T - t_p + \frac{1 - e^{\vartheta(1-p(y))(T-t_p)}}{\vartheta(1-p(y))}\right)\right] \quad (10.14)$$

To control the exceeding amount of CEs, carbon reduction investment has been considered to reduce the emissions.

Amount of CEs with carbon reduction green investment is:

$$\text{RCE} = \left[F + \left(\frac{C_{\text{HE}}}{\vartheta(1-p(y))} + C_{\text{DE}}\right)\left[P - D(x)\left(t_p + \frac{e^{-\vartheta(1-p(y))t_p} - 1}{\vartheta(1-p(y))}\right) - D(x)\left(T - t_p + \frac{1 - e^{\vartheta(1-p(y))(T-t_p)}}{\vartheta(1-p(y))}\right)\right]\right]\left(1 - \rho\left(1 - e^{-\eta R}\right)\right) \quad (10.15)$$

Now the carbon emission cost using "carbon tax" policy

$$\text{CEC} = \lambda\left[F + \left(\frac{C_{\text{HE}}}{\vartheta(1-p(y))} + C_{\text{DE}}\right)\left[P - D(x)\left(t_p + \frac{e^{-\vartheta(1-p(y))t_p} - 1}{\vartheta(1-p(y))}\right) - D(x)\left(T - t_p + \frac{1 - e^{\vartheta(1-p(y))(T-t_p)}}{\vartheta(1-p(y))}\right)\right]\right]\left(1 - \rho\left(1 - e^{-\eta R}\right)\right) \quad (10.16)$$

There may arise two scenarios based on the considered credit period durations:

- When producer's credit period (u) is greater than the credit period of customer (v).
- When manufacturer's credit period (u) is less than the customer's credit period (v).

According to above two scenarios there can be seven possible outcomes in this situation which is defined as follow

Case-i: $u < t_p$ **Case-ii:** $t_p < u < T$

Case-iii: $v < T < u$ **Case-iv:** $T < v < u$

Case-v: $u < v \le t_p$ **Case-vi:** $t_p \prec u < v \le T$

Case-vii: $T \le u < v$

Case-1: $u < t_p$

In this scenario, the producer accrues interest during the specified duration $[0, u]$ and settles the interest payment within the time $[u, T]$. For this case calculation of both interests paid and the interest earned are determined as follows:

$$\begin{aligned}\text{IP} &= \frac{\varepsilon l_p}{T}\left[\int_u^{t_p} I_1(t)\text{d}t + \int_{t_p}^{T} I_2(t)\text{d}t\right] \\ &= \frac{\varepsilon l_p}{T\vartheta(1-p(y))}\left[(P - D(x))\left(t_p - u + \frac{e^{-\vartheta(1-p(y))t_p} - e^{-\vartheta(1-p(y))u}}{\vartheta(1-p(y))}\right)\right. \\ &\left. -D(x)\left(T - t_p + \frac{1 - e^{\vartheta(1-p(y))(T-t_p)}}{\vartheta(1-p(y))}\right)\right] \end{aligned} \tag{10.17}$$

$$\text{IE} = \frac{1}{T}\left[xl_e\mu D(x)\int_0^u t\text{d}t + xl_e D(x)\int_v^u t\text{d}t\right]$$

$$\text{IE} = \frac{xl_e D(x)}{2T}\left[u^2 + (\mu - 1)v^2\right] \tag{10.18}$$

Therefore, manufacturer's profit for case-1 is

$$\text{TP}_1 = \text{SR-OC-HC-DC} + \text{-GTI-PTI-CEC-IP} + \text{IE}$$

$$\mathrm{TP}_1 = \frac{1}{T}\left[\begin{array}{l} xD(x)T - A - \left(\frac{C_H}{\vartheta(1-p(y))} + C_D\right)[P \\ -D(x)\left(t_p + \frac{e^{-\vartheta(1-p(y))t_p} - 1}{\vartheta(1-p(y))}\right) \\ -D(x)\left(T - t_p + \frac{1 - e^{\vartheta(1-p(y))(T-t_p)}}{\vartheta(1-p(y))}\right)\Bigg] - yT \\ -F - \mathrm{RT} - \lambda\Bigg[F + \left(\frac{C_{\mathrm{HE}}}{\vartheta(1-p(y))} + C_{\mathrm{DE}}\right)[P \\ -D(x)\left(t_p + \frac{e^{-\vartheta(1-p(y))t_p} - 1}{\vartheta(1-p(y))}\right) \\ -D(x)\left(T - t_p + \frac{1 - e^{\vartheta(1-p(y))(T-t_p)}}{\vartheta(1-p(y))}\right)\Bigg]\Bigg] \\ \left(1 - \rho\left(1 - e^{-\eta R}\right)\right) \\ -\frac{\varepsilon l_p}{T\vartheta(1-p(y))}\left[(P - D(x))\left(t_p\right.\right. \\ \left.-u + \frac{e^{-\vartheta(1-p(y))t_p} - e^{-\vartheta(1-p(y))u}}{\vartheta(1-p(y))}\right) \\ \left.-D(x)\left(T - t_p + \frac{1 - e^{\vartheta(1-p(y))(T-t_p)}}{\vartheta(1-p(y))}\right)\right] \\ +\frac{xl_e D(x)}{2T}\left[u^2 + (\mu - 1)v^2\right] \end{array}\right] \quad (10.19)$$

Case-2: $t_p < u < T$

In this case, producer accrues interest over the specified time period 0 to u and is obligated to make the interest payment within the designated timeframe u to T. The computation of the interest paid and earned are calculated as follows:

$$\begin{aligned} \mathrm{IP} &= \frac{\varepsilon l_p}{T}\left[\int_u^T I_2(t)\mathrm{d}t\right] \\ &= \frac{\varepsilon l_p D(x)}{(\vartheta(1-p(y)))^2 T}\left[e^{\vartheta(1-p(y))(T-u)}\right. \\ &\quad \left. -\vartheta(1-p(y))(T-u) - 1\right] \end{aligned} \quad (10.20)$$

$$\mathrm{IE} = \frac{1}{T}\left[xl_e\mu D(x)\int_0^u t\mathrm{d}t + xl_e D(x)\int_v^u t\mathrm{d}t\right]$$

$$\mathrm{IE} = \frac{xl_e D(x)}{2T}\left[u^2 + (\mu - 1)v^2\right] \tag{10.21}$$

Therefore, manufacturer's profit for case-2 is

$$\mathrm{TP}_2 = \text{SR-OC-HC-DC} + \text{-GTI-PTI-CEC-IP} + \mathrm{IE}$$

$$\mathrm{TP}_2 = \frac{1}{T}\left[\begin{array}{l} xD(x)T - A - \left(\dfrac{C_H}{\vartheta(1-p(y))} + C_D\right)[P \\ -D(x)\left(t_p + \dfrac{e^{-\vartheta(1-p(y))t_p} - 1}{\vartheta(1-p(y))}\right) \\ -D(x)\left(T - t_p + \dfrac{1 - e^{\vartheta(1-p(y))(T-t_p)}}{\vartheta(1-p(y))}\right)\Bigg] - yT \\ -F - \mathrm{RT} - \lambda\Bigg[F + \left(\dfrac{C_{\mathrm{HE}}}{\vartheta(1-p(y))} + C_{\mathrm{DE}}\right)[P \\ -D(x)\left(t_p + \dfrac{e^{-\vartheta(1-p(y))t_p} - 1}{\vartheta(1-p(y))}\right) \\ -D(x)\left(T - t_p + \dfrac{1 - e^{\vartheta(1-p(y))(T-t_p)}}{\vartheta(1-p(y))}\right)\Bigg]\Bigg](1 \\ -\rho\left(1 - e^{-\eta R}\right)) \\ -\dfrac{\varepsilon l_p D(x)}{(\vartheta(1-p(y)))^2 T}\left[e^{\vartheta(1-p(y))(T-u)}\right. \\ \left. -\vartheta(1-p(y))(T-u) - 1\right] \\ +\dfrac{xl_e D(x)}{2T}\left[u^2 + (\mu-1)v^2\right] \end{array}\right] \tag{10.22}$$

Case-3: $v < T < u$

In this scenario the producer is not required to pay the interest and he earned interest in the complete cycle which is calculated as follows:

$$\mathrm{IP} = 0 \tag{10.23}$$

$$\mathrm{IE} = \frac{1}{T}\left[xl_e\mu D(x)\int_0^v t\,\mathrm{d}t + xl_e D(x)\int_v^T t\,\mathrm{d}t + D(x)\int_T^u \mathrm{d}t\right]$$

$$\mathrm{IE} = \frac{xl_e D(x)}{2T}\left[2uT + (\mu - 1)v^2 - T^2\right] \tag{10.24}$$

Hence, manufacturer's profit for case-3 is

$$\mathrm{TP}_3 = \text{SR-OC-HC-DC} + \text{-GTI-PTI-CEC-IP} + \mathrm{IE}$$

$$\mathrm{TP}_3 = \frac{1}{T}\begin{bmatrix} xD(x)T - A - \left(\dfrac{C_H}{\vartheta(1-p(y))} + C_D\right)[P \\ -D(x)\left(t_p + \dfrac{e^{-\vartheta(1-p(y))t_p} - 1}{\vartheta(1-p(y))}\right) \\ -D(x)\left(T - t_p + \dfrac{1 - e^{\vartheta(1-p(y))(T-t_p)}}{\vartheta(1-p(y))}\right)\Bigg] - yT \\ -F - \mathrm{RT} - \lambda\Bigg[F + \left(\dfrac{C_{\mathrm{HE}}}{\vartheta(1-p(y))} + C_{\mathrm{DE}}\right)[P \\ -D(x)\left(t_p + \dfrac{e^{-\vartheta(1-p(y))t_p} - 1}{\vartheta(1-p(y))}\right) \\ -D(x)\left(T - t_p + \dfrac{1 - e^{\vartheta(1-p(y))(T-t_p)}}{\vartheta(1-p(y))}\right)\Bigg]\Bigg](1 \\ -\rho\left(1 - e^{-\eta R}\right)) \\ + \dfrac{xl_e D(x)}{2T}\left[2uT + (\mu - 1)v^2 - T^2\right] \end{bmatrix} \tag{10.25}$$

Case-4: $T < v < u$

In this case the producer earned only interest and he has no require pay the interest to the supplier

$$\mathrm{IP} = 0 \tag{10.26}$$

$$\mathrm{IE} = \frac{1}{T}\left[xl_e\mu D(x)\int_0^T t\mathrm{d}t + xl_e\mu T D(x)\int_T^v t\mathrm{d}t + T\int_v^u \mathrm{d}t\right]$$

$$\mathrm{IE} = xl_e D(x)\left[u + (\mu - 1)v - \frac{\mu T}{2}\right] \tag{10.27}$$

Therefore, manufacturer's profit for case-4 is

$$\mathrm{TP}_4 = \text{SR-OC-HC-DC} + \text{-GTI-PTI-CEC-IP} + \mathrm{IE}$$

$$\mathrm{TP}_4=\frac{1}{T}\left[\begin{array}{l} xD(x)T-A-\left(\frac{C_H}{\vartheta(1-p(y))}+C_D\right)[P \\ -D(x)\left(t_p+\frac{e^{-\vartheta(1-p(y))t_p}-1}{\vartheta(1-p(y))}\right) \\ -D(x)\left(T-t_p+\frac{1-e^{\vartheta(1-p(y))(T-t_p)}}{\vartheta(1-p(y))}\right)\Bigg]-yT \\ -F-\mathrm{RT}-\lambda\Bigg[F+\left(\frac{C_{\mathrm{HE}}}{\vartheta(1-p(y))}+C_{\mathrm{DE}}\right)[P \\ -D(x)\left(t_p+\frac{e^{-\vartheta(1-p(y))t_p}-1}{\vartheta(1-p(y))}\right) \\ -D(x)\left(T-t_p+\frac{1-e^{\vartheta(1-p(y))(T-t_p)}}{\vartheta(1-p(y))}\right)\Bigg]\Bigg](1 \\ -\rho\left(1-e^{-\eta R}\right)) \\ +xl_eD(x)\left[u+(\mu-1)v-\frac{\mu T}{2}\right] \end{array}\right] \tag{10.28}$$

Case-5: $u < v \le t_p$

In this scenario, the producer accrues interest during the specified duration $[0, u]$ and settles the interest payment within the time $[u, T]$. For this case calculation of both interests paid and the interest earned are determined as follows:

$$\begin{aligned} \mathrm{IP} &= \frac{\varepsilon l_p}{T}\left[\int_u^{t_p} I_1(t)\mathrm{d}t+\int_{t_p}^{T} I_2(t)\mathrm{d}t\right] \\ &= \frac{\varepsilon l_p}{T\vartheta(1-p(y))}\Bigg[(P-D(x))\left(t_p-u+\frac{e^{-\vartheta(1-p(y))t_p}-e^{-\vartheta(1-p(y))u}}{\vartheta(1-p(y))}\right) \\ &\quad -D(x)\left(T-t_p+\frac{1-e^{\vartheta(1-p(y))(T-t_p)}}{\vartheta(1-p(y))}\right)\Bigg] \end{aligned} \tag{10.29}$$

$$\mathrm{IE}=\frac{xl_e\mu D(x)}{T}\int_0^u t\mathrm{d}t$$

$$\mathrm{IE}=\frac{x\mu l_eD(x)u^2}{2T} \tag{10.30}$$

Therefore, manufacturer's profit for case-5 is

$$\mathrm{TP}_5=\text{SR-OC-HC-DC}+\text{-GTI-PTI-CEC-IP}+\mathrm{IE}$$

$$\mathrm{TP}_5 = \frac{1}{T}\left[\begin{array}{l} xD(x)T - A - \left(\frac{C_H}{\vartheta(1-p(y))} + C_D\right)[P \\ -D(x)\left(t_p + \frac{e^{-\vartheta(1-p(y))t_p} - 1}{\vartheta(1-p(y))}\right) \\ -D(x)\left(T - t_p + \frac{1 - e^{\vartheta(1-p(y))(T-t_p)}}{\vartheta(1-p(y))}\right)\Bigg] - yT \\ -F - \mathrm{RT} - \lambda\Bigg[F + \left(\frac{C_{\mathrm{HE}}}{\vartheta(1-p(y))} + C_{\mathrm{DE}}\right)[P \\ -D(x)\left(t_p + \frac{e^{-\vartheta(1-p(y))t_p} - 1}{\vartheta(1-p(y))}\right) \\ -D(x)\left(T - t_p + \frac{1 - e^{\vartheta(1-p(y))(T-t_p)}}{\vartheta(1-p(y))}\right)\Bigg]\Bigg](1 \\ -\rho\left(1 - e^{-\eta R}\right)) \\ -\frac{\varepsilon l_p}{T\vartheta(1-p(y))}\left[(P - D(x))\left(t_p\right.\right. \\ \left.-u + \frac{e^{-\vartheta(1-p(y))t_p} - e^{-\vartheta(1-p(y))u}}{\vartheta(1-p(y))}\right) \\ -D(x)\left(T - t_p + \frac{1 - e^{\vartheta(1-p(y))(T-t_p)}}{\vartheta(1-p(y))}\right)\Bigg] \\ +\frac{x\mu l_e D(x)u^2}{2T} \end{array}\right] \tag{10.31}$$

Case-6: $t_p < u < v \leq T$

In this case, interest paid amount and earn amount are calculated as:

$$\mathrm{IP} = \frac{\varepsilon l_p}{T}\left[\int_u^T I_2(t)\mathrm{d}t\right]$$

$$\mathrm{IP} = \frac{\varepsilon l_p D(x)}{(\vartheta(1-p(y)))^2 T}\left[e^{\vartheta(1-p(y))(T-u)} - \vartheta(1-p(y))(T-u) - 1\right] \tag{10.32}$$

$$\mathrm{IE} = \frac{x l_e \mu D(x)}{T}\int_0^u t\,\mathrm{d}t$$

$$\mathrm{IE} = \frac{x\mu l_e D(x)u^2}{2T} \tag{10.33}$$

Therefore, manufacturer's profit for case-6 is

$$\mathrm{TP}_6 = \text{SR-OC-HC-DC} + \text{-GTI-PTI-CEC-IP} + \text{IE}$$

$$\mathrm{TP}_6 = \frac{1}{T}\left[\begin{array}{l} xD(x)T - A - \left(\dfrac{C_H}{\vartheta(1-p(y))} + C_D\right)[P \\ -D(x)\left(t_p + \dfrac{e^{-\vartheta(1-p(y))t_p} - 1}{\vartheta(1-p(y))}\right) \\ -D(x)\left(T - t_p + \dfrac{1 - e^{\vartheta(1-p(y))(T-t_p)}}{\vartheta(1-p(y))}\right)\Bigg] - yT \\ -F - \mathrm{RT} - \lambda\Bigg[F + \left(\dfrac{C_{\mathrm{HE}}}{\vartheta(1-p(y))} + C_{\mathrm{DE}}\right)[P \\ -D(x)\left(t_p + \dfrac{e^{-\vartheta(1-p(y))t_p} - 1}{\vartheta(1-p(y))}\right) \\ -D(x)\left(T - t_p + \dfrac{1 - e^{\vartheta(1-p(y))(T-t_p)}}{\vartheta(1-p(y))}\right)\Bigg]\Bigg](1 \\ -\rho\left(1 - e^{-\eta R}\right)) \\ -\dfrac{\varepsilon l_p D(x)}{(\vartheta(1-p(y)))^2 T}\left[e^{\vartheta(1-p(y))(T-u)}\right. \\ \left. -\vartheta(1-p(y))(T-u) - 1\right] + \dfrac{x\mu l_e D(x) u^2}{2T} \end{array}\right] \tag{10.34}$$

Case-7: $T \leq u < v$

In this scenario, the producer is not obligated to remit any interest to the supplier. The computation of interest paid and earned are calculated as follows:

$$\mathrm{IP} = 0 \tag{10.35}$$

$$\mathrm{IE} = \frac{1}{T}\left[xl_e\mu D(x)\int_0^T t\,\mathrm{d}t + xl_e\mu T D(x)\int_T^u \mathrm{d}t + T\int_u^v \mathrm{d}t\right]$$

$$\mathrm{IE} = xl_e D(x)\left[v + (\mu - 1)u - \frac{\mu T}{2}\right] \tag{10.36}$$

Therefore, manufacturer's profit for case-7 is

$$\mathrm{TP}_7 = \text{SR-OC-HC-DC} + \text{-GTI-PTI-CEC-IP} + \text{IE}$$

$$\mathrm{TP}_7 = \frac{1}{T}\left[\begin{array}{l} xD(x)T - A - \left(\frac{C_H}{\vartheta(1-p(y))} + C_D\right)[P \\ -D(x)\left(t_p + \frac{e^{-\vartheta(1-p(y))t_p} - 1}{\vartheta(1-p(y))}\right) \\ -D(x)\left(T - t_p + \frac{1 - e^{\vartheta(1-p(y))(T-t_p)}}{\vartheta(1-p(y))}\right)\Bigg] - yT \\ -F - \mathrm{RT} - \lambda\Bigg[F + \left(\frac{C_{\mathrm{HE}}}{\vartheta(1-p(y))} + C_{\mathrm{DE}}\right)[P \\ -D(x)\left(t_p + \frac{e^{-\vartheta(1-p(y))t_p} - 1}{\vartheta(1-p(y))}\right) \\ -D(x)\left(T - t_p + \frac{1 - e^{\vartheta(1-p(y))(T-t_p)}}{\vartheta(1-p(y))}\right)\Bigg]\Bigg](1 \\ -\rho\left(1 - e^{-\eta R}\right)) \\ +xl_e D(x)\left[v + (\mu - 1)u - \frac{\mu T}{2}\right] \end{array}\right] \tag{10.37}$$

10.4 Solution Procedure

The profit of the integrated model is the function of four decision variable t_p, T, R, y and the necessary condition to maximize the total profit is

$$\frac{\partial TP_i}{\partial t_p} = 0, \tag{10.38}$$

$$\frac{\partial TP_i}{\partial T} = 0, \tag{10.39}$$

$$\frac{\partial TP_i}{\partial R} = 0, \tag{10.40}$$

$$\frac{\partial TP_i}{\partial y} = 0 \tag{10.41}$$

On solving the Eqs. (10.38–10.41), we get the values of t_p, T, R, y. Check the nature of the Hessian matrix

$$M\left(t_p, T, R, y\right) = \begin{bmatrix} \frac{\partial^2 TP_i}{\partial t_p^2} & \frac{\partial^2 TP_i}{\partial t_p \partial T} & \frac{\partial^2 TP_i}{\partial t_p \partial R} & \frac{\partial^2 TP_i}{\partial t_p \partial y} \\ \frac{\partial^2 TP_i}{\partial T \partial t_p} & \frac{\partial^2 TP_i}{\partial T^2} & \frac{\partial^2 TP_i}{\partial T \partial R} & \frac{\partial^2 TP_i}{\partial T \partial y} \\ \frac{\partial^2 TP_i}{\partial R \partial t_p} & \frac{\partial^2 TP_i}{\partial R \partial T} & \frac{\partial^2 TP_i}{\partial R^2} & \frac{\partial^2 TP_i}{\partial R \partial y} \\ \frac{\partial^2 TP_i}{\partial y \partial t_p} & \frac{\partial^2 TP_i}{\partial y \partial T} & \frac{\partial^2 TP_i}{\partial y \partial R} & \frac{\partial^2 TP_i}{\partial y^2} \end{bmatrix}$$

At obtained point. If H is negative definite the $TP_i\left(t_p, T, R, y\right)$ is the optimal profit of the system.

10.5 Numerical Illustration

To validate the proposed study numerical example is given for all the seven cases. All calculations are performed using MATHEMATICA 12.

Example 1: To demonstrate the first case following data is used $C_D = 1.6, O = 240, P = 180, C_H = 0.02, c = 120, d = 0.7, x = 80, \xi = 0.2, \eta = 0.1, \theta = 0.8, l_e = 0.1, u = 1.4, B = 1200, C_{\mathrm{HE}} = 0.9$

t_1	T	R	y	CE	TP_1
0.611633	1.68778	10.8872	10.4171	644.094	4661.19

Concavity of Manufacturer's Profit: Now, we examine the principal minor of matrix M at (0.611633, 1.68778, 10.8872, 10.4171).

$$M_{11} = -664.74 < 0, M_{22} = 102916.57 > 0$$
$$M_{33} = -10486.86 < 0, M_{44} = 1347979.45 > 0$$

Hence, the matrix M is negative semi-definite leading to the conclusion that profit attains its maximum at (0.611633, 1.68778, 10.8872, 10.4171).

Example 2: To validate the second case, the data remains unchanged except for the $v = 0.3, u = 0.7$.

t_1	T	R	y	CE	TP_2
0.534715	1.4708	12.161	9.43745	724.8	4781.6

Concavity of Manufacturer's Profit: Now, we calculate the principal minor of matrix M at (0.534715, 1.4708, 12.161, 9.43745).

$$M_{11} = -39.4857 < 0, M_{22} = 15572.009187539999999 > 0$$

$$M_{33} = -7079339.58 < 0, M_{44} = 2055935.72 > 0$$

Hence, the matrix M is negative semi-definite that means profit attains its maximum at (0.534715, 1.4708, 12.161, 9.43745).

Example 3: To validate the third scenario, the data remains unchanged except for the $v = 0.3, u = 1.4$.

t_1	T	R	y	CE	TP_3
0.487644	1.32957	13.1119	7.98297	792.119	5118.76

Concavity of Manufacturer's Profit: Now, we examine the principal minor of matrix M at (0.487644, 1.32957, 13.1119, 7.98297).

$$M_{11} = -39.4857 < 0, M_{22} = 15572.01 > 0$$
$$M_{33} = -1537.23 < 0, M_{44} = 465.91 > 0$$

Hence, the matrix M is negative semi-definite i.e. profit attains its maximum at (0.487644, 1.32957, 13.1119, 7.98297).

Example 4: To validate the fourth scenario, the data remains unchanged except for the $v = 2.9, u = 2.95$.

t_1	T	R	y	CE	TP_4
1.04595	2.85319	6.40183	10.5816	429.366	5105.14

Concavity of Manufacturer's Profit: Now, we examine the principal minor of matrix M at (1.04595, 2.85319, 6.40183, 10.5816).

$$M_{11} = -14.96 < 0, M_{22} = 589.45 > 0$$
$$M_{33} = -57.85 < 0, M_{44} = 17.394 > 0$$

Therefore, the matrix M is negative semi-definite leading to the conclusion that profit attains its maximum at (1.04595, 2.85319, 6.40183, 10.5816).

Example 5: To validate the fifth case, the data remains unchanged except for the $v = 0.4, u = 0.3$.

t_1	T	R	y	CE	TP_5
0.644911	1.77924	181.039	10.5573	566.222	4649.26

Concavity of Manufacturer's Profit: Now, we examine the principal minor of matrix M at (0.644911, 1.77924, 181.039, 10.5573).

$$M_{11} = -629.1 < 0, M_{22} = 92192.887575 > 0$$
$$M_{33} = -0.000358 < 0, M_{44} = 0.001051 > 0$$

Hence, the matrix M is negative semi-definite leading to the conclusion that profit attains its maximum value at (0.644911, 1.77924, 181.039, 10.5573).

Example 6: To illustrate the sixth scenario, the data remains unchanged except for the $v = 0.6, u = 0.55$.

t_1	T	R	y	CE	TP_6
0.56412	1.5593	159.954	10.4644	639.02	4700.85

Concavity of Manufacturer's Profit: Now, we examine the principal minor of the matrix M at (0.644911, 1.77924, 181.039, 10.5573).

$$M_{11} = -25.3953 <0, M_{22} = 6626.53 > 0$$
$$M_{33} = -0.000239 < 0, M_{44} = 0.0000709 > 0$$

Hence, matrix M is negative semi-definite leading to the conclusion that profit attains its maximum value at (0.644911, 1.77924, 181.039, 10.5573).

Example 7: To validate the seventh case, the data remains unchanged except for the $v = 2.9, u = 2.8$.

t_1	T	R	y	CE	TP_7
1.02006	2.78217	174.763	10.4818	386.893	5044.84

Concavity of Manufacturer's Profit: Now, we examine the principal minor of matrix M at (1.02006, 2.78217, 174.763, 10.4818).

$$M_{11} = -14.2142 < 0, M_{22} = 570.6595 > 0$$
$$M_{33} = -0.000002838 < 0, M_{44} = 0.0000008537 > 0$$

Hence, M is negative semi-definite i.e. profit attains its maximum at (1.02006, 2.78217, 174.763, 10.4818).

Table 10.3 Comparative study

Parameters	With preservation and green investment	Without green and with preservation investment	Without preservation and with green investment
t_p	0.487644	0.505251	0.605952
T	1.32957	1.3775	1.2665
R	13.1119	0	13.6056
y	7.98297	8.11537	0
CE	792.119	896.986	829.672
TP_3	5118.76	5105.22	5093.04

Source Own

10.6 Comparative Analysis

Based on aforementioned cases of trade credit, it is evident that maximum profit is obtained in third case i.e.$v < T < u$. So, this comparison is done for that case.

Government has implemented many policies intending to reduce the carbon footprint and promotes cleaner, sustainable practices. This model used a "carbon tax" policy, where a tax is a form of carbon pricing. Preservation technology is employed to diminish waste and minimize the environmental impact of their inventory operations (Table 10.3).

From the table it is cleared that by implementation of the green technology provides a substantial increase in the profit of the system 13.54, along with the noteworthy decrease of 104.867 in carbon emission. Similarly, the implementation of preservation investment gives an increment in the profit 25.76 along with the noteworthy decrease of 37.553. Hence, the results indicates that by integrating green and preservation investments into the system decision maker can contribute to a more sustainable future while earning various economic and environment benefits. The effect of change in "manufacturing time", "cycle time", "green investment", "preservation investment", "carbon emission" and the "total profit" is shown in Fig. 10.2.

10.7 Sensitivity Analysis

A sensitivity analysis is conducted to for third case to examine the variation in the decision variables, carbon emission and the total profit. This analysis is carried out by adjusting a single parameter's value by -30% and +30%, while keeping the values of the other parameters constant. The results of these variations to the optimal policies are detailed in Table 10.4.

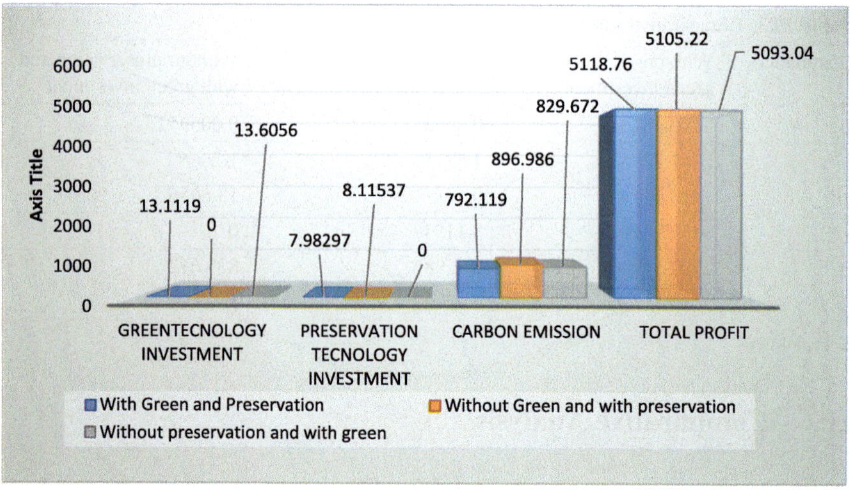

Fig. 10.2 Pictorial representation of comparative study. *Source* Own

10.8 Observations

1. The increasing production rate results a decreasing value of production time, cycle time and manufacturer's profit and an increasing value of preservation investment, green investment and carbon emission. As a result, manufacturer should not increase the production rate because the holding cost increases huge leads to lower profit and higher emission.
2. If the ordering cost increases, manufacturing time, cycle time, preservation investment increases while the carbon emission, and total profit decreases. This indicates that higher ordering cost leads to lower profit.
3. An increase in the demand parameter c results in the following: an increase in the production time, a decrease in the cycle time, an increase in the green investment cost, an increment in the carbon emission and an increase in the total profit.
4. If the demand parameter d increases then the preservation cost, green technology cost and total profit decreases. An increase in the price elasticity value indicates a decline in demand, leading to lower profits.
5. It is observed from the table when efficiency of greener technology rate increases then it gives the decreasing value of green investment, preservation investment and increasing value of carbon emission and total profit. Thus, the profit increases due to the lower investment in preservation and green.
6. The change in the deterioration rate decreases the total profit and increases the preservation cost with constant emission and green investment cost.

Table. 10.4 Sensitivity table

Parameter	Value	t_p	T	R	y	CE	TP_3
$C_D = 1.6$	2.08	0.48429	1.32959	13.1108	8.82803	927.541	5117.91
	1.84	0.485754	1.32958	13.1113	8.4323	927.588	5118.3
	1.36	0.40179	1.32956	13.1128	7.46312	927.729	5119.28
	1.12	0.493761	1.32954	13.114	6.84619	927.841	5119.9
$O = 240$	312	0.524762	1.43082	12.4205	8.23106	865.677	5066.59
	276	0.506547	1.38113	12.7527	8.11156	894.918	5092.2
	204	0.467967	1.2759	13.5026	7.84381	964.609	5146.39
	168	0.447413	1.21984	13.9305	7.69214	1006.78	5175.24
$P = 180$	234	0.374616	1.32828	13.1562	8.42967	931.765	5117.71
	207	0.42372	1.32884	13.137	8.24216	929.977	5118.16
	153	0.574297	1.33056	13.0778	7.59979	924.492	5119.59
	126	0.69845	1.33198	13.0288	6.96959	924.367	5120.87
$C_H = 0.02$	0.026	0.487519	1.32925	13.1142	7.98357	927.861	5118.59
	0.023	0.487581	1.32941	13.1131	7.98327	927.755	5118.67
	0.017	0.487706	1.32973	13.1108	7.98268	927.542	5118.84
	0.014	0.487768	1.32989	13.1096	7.98238	927.436	5118.92
$c = 120$	156	0.610383	1.07629	15.1433	7.38269	1136.59	8221.55
	138	0.55168	1.18145	14.2523	7.77639	1039.7	6665.56
	102	0.420013	1.54364	11.6581	8.00502	802.128	3670.24
	84	0.330719	1.99098	9.16057	7.76416	624.854	2075.59
$d = 0.7$	0.91	0.420863	1.54046	11.6783	8.00586	803.75	3687.19
	0.805	0.455291	1.4228	12.4534	8.01656	868.525	4401.17
	0.595	0.518316	1.25341	13.6828	7.90894	982.145	5839.24
	0.49	0.550322	1.18418	14.2301	7.78294	1037.39	6631.08
$x = 80$	104	0.371094	1.35812	12.8695	7.57583	905.427	4894
	92	0.425872	1.3308	13.0857	7.78962	925.218	5114.15
	68	0.559982	1.35419	12.9513	8.16903	912.867	4907.76
	56	0.648769	1.40955	12.5831	8.36347	877.991	4481.92
$\lambda = 0.2$	0.26	0.516557	1.4087	15.1904	8.19872	878.427	5072.82
	0.23	0.50234	1.36978	14.2281	8.0937	901.903	5095.41
	0.17	0.477558	1.30198	12.2569	7.90561	946.257	5134.8
	0.14	0.512065	0.97683	–	68.055	–	6728.3
$\eta = 0.1$	0.13	0.486096	1.32534	12.1275	7.97118	930.453	5122.08
	0.115	0.486768	1.32718	12.6318	7.97631	929.232	5120.56
	0.085	0.48883	1.33282	13.4867	7.992	925.512	5116.59
	0.07	0.490528	1.33746	13.556	8.00489	922.471	5113.96
$\vartheta = 0.8$	1.04	0.487644	1.32957	13.1119	8.85752	927.648	5117.88

(continued)

Table. 10.4 (continued)

Parameter	Value	t_p	T	R	y	CE	TP_3
	0.92	0.487644	1.32957	13.1119	8.44885	927.648	5118.29
	0.68	0.487644	1.32957	13.1119	7.44124	927.648	5119.3
	0.56	0.487644	1.32957	13.1119	6.79406	927.648	5119.95
$I_e = 0.1$	0.13	0.430558	1.17387	14.2978	7.56254	1044.45	5233.62
	0.115	0.456284	1.24403	13.7433	7.75842	988.104	5174.77
	0.085	0.527005	1.43694	12.3805	8.2455	862.22	5066.27
	0.07	0.578405	1.57716	11.5133	8.56066	790.6	5018.33
$u = 1.4$	1.82	0.487644	1.32957	13.1119	7.98297	927.648	5333.8
	1.61	0.487644	1.32957	13.1119	7.98297	927.648	5226.28
	1.19	0.487644	1.32957	13.1119	7.98297	927.648	5011.24
	0.98	0.487644	1.32957	13.1119	7.98297	927.648	4903.72
$F = 180$	1560	0.517656	1.41142	15.1019	8.18381	1131.9	5074.17
	1380	0.502879	1.37112	14.1814	8.08637	1032.36	5096.07
	1020	0.472348	1.28786	11.8811	7.87601	820.215	5141.68
	840	0.455601	1.24219	10.2918	7.5508	699.69	5167.01
$C_{HE} = 0.9$	1.17	0.486637	1.32696	13.2104	7.98712	936.831	5117.48
	1.035	0.487135	1.32825	13.1617	7.98507	932.278	5118.11
	0.765	0.48815	1.33089	13.0621	7.98089	923.043	5119.39
	0.63	0.488659	1.33221	13.012	7.97879	918.428	5120.03

Source Own

7. From the table it seems that an increasing of the interest earned rate gives the following results as: a decrease in production time, cycle time and preservation cost while an increment in green investment, carbon emission and the total profit.
8. The change in the holding cost and deterioration cost gives a negative impact on the manufacturer's profit. To earn more profit decision maker should focus on these costs.
9. Emission associated parameter B, C_{HE} gives a negative impact on the total profit. So, to make the system economically and environment friendly, retailer should be more conscious about that.
10. If the manufacturer's credit period increases, total profit increases while the values of other parameters remain unchanged.
11. An increasing value of the carbon tax results in the following: an increasing value of the cycle time, production time, preservation and green investment while a decreasing value of emission and total profit. It means that higher tax rate gives a good impact on the environment.

10.9 Managerial Insights

- Form the sensitivity table it is noted that the decision maker should select those suppliers where the rate of interest earned is higher as this is crucial for maintaining financial sustainability.
- From the comparative analysis it is observed that profit is higher by investing green investment and carbon emission is lower. So, the decision-maker can enhance their reputation and brand image through the green investment. A positive brand perception may lead to increased customer loyalty and a competitive edge in the market, influencing long term profitability and environment friendly.
- Results suggested that investment on preservation not only reduce the emission and deterioration but also increase the profit. Hence the preservation helps manufacturer's ability to make the system environmental and economical friendly (Figs. 10.3 and 10.4)

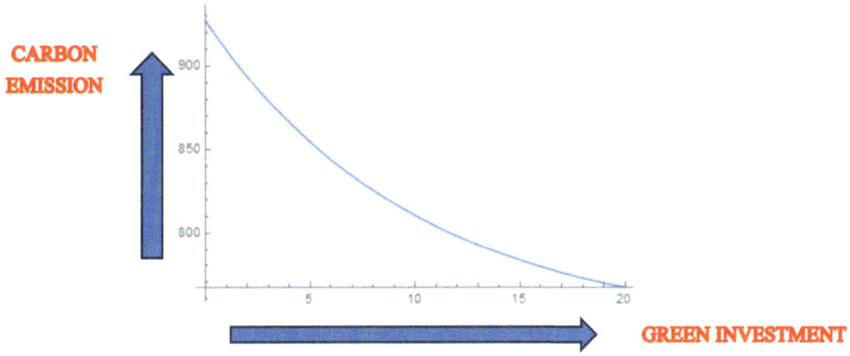

Fig. 10.3 Effect of green investment on carbon emission. *Source* Own

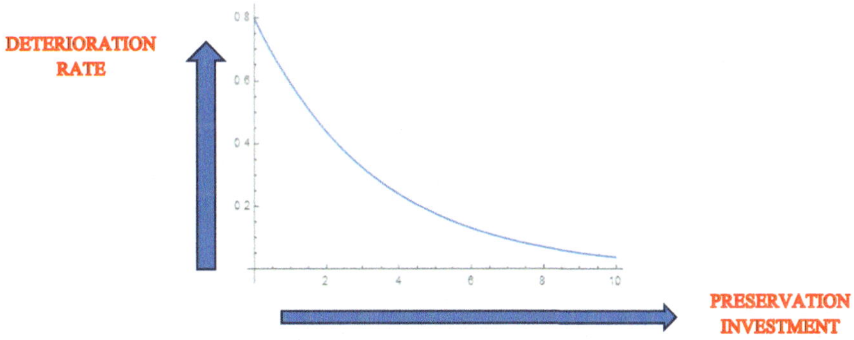

Fig. 10.4 Effect of preservation investment on deterioration. *Source* Own

10.10 Conclusion

The proposed study developed an inventory model for deteriorating items that considers price-reliant demand, preservation investment, green investment, carbon tax policy. A two-level trade-credit policy is implemented in which supplier offers full trade credit to the producer and producer provides a partial trade credit to the customer. The finding suggests that maximum profit \$5118.76 and minimum carbon emission 792.119 which is obtained when the producer's credit is greater than the cycle time. In contrast, the model without green investment yields a profit of \$5105.22 with carbon emission 896.986, similarly the model without preservation investment gives a profit of \$5093.04 with carbon emission of 829.672. Results suggested that when interest earned rate increased −30 to +30% total profit is increased 5018.33 to 5233.62 so that decision maker should select those suppliers where the rate of interest earned is higher as this is crucial for maintaining financial sustainability. In the previous research work, no policy of any kind was made for carbon reduction and in comparison, through this research, a model has been developed so that eco-friendly products can be manufactured using green technology under the carbon reduction policy. For further research can be extended as demand can be taken as greening degree dependent, stock dependent. Preservation can be taken as price dependent. The whole study can be done in inflationary and fuzzy environment.

Acknowledgement First author is funded by Senior Research Fellowship funded by CSIR (File No.-09/113(0032)/2020-EMR-I).

References

Das S, Khan MAA, Mahmoud EE, Abdel-Aty AH, Abualnaja KM, Shaikh AA (2021) A production inventory model with partial trade credit policy and reliability. Alexandria Eng J 60(1)1325–1338
Datta TK (2017) Effect of green technology investment on a production-inventory system with carbon tax. Adv Oper Res 1:4834839
Handa N, Singh SR, Punetha N (2022) Impact of carbon emission in two-echelon supply chain inventory decision with controllable deterioration and two-level trade-credit period. Opsearch 59(4):1555–1586
Hsieh TP, Dye CY (2013) A production–inventory model incorporating the effect of preservation technology investment when demand is fluctuating with time. J Comput Appl Math 239:25–36
Hua G, Cheng TCE, Wang S (2011) Managing carbon footprints in inventory management. Int J Prod Econ 132(2):178–185
Huo J, Zhang M, Wang D, Mujumdar AS, Bhandari B, Zhang L (2023) New preservation and detection technologies for edible mushrooms: a review. J Sci Food Agric 103(7):3230–3248
Kumar N, Kumari R, Yadav D (2024) Lot sizing model for multiple products over finite planning horizon under the effect of learning and time-value of money with cap-and-trade and carbon tax regulations: a fuzzy framework. Int J Oper Res 49(2):231–264
Ma Q, Song H, Chen G (2014) Dynamic optimal production strategies based on the inventory-dependent demand under the cap-and-trade mechanism. Mathematical Problems in Engineering 1:201708

Mohanta K, Jha AK, Dey A, Pal A (2022) An application of neutrosophic logic on an inventory model with two-level partial trade credit policy for time-dependent perishable products. Soft Comput 27(8):1–28
Moradi S, Gholamian MR, Sepehri A (2023) An inventory model for imperfect quality items considering learning effects and partial trade credit policy. Opsearch 60(1):276–325
Padiyar SVS, Kuraie VC, Bhagat N, Singh SR, Chaudhar R (2022) An integrated inventory model for imperfect production process having preservation facilities under fuzzy and inflationary environment. Int J Math Model Numer Optim 12(3):252–286
Padiyar SVS, Kuraie VC, Bhagat N, Singh SR, Dem H (2022) Green Integrated model for imperfect production process under reliability. J Math Control Sci Appl 8(1):1–13
Saha S, Sarkar B, Sarkar M (2023) Application of improved meta-heuristic algorithms for green preservation technology management to optimize dynamical investments and replenishment strategies. Math Comput Simul 209:426–450
Sarkar B, Guchhait R (2023) Ramification of information asymmetry on a green supply chain management with the cap-trade, service, and vendor-managed inventory strategies. Electron Commer Res Appl 60:101274
Sarkar B, Dey BK, Sarkar M, Hur S, Mandal B, Dhaka V (2020) Optimal replenishment decision for retailers with variable demand for deteriorating products under a trade-credit policy. RAIRO Oper Res 54(6):1685–1701
Shah NH (2015) Manufacturer-retailer inventory model for deteriorating items with price-sensitive credit-linked demand under two-level trade credit financing and profit sharing contract. Cogent Eng 2(1):1012989
Shah NH, Keswani M, Khedlekar UK, Prajapati NM (2024) Non-instantaneous controlled deteriorating inventory model for stock-price-advertisement dependent probabilistic demand under trade credit financing. Opsearch 61(1):421–459
Shah NH, Shah PH, Patel MB, Jauhari WA (2021) Inventory policies for non-instantaneous deteriorating items with preservation technology investment under price-sensitive time-dependent demand. Int J Procure Manag 14(6):702–723
Shen Y, Shen K, Yang C (2019) A production inventory model for deteriorating items with collaborative preservation technology investment under carbon tax. Sustainability 11(18):5027
Singh SR, Tayal S, Gaur A (2020) Replenishment policy for deteriorating items with trade credit and allowable shortages under inflationary environment. Int J Process Manag Benchmarking 10(4):462–478
Singh SR, Ummeferva U, Vaishali V (2022) An EPQ model with inflation under non-linear price stock dependent demand and time varying holding cost including shortages. In: AIP conference proceedings, vol 2481, no 1. AIP Publishing
Singh SR, Yadav D, Sarkar B, Sarkar M (2021) Impact of energy and carbon emission of a supply chain management with two-level trade-credit policy. Energies 14(6):1569
Singh S, Chaudhary R (2023) Effect of inflation on EOQ model with multivariate demand and partial backlogging and carbon tax policy. J Futur Sustain 3(1):35–58
Singh V, Singh SR, Padiyar SVS (2024) Benefits of preservation, green and quality improvement investment for waste management in sustainable supply chain under fuzzy learning and inflation. Contemp Math 5(2):326–364
Soni HN, Patel KA (2012) Optimal strategy for an integrated inventory system involving variable production and defective items under retailer partial trade credit policy. Decis Support Syst 54(1):235–247
Tayal S, Singh SR, Katariya C, Handa N (2021) An inventory model with quantity dependent trade credit for stock and price dependent demand, variable holding cost and partial backlogging. Reliab Theory Appl 16(64):225–240
Teng JT, Min J, Pan Q (2012) Economic order quantity model with trade credit financing for non-decreasing demand. Omega 40(3):328–335
Teng JT, Yang HL, Chern MS (2013) An inventory model for increasing demand under two levels of trade credit linked to order quantity. Appl Math Model 37(14–15):7624–7632

Tiwari S, Ahmed W, Sarkar B (2019) Sustainable ordering policies for non-instantaneous deteriorating items under carbon emission and multi-trade-credit-policies. J Clean Prod 240:118183

Tiwari S, Cárdenas-Barrón LE, Goh M, Shaikh AA (2018) Joint pricing and inventory model for deteriorating items with expiration dates and partial backlogging under two-level partial trade credits in supply chain. Int J Prod Econ 200:16–36

Toptal A, Özlü H, Konur D (2014) Joint decisions on inventory replenishment and emission reduction investment under different emission regulations. Int J Prod Res 52(1):243–269

Ullah M, Sarkar B, Asghar I (2019) Effects of preservation technology investment on waste generation in a two-echelon supply chain model. Mathematics 7(2):189

Ummeferva Z, Singh SR, Padiyar SVS (2023) Two-level trade credit policy approach for a production inventory model under greening degree dependent demand and reliability. Eur Chem Bull 12(10):4278–4291

Yadav D, Singh SR, Arora V (2016) Multi-item multi-constraint supply chain integrated inventory model with multi-variable demand under the effect of preservation technology. Cogent Eng 3(1):1272159

Chapter 11
Optimizing a Sustainable Leakage Inventory Model Under Fuzzy Environment

Nahakpam Roshni Devi, M. Kuber Singh, and Huidrom Malemnganbi

Abstract In today's highly competitive business environment, inventory management plays a very important role in supply chain management to ensuring smooth operation and maximizing profitability. This paper aims to create a simple leakage inventory model in a fuzzy environment with either instantaneous or finite production rates that avoids shortages. In any inventory system, goods in stock may possess the properties of deterioration, perishability, or leakage. A decline in quality with a relatively constant quantity is referred to as deterioration. On the other hand, leakage indicates the decrease in quantity over a predetermined period of time while retaining constant quality. The objective here is to determine the Optimal Economic order lot size (EOQ) to maximize the annual total profit. Since carbon emissions have an impact of carbon emissions on accelerating global warming, it is imperative to focus on reducing carbon emissions. The fuzzy numbers and fuzzy values are widely used in many applications for representing uncertain information. This paper integrates the cost of carbon emissions into the total inventory cost. Certain uncertain inventory parameters are represented by fuzzy numbers, and the optimal solution is obtained through the signed distance method. To validate the model, a numerical example is provided.

Keywords Leakage inventory · Fuzzy number · EOQ · Supply inventory model

11.1 Introduction

An inventory system is a vast area of various policies and controls and has economical values that determine any inventory levels in order to maximize the total profit and give the opportunity to run smooth operation of any business organization. The

N. R. Devi (✉) · M. Kuber Singh
Department of Mathematics, Dhanamanjuri University, Manipur 795001, India
e-mail: roshninahakpam21@gmail.com

H. Malemnganbi
Department of Mathematics, Manipur Technical University, Manipur 795003, India

N. H. Shah and M. Mittal (eds.), *Sustainable Inventory Management*, Inventory Optimization, https://doi.org/10.1007/978-981-97-6765-6_12

necessity potential in inventory control policy is to make appropriate decisions on the holding and ordering of items. Actually, inventory models deal with issues of inventory with interrelationship between a buyer and a seller. Many decision-making problems in real-life scenarios are too complicate to be aware of quantitatively, since the complications generally appear to uncertainty in the form of ambiguity. There are two type of inventory variables—control variables and uncontrolled variables. Controlled variables include the quantity acquired, frequency or timing of acquisition, the stage of completion of stocked items, etc. Uncontrolled variables include the holding or storage cost, shortage or penalty cost, setup cost or ordering cost, etc. Above all these variables, there are another two variables in the inventory system: They are leakage cost and carbon emissions cost. These two variables are considered as uncontrolled variables. Leakage cost involves a decline in quality while maintaining constant quality for a specified period. Loss of quantity may occur through liquid stock or breakages in the case of solid goods (like glass or bottles), damage caused by insects or animals (for food items), and transit loss in business due to the improper practices of sales personnel. These inventory system leakages might be perceived as very minute, escaping immediate detection by decision-makers or management. Further details are considered in Geeta's paper (Tomba and Geeta 2008; Geeta 2010).

In today's competitive environment, timely and adequate availability of goods and production resources is more substantial dynamics in inventory management and is more needed. Therefore, now is the time to support sustainable practices, recycling and environmental awareness as well as inventory models which help a supply chain. Efficient utilization of its resources lead to the inventory model for sustainable supply chains. Carbon emissions cost occurred affects the profitability of the firm or industry's organization. Too much emission of carbon dioxide to the atmosphere can cause global warming and greenhouse effect to the environment. That results in affecting to human and animal life with the occurrence of different types of diseases such as malaria, dengue, asthma, and other respiration-related diseases. So, to prevent all these circumstances, the government set a price to those who emit more carbon into the environment and to pay some amount called carbon emissions cost (Chaudhary 2023). In a classical inventory model, this cost is not included. If the decision-maker does not include this cost nowadays, it can lead to the loss of profit to any business or industry, or organization. Therefore, it is needed to add this cost to the classical model.

The term "supply chain management" was first introduced by Keith Oliver, a US industry consultant, in the early 1980s. However, the concept had been significant long before this, during the early twentieth century. Supply chain management can be defined as the coordination of upstream and downstream interactions with vendors and customers to provide superior customer value at the lowest possible cost. The primary goal of supply chain management is to meet customer needs, and the core objective of a supply chain is to efficiently coordinate the movement of materials, services, and information among its various components to optimize customer value. The essential functions typically encompass purchasing and procurement of materials and supplies, sales and order processing, operations, inventory and materials

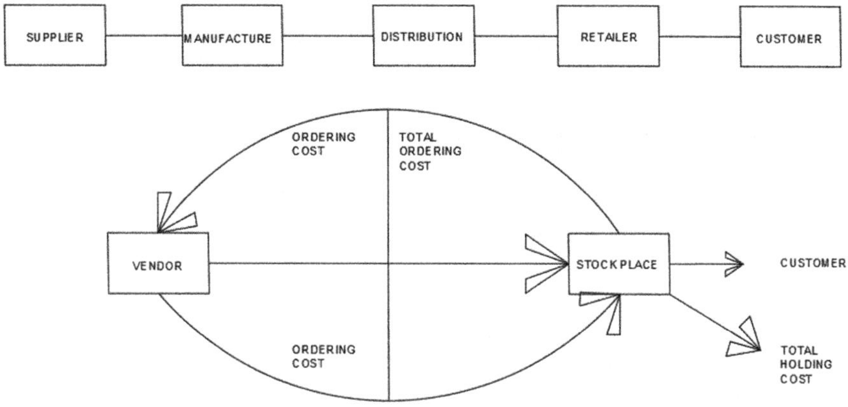

Fig. 11.1 Inventory management. (*Source* Own)

management, transportation and distribution, information management, finance, and customer service. To achieve this, various operations in supply chain management are employed, including "supply chain collaboration," "the role of the Internet in supply chain management," and "inventory management in the supply chain," among others.

Supply chain management is crucial for enhancing partnership performance. Numerous global companies such as Unilever, Nestle, Samsung, Sony, Apple, and IBM have relied heavily on supply chain collaboration with their partners to maintain a sustainable competitive advantage. The importance of supply chain collaboration lies in improving efficiencies in sourcing, planning, production, distribution, and other related activities. The Internet's greatest potential is being realized by accelerating communication between customers and suppliers, enhancing service levels, and reducing logistics costs.

A supply chain for goods production usually involves suppliers, manufacturers, distributors, retailers, and customers as illustrated in Fig. 11.1.

11.1.1 Streamlined and Adaptive Supply Chains

Streamlined Supply Chains:

It focuses on minimizing inventory and improving process flow efficiencies. It is best suited for products with predictable demand, stable product lines, long life cycles, and low profit margins. Strategies involve balancing supply and demand, maintaining low inventory levels, using large distribution centers to achieve economies of scale, and optimizing routing costs.

Adaptive Supply Chains: It emphasizes flexibility and the capability to rapidly adjust to changing market demands and requirements.

Key Concepts:

- **Contract Manufacturer**: A company specializing in specific types of goods production, such as customized design, manufacturing, assembly, and packaging, typically works under contract for end users.
- **Push System**: It produces goods in anticipation of customer demand based on sales forecasts and moves them through the supply chain to retail locations where they are stored as finished goods.

In this paper, we considered all the costs involved in the inventory model as uncertain. Under such uncertainty, fuzzy set theory and fuzzy parameters provide better and more acceptable inference compared to the crisp inventory model when dealing with uncertain data. Therefore, we developed an inventory model that includes inventory holding costs, ordering costs, leakage costs, and carbon emissions costs. We used triangular fuzzy numbers and the signed distance method for defuzzification. The primary objective of this paper is to explore the use of triangular fuzzy numbers to evaluate the fuzzy optimal order quantity.

Inventory management role in supply chain management

11.2 Literature Survey

Numerous studies have integrated EOQ models with aspects like leakage inventory models, carbon emissions, imperfect items, and fuzzy environments. After thorough investigation, analysis, and review of various methods and techniques, this paper primarily aims to address the costs of leakage and carbon emissions by incorporating them into the traditional EOQ model within a fuzzy environment. The concept of fuzzy set theory, introduced by Zadeh (1965), extends classical set theory. Zimmermann discussed the application of fuzzy set theory (Zimmerman 2021), highlighting its significance in addressing uncertainty within inventory control models. Fuzzy set theory is particularly useful for dealing with the uncertainty inherent in inventory systems, where holding costs and order placement costs may fluctuate. Organizations strive to minimize the total inventory cost, which includes all associated expenditures. An inventory model featuring at least one fuzzy parameter is termed a fuzzy inventory model. Lee and Yao (1990) pioneered the fuzzy inventory model, which has since been deemed more effective than the crisp inventory model. Following their work, many researchers, such as Chandrasiri (2016), have developed various classes of fuzzy inventory models. Chandrasiri's model, for example, considered holding and ordering costs as triangular fuzzy numbers and utilized signed distance methods for defuzzification. Similarly, Chaudhary et al. (2023) discussed a sustainable inventory model for defective items within a fuzzy environment.

With the rising awareness of Fuzzy Set Theory, numerous studies have applied these concepts to inventory management to create more realistic models. Traditional EOQ models often assume deterministic settings, which is unrealistic in today's dynamic business environment. Information required for inventory management is not always fully available or well-defined. Fuzzy Set Theory (FST), invented by Zadeh in (1965), offers a mathematical approach to handle vagueness and incomplete information in inventory systems. The sustainability of supply chains has gained significant attention, linking logistics with environmental concerns. This strategic approach aims to optimize operational procedures and resource efficiency, and reduce environmental impact (Zhang and Liu 2013) (Sazvar et al. 2014). Green supply chains influence decisions related to storage, decaying items, gas emissions, and remanufacturing processes.

One study explored the impact of carbon emissions (pricing/taxes, trades, and caps) within a transportation and inventory model through a multi-player dynamic game (Tang et al. 2020). Another study examined the influence of carbon emissions on a production-inventory model for a sustainable supply chain (Ghosh et al. 2020). A comprehensive assessment of quantitative models for sustainable supply chains categorized papers based on configuration, mathematical models, simulations, and algorithms (Becerra et al. 2021). A literature review highlighted contributions related to inventory models and greenhouse gas (GHG) emissions (Pattnaik et al. 2021). Studies have analyzed the effects of carbon emission regulations, such as carbon caps, taxes, and cap-and-trade systems, on inventory reclamation and investment decisions (Raiya and Mittal 2022, 2023).

Challenges related to perishable items with short shelf lives have been examined, including green product design and remanufacturing processes (Chung and Wee 2011; Wee et al. 2011). An inventory model was developed to address damaged goods and remanufacturing processes, aiming to reduce overall supply chain costs (Lin and Lin 2011; Widyadana and Wee 2012). The traveling agent problem within green supply chains, focusing on supplier selection, gas emissions, and storage, has also been studied (Karimi et al. 2016b). A three-layer green supply chain model considering uncertain holding costs and degrading products was developed (Khatua et al. 2017). Inventory management aims to minimize GHG emissions and enhance environmental performance (García-Alvarado et al. 2017). Sustainable supply chain inventory models often incorporate strategies to reduce carbon emissions, considering market, tax, and decision-making factors to improve procurement, manufacturing, transportation, and storage operations. Models have been created for decaying goods and greenhouse emissions under variable demands, backorders, and sustainability standards, using different transportation methods.

To address emissions, some models have included shipment policies, while others have focused on production systems with flaws, carbon emissions, backorders, and defect control strategies. Studies have examined Vendor Managed Inventory (VMI) models considering GHG emissions (Lu et al. 2015a; Mokhtari and Rezvan 2017a). The inverse relationship between inventory costs and carbon emissions has been studied to maximize supply chain profits by integrating carbon reduction strategies, delivery, and technology into production-inventory models. Policies have been developed to reduce carbon emissions related to inventory, distribution, storage, and the environment.

One study focused on a low carbon EOQ model with partial back-ordering and defective goods, distinguishing between perfect and defective products with varying demand rates, selling prices, and holding costs. The model assumed adherence to carbon tax regulations, with overall costs including carbon emissions from inventory and transportation operations. The study found that while carbon emission regulations effectively reduce emissions, they also impact the firm's profitability. Another study optimized retailer profits considering cycle length, learning effects under inflation, and carbon emissions, assuming defective items follow an S-shaped learning curve. A sustainable inventory model for non-instantaneous decaying items with partially backlogged shortages was also introduced, influenced by eco-friendly demand driven by herbal and chemical product usage.

Initially, we understood the classical EOQ model. As industries evolve, enhancements to the EOQ model are necessary. We incorporate leakage and carbon emissions costs as key elements in the EOQ model. To better reflect real-world scenarios, we integrate Fuzzy Set Theory with the inventory model for more accurate outcomes. This chapter considers two cases:

(a) The first case discusses the carbon emission and leakage inventory model with uniform demand and instantaneous production rate without shortages.
(b) The second case addresses leakage and carbon emissions with a uniform rate of demand and finite production rate without shortages.

Definition 2.1 (Fuzzy set) If X is a universe of discourse and x is any particular element of x, then a fuzzy set $\tilde{A}$ is defined on X may be expressed as a collection of ordered pairs:

$\tilde{A} = \left[(x, \mu_{\tilde{A}}(x)) : x \epsilon X\right]$ where $\mu_{\tilde{A}}(A) \rightarrow [0, 1]$ is a membership function. The value 0 denotes non-membership and 1 denotes full membership. The values between 0 and 1 represent partly membership (Zadeh 1965).

Definition 2.2 (Triangular fuzzy numbers) The three numbers a, m, and b are said to be a triangular fuzzy numbers, if these three numbers satisfied triangular membership function which is denoted as $\tilde{A} = (a, m, b)$.

Triangular membership function is defined as

$$\mu_{\tilde{A}}(x) = \begin{cases} 0 & \text{if} x < a \\ \frac{x-a}{m-a} & \text{if} a \leq x \leq m \\ \frac{b-x}{b-m} & \text{if} m \leq x \leq b \\ 0 & \text{if} b < x \end{cases}$$

The triplet (a, m, b) conventionally represents triangular fuzzy number. In this context, a denotes the lower boundary and b signifies the upper boundary, both having a degree of membership 0 and m is between a and b, corresponding to a degree of membership 1 (Fig. 11.2).

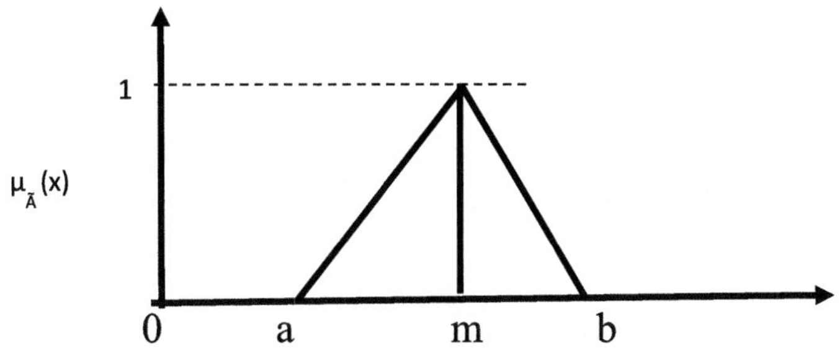

Fig. 11.2 Representation of triangular fuzzy number (*Source* Own)

Definition 2.3 (Fuzzy point) Let $\tilde{a}_1$ be a fuzzy set on R. It is called a fuzzy point if its membership function is

$$\mu_{\tilde{a_1}}(x) = \begin{cases} 1 \text{ if } x = a_1 \\ 0 \text{ if } x \neq a_1 \end{cases}$$

Definition 2.4 (The signed distance method) In the defuzzification process, sign distance method is a method for conversion of fuzzy number to crisp number and is briefly defined by Yao and Lee (1990). They interpret sign distance method as follows.

Definition 2.4(1) For any a and $0 \epsilon R$, the signed distance from a to 0 is defined as $d_o(a, 0) = a$, if $a > 0$. The distance from a to 0 is $-d_o(a, 0) = -a$, if $a < 0$. So we called $d_o(a, 0) = a$ the sign distance of a to 0.

Let β be the family of fuzzy sets $\tilde{A}$ on R with which the α-cut $A(\alpha) = [A_u(\alpha), A_v(\alpha)]$ exist for every $\alpha \in [0, 1]$ and $A_u(\alpha), A_v(\alpha)$ are continuous functions on $\alpha \in [0, 1]$.

Then for any $\widetilde{A} epsilon \beta$ we have $\tilde{A} = U_{0 \leq \alpha \leq 1}[A_u(\alpha), A_v(\alpha)]$.

Definition 2.4(2) The signed distance of the left end point $A_u(\alpha)$ of the α-cut $[A_u(\alpha), A_v(\alpha)]$ of $\tilde{A}$ to the origin O is $A_u(\alpha)$. And the signed distance of the right end point $A_v(\alpha)$ of the α-cut $[A_u(\alpha), A_v(\alpha)]$ of $\tilde{A}$ to the origin O is $A_v(\alpha)$.

Taking average we get $\frac{A_u(\alpha)+A_v(\alpha)}{2}$.

It is taken as signed distance of α-cut $[A_u(\alpha), A_v(\alpha)]$.

We defined the signed distance of the interval $[A_u(\alpha), A_v(\alpha)]$ to 0 as $\alpha_o([A_u(\alpha), A_v(\alpha)], 0) = \frac{1}{2}[d_o(A_u(\alpha), 0) + d_o(A_v(\alpha), 0)]$:

$$= \frac{1}{2}[A_u(\alpha) + A_v(\alpha)]$$

And for every $\alpha \in [0, 1]$, there is a one-to-one mapping between the α-level fuzzy interval:

$$[A_u(\alpha), A_v(\alpha)] \longleftrightarrow [A_u(\alpha)_\alpha, A_v(\alpha)_\alpha]$$

Also 1-level fuzzy point $\tilde{O}_1$ is mapped to the real number hence the signed distance of $[A_u(\alpha)_\alpha, A_v(\alpha)_\alpha)]$ to $\tilde{O}_1$ can defined as $d_o([(A_u(\alpha)_\alpha, A_v(\alpha)_\alpha], \tilde{O}_1)$:

$$= d_o([A_u(\alpha), A_v(\alpha)], 0)$$
$$= \frac{1}{2}[A_u(\alpha) + A_v(\alpha)]$$

Definition 2.4(3) For $\tilde{A}\,\epsilon\beta$, we defined the signed distance of $\tilde{A}$ to $\tilde{0}$ as

$$d(\tilde{0}) = \int_0^1 d_0[(A_u(\alpha)_\alpha, A_v(\alpha)_\alpha], \tilde{O}_1)$$
$$= \frac{1}{2}\int_0^1 [A_u(\alpha) + A_v(\alpha)]d\alpha$$

The signed distance measure for different types of fuzzy numbers such as Triangular, Trapezoidal, Gaussian, and Bell-shaped fuzzy number are discussed exhaustively in Berkachy et al. (2016).

For us we only discussed triangular fuzzy number (Berkachy et al. 2016).

Let $\tilde{A}$ be a triangular fuzzy number as $\tilde{A} = (a, m, b)$.

The $\alpha - cut$ are given by $A_u(\alpha) = a + (m - a)\alpha$.

and $A_v(\alpha) = b + (b - m)\alpha$.

The signed of the triangular fuzzy number

$\tilde{A} = (a, m, b)$ can be calculated as.

$$d(\tilde{A}, 0) = \frac{1}{2}\int_0^1 [A_u(\alpha) + A_v(\alpha)]d\alpha$$

where $A_\alpha = [A_u(\alpha), A_v(\alpha)]$

and $A_\alpha = [a + (m - a)\alpha + b - (b - m)\alpha]$

$$= \frac{1}{4}(a + 2m + b)$$

Thus putting all our parameters (a_1, b_1, c_1), (a_3, b_3, c_3), and (a_4, b_4, c_4) in the above formula, we get the result as follows:

$$d(\tilde{A}(\alpha), 0) = \frac{1}{2}\int_0^1 [a_3 + c_3 + (2b_3 - a_3 - c_3)\alpha]d\alpha$$
$$= \int_0^1 (a_3 + c_3)d\alpha + \frac{1}{2}\int_0^1 (2b_3 - a_3 - c_3)d\alpha$$
$$= \frac{1}{2}(a_3 + c_3) + \frac{1}{2}(2b_3 - a_3 - c_3)\left(\frac{1}{2} - 0\right).$$

$$= \frac{1}{2}(a_3 + c_3) + \frac{1}{4}(2b_3 - a_3 - c_3)$$
$$= \frac{1}{2}(a_3 + c_3) + \frac{1}{4}(2b_3 - a_3 - c_3)$$
$$= \frac{2a_3 + 2c_3 + 2b_3 - a_3 - c_3}{4}$$
$$= \frac{a_3 + 2b_3 + c_3}{4} \tag{11.1}$$

$$d\left(\tilde{A}(\alpha), 0\right) = \frac{1}{2}\int_0^1 [a_1 + c_1 + (2b_1 - a_1 - c_1)\alpha]\,\mathrm{d}$$
$$= \frac{1}{2}\int_0^1 (a_1 + c_1) = + + \mathrm{d}\alpha + \frac{1}{2}\int_0^1 (2b_1 - a_1 - c_1)\,\mathrm{d}\alpha$$
$$= \frac{1}{2}(a_1 + c_1)|\alpha|_0^1 + \frac{1}{2}(2b_1 - a_1 - c_1)\left|\frac{\alpha^2}{2}\right|_0^1$$
$$= \frac{1}{2}(a_1 + c_1) + \frac{1}{2}(2b_1 - a_1 - c_1)\left(\frac{1}{2} - 0\right)$$
$$= \frac{1}{2}(a_1 + c_1) + \frac{1}{4}(2b_1 - a_1 - c_1)$$
$$= \frac{2a_1 + 2c_1 + 2b_1 - a_1 - c_1}{4}$$
$$= \frac{a_1 + 2b_1 + c_1}{4} \tag{11.2}$$

$$d\left(\tilde{A}(\alpha), 0)\right) = \frac{1}{2}\int_0^1 [a_4 + c_4 + (2b_4 - a_4 - c_4)\alpha]\,d\,\alpha$$
$$= \frac{1}{2}\int_0^1 (a_4 + c_4)d\,\alpha + \frac{1}{2}\int_0^1 (2b_4 - a_4 - c_4)\,d\,\alpha$$
$$= \frac{1}{2}(a_4 + c_4)|\alpha|_0^1 + (a_4 + c_4) + \frac{1}{2}(2b_4 - a_4 - c_4)\left|\frac{\alpha}{2}\right|_0^1$$
$$= \frac{1}{2}(a_4 + c_4) + \frac{1}{2}(2b_4 - a_4 - c_4)\left(\frac{1}{2} - 0\right)$$
$$= \frac{1}{2}(a_4 + c_4) + \frac{1}{4}(2b_4 - a_4 - c_4)$$
$$= \frac{2a_4 + 2c_4 + 2b_4 - a_4 - c_4}{4}$$
$$= \frac{a_4 + 2b_4 + c_4}{4} \tag{11.3}$$

11.3 Algorithm for finding fuzzy total cost and fuzzy optimal order quantity:

Step 1: Calculate total (TC) for the crisp model sense for the given crisp value.
Step 2: Determine fuzzy total cost ($\widetilde{TC}$) by performing fuzzy arithmetic operations on the fuzzy carrying cost, fuzzy ordering cost, and fuzzy carbon emissions cost, all represented as triangular fuzzy numbers.
Step 3: Utilize the signed distance method to defuzzify the fuzzy total cost ($\widetilde{TC}$). Then, calculate the fuzzy optimal order quantity (q^*) accordingly.

11.4 Economic Order Quantity (EOQ)

The most common inventory challenge in the industry is managing stock levels that deplete over time and that are then replenished with new items. This inventory problem, where demand is assumed to be fixed and entirely predictable, is known as the Economic Order Quantity (EOQ) model. In inventory management, calculating the EOQ is essential to balancing ordering costs with holding costs and time, which was the first model, developed in the early 1900s.

11.4.1 Some of the Definitions Used in the EOQ Model

(a) Holding cost:

Holding costs refer to the expenses associated with storing inventory, such as warehousing, utilities, insurance, and depreciation. These costs increase with the amount of inventory held and the duration it remains in storage. Shortage costs, on the other hand, arise from not having enough inventory to meet demand, leading to lost sales, backorders, and potential damage to customer relationships. Balancing holding and shortage costs is essential for effective inventory management, ensuring optimal inventory levels to minimize overall expenses while meeting customer demand (Gupta 1992)

(b) Ordering cost:

Ordering costs encompass the expenses associated with the process of placing and receiving inventory orders, including administrative expenses, transportation costs, and any other costs incurred in the procurement process. The magnitude of this cost may vary based on the volume of goods purchased, influenced by factors like price breaks or quantity discounts (Gupta 1992).

(c) Demand:

Demand represents the quantity of items needed within a specific timeframe, which may not always align with the amount sold due to unmet demand caused by shortages or delays (Gupta 1992).

(d) Lead time:

Lead time refers to the duration between placing an order or commencing production and the arrival or delivery of goods to the inventory. Similarly, it also denotes the duration between demand initiation and fulfillment from the inventory. When lead time is known and greater than zero, one may opt to place orders in advance, offsetting the lead time duration (Gupta 1992).

11.4.2 Total Cost About Inventory

See Fig. 11.3.

11.5 Proposed Inventory Model in Crisp Sense and Fuzzy Sense

Case 1: Leakage inventory model with Carbon emission under uniform demand rate, instantaneous production rate without shortages (Fig. 11.4).

Fig. 11.3 Total cost about inventory. (*Source* Own)

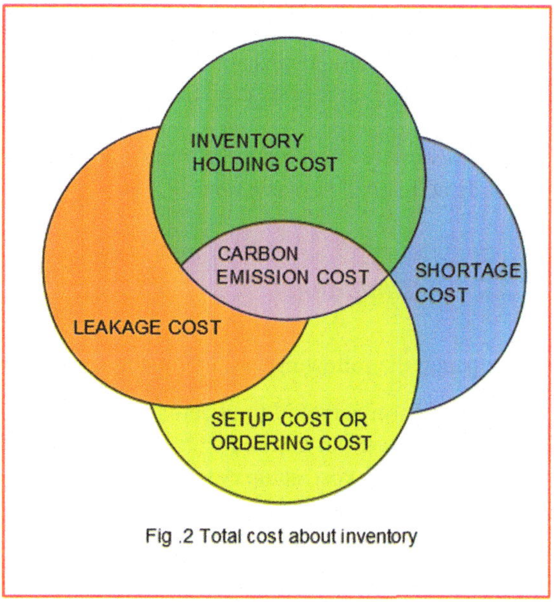

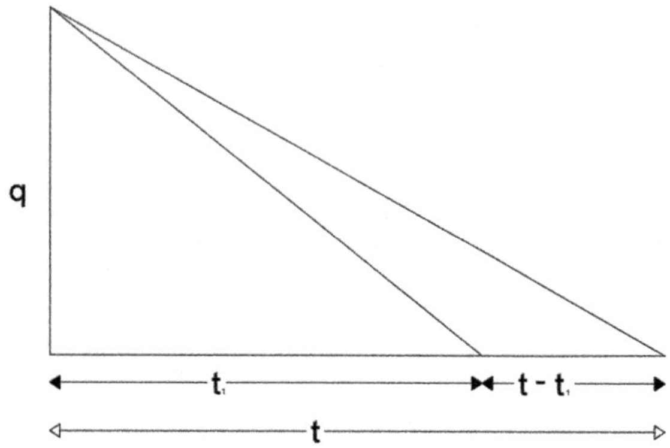

Fig. 11.4 Instantaneous production leakage and carbon emission (*Source* Own)

11.5.1 Assumptions and Notations

Some notations and assumptions that would be used to solve the problems are as follows:

q = Order quantity per run
r = Rate of demand per unit time
D_p = Defective percentage in a lot size of q (in units).
C_0 = Setup or ordering cost per order
C_h = holding cost per unit quantity per unit time
d_1 = leakage rate per unit time
TC = Total cost per unit time.
$\widetilde{Tc}$ = Fuzzy average total cost.
T_{ce} = Tax on carbon emission (in rupees/ton of CO_2).
E_{ce} = Average carbon emission from warehouse electricity (in ton of CO_2/kilowatt hour).
e_i = Electricity consumption per unit in the warehouses (in kwh/unit/per year).
t = Time interval between runs.

11.5.2 Assumptions

In this paper, the following assumption are considered:

(i) the uniform nature of total demand is taken
(ii) shortages are not allowed
(iii) only holding cost, setup cost, and carbon emissions cost are fuzzy in nature
(iv) lead time is zero
(v) production is instantaneous.

We have

$$q = rt \tag{11.3}$$

$$\text{The inventory holding cost} = \frac{1}{2}C_h qt \tag{11.4}$$

$$\text{The setup cost per production run} = C_0 \tag{11.5}$$

Average total cost per unit time $= \frac{1}{2}C_h q + \frac{C_0}{t}$

$$= \frac{1}{2}C_h q + \frac{C_0 r}{q} \tag{11.6}$$

If $d_1 > 0$ is the leakage rate per unit time, then the quantity q reduces to zero in time t_1 and q $= (r + d_1)t_1$.

Now,

$$rt - (r + d_1)t_1 = 0$$

$$\Rightarrow r = \frac{d_1 t_1}{t - t_1}$$

$$\Rightarrow t - t_1 = \frac{d_1 q}{r(r + d_1)} \quad q = (r + d_1)t_1 \tag{11.7}$$

$$\text{Quantity loss (due to leakage)} = r(t - t_1) = \frac{d_1 q}{(r + d_1)} \tag{11.8}$$

$$\begin{aligned}\text{Average additional cost incurred} &= \frac{1}{2}(t - t_1)C_h q\frac{1}{t}\\ &= \frac{1}{2}\frac{d_1 C_h q}{(r + d_1)}\end{aligned} \tag{11.9}$$

And the perfect quantity items are

$$\left(\mathrm{q} - D_p q\right) = \left(1 - D_p\right)q \tag{11.10}$$

In the inventory management, preservation in production process right temperature or some fuels are use such as in the form of electricity, electric generator as well as petrol, diesel, and natural gases to generate energy of any kind of Machine.

Hence, it results in carbon emissions, necessitating the reduction of extensive reliance on high-carbon fuels across various sectors of the economy to protect the environment from the adverse effects of excessive carbon emissions produced by diverse industries and companies. This introduces a new expense referred to as the carbon emission cost, which is included in the overall expenditures. The carbon emissions cost incurred during electricity consumption is determined by factors such as the average electricity usage "e_i", standard electricity emission "E_{ce}", and the carbon tax rate "T_{ce}" (Chaudhary 2023).

$$\text{It is given as the carbon emissions cost } = e_i E_{ce} T_{ce} \frac{1}{2}\left(1 - D_p\right) qt \tag{11.11}$$

$$\text{The average carbon emission cost} = e_i E_{ce} T_{ce} \frac{1}{2}\left(1 - D_p\right) q \tag{11.12}$$

∴ The required inventory total cost is

$$TC = \frac{1}{2} C_h q + \frac{C_0 r}{q} + \frac{1}{2} \frac{d_1 C_h q}{(r + d_1)} + e_i E_{ce} T_{ce} \frac{\left(1 - D_p\right) q}{2} \tag{11.13}$$

To obtain the optimum q^* and TC^*, we have to equate the first order derivative of TC to zero and solve the resulting equations.

Using $\frac{dTC}{dq} = 0$ and $\frac{d^2 TC}{dq^2} > 0$,

We have,

$$q^* = \sqrt{\frac{2 C_0 r (r + d_1)}{C_h (r + 2d_1) + e_i E_{ce} T_{ce} \left(1 - D_p\right)(r + d_1)}} \tag{11.14}$$

and the minimum total cost

$$C_{\min} = \sqrt{\frac{2 C_0 r \left\{ C_h (r + 2d_1) + e_i E_{ce} T_{ce} \left(1 - D_p\right)(r + d_1) \right\}}{(r + d_1)}} \tag{11.15}$$

When $d_1 \to 0$, i.e. there is no leakage then we have

$$q^* = \sqrt{\frac{2 C_0 r}{C_h + e_i E_{ce} T_{ce} \left(1 - D_p\right)}} \tag{11.16}$$

and

Minimum Total cost

$$C_{\min} = \sqrt{2 C_0 r \left\{ C_h + e_i E_{ce} T_{ce} \left(1 - D_p\right) \right\}} \tag{11.17}$$

In practical scenarios, determining the ordering cost and carrying cost over an extended period proves challenging due to uncertainties. Consequently, we characterize inventory holding cost, ordering cost, and carbon emission cost as possessing a fuzzy nature. To address this, we adopt a fuzzy environment model utilizing triangular fuzzy numbers.

Let

$\tilde{C}_h$ = Fuzzy carrying or holding cost per unit quantity per unit time

$\tilde{C}_o$ = fuzzy setup ordering cost per order.

$\tilde{T}_{ce}$ = fuzzy carbon emissions cost (in rupees per ton of CO_2).

The nature of total demand and time of plan are taken as constant. The fuzzy total cost is given by

$$\widetilde{TC} = \left(\frac{q}{2}\right)\tilde{C}_h + \left(\frac{r}{q}\right)\tilde{C}_o + \frac{1}{2}\frac{d_1 q}{(r+d_1)}\tilde{C}_h + e_i \tilde{T}_{ce} E_{ce}\left(\frac{1-D_p}{2}\right)q+ \tag{11.18}$$

Therefore, we define inventory holding cost, ordering cost, and carbon emission tax as.

$$\tilde{C}_h = (a_1, b_1, c_1), \quad \tilde{C}_0 = (a_3, b_3, c_3) \quad \text{and} \quad \tilde{T}_{ce} = (a_4, b_4, c_4)$$

Now,

$$\begin{aligned}\widetilde{TC} &= \left(\frac{q}{2}\right)(a_1,\ b_1, c_1) + \left(\frac{r}{q}\right)(a_3, b_3, c_3)\\ &+ \frac{1}{2}\frac{d_1}{(r+d_{1)}}(a_1, b_1, c_1) + e_i E_{ce}\left(\frac{1-D_p}{2}\right)q(a_4, b_4, c_4)\end{aligned} \tag{11.19}$$

where

$$\begin{aligned}a &= \left(\frac{q}{2}\right)a_1 + \left(\frac{r}{q}\right)a_3 + \frac{1}{2}\frac{d_1 q}{(r+d_1)}a_1 + e_i E_{ce}\left(\frac{1-D_p}{2}\right)qa_4.\\ b &= \left(\frac{q}{2}\right)b_1 + \left(\frac{r}{q}\right)b_3 + \frac{1}{2}\frac{d_1 q}{(r+d_1)}b_1 + e_i E_{ce}\left(\frac{1-D_p}{2}\right)qb_4.\\ c &= \left(\frac{q}{2}\right)c_1 + \left(\frac{r}{q}\right)c_3 + \frac{1}{2}\frac{d_1 q}{(r+d_1)}c_1 + e_i E_{ce}\left(\frac{1-D_p}{2}\right)qc_4.\end{aligned}$$

Defuzzification of fuzzy number $\widetilde{TC}$ by using signed distance method is given as.

$$d\left(\widetilde{TC}, 0\right) = \frac{1}{2}\int_0^1 [A_u(\alpha) + A_v(\alpha)]d\alpha$$

where $A_L(\alpha) = a + (b-a)\alpha, \quad A_R(\alpha) = c - (c-b)\alpha.$

Now, $A_u(\alpha) = a + (b-a)\alpha$

$$= \left[\left(\frac{q}{2}\right)a_1 + \left(\frac{r}{q}\right)a_3 + \frac{1}{2}\frac{d_1 q}{(r+d_1)}a_1 + e_i E_{ce}\left(\frac{1-D_p}{2}\right)qa_4\right] + \left[\begin{array}{l}\left(\frac{q}{2}\right)b_1 + \left(\frac{r}{q}\right)b_3 + \frac{1}{2}\frac{d_1 q}{(r+d_1)}b_1 + e_i E_{ce}\left(\frac{1-D_p}{2}\right)qb_4\\ -\left(\frac{q}{2}\right)a_1 - \left(\frac{r}{q}\right)a_3 - \frac{1}{2}\frac{d_1 q}{(r+d_1)}a_1 - e_i E_{ce}\left(\frac{1-D_p}{2}\right)qa_4\end{array}\right]\alpha$$

$$= \left[\left(\frac{q}{2}\right)a_1 + \left(\frac{r}{q}\right)a_3 + \frac{1}{2}\frac{d_1 q}{(r+d_1)}a_1 + e_i E_{ce}\left(\frac{1-D_p}{2}\right)qa_4\right]$$
$$+ \left[\begin{array}{l}\left(\frac{q}{2}\right)(b_1 - a_1) + \left(\frac{r}{q}\right)(b_3 - a_3) + \frac{1}{2}\frac{d_1 q}{(r+d_1)}(b_1 - a_1)\\ +e_i E_{ce}\left(\frac{1-D_p}{2}\right)q(b_4 - a_4)\end{array}\right]\alpha$$

And

$$A_v(\alpha) = c - (c-b)\alpha$$
$$= \left[\left(\frac{q}{2}\right)c_1 + \left(\frac{q}{r}\right)c_3 + \frac{1}{2}\frac{d_1 q}{(r+d_1)}c_1 + e_i E_{ce}\left(\frac{1-D_p}{2}\right)qc_4\right]$$
$$- \left[\begin{array}{l}\left(\frac{q}{2}\right)c_1 + \left(\frac{q}{r}\right)c_3 + \frac{1}{2}\frac{d_1 q}{(r+d_1)}c_1 + e_i E_{ce}\left(\frac{1-D_p}{2}\right)qc_4\\ -\left(\frac{q}{2}\right)b_1 - \left(\frac{q}{2}\right)b_3 - \frac{1}{2}\frac{d_1 q}{(r+d_1)}b_1 - e_i E_{ce}\left(\frac{1-D_p}{2}\right)qb_4\end{array}\right]\alpha$$
$$= \left[\left(\frac{q}{2}\right)c_1 + \left(\frac{q}{r}\right)c_3 + \frac{1}{2}\frac{d_1 q}{(r+d_1)}c_1 + e_i E_{ce}\left(\frac{1-p}{2}\right)qc_4\right]$$
$$- \left[\begin{array}{l}\left(\frac{q}{2}\right)(c_1 - b_1) + \left(\frac{q}{r}\right)(c_3 - b_3) + \frac{1}{2}\frac{d_1 q}{(r+d_1)}(c_1 - b_1)\\ +e_i E_{ce}\left(\frac{1-D_p}{2}\right)q(c_4 - b_4)\end{array}\right]\alpha$$

Then,

$$d\left(\widetilde{TC}, 0\right) = \left(\frac{q}{2}\right)\left(\frac{a_1 + c_1 + 2b_1}{4}\right) + \left(\frac{r}{q}\right)$$
$$\left(\frac{a_3 + c_3 + 2b_3}{4}\right) + \frac{d_1 q}{2(r+d_1)}\left(\frac{a_1 + c_1 + 2b_1}{4}\right)$$
$$+ e_i E_{ce}\left(\frac{1-D_p}{2}\right)q\left(\frac{a_4 + c_4 + 2b_4}{4}\right)$$
$$= C_r(q) \text{ (say); } \{\because \text{ from } (A),\ (B), (C)\}$$

Now,

$$d\left(\widetilde{TC}, 0\right) = \left(\frac{q}{2}\right)\left(\frac{a_1 + c_1 + 2b_1}{4}\right) + \left(\frac{r}{q}\right)$$
$$\left(\frac{a_3 + c_3 + 2b_3}{4}\right) + \frac{d_1 q}{2(r+d_1)}\left(\frac{a_1 + c_1 + 2b_1}{4}\right)$$

$$+ e_i E_{ce}\left(\frac{1-D_p}{2}\right) q\left(\frac{a_4+c_4+2b_4}{4}\right) = C_r(q)(say);\ \{\because from(A), (B), (C)\} \tag{11.20}$$

For the minimum value $C_r(q)$.

Differentiate the above $C_r(q)$ with respect to q and equating it to zero, $C_r'(q) = 0$ and

$$C_r''(q) > 0$$

Then,

$$q^* = \sqrt{\frac{2r(r+d_1)(a_3+c_3+2b_3)}{(r+d_1)(a_1+c_1+2b_1)+d_1(a_1+c_1+2b_1)+e_iE_{ce}(1-D_p)(a_4+c_4+2b_4)(r+d_1)}}$$

$$q^* = \sqrt{\frac{2r(r+d_1)(a_3+c_3+2b_3)}{(r+2d_1)(a_1+c_1+2b_1)+e_iE_{ce}(1-D_p)(a_4+c_4+2b_4)(r+d_1)}} \tag{11.21}$$

$$C_{\min} = \sqrt{\frac{2r(a_3+c_3+2b_3)\{(a_1+c_1+2b_1)(r+2d_1)+e_iE_{ce}(1-D_p)(a_4+c_4+2b_4)(r+d_1)\}}{16(r+d_1)}} \tag{11.22}$$

When $d_1 \to 0$ (I.e. there is no leakage),

$$q^* = \sqrt{\frac{2r(a_3+c_3+2b_3)}{(a_1+c_1+2b_1)+e_iE_{ce}(1-D_p)(a_4+c_4+2b_4)}} \tag{11.23}$$

$$C_{\min} = \frac{1}{4}\sqrt{2r(a_3+c_3+2b_3)\{(a_1+c_1+2b_1)+e_iE_{ce}(1-D_p)(a_4+c_4+2b_4)\}} \tag{11.24}$$

11.6 Numerical Analysis

With the help of numerical example the above theory can be illustrated.

Model (Crisp): Let us consider the inventory system with the following data in usual notation as

r =500 unite per unite per year, C_h = ₹11, C_0 = ₹105 per order, $d_1 = 5$ units per year, $k = 1000$, T_{ce} = ₹75/ton CO_2, $e_i = 1.44$ kwh/unit/year, E_{ce} =0.005 ton CO_2/kwh and $D_p = 0.02$s (Chandrasiri 2016; Chaudhary 2023).

Solution

See Fig. 11.5 and Tables 11.1 and 11.2.

Fig. 11.5 Finite production leakage inventory (*Source* Own)

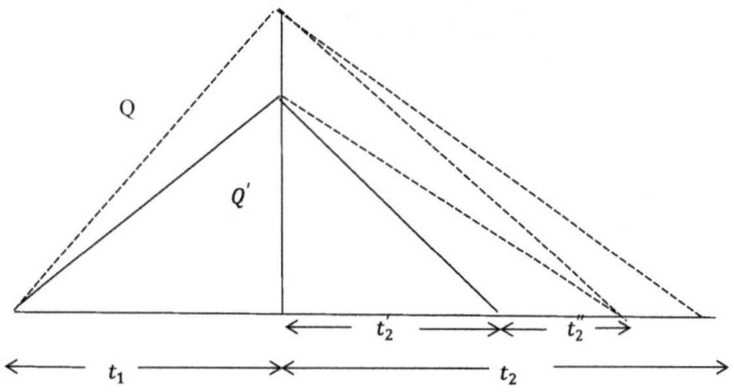

Table 11.1 Sensitivity analysis (For crisp model)

Sl. No.	Demand (r)	$q*$	$C_{\min}$	$d_1 \to 0$ $q*$	$d_1 \to 0$ $C_{\min}$
1	500	96.989993	₹1,082.5859	97.466717	₹1,077.29133

Table 11.2 Sensitivity analysis (For the fuzzy model)

Sl. No.	Demand (r)	$C_h = (9, 11, 13)$ $C_o = (90, 100, 110)$ $T_{ce} = (60, 75, 90)$	$C_h = (9, 11, 13)$ $C_o = (90, 100, 110)$ $T_{ce} = (60, 75, 90$	$C_h = (9, 11, 13)$ $C_o = (90, 100, 110)$ $T_{ce} = (60, 75, 90)$	$C_h = (9, 11, 13)$ $C_o = (90, 100, 110)$ $T_{ce} = (60, 75, 90)$
		$q*$	$C_{\min}$	$d_1 \to 0$ $q*$	$d_1 \to 0$ $C_{\min}$
1	500	94.6525418	₹1,053.99315	95.117732	₹1051.32

Case 2: Leakage inventory model with carbon emission under uniform demand rate, instantaneous production rate without shortages

11.7 Assumptions and Notations

Some notations and assumptions that would be used to solve the problems are as follows:

$q =$ Order quantity per run

$r =$ rate of demand per unit time

$D_p =$ Defective percentage in a lot size of q (in units)

$C_0 =$ Setup or ordering cost per order

$C_h =$ holding cost per unit quantity per unit time

d_1 =leakage rate per unit time

TC = Total cost per unit time.

$\widetilde{Tc}$ = Fuzzy average total cost.

T_{ce} = Tax on carbon emission (in rupees/ton of CO_2).

E_{ce} = Average carbon emission from warehouse electricity (in ton of CO_2/kilowatt hour).

e_i = Electricity consumption per unit in the ware houses (in kwh/unit/per year).

t = Time interval between runs.

k = Finite production rate per unit time.

Q = Denote the inventory level at the end of t_1.

Q' = Denote the inventory level with the occurrence of leakage in the system at the moment when the production stopped.

11.7.1 Assumptions

In this paper, the following assumption are considered:

(i) the uniform nature of total demand is taken
(ii) shortage are not allowed
(iii) only holding cost, setup cost, and carbon emissions cost are fuzzy in nature
(iv) lead time is zero
(v) production is finite.

Let q be the number of units produced per run and t the time interval between successive runs. Let the production continue for a time t_1. Then $q = kt_1$

$$q = rt$$

If Q is the inventory level at the moment the production is stopped (i.e. at the end of time t_1)

$$\begin{aligned} Q &= q - rt_1 \\ &= q - r\frac{q}{k} \\ &= q\left(1 - \frac{r}{k}\right) \end{aligned}$$

Inventory holding cost, $C_h = \frac{1}{2}C_h Qt$

$$= \frac{1}{2}qC_h\left(1 - \frac{r}{k}\right)t.$$

Setup cost $= C_o$.

Total cost $= C_o + \frac{1}{2}qC_h\left(1 - \frac{r}{k}\right)t$.

Average total cost$= \frac{1}{2}qC_h\left(1 - \frac{r}{k}\right)t + C_o\frac{r}{k}$.

Let K-$(r + d_1) > 0$ and $d_1 > 0$ and Q' is the inventory level at the moment when the production is stopped.

Quantity loss with leakage in time $t_1 = Q - Q' = d_1t_1 = q\frac{d_1}{k}$

$$Q' = q - (r + d_1)t = q - (r + d_1)\frac{q}{k} = q\left(1 - \frac{(r + d_1)}{k}\right)$$

Additional cost incurred (due to leakage) in time $t_1 = \frac{1}{2}(Q - Q')t_1C_o = \frac{1}{2}C_od_1\left(\frac{q}{k}\right)^2$.

If the leakage is not detected at the end of time t_1 then the quantity Q' reduces to zero at time t_2'

$$Q' = (d_1 + r)t_2'$$

If the leakage is detected at the end of time t_1, then the quantity Q' reduces to zero at time t_2'

Thus $Q' = d\left(t_1' + t_2\right)$.

Additional cost incurred with leakage in time

$$\begin{aligned} t_2 &= \frac{1}{2}C_hQ't_2'' \\ &= \frac{1}{2r}\frac{d_1}{(r + d_1)}C_hq^2\left(1 - \frac{(r + d_1)}{k}\right)^2 \end{aligned}$$

Total additional cost with leakage in one run $= \frac{1}{2}C_hd_1\left(\frac{q}{k}\right)^2 + \frac{1}{2r}\frac{d_1}{(r+d_1)}C_hq^2\left(1 - \frac{(r+d_1)}{k}\right)^2$

Average additional cost with leakage

$$\begin{aligned} &= \frac{1}{2}C_hd_1\left(\frac{q}{k}\right)^2\frac{r}{q} + \frac{r}{q}\frac{1}{2r}\frac{d_1}{(r + d_1)}C_hq^2\left(1 - \frac{(r + d_1)}{k}\right)^2 \\ &= \frac{1}{2}C_hd_1\frac{rq}{k^2} + \frac{1}{2}\frac{d_1}{(r + d_1)}C_hq\left(1 - \frac{(r + d_1)}{k}\right)^2 \end{aligned}$$

And the perfect quantity items $= \left(q - D_pt_1\right)\left(q - D_pt_1\right) = \left(q - D_p\frac{q}{k}\right) = q\left(1 - \frac{D_p}{k}\right)$

Thus, the carbon emissions cost $= e_iE_{ce}T_{ce}\frac{1}{2}\left(1 - \frac{D_p}{k}\right)qt$

Average carbon emission cost $= e_i E_{ce} T_{ce} \frac{1}{2}\left(1 - \frac{D_p}{k}\right) q.$

Therefore, the required average additional total cost with leakage and carbon emissions cost in economic lot size model is

$$C = \frac{1}{2} C_h \left(1 - \frac{r}{k}\right) q + C_o \frac{r}{q} + \frac{1}{2} C_h d_1 \frac{r}{k^2} q + \frac{1}{2} \frac{C_h d_1}{(r + d_1)} q \left(1 - \frac{r + d_1}{k}\right)^2 + \frac{1}{2} e_i E_{ce} T_{ce} \left(1 - \frac{D_p}{k}\right) q$$

Using $\frac{dC}{dq} = 0$ and $\frac{dC^2}{dq^2} > 0$, we have

$$\frac{1}{2} C_h \left(1 - \frac{r}{k}\right) + C_o \frac{(-r)}{q^2} + \frac{1}{2} C_h d_1 \frac{r}{k^2} + \frac{1}{2} \frac{C_h d_1}{(r + d_1)} \left(1 - \frac{r + d_1}{k}\right)^2 + \frac{1}{2} e_i E_{ce} T_{ce} \left(1 - \frac{D_p}{k}\right) = 0$$

$$=> C_o \frac{r}{q^2} = \frac{1}{2} C_h \left(\frac{k - r}{k}\right) + \frac{1}{2} C_h d_1 \frac{r}{k^2} + \frac{1}{2} \frac{C_h d_1}{(r + d_1)} \left(\frac{k - r - d_1}{k}\right)^2 + \frac{1}{2} e_i E_{ce} T_{ce} \left(\frac{k - D_p}{k}\right)$$

$$=> C_o \frac{r}{q^2} = \frac{1}{2} \left[\frac{C_h k (k - r)(r + d_1) + C_h d_1 r (r + d_1) + C_h d_1 (k - r - d_1)^2 + e_i E_{ce} T_{ce} k \left(k - D_p\right)(r + d_1)}{k^2 (r + d_1)} \right]$$

$$=> 2 C_o r k^2 (r + d_1) = q^2 \{ C_h k (k - r)(r + d_1) + C_h d_1 r (r + d_1) + C_h d_1 (k - r - d_1)^2 + e_i E_{ce} T_{ce} k \left(k - D_p\right)(r + d_1)$$

$$=> q^* = \sqrt{\frac{2 C_o r k^2 (r + d_1)}{\{ C_h k (k - r)(r + d_1) + C_h d_1 r (r + d_1) + C_h d_1 (k - r - d_1)^2 + e_i E_{ce} T_{ce} k \left(k - D_p\right)(r + d_1)}}$$

which is the required economic quantity.

When $d_1 \rightarrow 0$,

$$=> q^* = \sqrt{\frac{2 C_o r^2 k^2}{\{ C_h k (k - r) r + e_i E_{ce} T_{ce} k \left(k - D_p\right) r}}$$

$$=> q^* = \sqrt{\frac{2C_o r^2 k^2}{kr\{C_h(k-r) + e_i E_{ce} T_{ce}(k - D_p)\}}}$$

$$=> q^* = \sqrt{\frac{2C_o rk}{\{C_h(k-r) + e_i E_{ce} T_{ce}(k - D_p)}}$$

We consider the model in a fuzzy environment since the ordering, carbon emission, and holding costs are fuzzy in nature. We represent them by triangular fuzzy numbers.

Let $\widetilde{C}_h$: fuzzy carrying or holding cost per unit quantity per unit time

$\widetilde{C}_o$: fuzzy set up or ordring cost per order

$\widetilde{T}_{ce}$: fuzzy carbon emission cost (rupees per ton of CO_2)

The nature of total demand and time of plan is taken as constant. The fuzzy total cost is obtained by

$$\widetilde{TC} = \frac{1}{2}(a_1, b_1, c_1)\left(1 - \frac{r}{k}\right)q + \frac{r}{q}(a_3, b_3, c_3) + \frac{1}{2}(a_1, b_1, c_1)d_1\frac{r}{k^2}q$$
$$+ \frac{1}{2}\frac{(a_1, b_1, c_1)}{(r+d_1)}d_1 q\left(1 - \frac{r+d_1}{k}\right)^2 + \frac{1}{2}e_i E_{ce}(a_4, b_4, c_4)\left(1 - \frac{D_p}{k}\right)q.$$

where

$$a = \frac{1}{2}\left(1 - \frac{r}{k}\right)qa_1 + \frac{r}{q}\ a_3 + \frac{1}{2}d_1\frac{r}{k^2}qa_1$$
$$+ \frac{1}{2}\frac{d_1 q}{(r+d_1)}a_1\left(1 - \frac{r+d_1}{k}\right)^2 + \ \frac{1}{2}e_1 E_{ce}\left(1 - \frac{D_p}{k}\right)qa_4$$
$$b = \frac{1}{2}\left(1 - \frac{r}{k}\right)qb_1 + \frac{r}{q}\ b_3 + \frac{1}{2}d_1\frac{r}{k^2}qb_1$$
$$+ \frac{1}{2}\frac{d_1 q}{(r+d_1)}b_1\left(1 - \frac{r+d_1}{k}\right)^2 + \ \frac{1}{2}e_1 E_{ce}\left(1 - \frac{D_p}{k}\right)qb_4$$
$$c = \frac{1}{2}\left(1 - \frac{r}{k}\right)qc_1 + \frac{r}{q}\ c_3 + \frac{1}{2}d_1\frac{r}{k^2}qc_1$$
$$+ \frac{1}{2}\frac{d_1 q}{(r+d_1)}c_1\left(1 - \frac{r+d_1}{k}\right)^2 + \ \frac{1}{2}e_1 E_{ce}\left(1 - \frac{D_p}{k}\right)qc_4$$

Signed distance method for defuzzification of fuzzy number $\widetilde{TC}$ is given as

$$d\left(\widetilde{TC}, 0\right) = \frac{1}{2}\int_0^1 [A_u(\alpha) + A_v(\alpha)]d\alpha$$

where $A_u(\alpha) = a + (b - a)\alpha, A_v(\alpha) = c - (c - b)\alpha$

Now,

$$
\begin{aligned}
(\widetilde{TC},0) &= \frac{1}{2}q\left(1-\frac{r}{k}\right)\left(\frac{a_1+c_1+2b_1}{4}\right)+\frac{r}{q}\left(\frac{a_3+c_3+2b_3}{4}\right)\\
&+\frac{1}{2}d_1\frac{r}{k^2}q\left(\frac{a_1+c_1+2b_1}{4}\right)+\frac{1}{2}\frac{d_1q}{(r+d_1)}\left(1-\frac{r+d_1}{k}\right)^2\left(\frac{a_1+c_1+2b_1}{4}\right)\\
&+\frac{1}{2}e_1E_{ce}\left(1-\frac{D_p}{k}\right)q\left(\frac{a_4+c_4+2b_4}{4}\right)\\
&= C_r(q)(\text{say})
\end{aligned}
$$

For the minimum value $C_r(q)$Differentiate the above $C_r(q)$ with respect to q and equate it to zero

$$
\begin{aligned}
&C_r'(q)=0 \text{ and } C_r''>0\\
&\Rightarrow \frac{1}{2}\left(1-\frac{r}{k}\right)\left(\frac{a_1+c_1+2b_1}{4}\right)+\frac{(-r)}{q^2}\left(\frac{a_3+c_3+2b_3}{4}\right)\\
&+\frac{1}{2}d_1\frac{r}{k^2}\left(\frac{a_1+c_1+2b_1}{4}\right)+\frac{1}{2}\frac{d_1}{(r+d_1)}\left(1-\frac{r+d_1}{k}\right)^2\left(\frac{a_1+c_1+2b_1}{4}\right)\\
&+\frac{1}{2}e_1E_{ce}\left(1-\frac{D_p}{k}\right)\left(\frac{a_4+c_4+2b_4}{4}\right)=0\\
&\Rightarrow \frac{r}{q^2}\left(\frac{a_3+c_3+2b_3}{4}\right)=\frac{1}{2}\left(\frac{k-r}{k}\right)\left(\frac{a_1+c_1+2b_1}{4}\right)+\frac{1}{2}d_1\frac{r}{k^2}\left(\frac{a_1+c_1+2b_1}{4}\right)\\
&+\frac{1}{2}\frac{d_1}{(r+d_1)}\left(\frac{k-r-d_1}{k}\right)^2\left(\frac{a_1+c_1+2b_1}{4}\right)+\frac{1}{2}e_1E_{ce}\left(\frac{k-D_p}{k}\right)\left(\frac{a_4+c_4+2b_4}{4}\right)\\
&\Rightarrow \frac{r}{q^2}\left(\frac{a_3+c_3+2b_3}{4}\right)\\
&=\frac{1}{8}\left\{\frac{\begin{array}{l}k(k-r)(r+d_1)(a_1+c_1+2b_1)+d_1r(r+d_1)(a_1+c_1+2b_1)\\+d_1(k-r-d_1)^2(a_1+c_1+2b_1)\\+e_1E_{ce}k(r+d_1)(k-D_p)(a_4+c_4+2b_4)\end{array}}{k^2(r+d_1)}\right\}\Rightarrow q^*\\
&=\sqrt{\frac{2rk^2(r+d_1)(a_3+c_3+2b_3)}{\begin{array}{c}k(k-r)(r+d_1)(a_1+c_1+2b_1)+d_1r(r+d_1)\\(a_1+c_1+2b_1)+d_1(k-r-d_1)^2(a_1+c_1+2b_1)\\+e_1E_{ce}k(r+d_1)(k-D_p)(a_4+c_4+2b_4)\end{array}}}
\end{aligned}
$$

When $d_1 \to 0$

$$
q^*=\sqrt{\frac{2rk(a_3+c_3+2b_3)}{(k-r)(a_1+c_1+2b_1)+e_1E_{ce}(k-D_p)(a_4+c_4+2b_4)}}
$$

Table 11.3 Sensitivity analysis (For crisp model)

Sl. No.	Demand (r)	q^*	$d_1 \to 0$ q^*
1	500	136.830552	137.4945

Table 11.4 Sensitivity analysis (For fuzzy model)

Sl. No.	Demand (r)	$C_h = (9, 11, 13)$ $C_o = (90, 100,1\ 10)$ T_{ce} =(60, 75, 90)	$C_h = (9, 11, 13)$ $C_o = (90, 100, 110)$ T_{ce} =(60, 75, 90)
		q^*	$d_1 \to 0$ q^*
1	500	133.53306	134.182879

11.8 Numerical Example (Chandrasiri 2016; Chaudhary 2023)

Model (Crisp): Let us consider the inventory system with the following data in usual notation as

r =500 units per unite per year, C_h = ₹11, C_0 = ₹105 per order, $d_1 = 5$ units per year, $k = 1000$, T_{ce} = ₹75/ton CO_2, $e_i = 1.44$ kwh/unit/year, E_{ce} =0.005 ton CO_2/kwh and $D_p = 0.02s$

Solution

See Tables 11.3 and 11.4.

11.9 Conclusion

In this paper, we developed models focusing on carbon emissions and leakage with a uniform demand rate, instantaneous and finite production rates, and no shortages within the Economic Order Quantity (EOQ) framework. We incorporated both leakage and carbon emissions costs into the inventory model without shortages. The signed distance method was used for defuzzifying the total cost, and we computed the EOQ in both crisp and fuzzy environments. We demonstrated that holding costs, ordering costs, and carbon emissions costs can be represented as triangular fuzzy numbers. Our findings indicate that the EOQ derived using the signed distance method closely aligns with the crisp EOQ, while the total cost calculated through the signed distance method exceeds the crisp total cost. The EOQ is particularly sensitive to variations in demand, causing an increase in total cost with higher demand levels. Additionally, our observations highlight that the total cost of the EOQ model is influenced by environmental conditions.

References

Bazan E, Jaber MY, Zanoni S (2017) Carbon emissions and energy effects on a two-level manufacturer-retailer closed-loop supply chain model with remanufacturing subject to different coordination mechanisms. Int J Prod Econ 183:394–408. https://doi.org/10.1016/J.IJPE.2016.07.009

Becerra P, Mula J, Sanchis R (2021) Green supply chain quantitative models for sustainable inventory management: a review. J Clean Prod 328:129544. https://doi.org/10.1016/J.JCLEPRO.2021.129544

Berkachy R, Donze L (2016) Linguistic questionnaire evaluation. an application of signed distance defuzzification method on different fuzzy number. The impact on the skewness of the output on the skewness distribution. Int J Fuzzy Syst Adv Appl 3

Chung CJ, Wee HM (2011) Short life-cycle deteriorating product remanufacturing in a green supply chain inventory control system. Int J Prod Econ 129:195–203. https://doi.org/10.1016/J.IJPE.2010.09.033

Chandrasiri AM (2016) Fuzzy inventory model without shortages using triangular fuzzy number and singed distance method. Int J Sci Res (IJSR)

Chaudhary R, Mittal M, Jayaswal MK (2023) A Sustainable inventory model for defective items under fuzzy environment. Decision Anal J 7:100207

Chopra S, Meindl P (2016) Supply chain management strategy, planning and operation. 6th edn. ISBN 13:978-0-13-380020-3

Dhivya Lakshmi M, Pandian P (2018) A review on inventory models in fuzzy environment. 9:113–123

Dutta D, Kumar P (2013) Fuzzy inventory model for deteriorating items with shortages under fully backlogged condition. Int J Soft Comput Eng (TJSCE) 3:393–398

García-Alvarado M, Paquet M, Chaabane A, Amodeo L (2017) Inventory management under joint product recovery and cap-and-trade constraints. J Clean Prod 167:1499–1517. https://doi.org/10.1016/J.JCLEPRO.2016.10.074

Geeta O (2010) Some deterministic and stochastic leakage inventory control. Ph D Thesis, Manipur University, Imphal

Ghare P (1963) A model for an exponentially decaying inventory. J Ind Eng 14:238–243

Ghosh A, Jha JK, Sarmah SP (2020) Production-inventory models considering different carbon policies: a review. Int J Prod Qual Manag 30:1–27. https://doi.org/10.1504/IJPQM.2020.107280

Gupta RK (1992) Operation Research, Krishna Prakshashan Media (P) Ltd. Meerut

Halat K, Hafezalkotob A (2019) Modeling carbon regulation policies in inventory decisions of a multi-stage green supply chain: a game theory approach. Comput Ind Eng 128:807–830

Kang K, Sung Hong K, Kim KH, Lee C (2017) Shipment consolidation policy under uncertainty of customer order for sustainable supply chain management. Sustainability 9:1675. https://doi.org/10.3390/SU9091675, https://www.mdpi.com/2071-1050/9/9/1675/htm

Karimi M, Niknamfar AH, Pasandidesh SHR (2016) Two-stage single period inventory management for a manufacturing vendor under green–supply chain. Int J Syst Assuring English Manag 8:704/718

Karimi M, Niknamfar AH, Pasandideh SHR (2016) Two-stage single period inventory management for a manufacturing vendor under green-supplier supply chain. Int J Syst Assur Eng Manag 8:704–718. https://doi.org/10.1007/S13198-016-0557-5, https://link.springer.com/article/10.1007/s13198-016-0557-5

Khatua D, Roymahapatra G, Maity K (2017) A green supply chain production inven tory model with uncertain holding cost. Int J Process Manag Benchmarking 7:277–304. https://doi.org/10.1504/IJPMB.2017.084905

Lee HM, Yao JS (1990) Economic order quantity in fuzzy sense for inventory without backorder model. Fuzzy Sets and Syst 105:311–337

Lin CC, Lin CW (2011) Defective item inventory model with remanufacturing or replenishing in an integrated supply chain. Int J Integr Supply Manag 6:254–269. https://doi.org/10.1504/IJISM.2011.044889

Lu X, Shang J, Wu SY, Hegde GG, Vargas L, Zhao D (2015a) Impacts of supplier hubris on inventory decisions and green manufacturing endeavors, European. J Oper Res 245:121–132. https://doi.org/10.1016/J.EJOR.2015.02.051

Lu X, Shang J, Wu SY, Hegde GG, Vargas L, Zhao D (2015b) Impacts of supplierhubris on inventory decisions and green manufacturing endeavors, European. J Oper Res 245:121–132. https://doi.org/10.1016/J.EJOR.2015.02.051

Mokhtari H, Rezvan MT (2017) A single-supplier, multi-buyer, multi-product VMI production-inventory system under partial backordering. Oper Res 20:37–57. https://doi.org/10.1007/S12351-017-0311-Z, https://link.springer.com/article/10.1007/s12351-017-0311-z

Mokhtari H, Rezvan MT (2017) A single-supplier, multi-buyer, multi-product VMI production-inventory system under partial backordering. Oper Res 20:37–57. https://doi.org/10.1007/S12351-017-0311-Z, https: //link.springer.com/article/ https://doi.org/10.1007/s12351-017-0311-z

Montgomery DC, Chung CJ, Wee HM (2011) Short life-cycle deteriorating product remanufacturing ina green supply chain inventory control system. Int J Prod Econ 129:195–203. https://doi.org/10.1016/J.IJPE.2010.09.033

Panja S, Mondal SK (2019) Analyzing a four-layer green supply chain imperfect production inventory model for green products under type-2 fuzzy credit period. Comput Ind Eng 129:435–453

Pattnaik S, Nayak MM, Abbate S, Centobelli P (2021) Recent trends in sustainable inventory models: a literature review. Sustainability 13:11756. https://doi.org/10.3390/SU132111756, https://www.mdpi.com/2071-1050/13/21/11756/htm

Raiya G, Mittal M (2023) Joint decisions on imperfect production process and carbon emission reduction under carbon regulations. In: Frontiers in industrial and applied mathematics: FIAM-2021, Punjab, India, December 21–22, Springer, pp 411–426

Raiya G, Mittal M (2022) Economic order quantity model for imperfect quality items with environmental regulations, Yugosl. J Oper Res 32(4):483–501

Sazvar Z, Al-E-Hashem SMJM, Baboli A, Jokar MRA (2014) A bi-objective stochas tic programming model for a centralized green supply chain with deteriorating products. Int J Prod Econ 150:140–154. https://doi.org/10.1016/J.IJPE.2013.12.023

Taleizadeh AA, Hazarkhani B, Moon I (2018) Joint pricing and inventory decisions with carbon emission considerations, partial backordering and planned discounts. Ann Oper Res 290:95–113. https://doi.org/10.1007/S10479-0182968-Y, https://link.springer.com/article/10.1007/s10479018-2968-y

Tang Z, Liu X, Wang Y (2020) Integrated optimization of sustainable transportation and inventory with multiplayer dynamic game under carbon tax policy. Math Probl Eng. https://doi.org/10.1155/2020/4948383

Tomba I, Geeta O (2008) Some deterministic Leakage inventory models. Bullet Pure and Appl Sci 27(2):267–276

Wee HM, Lee MC, Yu JCP, Wang CE (2011) Optimal replenishment policy for a deteriorating green product: life cycle costing analysis. Int J Prod Econ 133:603–611. https://doi.org/10.1016/J.IJPE.2011.05.001

Wagner HM, Whitin TM (1958) Dynamic version of the economic lot size model. Manage Sci 5(1):89–96

Widyadana GA, Wee HM (2012) An economic production quantity model for dete riorating items with multiple production setups and rework. Int J Prod Econ 138:62–67. https://doi.org/10.1016/J.IJPE.2012.02.025

Zadeh LA (1965) Fuzzy sets, information and control. 8(3):338–353

Zhang CT, Liu LP (2013) Research on coordination mechanism in three-level green supply chain under non-cooperative game. Appl Math Model 37:3369–3379. https://doi.org/10.1016/J.APM.2012.08.006

Zimmerman HJ (2001) In: Fuzzy set theory and its applications. Springer Science Business Media, LLC

Chapter 12
Inventory Decisions with Carbon Emissions, Partial Backlogging and Price-Stock-Dependent Demand

Nita H. Shah, Ekta Patel, and Kavita Rabari

Abstract In light of growing awareness surrounding carbon emissions, companies are urged to integrate sustainability into their conventional inventory systems, aligning both monetary and environmental goals. Regulatory policies aimed at reducing carbon emissions have significantly impacted profit-driven enterprises. So, the proposed research delves the complex interplay between inventory management, carbon emissions, partial backlogging, price-stock-dependent demand, and deterioration within a unified framework. In this article, the authors propose a comprehensive model that accounts for these factors simultaneously, aiming to optimize inventory decisions while minimizing environmental impact and meeting customer demand. The model considers the carbon emissions associated with inventory holding and transportation, highlighting the significance of sustainable practices in managing supply chains. Additionally, partial backlogging is incorporated to reflect situations where only a portion of unfilled demand is satisfied in subsequent periods, enhancing the realism of the model. Moreover, we incorporate the impact of both price and stock levels on demand, acknowledging their dynamic nature in shaping consumer behavior. Deterioration is another critical aspect considered in the model, recognizing the natural decay of perishable goods over time. The authors employ mathematical optimization techniques to derive optimal policies for inventory replenishment, order quantities, and pricing strategies, considering both economic objectives and environmental sustainability goals. Numerical experiments are performed to demonstrate the efficacy of the proposed model in achieving a balance between competing objectives and to offer insights into the trade-offs involved in sustainable inventory management practices.

Keywords Stock and price dependent demand · Deterioration · Carbon emissions · Carbon tax · Backorder

N. H. Shah (✉) · K. Rabari
School of Emerging Science and Technology, Department of Mathematics, Gujarat University, Ahmedabad, Gujarat 380009, India
e-mail: nitahshah@gmail.com

E. Patel
Department of Mathematics, Nirma University, Ahmedabad, India

N. H. Shah and M. Mittal (eds.), *Sustainable Inventory Management*, Inventory Optimization, https://doi.org/10.1007/978-981-97-6765-6_13

MSC Classification Code 90B05

12.1 Introduction

In the contemporary business landscape, the imperative to address climate change has become a central focus, reshaping corporate strategies and operational paradigms. Firms are navigating this new terrain by reimagining their corporate plans, integrating climate change considerations into their core operations. This shift not only aligns with broader environmental goals but also presents a spectrum of novel opportunities for businesses. At the forefront of these opportunities lies the urgent task of reducing carbon emissions. Recognized as a primary contributor to climate change, carbon emissions predominantly stem from human activities, notably the combustion of fossil fuels within industrial processes. The ramifications of this extend beyond ecological concerns, directly impacting the international economy. Consequently, companies face a monumental challenge in not only curtailing their carbon footprint but also in mitigating the broader effects of global warming. Nevertheless, amidst these challenges lie avenues for innovation and growth. Embracing sustainable technologies emerges as a pivotal strategy in mitigating carbon emissions. By adopting technologies that prioritize environmental sustainability, businesses can navigate both the immediate exigencies and the long-term implications of their operations. These sustainable solutions include a range of strategies, such as energy efficiency, recycling programs, health and safety measures, and the use of renewable resources. Central to this paradigm shift is the emergence of green products. These innovative offerings epitomize environmentally conscious design, encompassing a multifaceted approach that integrates various eco-friendly elements. From enhancing energy efficiency to promoting recycling practices, green products epitomize a holistic commitment to environmental stewardship. Furthermore, the burgeoning adoption of green products underscores a broader trend towards sustainability across consumer preferences and regulatory frameworks. In tandem with these developments, authorities in developed nations are spearheading measures to incentivize sustainable practices and mitigate carbon emissions. Through regulatory interventions and policy frameworks, governments are catalyzing the transition towards a more sustainable economic landscape. This regulatory impetus not only fosters an enabling environment for green innovation but also underscores the imperative for businesses to align with evolving environmental standards.

Moreover, the dynamics of demand in the marketplace introduce additional complexity to inventory management strategies. While traditional inventory models often operate under the assumption of constant demand rates, real-life scenarios are characterized by fluctuating demand dynamics. Factors such as selling price and product availability exert a profound influence on consumer behavior, necessitating a more nuanced approach to inventory optimization.

Furthermore, the presence of deteriorating items within inventory introduces additional challenges to profitability. The management of perishable goods requires a judicious balance between minimizing waste and maximizing revenue streams. In this context, leveraging advanced inventory management techniques, such as dynamic pricing algorithms and predictive analytics, becomes imperative in optimizing inventory turnover and maximizing profitability.

In summation, the convergence of climate change imperatives and business imperatives heralds a transformative era for corporate strategy and operations. As businesses navigate the complexities of mitigating carbon emissions and embracing sustainability, they must concurrently contend with evolving market dynamics and regulatory frameworks. Through strategic innovation and a steadfast commitment to environmental stewardship, businesses can not only mitigate their ecological footprint but also position themselves as leaders in a rapidly evolving global economy.

In the proposed article, the subsequent section delineates a structured framework aimed at comprehensively addressing the intersection of climate change considerations and corporate strategy. Organized into distinct segments, each section contributes to a cohesive narrative aimed at elucidating the proposed approach and its implications for managerial decision-making. Section 12.2 embarks on an exploration of relevant literature, contextualizing the proposed framework within the broader scholarly discourse. Section 12.3 presents the symbolic notation and outlines the fundamental assumptions that support the proposed mathematical model. Section 12.4 constitutes the heart of the article, presenting the mathematical model in a structured and systematic manner. Drawing upon established mathematical principles and optimization techniques, this section articulates the framework for optimizing carbon emissions reduction strategies within a corporate context. By elucidating the model's formulation and solution methodology. Following the presentation of the mathematical model, Sect. 12.5 endeavours to concretize the theoretical framework through a numerical example. Through a step-by-step illustration, this section elucidates the application of the model in a real-world context, reaffirming its efficacy and practical relevance. By showcasing a numerically validated solution, Sect. 12.5 bolsters the credibility and applicability of the proposed methodology. Section 12.6 advances the analytical discussion by performing a sensitivity analysis, examining the model's robustness to changes in key parameters. By systematically varying input parameters and assessing their impact on the optimal solution, this section offers valuable insights into the model's sensitivity to underlying assumptions. Through a nuanced exploration of potential scenarios, Sect. 12.6 informs managerial decision-making by delineating the trade-offs inherent in carbon emissions reduction strategies.

Ultimately, Sect. 12.7 serves as the denouement of the proposed article, synthesizing key findings and delineating avenues for future research. By summarizing the salient insights gleaned from the preceding sections, Sect. 12.7 encapsulates the suggested approach's contribution to scholarly discourse and managerial practice.

12.2 Literature Survey

This part provides a thorough examination of the current body of literature on traditional inventory models, taking into account different demand patterns and their influence on carbon emissions. It highlights the shortcomings in the current comprehension and analyses their importance in the present circumstances. Market demand rate assumptions are based on factors such as pricing, stock levels, or other relevant considerations, and can either remain constant or vary. Sana and Chaudhuri (2004) established an Economic Order Quantity (EOQ) model for perishable items with constant replenishment rate, considering demand to be dependent on stock levels, in which due to storage capacity limitations, the associated cost function is optimized under certain constraints. Min and Zhou (2009) proposed an inventory model that accounts for item decay, where the demand is influenced by the quantity of stock on hand, and also permits partial backlogging. Later, Yang et al. (2010) developed a specialized inventory model for perishable goods. This model considers the influence of inventory levels on demand, permits for partial backlogging, and integrates the effects of inflation. The study conducted by Lee and Dye (2012) extensively examined a degrading inventory model that integrated demand determined by stock levels and also considered a limited number of backorders. In Mondal et al. (2003) developed an inventory model aimed at enhancing goods by considering the demand rate's sensitivity to price and utilizing the Weibull distribution.

Mukhopadhyay et al. (2005) did a study where they introduced an Economic Order Quantity (EOQ) model that includes a two-parameter Weibull distribution. This model incorporates the dynamic demand rates in response to price fluctuations and the fluctuating deterioration rates of stored items over time. In their study, Xiao et al. (2016) devised a sustainable supply chain consisting of two tiers. They focused on the reduction of carbon footprint in order to address demand that is sensitive to price changes. In their study, Panda et al. (2017) investigated a model for inventory management model for a manufacturing system that accounts for both deterioration and fluctuations in volume. The study specifically considered the influence of price elasticity of demand. Ruidas et al. (2021) devised a production inventory model that incorporates regulations on carbon emissions, in which demand decreases linearly as the selling price rises. Hou and Lin (2006) examined an Economic Order Quantity (EOQ) model for products that undergo deterioration. Their study considered the impact of inflation and accounted for the responsiveness of demand to changes in both price and stock levels. In a further study, You and Hsieh (2007) created a model to effectively handle the inventory of seasonal goods over a specified timeframe. The model takes into account the impact of both stock levels and pricing on demand. Panda et al. (2010) investigated a two-warehouse inventory model that incorporates a solitary supplier and many retailers. In this model, the demand exhibits a direct correlation with the stock and an inverse correlation with the selling price. Chowdhury et al. (2015) developed an inventory model for a firm selling seasonal items over a finite planning period. It considers customer behavior, where higher stock levels attract more buyers and demand varies with inventory levels. The model addresses product deterioration, seeking to maximize the firm's expected profit by optimizing ordering quantities and pricing strategies. Shah and Naik's study introduced inventory techniques for deteriorating items that consider impact of demand on pricing and incorporation of conditional discount. Lu et al. (2020) investigated an intricate inventory model for sustainable production that encompassed several stages. The researchers employed the Stackelberg game approach to examine the dynamics of the model in relation to the deterioration of items and carbon emissions. Halim et al. (2021) proposed a model for effectively controlling the inventory of perishable products. The model considers non-linear demand that is responsive to price fluctuations, which are impacted by the present inventory levels. Mahato et al. (2021) explored a two-echelon supply chain for growing items, considering a hybrid price-stock-dependent demand under a trade credit policy. It examines a supplier-retailer scenario where the supplier raises and slaughters animals, which are then subject to deterioration at the retailer. Demand depends on the selling price and inventory level. The model is analyzed in both decentralized and centralized structures.

Carbon emissions are the main factor that determines environmental pollution. Hovelaque and Bironneau (2015) introduced an Economic Order Quantity (EOQ) framework that integrates the impact of pricing, environmental factors and carbon emissions on demand. Sarkar et al. (2016) examined the implementation of a Stackelberg game strategy within an integrated inventory model that took into account the effects of carbon emissions Saga et al. (2019) proposed research on a production inventory model that incorporates imperfect production and its impact on carbon emissions. Mishra et al. (2020) conducted a study to investigate a model that predicts the quantity of sustainable economic output. The approach prioritized investment in environmentally-friendly technologies while complying with legislation pertaining to carbon emissions limits and carbon taxation. Mashud et al. (2021) proposed a study on a sustainable inventory model that focuses on managing deteriorating products and reducing carbon emissions. The authors of this research proposed the utilization of green and preservation technology as a strategy to mitigate carbon emissions and safeguard against product degradation. Additionally, they deliberated about the utilization of contemporary payment mechanisms. Sepehri et al. (2021) presented a joint pricing and inventory model tailored for deteriorating items with a defined maximum lifespan. In their study, the authors identified the optimal replenishment cycle and selling price for these perishable goods, considering a specific allowable delay in payment to generate revenue. Additionally, the model accounts for carbon emissions resulting from ordering and storage processes. The authors also incorporated a carbon reduction policy within a regulated carbon cap and trade framework. Shah et al. (2022) conducted a study on an EPQ (Economic Production Quantity) model for items that experience degradation over time. They considered the influence of stock levels on demand, which is responsive to price, as well as the carbon emissions linked to the production process. Shah et al. (2022) established an inventory model for perishable products for price and stock-dependent demand rate incorporating greening efforts, in which inventory model deals with order size purchase cost by considering all unit quantity discounts and also consider holding cost as a function of storage time and purchase cost. In addition, they analyzed the impacts of investing in environmentally-friendly and conservation technology. Shah et al. (2022) presented an inventory model of investigation of carbon emissions due to vaccine of covid-19. The model uses a non-linear formulation to determine the optimal cycle time without shortages, demonstrating the convexity of the objective function with numerical data. The study aims to understand the relationship between COVID-19 vaccine inventory and carbon emissions, highlighting the environmental impact and the need for sustainable practices. Shah et al. (2022) investigated an Economic Production Quantity model for deteriorating items by considering carbon cap and carbon tax policy in which demand is stock dependent and price sensitive. In this model, the authors analyzed under different scenario of controllable carbon emissions like under green technology, under preservation technology and under both the technologies are together. De-la-Cruz-Márquez et al. (2022) introduced an optimization model for a three-stage supply chain involving farmers, processors, and retailers, addressing issues of imperfect quality, mortality, shortages with full backordering, and carbon emissions. The model considers survival probabilities during the growing period and imperfections at the retailer stage, impacting consumer perceptions. It aims to maximize expected total profit for a single type of growing item with price-dependent polynomial demand. Mahato et al. (2023) devised a model for effectively handling inventories of perishable commodities with a specific lifespan, while also accommodating partial backorders. The model additionally considers carbon emissions. Singh (2022)presented a new inventory model that considers the influence of inflation and carbon emissions on the variable holding cost of deteriorating goods. Bhavani et al. (2022) studied a sustainable inventory model for non-instantaneous decaying items focusing on novel eco-friendly demand given by herbal and chemical substances under partially backlogged shortages by considering fuzziness, in which carbon emissions during different activities were estimated under cap and tax policies. Mondal et al. (2023) deliberated an Economic Order Quantity model with continuous time dependent demand with constant rate of deterioration by considering partial backordering including delay in payment and time period.

12.3 Notations and Assumptions

12.3.1 Notations

Notations utilized to formulate an inventory model are provided in Table 12.1.

12.3.2 Assumption

The model presented is developed based on the following specified characteristics.

I. Proposed inventory system considers single item.

Table 12.1 *Source* Own

Parameters	
A	Ordering cost
h	Unit holding cost per unit time
η	Annual rate of average inventory obsolescence
w	Weight of an obsolete units in the warehouse
C	Purchase cost per unit in dollars
C_b	Unit backordering cost
C_l	Unit lost sales cost
C_{GL}	Unit goodwill loss
i	Inventory carrying charge fraction
Carbon emissions parameters	
C_{eo}	Average cost of carbon emission coefficients of average waste for emissions during collection and disposal
C_{EO}	Carbon emission unit associated with order replenishment
C_{EH}	Carbon emission unit in the inventory system that is related to stock-level per unit of time
C_{EP}	Carbon emission units associated per unit purchased/produced
C_T	Carbon tax per unit ($/ton) (money units for each unit of carbon emitted as tax)
C_s	Unitary scrape price
Constants	
α	Variable component
β	Constant fraction of backordering
λ	% of demand that will be filled from stock
c	Constant
Demand and spoilage parameter	
a	Potential scale demand
b	Elasticity of stock-dependent demand
θ	Rate of deterioration per item
Other parameters	
Q	Maximum order level
MI	Maximum level of inventory
T	Cycle time
$R(I(t))$	Annual stock-dependent demand rate
B	Backordered quantity
L	Lost sales quantity
TP	Total profit
t_1	Positive inventory level

II. The holding cost demonstrates a linear escalation with the unit purchasing cost, indicating a direct proportionality between the unit carrying cost and the unit purchase cost, $h = i + \alpha C$ where, α is a variable component. (The relationship between the holding cost and the unit purchasing cost is characterized by a linear increase, implying a direct correlation between the unit carrying cost and the unit purchase cost.)
III. Demand rate is assumed to be price sensitive and stock dependent, which is given by $R(P, I(t)) = a + bI(t) - cP$ where, a is potential scale demand, b denotes elasticity of stock dependent demand, c is price elasticity and selling price is denoted by P.
IV. Deterioration is considered.
V. Carbon emissions during the activities like set-up, order process, transportation, inventory holding, material holding and from obsolete material is considered.
VI. Partial backordering is allowed.

12.4 Mathematical Model

In this segment, proposed inventory model is structured under consideration of all assumptions stated in Sect. 12.3. Initially the inventory level is Q, which declines due to demand and deterioration is represented in Fig. 12.1.

Here, the term "percentage of demand that will be filled from stock" refers to the portion of customer demand that can be satisfied using the available inventory on hand. This metric indicates the extent to which the current stock levels can meet customer orders without requiring additional procurement or production. It essentially quantifies the ability of a company to fulfill orders from its existing inventory, thereby minimizing backorders or stock outs. This percentage is crucial for inventory management as it directly impacts customer satisfaction, operational efficiency, and overall supply chain performance.

Therefore, the differential equation governing the rate of change of the inventory level is expressed as follows:

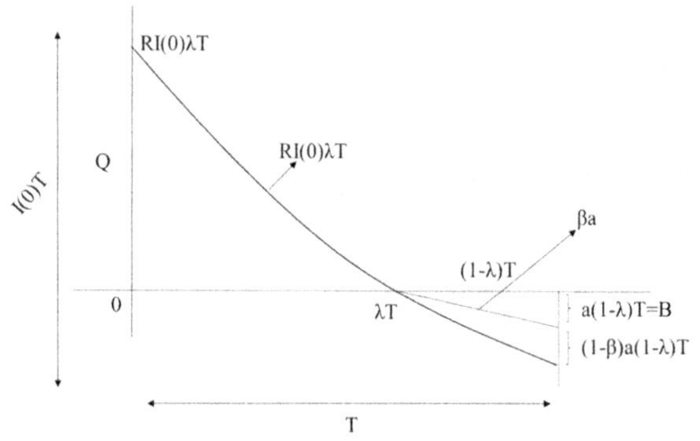

Fig. 12.1 Inventory model with partially backordering (*Source* Own)

$$\frac{dI(t)}{dt} + \theta(t) = -R(I(t), P), I(0) = T, 0 \leq t \leq t_1 \tag{12.1}$$

On solving equation given in (12.1) and applying boundary condition, we have the inventory is

$$I(t) = \frac{(a - cP)}{(b + \theta)}\left[e^{(b+\theta)(T\lambda - t)} - 1\right], 0 \leq t \leq t_1 \tag{12.2}$$

Switching the boundary condition $I(0) = Q$, the order quantity is determined by

$$Q = I(t) = \frac{(a - cP)}{(b + \theta)}\left[e^{(b+\theta)T\lambda} - 1\right]\lambda T + (1 - \lambda)\beta(a - cP)T \tag{12.3}$$

The associated costs are:

The fixed ordering cost per unit time is

$$OC = A \tag{12.4}$$

Here, C represents the purchasing cost per order. Consequently, the purchase cost per unit time for the order quantity Q is given by

$$PC = \frac{CQ}{T} = \frac{1}{T}C\left(\frac{(a - cP)\left(e^{(b+\theta)\lambda T} - 1\right)\lambda T}{(b + \theta)} + (1 - \lambda)\beta(a - cP)T\right) \tag{12.5}$$

Holding cost is based on the average inventory level in stock, because is the cost of holding of an item in each year and it is expressed as:

$$HC = \frac{h(a - cP)\left(\lambda Tb + \lambda T\theta - e^{(b+\theta)\lambda T} + 1\right)}{(b + \theta)^2 T} \tag{12.6}$$

The backordering cost considers the average number of backorders occurring within a specified percentage each year, calculated as follows:

$$BC = \frac{1}{2}C_b\beta(a - cP)(1 - \lambda)^2 T \tag{12.7}$$

The cost of lost sales is determined by accounting for the number of orders lost at a fixed percentage rate.

$(1 - \beta)$ per year. $(P - c + cl)$ factors in both lost profit and goodwill loss, considering,

$$LC = (P - c + cl)(1 - \beta)(a - cP)(1 - \lambda) \tag{12.8}$$

The cost of waste encompasses the expenses associated with collecting and disposing of stored products that become wasted or obsolete. Consequently, the annual cost for removing obsolete products is determined by this factor.

$$WC = \frac{(P - cs)n\lambda(a - cP)\left(e^{(b+\theta)\lambda T} - 1\right)}{(b + \theta)T} \tag{12.9}$$

Carbon emissions cost:

The cost related to carbon emissions consists of three components: the first is associated with replenishment, the second with the quantity of inventory in stock, and the third with environmental impact.

Due to replenishment

$$CER = \frac{C_{EO}}{T}. \tag{12.10}$$

Due to quantity of inventory in stock

$$CECP = \frac{C_{EP}(a - cP)\left(e^{(b+\theta)\lambda T} - 1\right)}{(b + \theta)T} \tag{12.11}$$

Due to storage amounts

$$CES = C_{EH}\int_{0}^{\lambda T} I(t)dts$$

$$CES = \frac{C_{EH}(a - cP)\left(-\lambda T(b + \theta) + e^{(b+\theta)\lambda T} - 1\right)}{(b + \theta)^2 T} \tag{12.12}$$

Environmental impact

$$EI = \frac{C_{EP}\left(\frac{(a-cP)\left(e^{(b+\theta)\lambda T}-1\right)\lambda T}{(b+\theta)} + (1 - \lambda)\beta(a - cP)T\right)}{T} \tag{12.13}$$

Due to obsolete material

$$OM = \frac{\eta w C_{eo}(a - cP)\left(-\lambda T(b + \theta) + e^{(b+\theta)\lambda T} - 1\right)}{(b + \theta)^2 T} \tag{12.14}$$

Revenue from carbon taxes can be utilized by governments for diverse purposes, including financing renewable energy projects, bolstering energy efficiency efforts, subsidizing clean technologies, or offering rebates to low-income households. The efficacy of a carbon tax hinges on its structure, encompassing factors like the tax rate, the sectors and activities subject to it, and any accompanying policies or regulations put in place.

So, total Carbon emissions cost due to activities like replenishment, quantity of inventory in stock, storage, environmental impact and obsolete material is given by

$$CTE = C_T(CER + CECP + CES + EI + OM)$$

$$CTE = C_T\left(\begin{array}{l}\dfrac{C_{EO}}{T} + \dfrac{C_{EP}(a - cP)\left(e^{(b+\theta)\lambda T} - 1\right)}{(b+\theta)T} \\ -\dfrac{C_{EH}(cP - a)\left(-\lambda Tb - \lambda T\theta + e^{(b+\theta)\lambda T} - 1\right)}{(b+\theta)^2 T} \\ +\dfrac{C_{EP}}{T}\left(\begin{array}{l}\dfrac{(-cP + a)\left(e^{(b+\theta)\lambda T} - 1\right)\lambda T}{b+\theta} \\ +(1-\lambda)\beta(-cP + a)T\end{array}\right) \\ -\dfrac{\eta w C_{eo}(cP - a)\left(-\lambda Tb - \lambda T\theta + e^{(b+\theta)\lambda T} - 1\right)}{(b+\theta)^2 T}\end{array}\right) \tag{12.15}$$

The sales revenue derived from the inventory results from the timely sale of products and the backorder level, as indicated by:

$$SR = \frac{P}{T}\left(\frac{(a - cP)\left(e^{(b+\theta)\lambda T} - 1\right)\lambda T}{b+\theta} + (1-\lambda)\beta(a - cP)T\right) \tag{12.16}$$

Hence, total profit is given by

$$TP = SR - OC - PC - HC - BC - LC - WC - C_T$$
$$(CER + CECP + CES + EI + OM)$$

$$TP = \left[\begin{array}{l} \dfrac{P}{T}\left(\dfrac{(-cP+a)\left(e^{(b+\theta)\lambda T}-1\right)\lambda T}{b+\theta}+(1-\lambda)\beta(a-cP)T\right)-\dfrac{A}{T}-\dfrac{C}{T} \\ \left(\begin{array}{l}\dfrac{(-cP+a)\left(e^{(b+\theta)\lambda T}-1\right)\lambda T}{b+\theta} \\ +(1-\lambda)\beta(-cP+a)T\end{array}\right) \\ +\dfrac{h(cP-a)\left(-\lambda Tb-\lambda T\theta+e^{(b+\theta)\lambda T}-1\right)}{(b+\theta)^2 T} \\ -\dfrac{1}{2}C_b\beta(a-cP)(1-\lambda)^2 T-(P-C+C_l)(1-\beta) \\ (a-cP)(1-\lambda)-\dfrac{(P-Cs)\eta\lambda(-cP+a)\left(e^{(b+\theta)\lambda T}-1\right)}{(b+\theta)T} \\ -C_T\left(\begin{array}{l}\dfrac{C_{EO}}{T}+\dfrac{C_{EP}(-cP+a)\left(e^{(b+\theta)\lambda T}-1\right)}{(b+\theta)T} \\ -\dfrac{C_{EH}(cP-a)\left(-\lambda Tb-\lambda T\theta+e^{(b+\theta)\lambda T}-1\right)}{(b+\theta)^2 T} \\ +\dfrac{C_{EP}}{T}\left(\dfrac{(-cP+a)\left(e^{(b+\theta)\lambda T}-1\right)\lambda T}{b+\theta}+(1-\lambda)\beta(-cP+a)T\right) \\ -\dfrac{\eta w C_{eo}(cP-a)\left(-\lambda Tb-\lambda T\theta+e^{(b+\theta)\lambda T}-1\right)}{(b+\theta)^2 T}\end{array}\right)\end{array}\right] \tag{12.17}$$

The primary objective of the retailer is to optimize inventory management decisions to minimize costs while meeting customer demand, complying with carbon emissions regulations, and considering the impact of partial backlogging on service levels. By integrating these factors into the decision-making process, the retailer aims to achieve a balance between economic efficiency, environmental sustainability, and customer satisfaction in their supply chain operations.

12.5 Numerical Analysis

To guarantee the concavity of the profit function and secure an optimal value, the algorithm outlined below is employed:

Step 1: Differentiating Eq. (12.17) partially with respect to decision variable T and P by using the mathematical software Maple 18.

Step 2: Assigning all the inventory parameters to some hypothetical values other than decision variables.

Step 3: For finding the solution, set all the equations equal to zero.

Step 4: Solve the equations for profit function and decision variables.

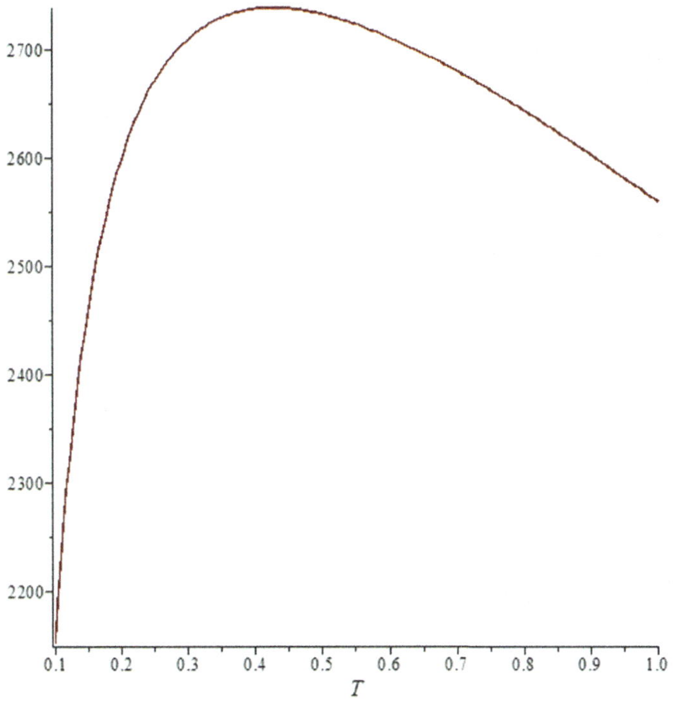

Fig. 12.2 Optimal solution (*Source* Own)

The provided numerical values for inventory parameters are taken into account to validate the proposed model

$$\begin{aligned}&[C = \$20\,\text{per unit},\ A = \$100\,\text{per order},\ a = 1000,\ b = 0.35,\ \theta = 0.1,\ c = 8,\ \beta = 0.6,\\&c_b = \$8\,\text{perunit},\ c_l = \$5\,\text{per unit},\ C_{GL} = 0.1,\ h = \$8\,\text{per unit}\,\lambda = 0.09,\ C_{EO} = 1,\\&C_{EH} = 1,\ C_{EP} = 2,\ C_T = 0.10,\ C_s = 5,\ w = 0.003,\ C_{eo} = 13,\ \eta = 0.1,\ \alpha = 0.3]\end{aligned}$$

Based on the numerical values as stated above, cycle time c, selling price $P =$ \$80.14 gaining total profit $TP =$ \$2738.22 and have $\frac{\partial^2(TP)}{\partial T^2} = -2482.32 < 0$ is a sufficient condition for concavity which is graphically represented by Fig. 12.2.

12.6 Sensitivity Analysis

This section conducts an assessment to measure the varying impact of different inventory parameters on cycle time, selling price, total profit, and the corresponding costs related to carbon emissions.

The foundation of this study lies in the examination of scenarios where only a single parameter undergoes modification, while the remaining parameters are maintained at their initial values. This analytical approach enables a focused investigation into the effects of individual parameter adjustments, providing a distinct and isolated understanding of the impact of changing one variable on the overall study framework. The following managerial insights can be observed from Figs. 12.3 and 12.4. A rise in ordering costs leads to an extension of the cycle time and an elevation in the selling price, concurrently resulting in a reduction of total profit. The variable component has negligible impact on selling price, cycle time and profit. While the holding cost exerts minimal influence on both cycle time and selling price, its impact is evident in diminishing overall profit. Cycle time and selling price get increases whereas profit gets decreases due to purchase cost. As the rate of potential scale demand increases, overall profit also increases by raising the selling price and reducing the replenishment cycle. It is recommended to consider reducing the selling price of the declining product as a strategy to increase overall profit. Therefore, when the price dependent coefficient is bigger, it leads to the collapse of the total profit. Therefore, when the rate of deterioration escalates, the organizations proposed reducing the price in order to liquidate the inventory and enhance the profit. The yearly rate of average inventory obsolescence significantly affects the overall profit from a managerial perspective. The weight of an old unit in the warehouse has no impact on the selling price or profit. The costs associated with backordering and lost sales have a favorable impact on the selling price and cycle time, but they have a negative impact on the overall profit. Total profit gets positively affected by a Constant fraction of backorder while negatively affected by the proportion of demand that can be satisfied from existing inventory varies. The impact of the elasticity of stock-dependent demand on both total profit and selling price is considered negligible. Profit is not affected by unit goodwill loss. Carbon emission during purchase activity increases total profit. Total profit is not much affected by Carbon emission during holding the inventory and with order replenishment. With a rise in unit scrape price, total profit will increase. Average waste for emissions during collection and disposal has a managerial effect on profit. As the carbon tax experiences an escalation, there is a corresponding rise in the selling price. This increase, however, triggers a heightened replenishment cycle, leading to a notable decrease in total profit. The intricacies of this scenario necessitate the organization to make strategic investments in emission control measures. Consequently, the selling price must be adjusted upwards to offset these additional expenses.

12.7 Conclusion

The exploration of inventory decisions under the nuanced lens of carbon emissions, partial backlogging, price-stock-dependent demand, deterioration, and carbon tax policy unveils a multifaceted landscape ripe with opportunities for businesses

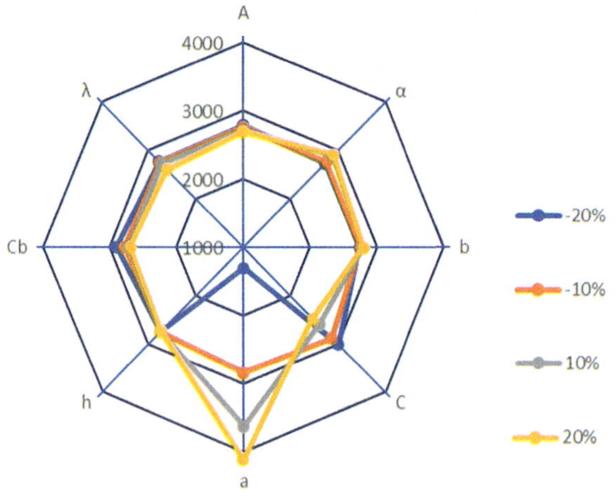

Fig. 12.3 The effect of parameters on profit (*Source* Own)

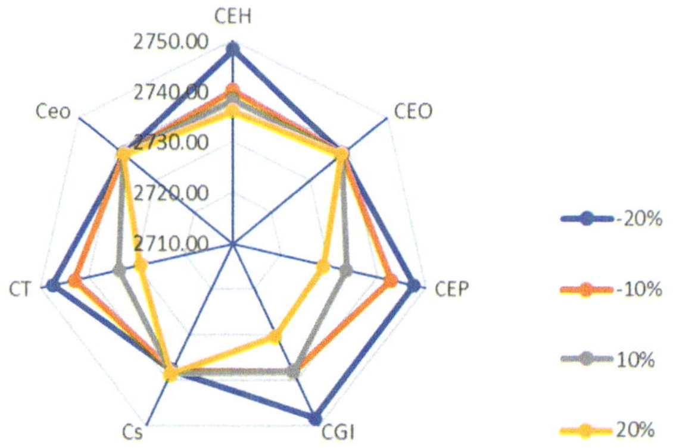

Fig. 12.4 Effect of carbon emissions parameters on profit (*Source* Own)

to address the challenges of sustainability and supply chain management effectively. Through a meticulous analysis of these interconnected variables, our study has shed light on the intricate dynamics shaping contemporary inventory decision-making processes. Our findings underscore the imperative for businesses to adopt a holistic approach that transcends traditional paradigms, integrating environmental, economic, and operational considerations into their inventory management strategies. By embracing this comprehensive perspective, companies can not only optimize their inventory policies to minimize carbon footprint and meet customer demand efficiently but also enhance overall profitability in a rapidly evolving marketplace. Moreover, our study underscores the pivotal role of regulatory frameworks, such as carbon tax policies, in incentivizing sustainable practices and shaping corporate behavior. By aligning with these regulatory imperatives and embracing proactive measures to mitigate carbon emissions, businesses can not only enhance their environmental stewardship but also foster long-term resilience and competitiveness in an increasingly conscientious global economy.

Looking ahead, further research in this domain holds immense promise in refining and advancing our understanding of sustainable supply chain management practices. By delving deeper into the intricate interplay of emerging technologies, regulatory frameworks, and market dynamics, researchers can unlock innovative solutions that offer unprecedented levels of transparency, efficiency, and sustainability across the supply chain. In essence, our study serves as a clarion call for businesses to embrace sustainability as a cornerstone of their strategic vision, recognizing that the pursuit of environmental stewardship is not only a moral imperative but also a source of enduring competitive advantage and business success in the twenty-first century.

Further research could delve into developing comprehensive methodologies for assessing and quantifying the carbon footprint associated with different inventory policies. This would enable businesses to make informed decisions that minimize their environmental impact while maximizing operational efficiency and profitability.

Acknowledgements The authors thank DST-FIST file # MSI-097 for the technical support to the department. Second author (Ekta Patel) would like to extend sincere thanks to the Education Department, Gujarat State for providing scholarship under scheme of Developing High quality research (Student Ref No : 201901380184).

References

Bhavani GD, Meidute-Kavaliauskiene I, Mahapatra GS, Činčikaitė R (2022) A sustainable green inventory system with novel eco-friendly demand incorporating partial backlogging under fuzziness. Sustainability 14(15):9155

Chowdhury RR, Ghosh SK, Chaudhuri KS (2015) An inventory model for deteriorating items with stock and price sensitive demand. Int J Appl Comput Mathem 1(2):187–201

De-la-Cruz-Márquez CG, Cárdenas-Barrón LE, Mandal B, Smith NR, Bourguet-Díaz RE, Loera-Hernández IDJ, … Treviño-Garza G (2022) An inventory model in a three-echelon supply chain for growing items with imperfect quality, mortality, and shortages under carbon emissions when the demand is price sensitive. Mathematics 10(24):4684

Halim MA, Paul A, Mahmoud M, Alshahrani B, Alazzawi AY, Ismail GM (2021) An overtime production inventory model for deteriorating items with nonlinear price and stock dependent demand. Alex Eng J 60(3):2779–2786

Hou KL, Lin LC (2006) An EOQ model for deteriorating items with price-and stock-dependent selling rates under inflation and time value of money. Int J Syst Sci 37(15):1131–1139

Hovelaque V, Bironneau L (2015) The carbon-constrained EOQ model with carbon emission dependent demand. Int J Prod Econ 164:285–291

Lee YP, Dye CY (2012) An inventory model for deteriorating items under stock-dependent demand and controllable deterioration rate. Comput Ind Eng 63(2):474–482

Lu CJ, Lee TS, Gu M, Yang CT (2020) A multistage sustainable production-inventory model with carbon emission reduction and price-dependent demand under stackelberg game. Appl Sci 10(14):4878

Mahato C, De SK, Mahata GC (2021) Joint pricing and inventory management for growing items in a supply chain under trade credit. Soft Comput 25(11):7271–7295

Mahato F, Choudhury M, Das S, Mahata GC (2023) Optimal pricing and replenishment decisions for non-instantaneous deteriorating items with a fixed lifetime and partial backordering under carbon regulations. Environ Develop Sustain 1–34

Mashud AHM, Roy D, Daryanto Y, Chakrabortty RK, Tseng ML (2021) A sustainable inventory model with controllable carbon emissions, deterioration and advance payments. J Clean Prod 296:126608

Min J, Zhou YW (2009) A perishable inventory model under stock-dependent selling rate and shortage-dependent partial backlogging with capacity constraint. Int J Syst Sci 40(1):33–44

Mishra U, Wu JZ, Sarkar B (2020) A sustainable production-inventory model for a controllable carbon emissions rate under shortages. J Clean Prod 256:120268

Mondal B, Bhunia AK, Maiti M (2003) An inventory system of ameliorating items for price dependent demand rate. Comput Ind Eng 45(3):443–456

Mondal P, Das AK, Roy TK (2023) An EOQ model for deteriorating item with continuous linear time dependent demand with trade of credit and replenishment time being demand dependent. Int J Mathemat Operat Res 24(1):104–127

Mukhopadhyay S, Mukherjee RN, Chaudhuri* KS (2005) An EOQ model with two-parameter Weibull distribution deterioration and price-dependent demand. Int J Math Educ Sci Technol 36(1):25–33

Nita SHAH, Patel E, Rabari K (2022) EPQ model to price-sensitive stock dependent demand with carbon emission under green and preservation technology investment. Econ Comput Econ Cybern Stud Res 56:209–222

Panda D, Maiti MK, Maiti M (2010) Two warehouse inventory models for single vendor multiple retailers with price and stock dependent demand. Appl Math Model 34(11):3571–3585

Panda S, Saha S, Modak NM, Sana SS (2017) A volume flexible deteriorating inventory model with price sensitive demand. Tékhne 15(2):117–123

Ruidas S, Seikh MR, Nayak PK (2021) A production inventory model with interval-valued carbon emission parameters under price-sensitive demand. Comput Ind Eng 154:107154

Saga RS, Jauhari WA, Laksono PW, Dwicahyani AR (2019) Investigating carbon emissions in a production-inventory model under imperfect production, inspection errors and service-level constraint. Int J Logist Syst Manag 34(1):29–55

Sana S, Chaudhuri KS (2004) A stock-review EOQ model with stock-dependent demand, quadratic deterioration rate. Adv Model Optimizat 6(2):25–32

Sarkar B, Saren S, Sarkar M, Seo YW (2016) A Stackelberg game approach in an integrated inventory model with carbon-emission and setup cost reduction. Sustainability 8(12):1244

Shah NH, Naik MK (2018) EOQ model for deteriorating item under full advance payment availing of discount when demand is price-sensitive. Int J Supply Chain Operations Resilience 3(2):163–197

Sepehri A, Mishra U, Tseng ML, Sarkar B (2021) Joint pricing and inventory model for deteriorating items with maximum lifetime and controllable carbon emissions under permissible delay in payments. Mathematics 9(5):470

Shah NH, Patel E, Rabari K (2022) Vendor-buyer pollution sensitive inventory system for deteriorating items. Process Integrat Optimizat Sustain 6(2):285–293

Shah NH, Patel E, Rabari K (2022) Investigation of carbon emissions due to COVID-19 vaccine inventory. Int J Syst Assurance Eng Managem 13(1):409–420

Shah NH, Rabari K, Patel E (2023) Greening efforts and deteriorating inventory policies for price-sensitive stock-dependent demand. Int J Syst Sci: Operat Logist 10(1):2022808

Singh SR (2022) A sustainable inventory model for deteriorating items with variable holding cost under controllable carbon emission and inflation

Xiao Y, Yang S, Zhang L, Kuo YH (2016) Supply chain cooperation with price-sensitive demand and environmental impacts. Sustainability 8(8):716

Yang HL, Teng JT, Chern MS (2010) An inventory model under inflation for deteriorating items with stock-dependent consumption rate and partial backlogging shortages. Int J Prod Econ 123(1):8–19

You PS, Hsieh YC (2007) An EOQ model with stock and price sensitive demand. Math Comput Model 45(7–8):933–942

Chapter 13
A Medication Inventory Model for Hospital Management Problem Having Weibull Deterioration with Lead Time and Shortages During Any Medical Emergency

Swadhin Banerjee and Tripti Chakrabarti

Abstract In this short study, authors have derived an EOQ model for medication inventory in case of medical emergency or epidemic. Time-dependent exponential demand with initial quantity as Single Valued Gaussian Neutrosophic Number (SVGNN) is used and shortages of drugs as well as lead time are also considered to formulate the model. Finally, the model is supported with a numerical example.

Keywords Exponential demand · Shortages · Lead time · Neutrosophic environment · EOQ model · Weibull deterioration

13.1 Introduction

In this study, we would develop an EOQ model for medication inventory of any healthcare facilities. Inventory management for a healthcare provider is to maintain its inventory in hand so that treatment process may remain uninterrupted. The problem of inventory management for a healthcare facility is to keep total inventory cost minimum as well as to achieve satisfactory service-level output. In recent past COVID-19, we have seen massive and uncertain demand for medical items. So, in this model we have considered exponential demand of drugs with parameter $\mu(>0)$, which is considered as emergency level i.e. μ will fluctuate with the fluctuation of infection-rate or demand. Also to account the imprecise, random and inconsistent nature of demand, we have used Single Valued Gaussian Neutrosophic Number as initial demand quantity. Advantage of SVGNN is that, its truth-membership function

S. Banerjee (✉)
Department of Mathematics, Techno India University, Kolkata, India
e-mail: swadhin.banerjee06@gmail.com

T. Chakrabarti
Techno India University, Kolkata, India

N. H. Shah and M. Mittal (eds.), *Sustainable Inventory Management*, Inventory Optimization, https://doi.org/10.1007/978-981-97-6765-6_14

is almost same as p.d.f. of Normal distribution. Since any unknown distribution can be approximated to Normal distribution, so SVGNN can handle random nature of data along with imprecise and inconsistent natures. Covert and Philip (1973) have discussed that, two parameter Weibull deterioration with $0 < \alpha \ll 1$ and $1 < \beta < 2$, is the best choice for drugs and pharmaceuticals. In this study, we would use two parameter Weibull deterioration having scale parameter α and shape parameter β. In our proposed model, we would consider shortages of drugs and a positive lead time, which are very common phenomena during any medical emergency or epidemic. Moon and Choi (1998) discussed the continuous review inventory model with lead time and they introduced the reorder point as a new decision variable. Like them, we too have considered the reorder point as our decision variable. Park (2007) discussed the lead time demand distribution in stochastic environment. But in present study, uncertain nature of demand is accounted with the help of SVGNN as initial demand quantity.

13.2 Mathematical Preliminaries

The Neutrosophic set was first introduced by Smarandache (2005). This is a generalization of fuzzy set and intuitionistic fuzzy set. Neutrosophic sets and numbers are used to the real-life problems where the information is indeterminate and inconsistent. A Neutrosophic set is characterized by three membership functions, viz. truth, indeterminacy and falsity. In this section, we would present some basics of SVGNN in outline. For details of Neutrosophic techniques, readers may refer to Wang et al. (2010) and Karaaslan (2018).

Definition 14.1 A quantity $\tilde{A} = ((m_t, \sigma_t), (m_i, \sigma_i), (m_f, \sigma_f))$ is called a SVGNN if truth-membership function, indeterminacy-membership function and falsity-membership function are given by

$$\varphi_t(x) = \exp\left(-\frac{1}{2}\left(\frac{x - m_t}{\sigma_t}\right)^2\right)$$

$$\varphi_i(x) = 1 - \exp\left(-\frac{1}{2}\left(\frac{x - m_i}{\sigma_i}\right)^2\right)$$

$$\varphi_f(x) = 1 - \exp\left(-\frac{1}{2}\left(\frac{x - m_f}{\sigma_f}\right)^2\right)$$

respectively, where $x \in \boldsymbol{R}$. Here m_t, m_i, m_f denote mean of truth-membership, indeterminacy-membership, falsity-membership values respectively. And $\sigma_t, \sigma_i, \sigma_f$ denote standard deviation of truth-membership, indeterminacy-membership, falsity-membership values respectively.

Definition 14.2 The **α-cuts** of a SVGNN, $\tilde{A} = ((m_t, \sigma_t), (m_i, \sigma_i), (m_f, \sigma_f))$, are given by

$$A_{t\alpha} = [m_t - \sigma_t\sqrt{-2\log\alpha},\ m_t + \sigma_t\sqrt{-2\log\alpha}]$$
$$A_{i\alpha} = m_i - \sigma_i\sqrt{-2\log(1-\alpha)}, m_i + \sigma_i\sqrt{-2\log(1-\alpha)}], \text{ and}$$
$$A_{f\alpha} = [m_f - \sigma_f\sqrt{-2\log(1-\alpha)}, m_f + \sigma_f\sqrt{-2\log(1-\alpha)}]$$

respectively, where $0 < \alpha < 1$.

Definition 14.3 Let $[A^L_{t\alpha}, A^U_{t\alpha}]$, $[A^L_{i\alpha}, A^U_{i\alpha}]$ and $[A^L_{f\alpha}, A^U_{f\alpha}]$ be the α-cuts of a SVGNN $\tilde{A}$, then the De-Neutrosophic value (by using mean interval method) of $\tilde{A}$, denoted as A^D, is defined by

$$A^D = \frac{1}{3}\left[\frac{1}{2}\left[\int_0^1 [A^L_{t\alpha} + A^U_{t\alpha}\Big]d\alpha + \int_0^1 [A^L_{i\alpha} + A^U_{i\alpha}\Big]d\alpha + \int_0^1 \left[A^L_{f\alpha} + A^U_{f\alpha}\right]d\alpha\right]\right]$$

Example 14.1 If $\tilde{A} = ((m_t, \sigma_t), (m_i, \sigma_i), (m_f, \sigma_f))$ be a SVGNN, then its De-Neutrosophic value using above definition is clearly given by $A^D = \frac{1}{3}(m_t + m_i + m_f)$.

It should be noted that, if τ be any scalar and $\tilde{A}$ be any SVGNN, then the De-Neutrosophic value of $\tau\tilde{A}$ is given by τA^D, by using above definition.

13.3 Mathematical Model

We first state the required assumptions and notations for our model:

13.3.1 Assumptions and Notations

(1) Replenishment rate is infinite.
(2) T is the constant time cycle.
(3) L is the average lead time, where $0 < L < T$.
(4) Shortages are allowed and fully backlogged.
(5) Time dependent exponential demand $\Omega e^{\mu t}$ is considered, where $\Omega > 0$ and $\mu > 0$. Here μ is the level of emergency.
(6) Weibull distributed deterioration rate function $\alpha\beta t^{\beta-1}$ is considered, where $0 < \alpha << 1$ and $1 < \beta < 2$ is assumed.
(7) C_1 is the ordering cost per unit.
(8) C_2 is the holding cost per unit.
(9) C_3 is the shortage cost per unit.
(10) $I(t)$ be instantaneous inventory level at time t.
(11) Q is the level of inventory at time $t = L$.

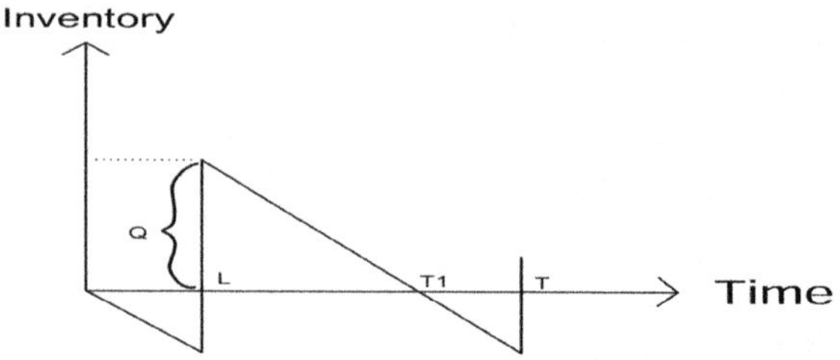

Fig. 13.1 Graphical representation of the model. *Source* Own

(12) T_1 is the time at which inventory level drops to 'zero' due to demand and deterioration, where $L < T_1 < T$.
(13) During lead time, demand is fulfilled.
(14) Tilde ($\sim$) symbols are used for Neutrosophic quantities.

Figure 13.1 shows that, at the beginning of any intermediate cycle, there is inventory due to delay of supply and at the end of lead time (L), inventory reaches at the highest-level Q. Then due to deterioration and demand, inventory reaches to 'zero' at the time T_1, which is the reorder point. Thereafter shortages begin until the end of the cycle (T). But the shortages will be fully backlogged to continue the treatment uninterrupted.

13.3.2 Model Description

The differential equation of our proposed model is given by

$$\frac{dI(t)}{dt} + \alpha\beta t^{\beta-1} I(t) = -\Omega e^{\mu t} \tag{13.1}$$

$$(L \leq t \leq T_1)$$

and

$$\frac{dI(t)}{dt} = -\Omega e^{\mu t} \tag{13.2}$$

$$(T_1 \leq t \leq T)$$

With the conditions $I(L) = Q$ and $I(T_1) = 0 = 0$
Now solving (13.1), we find

$$I(t) = e^{-\alpha t^\beta}[Qe^{\alpha L^\beta} - \Omega \int_L^t e^{\mu x} e^{\alpha x^\beta} dx] \tag{13.3}$$

$$(L \le t \le T_1)$$

Again solving (13.2), we get

$$\text{I(t)} = -\Omega \int_{T_1}^{t} e^{\mu x} dx \tag{13.4}$$

$$(T_1 \le t \le T)$$

Now using the condition $I(T_1) = 0$, we get from (13.3),

$$Q = \Omega e^{-\alpha L^\beta} \int_{L}^{T_1} e^{\mu x} e^{\alpha x^\beta} dx \tag{13.5}$$

The total deteriorated unit D is given by

$$\begin{aligned} D &= Q - \Omega \int_{L}^{T_1} e^{\mu x} dx \\ &= \Omega \left[\int_{L}^{T_1} e^{\mu x} \left[e^{-\alpha L^\beta} e^{\alpha x^\beta} - 1 \right] dx \right] \end{aligned} \tag{13.6}$$

The demand during lead time D_L is given by

$$D_L \Omega \int_{0}^{L} e^{\mu x} dx$$

Now the total inventory I_1, during $[L, T_1]$ is given by

$$\begin{aligned} I_1 &= \int_{L}^{T_1} I(t) dt \\ &= \int_{L}^{T_1} e^{-\alpha t^\beta} \left[Q e^{\alpha L^\beta} - \Omega \int_{L}^{t} e^{\mu x} e^{\alpha x^\beta} dx \right] dt \\ &= \Omega \int_{L}^{T_1} e^{-\alpha t^\beta} [\int_{t}^{T_1} e^{\mu x} e^{\alpha x^\beta} dx] dt \end{aligned}$$

[by using (13.5)]
On changing the order of integration, we find

$$I_1 = \int_{L}^{T_1} e^{\mu x} e^{\alpha x^{\beta}} \left[\int_{L}^{x} e^{-\alpha t^{\beta}} dt \right] dx \tag{13.7}$$

Again, the total shortages I_2, during $[T_1, T]$ is given by
$I_2 = -\int_{T_1}^{T} I(t)dt = \Omega \int_{T_1}^{T} \left[\int_{T_1}^{t} e^{\mu x} dx \right] dt$ [by using (13.4)]
On changing the order of integration, we find

$$\begin{aligned} I_2 &= \Omega \int_{T_1}^{T} e^{\mu x} \left[\int_{x}^{T} dt \right] dx \\ &= \Omega \int_{T_1}^{T} [T - x] e^{\mu x} dx \end{aligned} \tag{13.8}$$

Thus, total cost per unit time is given by

$$\begin{aligned} C(T_1) &= \frac{1}{T} = [C_1(D + D_L) + \ C_2 I_1 + \ C_3 I_2] \\ &= \frac{\Omega}{T}[C_1 \left[\int_{L}^{T_1} e^{\mu x} \left[e^{-\alpha L^{\beta}} e^{\alpha x^{\beta}} - 1 \right] dx + \ \int_{0}^{L} e^{\mu x} dx \right] \\ &\quad + C_2 \int_{L}^{T_1} e^{\mu x} e^{\alpha x^{\beta}} \left[\int_{L}^{x} e^{-\alpha t^{\beta}} dt \right] dx + C_3 \int_{T_1}^{T} [T - x] e^{\mu x} dx] \end{aligned} \tag{13.9}$$

To obtain the minimum value of $C(T_1)$, we first have to solve $\frac{dC(T_1)}{dT_1} = 0$ and then we will verify whether $\frac{d^2 C(T_1)}{dT_1^2} > 0$ for the sufficient condition.

13.3.3 Cost Function in Neutrosophic Environment

Let $\widetilde{\Omega}$ be the SVGNN as initial demand quantity with de-Neutrosophic value Ω^D, which is obtained by mean interval method and is given by $\Omega^D = \frac{1}{3}\left(m_t + m_i + m_f\right)$. Then the Neutrosophic cost is given by,

$$\begin{aligned} \widetilde{C(T_1)} &= \tilde{\Omega} * \frac{1}{T}[C_1[\int_{L}^{T_1} e^{\mu x} \left[e^{-\alpha L^{\beta}} e^{\alpha x^{\beta}} - 1 \right] dx \\ &+ \ \int_{0}^{L} e^{\mu x} dx] + C_2 \int_{L}^{T_1} e^{\mu x} e^{\alpha x^{\beta}} \left[\int_{L}^{x} e^{-\alpha t^{\beta}} dt \right] dx + C_3 \int_{T_1}^{T} [T - x] e^{\mu x} dx] \end{aligned} \tag{13.10}$$

Now using de-Neutrosophication by mean interval method, the de-Neutrosophic value of cost is given by,

$$C(T_1)^D = \frac{\Omega^D}{T}[C_1[\int_L^{T_1} e^{\mu x}\left[e^{-\alpha L^\beta} e^{\alpha x^\beta} - 1\right]dx$$
$$+ \int_0^L e^{\mu x} dx] + C_2 \int_L^{T_1} e^{\mu x} e^{\alpha x^\beta}\left[\int_L^x e^{-\alpha t^\beta} dt\right]dx + C_3 \int_{T_1}^T [T - x]e^{\mu x} dx] \quad (13.11)$$

Differentiating (13.11) under the sign of integration, we get

$$\frac{dC(T_1)^D}{dT_1} = \frac{\Omega^D}{T}[C_1 e^{\mu T_1}\left[e^{-\alpha L^\beta} e^{\alpha T_1^\beta} - 1\right]$$
$$+ C_2 e^{\mu T_1} e^{\alpha T_1^\beta} \int_L^{T_1} e^{-\alpha t^\beta} dt + C_3(T_1 - T)e^{\mu T_1}] \quad (13.12)$$

Now, to solve $\frac{dC(T_1)^D}{dT_1} = 0$, let us consider the function,

$$\psi(T_1) = C_1\left[e^{-\alpha L^\beta} e^{\alpha T_1^\beta} - 1\right] + C_2 e^{\alpha T_1^\beta} \int_L^{T_1} e^{-\alpha t^\beta} dt + C_3(T_1 - T) \quad (13.13)$$

Clearly ψ is continuously increasing function on $[L, T]$ and $\psi(L) < 0$ and $\psi(T) > 0$, hence we must have a unique solution of $\psi = (T_1) - 0 = 0$ in (L, T).

Suppose $T_1 = T_1^*$ be the solution of $\psi(T_1) = 0$, which clearly satisfy the sufficient condition $\frac{d^2C(T_1)^D}{dT_1^2} > 0$. This proves that, our cost function has a global minimum at $T_1 = T_1^*$. Then the optimal reorder time would be T_1^* and the optimal value of initial inventory Q be given by

$$Q^* = \Omega^D e^{-\alpha L^\beta} \int_L^{T_1^*} e^{\mu x} e^{\alpha x^\beta} dx \quad (13.14)$$

[using (13.5)]

Again, total number of backorders $= \Omega^D \int_{T_1^*}^T e^{\mu x} dx$.

Therefore, total number of inventories to be purchased is given by

$$S^* = Q^* + \Omega^D\left[\int_0^L e^{\mu x} dx + \int_{T_1^*}^T e^{\mu x} dx\right] \quad (13.15)$$

The optimal total cost C^* is obtained by putting $T_1 = T_1^*$ in the Eq. (13.11).

13.4 Numerical Result

To obtain the numerical result of our model, we have used Python programming language. First we consider the hypothetical values of input parameters in crisp environment as: $T = 180$ days, $L = 10$ days, $C_1 = \$5$, $C_2 = \$2$, $C_3 = \$3$, $\mu = 0.005$, $\alpha = 0.0035$, $\beta = 1.3125$, $\Omega = 10$ units. We find the output values in crisp sense as:$T_1^* = 83.42$ days, $C^* = \$2029.93$/day, $Q^* = 1664.92$ units, $S^* = 3650.23$ units.

Now to obtain the numerical result in Neutrosophic sense, we put the hypothetical data as: $m_t = 10$ units, $m_i = 11$ units and $m_f = 7$ units and keep all other input values unaltered. We get the output values as: $T_1^* = 83.42$ days, $C^* = \$1894.53$/day, $Q^* = 1535.87$, $S^* = 3406.76$ units. Thus, in Neutrosophic environment we get better optimal cost and optimal inventory than that of the crisp environment. It should be noted that, for different De-Neutrosophication method, optimal output would be different.

13.5 Conclusion

This paper presents a medication inventory model in Neutrosophic environment for healthcare facilities to combat the uncertainties of any medical emergency or epidemic. The demand rate is assumed to be time dependent exponential function, which is an essential criterion for epidemic or medical emergency. We have considered stock out of drugs and that will be fully backlogged. This model would allow to achieve appropriate managerial decision to maintain medication inventory for a hospital during medical emergency. Also, this study would contribute to existing literature by making use of SVGNN in inventory modeling. As we didn't consider variable or stochastic lead time, this study can be modified by using either variable or stochastic lead time. Also, one can consider the case of multi-drug items for future research.

References

Balkhi ZT (1998) On the global optimality of a general economic order quantity model for deteriorating items. Optimization 43(2):169–183. https://doi.org/10.1080/02331939808844381

Chakrabarti T, Giri BC, Chaudhuri KS (1998) An EOQ model for items with Weibull distribution deterioration, shortages trended demand: an extension of Philip's model. Comput Oper Res 25(7–8):649–657

Covert PR, Philip GC (1973) An EOQ model for items with Weibull distributed deterioration. AIIE Trans 5:323–326

Karaaslan F (2018) Gaussian single-valued neutrosophic numbers and its application in multi-attribute decision making. Neutrosophic Sets and Syst 22:101–117

Maragatham M, Palani R (2017) An inventory model for deteriorating items with lead time price dependent demand and shortages. Adv Comput Sci Technol 10(6):1839–1847

Mishra U (2016) An inventory model for Weibull deterioration with stock and price dependent demand. Int J Appl Comput Mathemat 3:1951–1967. https://doi.org/10.1007/s40819-016-0217-0

Moon I, Choi S (1998) A note on lead time and distribution assumptions in continuous review inventory models. Comput Oper Res 25(11):1007–1012. https://doi.org/10.1016/S0305-0548(97)00105-2

Park C (2007) An analysis of lead time demand distribution derivation in stochastic inventory systems. Int J Prod Econ 105:263–272

Smarandache F (2005) Neutrosophic set—a generalization of the intuitionistic fuzzy set. Int J Pure and Appl Mathemat 24(3):287–297

Wang H, Smarandache F, Zhang Y, Sunderraman R (2010) Single valued neutrosophic sets. Multispace and Multistructure 4:410–413

Wu JW, Lee WC (2003) An EOQ inventory model for items with Weibull deterioration, shortages and time varying demand. J Inf Optim Sci 24(1):103–122. https://doi.org/10.1080/02522667.2003.10699558

Wu J-W, Lin C, Tan B, Lee W-C (2000) An EOQ inventory model with time-varying demand and Weibull deterioration with shortages. Int J Syst Sci 31(6):677–683. https://doi.org/10.1080/00207720050030716

Yang G, Lin R, Lin J, Hung K-C, Chu P, Chouhuang W (2011) Note on inventory models with Weibull distribution deterioration. Prod Planning and Control 22(4):437–444. https://doi.org/10.1080/09537287.2010.499251

The manufacturer's authorised representative in the EU is Springer Nature Customer Service Centre GmbH, Europaplatz 3, 69115 Heidelberg, Germany. If you have any concerns regarding our products, please contact ProductSafety@springernature.com

Printed and bound by CPI Group (UK) Ltd, Croydon, CR0 4YY
01/10/2026
02225907-0006